Introduction to Communication

Second Edition

ISBN 978-1-934920-64-0

Publisher: Words of Wisdom, LLC — Schaumburg, IL
Book Title: Introduction to Communication
Author: Editorial Board
Rights: Words of Wisdom, LLC
Publication Date: 2012
Edition: 2

VS 1 1

Acknowledgments

We would like to thank the Editorial Board for their time and dedication to the creation of this book.

Dr. Dale Mancini
June McEldowney
Dr. Daryl Korinek
Dr. Bram Duffee
Shannon Powell
Tremayne Simpson

TABLE OF CONTENTS

Part I: Fundamentals of Communication

CHAPTER 1

The Communication Process

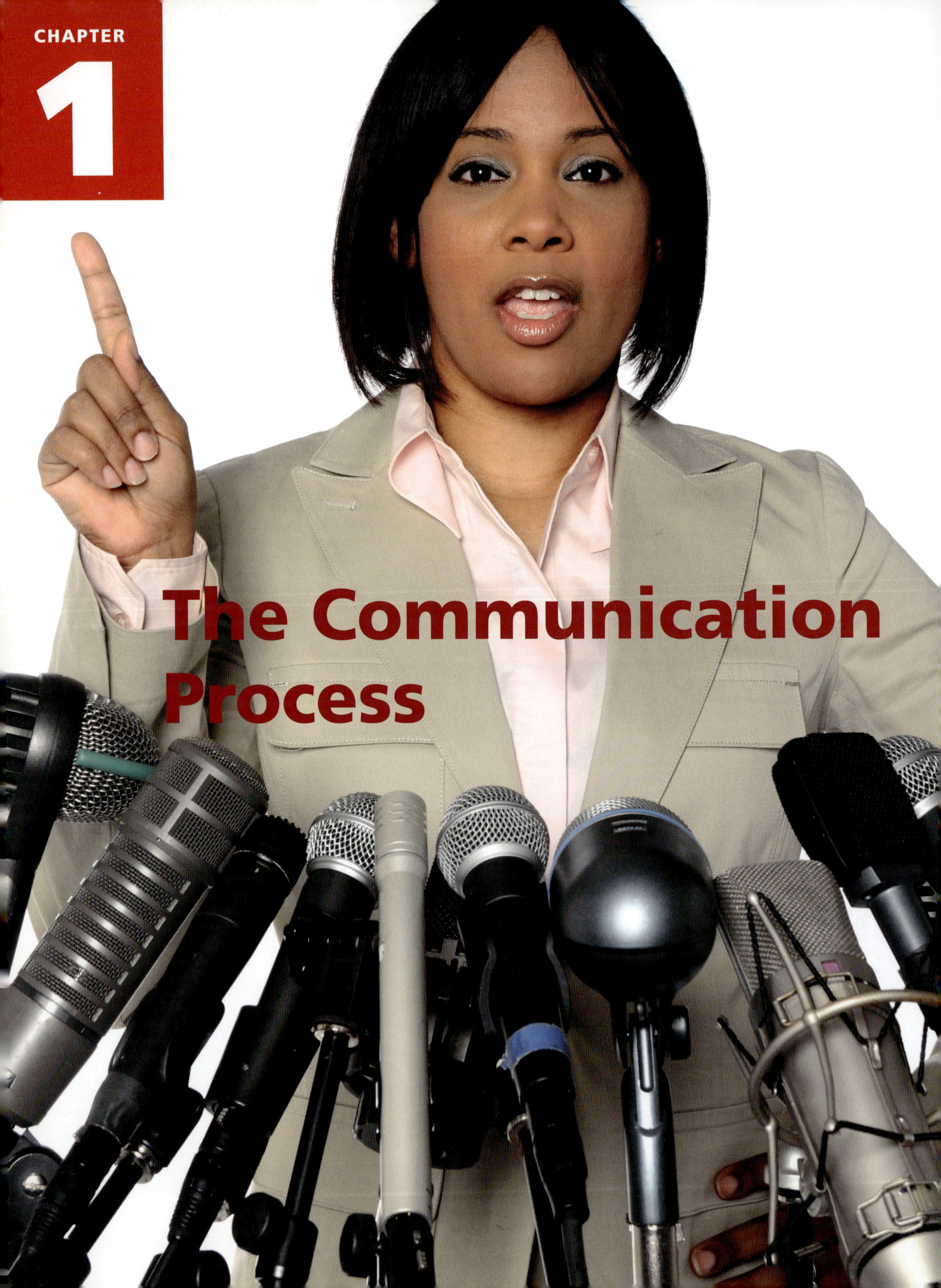

KEY CONCEPTS

1. The contemporary model of communication includes the sender, the receiver, channels of communication, the message, and other important components. See page 4.

2. Communication is both irreversible and inevitable. See page 9.

3. Ethical communication is civil and not misleading. The ethical communicator must always be well prepared. See page 11.

4. There are six types of communicative settings: interpersonal, intrapersonal, mediated, small group, virtual, or mass communication. See page 14.

Raisa Clark is giving a presentation at her local library about how to use the library's resources to find job listings and apply for jobs. How can Raisa make sure that her audience, a small group of five library patrons, knows what is expected of them? Should Raisa provide the audience with a written outline of her presentation before she begins? Should she give a brief overview before the presentation begins? Or should she use a combination of these communication options?

Even if Raisa provides both a written outline and a verbal overview of her presentation, how can she be sure that these two devices will make everything clear to her audience? How will she understand what is expected of them? In other words, how can she be certain that her audience will get her message?

WHAT IS COMMUNICATION?

Communication is a key element of our daily lives. There is no denying the nonverbal communication of a dog's wagging tail or a boss's slammed door. Simply enabling communication does not make it better. In fact, anyone who has ever played the children's game "Telephone" knows that spreading a story by word of mouth can change its meaning in just a few turns. Efficient communication is not necessarily the fastest communication, and quantity certainly does not equal quality. Instant and text messages are very fast, of course, but heavy reliance on the shorthand terms (LOL, TTYL) used in those channels, as well as their relaxed boundaries and filters, may erode your overall communication skills. While you may be confident communicating with familiar audiences like friends or family, developing the communication skills needed to be successful at school and throughout your career will serve you well in this rapidly changing world.

Why is communication so important? Opportunities for communication have increased, yet the ability to communicate well has not. A repeated finding of an annual survey conducted by the National Association of Colleges and Employers reports that communication ranks first in the list of desirable traits employers want from employees, beating out moral characteristics like honesty and integrity and technical skills like computer literacy. However, those same employers reported that they often find new graduates' communication skills to be lacking.

If you need further evidence of the need to develop strong communication skills, take a moment to think of effective examples of communication: compelling public speakers, commercials that moved you to try a product, or textbooks that helped you better understand difficult concepts. How many did you come up with? Next, think of examples of ineffective communication: commercials you did not understand, presentations that put you to sleep, or long, boring meetings in which you learned nothing. How many of those examples did you come up with? Last, consider this: Which would you rather be exposed to—effective or ineffective communication?

THE CONTEMPORARY MODEL OF COMMUNICATION

Part of conveying a message involves understanding the background, experience, and motivations of your audience—in this case, the members of Raisa's audience at the library. Raisa's particular audience includes an 18-year-old fresh out of high school, an adult for whom English is a second language, the parents of a young child, and a student currently juggling college classes and part-time work. Even though Raisa's audience is diverse, she must ensure that her communication is meaningful and productive for each person in attendance.

Communication is a multidimensional process. In this chapter, you will examine the process of communication with the help of the example above. As a presenter of a lecture on job search skills, Raisa is expected to communicate a variety of messages not only to each audience member, but also to the group as a whole. Additionally, Raisa is expected to communicate with the director at the library, peers who offer suggestions for her presentation, the library's administrators, and the professionals she works with in various businesses organizations—just to name a few of Raisa's co-communicators.

There are countless types of organizations; friends, families, coworkers, classmates, and even groups of strangers can be considered organizations. At the heart of every organization is communication, regardless of what the organization seeks to accomplish. In order to communicate successfully, you must first understand the communication process, which is modeled in Figure 1.1. Refer back to it as you read the rest of the chapter and note the following terms used in Figure 1.1.

- **Code** refers to preparing a message.
- **Encode** means senders put the message into their own words or meaning.
- The **sender** is the same as an initiator, the person who encodes or puts the message into words and meaning.
- The interpreter is the **receiver** of the message who **decodes**, or makes sense of the message by using their knowledge of language from personal experience.
- The sender and receiver both can be influenced by cultural factors such as beliefs and values.

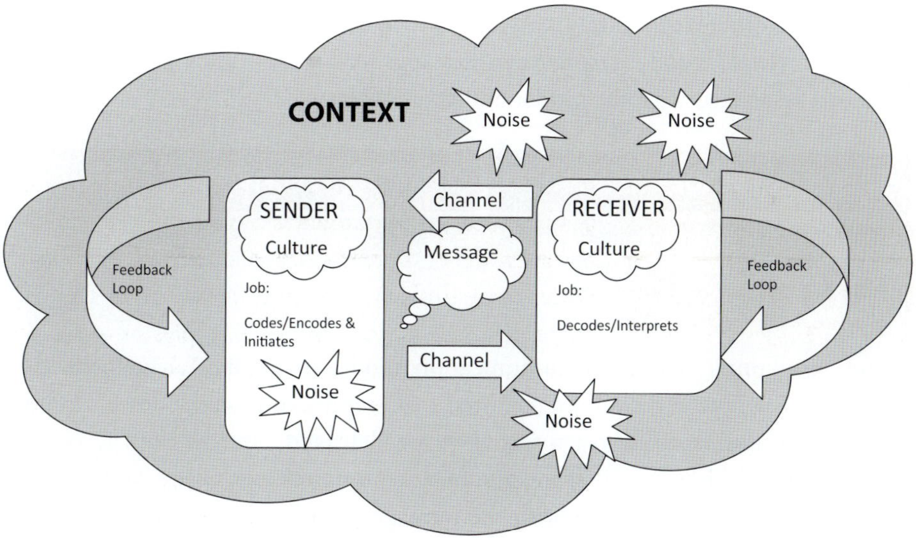

FIGURE 1.1 **Contemporary Communication Model**

During communication, a message is sent through a channel, which is the route by which it travels from sender to receiver. Think of communication as any means by which living things send information to one another. It is a process composed of the following components:

- Models of sender and receiver (affected by culture)
- Noise
- Feedback loop
- Channels
- Message
- Coding (encoding) and decoding messages
- Initiator
- Context

This chapter will examine each component individually and bring each part of the communication process to life by relating it to the classroom example you read at the beginning of the chapter.

The Models of Sender and Receiver

Figure 1.1 shows that the communication process begins with the sender, the individual who sends or initiates a **message**. The message, which is the physical product of the communication process (for example, an e-mail or a lecture), is sent to the receiver, who is also sometimes known as the interpreter.

Senders and receivers are the communicators shown in Figure 1.1. The sender begins the communication process with creating a message by thinking about how to approach the receiver with a message they can understand. This is called "encoding" the message. In the previous example, Raisa as the presenter of the lecture at the library is the message's sender and the receivers in the audience are the job seekers.

Early models of communication envisioned the sender and receiver as distinct and separate entities, but today the communication process is considered to be interactive, dynamic, and interdependent. When they communicate, senders and receivers are practicing both expressive and receptive skills, both of which are related and complementary. Senders use expressive skills like speaking and writing, and receivers use receptive skills like listening and reading. Keep in mind that culture plays a major role in sending and receiving messages. The sender may come from a different cultural background than the receiver. This can affect how the receiver decodes and interprets the message. See Figure 1.2 for a breakdown of the terms associated with the sender and the receiver.

SENDER		RECEIVER	
Encoder	Initiator	Decoder	Interpreter

FIGURE 1.2 **Sender and Receiver**

You may think that the communication model in Figure 1.1 suggests that messages are simply and easily transmitted from sender to receiver; however, most messages are not received exactly as they are delivered. The receiver receives a message through the channel(s) in spite of the interference or noise. Noise is considered anything that interferes with the message's delivery (e.g., cell phones ringing during a lecture). Given that noise has nothing to do with the message and is only an unnecessary by-product of the various components of the communication process, noise may affect the receiver's ability to decode or interpret the message. When the receiver decodes or interprets the message, the receiver determines what the message means—and noise may well play a role in the receiver's interpretation of that message.

Sender and Receiver

The sender is the initiator and begins the communication process by coding the message. Noise (cell phones ringing, traffic noise, and so on) may impact the receiver's ability to decode the message or determine what the message means. After all, it is not simply a matter of decoding the message; the receiver also must decode the intention behind the sender's message. The sender, through thoughtful coding, tries to influence how the receiver will perceive the intention.

Perception is the primary reason why the communication process is so complex. Perception is ever changing and continual, as sending and receiving the message affects the perceptions of both the sender and the receiver. Those perceptions change along with the ongoing communication. In the library presentation example, the receivers are the job-seeking audience members. However, as the communication continues and naturally grows, the audience members interchangeably assume the roles of sender and receiver as they talk with each other about the presentation.

In the process of perception, the receiver applies meaning borrowed from past experiences to make sense of the present message. Since the sender and receiver do not have identical past experiences, identical meaning will not flow from sender to receiver. Have you ever interpreted a piece of art—a painting, perhaps, or a poem—with a friend, and each of you come away with different interpretations of the art's meaning? Most likely, you and your friend did not "see" the same thing. Interpretation is highly subjective and dependent on many different internal and external components.

Noise

Noise refers to the distractions, the unwanted background input, the interference, or any other barriers that may cause complications or distort a message for both sender and receiver. **Internal noise** includes psychological distractions—such as thoughts, feelings, or reactions—that interfere with the communication process. Suppose that during a professor's lecture, you begin to worry about a fight you had with a friend earlier in the day. If you are so distracted by your thoughts and feelings about the fight that you fail to hear the professor's message, you are experiencing internal noise.

External noise, which is sometimes called "physical noise," includes environmental factors—such as sounds and visual stimuli—that distract from the intended message. Imagine trying to have a conversation with a friend while exposed to the external noise of a car alarm. It would be very difficult to send and receive messages. Both internal and external noise hamper an individual's ability to concentrate on the message and understand it. The sender may have to work to code or choose the language needed for the message so that the meaning will not be altered by the noise.

Similarly, the receiver may have to work to ensure that decoding is not affected by the noise. In the classroom example, this noise may include external noise, such as the chatter of the students, the odor of microwave popcorn coming from a neighboring office, the rustle of backpacks and papers, or the roar of a lawnmower outside. Noise is not just unwanted sound—it also may include the foggy haze induced by a cold and the medicines you might take to treat its symptoms. After all, illness definitely has the ability to distort the coding and decoding process.

Feedback Loop

The **feedback loop** is the space in which the sender adjusts the message based on responses from the receiver. It is the mechanism by which one-way communication becomes two-way communication—a **dialogue** or conversation. The receiver may respond to the sender through the feedback loop with a new message, but at the very least, the receiver should always confirm his or her interpretation of the message with the sender.

The sender may respond to the receiver through the feedback loop as well. Once the sender has passed along the information to the receiver, the process becomes two-way, as shown in Figure 1.1. In the figure, the channel arrows point in both directions, reflecting the fluid, continual nature of the feedback loop.

The feedback loop in the example about making a presentation at the library is actually much more dynamic than Figure 1.1 suggests. Imagine that Raisa, the presenter at the library, announces that she has a surprise guest. The audience will provide feedback right away by, whispering about who they think the guest is. In doing so, they will assume the roles of sender and receiver as needed. Decoding, coding, and feedback loop continue as communication occurs. The receivers (job seekers) are not only influenced by the sender (Raisa) but also by other audience members (other senders and receivers). Raisa must consider the totality of the environment where the communication is taking place.

The feedback loop also reveals the receiver's perception of the message. Perhaps a sender intended a message to be a joke, but instead, the receiver took offense to it. In the feedback loop, the receiver may not necessarily respond to the message the sender intended to send—instead, the receiver will respond to an interpretation of the message.

Channels

A sender sends a message through the appropriate **communication channels**, which are the means, methods, vehicles, modes, and techniques used to send messages. Some communication channels include oral or verbal communication (including face-to-face conversations or meetings, or perhaps virtual or otherwise technologically facilitated communication such as videoconferencing), nonverbal communication, written communication (including e-mail and online communication, such as chat/instant messages or postings on discussion boards), and mass communication (including television, radio, magazines, or newspapers).

In the library presentation example, Raisa's channels might include verbal (voice), written (handouts or whiteboard notes), and nonverbal (perhaps a cold glare at an audience member whose cell phone rings) elements. Channels are usually categorized by determining each channel's strengths and weaknesses. For instance, among the strengths of e-mail as a communication channel are its speed and convenience. However, e-mail communication does not allow communicators to hear each other's tone of voice or see facial expressions and body language. Accordingly, e-mail users have developed an elaborate system of **emoticons** designed to stand in for common face-to-face communication markers.

Do you think the message is more important than the channel? Or vice versa? The debate over whether message and channel are equally important, or if one is more important than the other, has raged for some time. **Media richness theory** categorizes communication channels and ranks them according to their "richness." The richest channel, such as a face-to-face conversation, allows for a variety of signals and feeds multiple senses. The least rich channels would include brochures, Web pages, or letters and e-mail messages. Typically, the richer the channel, the more likely it is that the message will be received and interpreted as it was intended.

CHARACTERISTICS OF COMMUNICATION

Although there is little consensus about which is the best model to represent the communication process, the following characteristics of communication are more or less universally agreed upon:

- Communication is irreversible.
- Communication is inevitable.
- Communication is multidimensional.
- Communication is transactional.

Communication Is Irreversible

You cannot take back a message you send—not really. Decoding and interpretation are automatic processes. This is why it is usually not a good idea to hit "send" on an angry e-mail message without first carefully considering what the possible repercussions of that message may be. It is also why communicators must carefully plan important conversations, like job interviews or public speeches. Whether a message is intentional or unintentional, or conscious or subconscious, you cannot unsend it or "uncommunicate" it. Communication is always happening, and this nonstop nature makes it incredibly difficult, if not impossible, to reverse the effects of a message.

Communication Is Inevitable

You have heard the message that communication is constant, consistent, and continuous, but just for a moment, try your best not to communicate. Are you finding it difficult to do so? In fact, it is actually impossible to not communicate.

Have you ever given a friend or family member the silent treatment? Even that silence was still communicating pretty loudly. Despite the "noise" of your silence, your message of being annoyed was getting through. Communication happens whether you want it to or not and whether you are in control of it or not. Of course, it is always better to be in control.

Instructors often use silence to effectively quiet a classroom at the start of class or before an important announcement. When students notice an instructor standing silently in the front of the classroom, they know that the attention is wanted: the instructor is communicating, or is about to communicate, something important.

DID YOU KNOW?

You Can Listen Faster Than You Can Speak

The average person speaks at a rate of 100 to 200 words per minute, but an average listener can process 400 words per minute. You would think that this fact would mean that listeners would be equipped to fully understand any message sent their way, but in fact, the opposite is true. Because the listener is able to process so much more input than a speaker can deliver, the listener is likely to use that capacity in other ways: predicting what the speaker is about to say, zeroing in on one of the speaker's points and going off on a mental tangent on it, engaging in other types of daydreaming, focusing on some of the noise present in the communication space, and so on. In short, this excess capacity results in a higher likelihood of a listener "tuning out" a sender. Communication is inevitable, and so is noise. Communicators must develop skills to successfully push their messages through this noise.

Communication Is Multidimensional

Using what you have just read about communication channels, consider the ways in which communication is multidimensional, which means that it covers different formats and modes often at the same time. You can think of communication in terms of being verbal, vocal, or visual. Verbal typically refers to words, vocal typically refers to spoken communication, and visual refers to pictures or symbols. Each of these types overlap, of course. Brochures and Web pages are both visual and written communication modes that use a mixture of language and images. In the case of Web pages, perhaps even audio (sound) is involved (verbal/visual/audio). Likewise, letters may be received in paper form in the mail or they may be delivered online in the form of e-mail, but either form uses both words and symbols (verbal/visual). Face-to-face communication (verbal/vocal/visual) engages multiple senses. How does your fellow communicator look or smell? How close is your fellow communicator to you? What does the environment that you are in communicate to you and your fellow communicator? Clearly, communication can be expressed in a multitude of ways, including words, letters, pictures, gestures, signals, and colors.

The ways in which you communicate are multidimensional, and so are the skills you use to do so. Effective communication involves both expression and reception. How do you express yourself to others? Speaking and writing are two of the most common ways you express yourself. How do you receive information from others? Most commonly, you receive information by listening and reading.

The communication process is complex and multidimensional. It involves the mechanics of cognition, language, speech, and less predictable variables, such as cultural beliefs, social constraints, and motivations. In addition to its mechanics, communication is rooted in context; a message does not transpire between sender and receiver in a vacuum. Instead, communication always occurs in both a social and a cultural context, and it is a means to achieve social action, or to get something done.

Communication Is Transactional

Although some models portray the communication process as one-way and occurring in a series of consecutive steps, the reality of the communication process is more complex than that. All communicators—that is, senders and receivers—are exchanging messages concurrently, or at the same time. At any given moment in the communication process, senders and receivers are playing interchangeable roles, and the feedback and noise that go on continuously play a large role in the messages' encoding and decoding process. As a result of this constant interchange, it is difficult to separate aspects of the communication model (see Figure 1.1) from one another.

Interconnectivity and dynamism are characteristics of the transactional nature of communication, so perhaps the best way to describe communication is with the word *transactional*. **Transactional** means that the communication process is completely integrated, simultaneous, and interrelated, including the encoding and decoding of messages, the sending and receiving of feedback, the social and physical context, and other components of the process.

Conscious versus Subconscious Messages

What subconscious message are you sending when you show up late for a job interview? Are you telling a potential employer that you will be late for work most days? Are you saying that you do not take the interview seriously, and thus you probably will not take the job seriously?

It may help to think about communication across a continuum of consciousness. For instance, when you sigh or exclaim angrily about a traffic jam, you may not be conscious—or at least not very conscious—of those forms of communication. Yet when you are engaging in a conversation during a job interview or giving a presentation in front of your speech class, you are engaging in a very formal, very conscious type of communication.

In their book *Communicate!*, authors Rudolph Verderber, Kathleen Verderber, and Deanna Sellnow (2010) distinguish three common types of communication along the consciousness spectrum: spontaneous (unconscious) messages, scripted (somewhat conscious) messages, and constructed (highly conscious) messages.

- **Spontaneous messages** are the ones you blurt out without thinking at all—for example, laughing at a person who slips and falls.
- **Scripted messages** are messages you use over and over again without putting much thought into them. For example, if you are feeling ill, you might respond to a friend's greeting of "Hi, how are you?" with a brief, "Good," even though you do not feel well at all. The scripted message just falls out quickly, before your brain has a chance to correct it.
- **Constructed messages** are highly thoughtful, carefully formulated messages. Building constructed messages is often the most difficult type of communication, because it necessarily involves a great deal of thought. Return for a moment to the college classroom scenario discussed previously. As a presenter of a lecture on job search skills at your local library, Raisa would choose to deliver a constructed message, with carefully prepared remarks.

The subconscious is also involved in the interpretation of a message. Many components of the communication process affect the sender's coding of the message and the receiver's decoding and interpretation. These components often relate to the sender personally, particularly on a subconscious basis. Who exactly is the sender? The sender's age, cultural background, hair color, level of attractiveness—all are encoded signals that the receiver subconsciously interprets. Similarly, the sender should subconsciously consider his or her audience's personal characteristics when shaping the message.

ETHICS AND COMMUNICATION

You may never have thought about the ethics of communication. But if you stop for a moment, you may be able to come up with more than a few examples of unethical communication. Has a President of the United States ever lied to the American public? If so, that certainly would be an unethical communication. You can probably think of additional examples—telling a lie on the witness stand at a court trial, or even misleading an audience who is placing their trust in you. A car salesman may try to convince you that a car is a better deal than it is. How would you interact with such a salesperson? If you don't believe she is credible, it is unlikely you will buy a car from her. And so it goes with any communication—if you do not engender the trust of your audience, it is unlikely that they will listen or believe your message.

What guidelines can you follow to ensure that your communications are ethical? In *Communicate!,* Verderber, Verderber, and Sellnow (2010) list five standards for keeping communication ethical and forthright:

1. Be truthful and honest.
2. Have integrity, which means that you will do what you say you will do.
3. Be fair. Give equal time to all sides of an issue. Do not take sides.

ETHICS AND JOURNALISM

In the late 19th century, yellow journalism, or what today is called tabloid journalism, first posed a challenge to the lofty primary goal of journalism: to inform a free and democratic society. Publishers began to discover that they sold more newspapers when the paper contained a sensational story—a lurid tale of murder, for example, or perhaps a compelling scandal involving a highly regarded public official.

Of course, journalism has another goal as well: In a capitalist society, owners of media outlets are in business to make money. Media companies want to sell newspapers, attract viewers, court listeners, and so on in order to make a profit. Today, media outlets must walk a fine line between reporting and entertaining, trying to secure a majority share of the public market in order to turn a profit.

4. Be respectful. Communication means that communicators will not always arrive at mutual understanding; should this happen, respect others' interpretations.
5. Be responsible. The messages you encode and decode may have meanings you did not intend or anticipate. Be accountable for how your messages may be received.

Ethical speakers begin by always keeping their audience and the backdrop of the message in mind. They attempt to shape and match their message in order to accommodate the audience, the situation in which the message will transpire, and the context of the communication. In order to achieve this match, ethical senders must study their receivers carefully and pay close attention to how the message is being received. Failure to do so could create confusion, or, worse yet, inadvertent or intentional fraud.

ASSESSING COMMUNICATION GOALS

Rather than an end goal itself, the communication process is instead a route to achieve a goal. Communication involves meeting the needs of others. In fact, Verderber, Verderber, and Sellnow identify that the five most common goals of communication are to

- meet social needs,
- develop and maintain a sense of self,
- develop relationships,
- exchange information, and
- influence others.

You might constrain these goals even further by stating that communication is a means to inform, influence, persuade, or entertain an audience.

Communicating with Civility

The message is not all that matters. How it is delivered can be just as important. A message that is rudely delivered may not be heard at all. Instead, the receiver may hear only the rudeness and completely discount the meaning of the message. A civil speaker is well mannered, appropriate, courteous, gracious, and considerate. If you are thoughtful not only in the coding of the message but also in its delivery, you are doing all you can to ensure successful communication.

Effective speakers follow rules of **etiquette**, which are the ground rules of polite, civil communication. Rules of etiquette include how to start, sustain, and stop communication—the sender(s) and the receiver(s) taking turns and working together in order to effectively transfer information. Effective use of etiquette can help you navigate difficult situations, including communicating with a diverse audience or in diverse contexts.

The cooperative nature of civil communication means that as conversations go on, all the parties involved build their own respective understanding together, and not separately. Rather than involving an active party—the sender—and a passive party—the receiver—a conversation actively engages both parties at all times. Senders and receivers engage in a constant negotiation of understanding.

Never Mislead an Audience

Speeches can and do affect their audiences, and this effect can be either positive or negative. Speakers are responsible for the effects of their messages on their audience, and they must carefully prepare in order to ensure that the messages do not contain wrong information or bad (or easily misconstrued) advice.

Speakers and audiences enter a basic contract during the communication process. It is a contract of mutual understanding. If the communicator is honest and has goodwill towards the audience, the communicator is likely to receive trust and goodwill from the audience. Receivers assemble an idea of a sender's credibility early on in this contract. If credibility is established and maintained, the sender can count on the audience's acceptance of the message. After all, if an audience thinks a speaker is an authority on a topic, the audience will invest trust in that speaker. The audience will believe the speaker to be very knowledgeable about the issue at hand, and it will believe that the message is accurate and earnest.

Preparation

When cautioning speakers about the importance of preparation, talk show host Larry King remarked that an audience is always "worthy of your best effort." Of course, this does not necessarily mean that you can only talk about topics that you are an expert about—King himself could not possibly have known all there was to know about all the topics his show covered. Instead, King's point is that a speaker must instill some sense of expert credibility with his or her audience, and the quickest route to doing so is to thoroughly prepare for the communication. An ethical speaker respects two important phases of preparation: research and personalization.

Research, no matter how thorough or light, will show when you communicate a message. Doing your homework before speaking is key to creating a sense of authority. If you spend time learning details about a topic

DID YOU KNOW?

Advertorials

Have you ever noticed a newspaper or magazine article with the word "advertisement" printed at the top of the page in small letters? Did you happen to notice that this type of ad looks entirely different from most of the other ads? These ads, which are known as advertorials, are designed to grab the attention of readers who usually skip over traditional ads. The term *advertorial* refers to an advertising message that pretends to be news—in other words, a message that attempts to confuse its receiver by implying that it comes from a different channel. This subtly suggests that the message of the advertorial is endorsed by the media channel in which it appears—credibility by association. Do you believe this practice is ethical?

and honing your presentation, your audience will be far more likely to listen to you and trust your message. Research involves reading and learning about what others have had to say about a particular topic, so the second part of ethical preparation involves processing the research—the thoughts of others—and then coming up with your own interpretations and opinions about the topic.

COMMUNICATIVE SETTINGS

Setting is an integral part of the communication process. **Settings** are also referred to as **contexts,** but you may find it easier to think of settings as environments where communication takes place. The setting of a communication is directly affected by the number of communicators involved and the level of consciousness with which communicators exchange messages—that is, whether the communication is formal or informal. These settings include:

- Intrapersonal, which is one's internal communication with oneself
- Interpersonal, which is one's communication with others
- Mediated, which is somehow facilitated by someone or something in the middle of, and in addition to, the communicators
- Small group, which may be formal or informal and usually involves a group of at least 3, and no more than 20, people
- Public, which typically applies to groups of 20 or more people and is the most formal environment for communication
- Virtual, which is any message destined for many receivers that must travel through some other means than direct to get from the sender to the receivers, and receivers may not be able to provide immediate feedback

Intrapersonal

The prefix *intra* means *within*, so simply put, **intrapersonal communication** is communication that occurs within you. Typically, this communication takes place within your mind, including your personal thoughts, emotions, and your internal perceptions of yourself and other people. When you talk to yourself (out loud or silently) and when you imagine (play scenes in your mind), you are experiencing intrapersonal communication. Students communicate intrapersonally when they solve problems during a test. You communicate intrapersonally when you make decisions, carefully weigh pros and cons, and play out what-if scenarios in your head. Other forms of silent intrapersonal communication include fantasies, self-reflection, creative thinking, daydreams, or dreams. While intrapersonal communication generally refers to internal dialogue, it also can be external—such as talking to yourself or using a voice recorder, e-mail, or voicemail to set reminders for yourself.

Intrapersonal communication is centered on **self-awareness**, a level of knowledge and understanding about your own biases, prejudices, motives, intentions, triggers, perceptions, and cultural filters that you as a conscious communicator can choose to either use or overcome to ensure your message is received and interpreted well. You must be able to honestly communicate with yourself if you have any hope of communicating honestly with others.

Intrapersonal communication also affects your interpersonal communication, as the initial encoding of a message happens within you. Before you communicate with others, you must first make a series of choices about a variety of messages you wish to share. Academics who study intrapersonal communication often examine its role in forming perceptions and anxiety as it relates to communicating in other environments, like interpersonal, small group, or public communication.

Noise may also play a role in intrapersonal communication—for example, consider the physiological noise of suffering the symptoms of a cold, or the psychological noise of feeling nervous as you plan a big sales pitch. Although it is typically informal, intrapersonal communication can become more formalized—such as the preparation you undergo before a job interview or an important speech, or the internal mental process of self-help.

Intrapersonal communication may often be subconscious. Things that you do out of habit may qualify as subconscious intrapersonal communication. For example, dialing a phone number you know "by heart" is an example of subconscious intrapersonal communication. However, when it matters—as in work and school settings—effective communicators are conscious even when communicating intrapersonally. Effective communicators remain mindful of that inner voice or **conscience** that guides them. They remain mindful of both the short- and long-term effects of the messages they send and how those messages are sent, and they take the time to understand their own mental processes—and thus be conscious of them—while communicating with others.

Interpersonal

The prefix *inter-* means *between;* thus, **interpersonal communication** is communication between or among two or more people. The scenario that cast Raisa as the presenter of a library lecture is an example of interpersonal communication. Interpersonal communication includes a variety of communicative settings—mediated, small group, public, and virtual or mass communication, among others—and has two distinguishing markers: the social structure within which the communication is taking place and the influence that communicators exert over one another.

Interpersonal communication is probably the communication environment of which you are most aware, as you are in a constant state of interpersonal communication (and now you realize you are also in a constant state of intrapersonal communication). Interpersonal communication is an informal

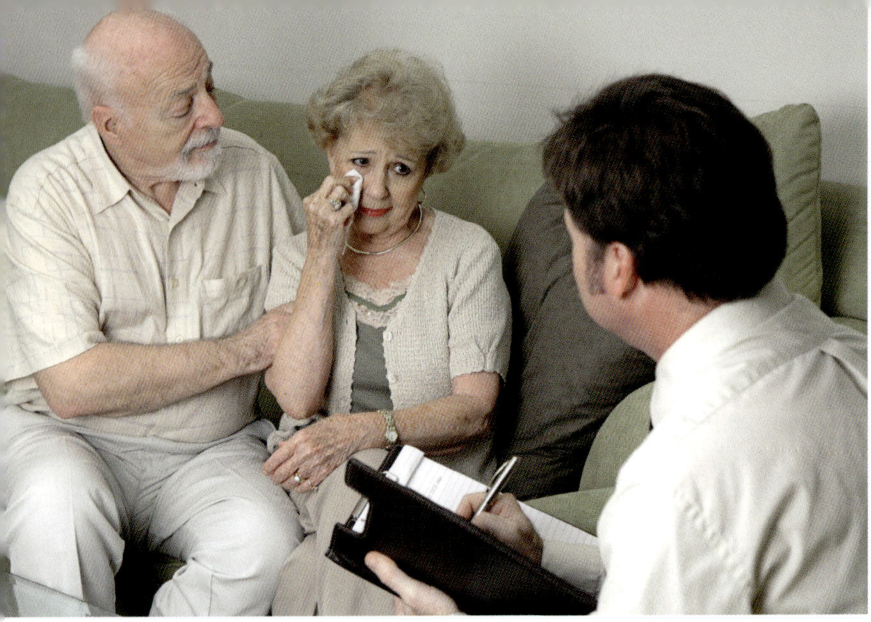

exchange between communicators who have a known connection to each other. Often the known connection, or **relationship**, between these parties comes from the roles communicators play in each other's lives. Some of the relationships present in the example of the library presentation on job search skills are speaker–audience, speaker–group member, group member–group member, or any variation of these pairs. Interpersonal communication plays a significant role in how a speaker gives information to an audience, how the audience members exhibit that they have received and understood that information, and how everyone in the group works together to create and transmit information.

Mediated Communication

Mediated communication is communication that is somehow facilitated by someone or something in the middle of, and in addition to, the communicators. Technology offers a multitude of ways to have mediated communication—for example, via computer, including instant messages, chat rooms, and e-mail. Other than face-to-face communication, technology has made sure that much of today's communication is mediated. In the classroom example, students logging into an online classroom management system to download audio files of lectures are using mediated communication. Other examples of mediated communication include cell phones, blogs, and social media.

A face-to-face mediated communication might be a joint marriage counseling session or a couple's appearance in a divorce court, when the communication is assisted by a professional attorney.

E-mails are an excellent example of computer-mediated communication. They are speedy, provide a durable record of the communication, and enable mass communication with a push of a button. However, e-mail communication can be problematic. E-mails, as well as other types of virtual communication, lack many of the rich dimensions of communication that takes place either face-to-face, ear-to-ear, or Web camera to Web camera. In e-mail, subtlety and nuance disappear, and much can be left up to interpretation. Many people use an elaborate, usually informal, system of emoticons to fill in some of the interpretive space when using e-communications. An emoticon is a symbol, such as a smiley face, meant to stand in for the missing nonverbal cues and to convey tone. A sender adds these emoticons to a message to aid a receiver in decoding the message.

It is important to be aware of when more formality is necessary. For instance, when you are at work, it is more critical to use spell check before sending an e-mail than when you are sending messages to friends from a home account. When sending an e-mail, you should also think about who owns the messages you send. For example, are you using your employer's equipment, or sending the messages from your work e-mail account? If so, you do not own the message within—your employer does. Consider the length of time that messages are kept at your workplace, school, or other institutions. Ask yourself if you would mind if the message you are about to send became public. Before hitting the "send" button, take a moment to proofread your message, check your coding, and anticipate your receiver's decoding and interpreting process. An effective communicator thinks ahead about how to set and manage a receiver's expectations. Even if you are not sending an e-mail message via a work account, always remember to be a conscientious communicator so your message is correctly interpreted.

Academic studies of computer-mediated communication have attempted to address whether the involvement of the computer as an intermediary has been beneficial for the development of interpersonal communication. These researchers hoped to figure out whether computer-mediated communication hinders or enhances interpersonal communication. Some have found that the ease of this communication and the ready access to computer-mediated communication cannot replace the communicator's ability to make a deeper connection in person. Computer-mediated messages must still struggle to get through noise that is only intensified by the Web.

In addition, mediation via computer may change the way communicators represent themselves. Online dating provides a good example of this phenomenon. A sender may choose to present messages that reflect only his or her most positive personal aspects, thus leading the receiver to interpret an idealized version of the message and the sender.

At the same time, computer-mediated communication can be helpful in the unique interpersonal dynamic of groups. The absence of any social cues and obvious status indicators can help unify a group and can help people work together better. The more anonymous nature of this communication can lead to less identification as an individual and more identification as a member of a group.

Small Group

Your family, friends, and classmates are all examples of small groups. A small group is interdependent and is made up of individuals who share common goals, play roles, have relationships with one another, share a sense of mutual belonging, observe standards for membership in the group, and communicate interactively with one another. **Small-group communication** may be formal or informal and usually involves a group of at least 3, and no more than 20, people.

Why is small-group communication important? As a student, working in small groups is necessary to complete assignments, gain knowledge, and obtain credit for your coursework. As a family member or friend, participation in small-group communication provides a social interaction outlet. Additionally, small-group communication is often the key method used by groups to do business.

In small-group communication, the group members constantly change roles, acting as both senders and receivers to simultaneously send and receive verbal and nonverbal messages. One of the many keys to successful small-group communication is having a better understanding of how social factors play a role in perception.

Think again about the library presentation scenario. Suppose that Raisa decides to arrange the audience into small groups to discuss job search skills. As the presenter (and group leader), how can Raisa best assess the participation of each member of the group? Successful small-group communication is based on three components: participants' attitudes, participants' contributions, and the quality of the participants' contributions.

Small-group communication is more effective if you adhere to the following guidelines:

- Adopt a cooperative attitude.
- Assume your share of responsibility.
- Avoid a passive attitude.
- Contribute effectively.
- Be a good listener.

Public Communication

The library presentation scenario also applies to public communication. A presenter addressing a group is an example of public communication. The term **public communication** typically applies to groups of 20 or more people. Typically, public communication is the most formal environment for communication—including clear identification of the roles of speaker and audience. That formality also comes with a certain fear factor. Roscoe Drummond, a journalist, once said of public speaking: "The mind is a wonderful thing. It starts working the moment you are born and never stops until you get up to speak in public."

The communication process has many components that are working in a coordinated and interrelated effort. So what is happening to the speaker and audience in a public communication setting?

- The presenter is making a commitment to the audience and is working to prove a point that will win the support of the audience or that will generate action.
- The audience is making a judgment about the presenter and asking questions like, "Do I really trust this person? Does this information make any sense? Are the facts presented here accurate?"

Components of the speech communication process include some familiar and some new concepts, including speaker, message, channel, listener, feedback, interference, and situation. How do these concepts relate to the communication model that began this chapter? The speaker is the sender and the initiator and is responsible for coding or encoding the message. The listener is the receiver and is responsible for decoding the message. Interference can be referred to as noise. The situation is the context in which you are expected to deliver your speech and includes the purpose and the physical location of the speech. (Is this a speech for a final class project? Is this a speech you are giving to a client? If you are giving a speech at work, will you be speaking to your peers or supervisors?)

As you know, common goals for speaking include informing, influencing, persuading, or entertaining. In work and school settings, informing and persuading are the most common goals. So how should you tackle a public speaking commitment when public speaking still ranks as Americans' top fear? Extensive preparation will cancel out your fears. Then, if you are confident about what you plan to say, you have little to worry about.

Next, review the information on the nature of ethical speaking earlier in this chapter. As you know, speakers are charged with a heavy ethical burden, as the position of delivering a speech confers deep knowledge and authority about a subject. Audiences assume that a speaker is an expert, and thus the role of speaker comes with a certain degree of power. Of course, the goal of a speech is to persuade or inform, but not at the expense of honesty and truth. As you prepare for the speech, consider whether your goals for your presentation are ethical and just.

Finally, consider whether the goals you have for your presentation are representative of who you are and what you want to say. Are you proud of the message you plan to deliver? Do you know your audience well—perhaps not personally, but do you know generally (characteristics, interests) who will be in attendance? Do you know what they expect of your presentation? Knowing these facts can help you gain the confidence to present your speech without fear.

Virtual (Mass) Communication

Telecommuting is when employees virtually communicate from home or another off-site location with their colleagues. Those colleagues may be located in a central office, or they may be telecommuters as well. While many telecommute exclusively via computer and telephone, some telecommuters communicate through videoconferencing, which adds a visual component to the audio exchange.

In recent years, many colleges and universities have begun to offer videoconferencing in their distance education programs as well. Students who view videoconferences also use virtual blackboards and online chats as part of their participation in the course.

Traditional mass communication outlets, such as print, radio, and television media, are now reinforced (and in some cases replaced) by virtual communication, the Internet, YouTube, and social media. These new mass communication outlets allow people to communicate with others regardless of time and physical boundaries. Think of **mass communication** as meaning any message destined for many receivers that must travel through some means other than direct to get from the sender to the receivers, and for which receivers may not be able to provide feedback.

- Mass communication includes newspapers, magazines, Internet, radio, and television.
- Mass communication messages are received by a large and diverse group of participants.
- With the exception of print media, mass communication messages have the capacity to be received with the same speed to all receivers with no, or very little, delay.

Of course, the rise of the Internet and social media has made mass communication much more of a two-way street; for example, now, a receiver can read a news story online and immediately provide feedback by "liking" it and sharing it with others. Before computers and the Internet, mass communication was more of a one-way communication process, but now receivers are a part of the mass media process. Virtual communication empowers receivers to move from a totally passive position to a range of active options.

Mass communication and culture are often so closely entwined that it may be difficult to tell the difference between culture and the communication channels used to reach receivers. In fact, many believe that mass media institutions are cornerstones of culture, in that they reflect and directly impact society itself.

SUMMARY

- The contemporary communication model includes the sender and receiver, noise, the feedback loop, channels, message, coding and decoding of the message, and context.
- Communication is irreversible, inevitable, multidimensional, and transactional, and it covers different formats and modes.
- Communication also involves the conscious and subconscious mind.
- Ethical communication means assessing communication goals and communicating with civility. An ethical communicator would never mislead an audience.
- Preparing for communication is vital to ethical communication. An audience's time must never be wasted or misused with an ill-prepared or inaccurate speech or other communication.
- Communication can take place either intrapersonally or interpersonally.
- Interpersonal communication settings include mediated, small group, public, and virtual (mass).

REFERENCES

Beebe, S., Beebe, S., & Ivy, D. K. (2009). *Communication: Principles for a lifetime*: Vol. 4. *Presentational speaking* (portable ed.). Needham Heights, MA: Allyn & Bacon/Pearson Education.

Brenner, D. M. (2007). *Move the world: Persuade your audience, change minds, and achieve goals*. New York, NY: John Wiley & Sons.

Brignall, M. (2007). Describing the transactional communications model. Retrieved from http://www.wisc-online.com/objects/ViewObject.aspx?ID=oic100

Capp, G., Capp, C., & Capp, G. R. (1990). *Basic oral communication* (5th ed.). Englewood Cliffs, NJ: Prentice-Hall.

Cherney, L. R. (2005). Communication. In G. Albecht (Ed.), *Encyclopedia of disability* (Vol. 1, pp. 279–282). Thousand Oaks, CA: Sage.

Christians, C. G. (2007). Communication ethics. In *Encyclopedia of science, technology and ethics.* Farmington Hills, MI: Gale Cengage (Macmillan Reference).

Communication; Nonverbal communication. (2008). In *International encyclopedia of the social sciences* (2nd ed.). Farmington Hills, MI: Gale Cengage (Macmillan Reference).

Communication channels; Speaking skills in business. (2007). In *Encyclopedia of business and finance* (2nd ed.). Farmington Hills, MI: Gale Cengage (Macmillan Reference).

Dellinger, S., & Deane, B. (1980). *Communicating effectively: A complete guide to better managing.* Radnor, PA: Chilton Book Company.

Duckworth, C., & Frost, R. (2008). Noise pollution. In *Gale encyclopedia of science* (Vol. 4). Farmington Hills, MI: Gale Cengage (Macmillan Reference).

Hargrave, J. (2007). Listening skills in business. In *Encyclopedia of business and finance* (2nd ed.). Farmington Hills, MI: Gale Cengage (Macmillan Reference).

Harris, T., & Sherblom, J. (2011). *Small group and team communication* (5th ed.). Needham Heights, MA: Allyn & Bacon/Pearson Education.

Headrick, D. (2005). Communication overview. In *Berkshire encyclopedia of world history*. Retrieved from http://www.scribd.com/doc/36159228/Ency-of-World-Hist

Hu, Y., & Sundar, S. (2007). Computer-mediated communication (CMC). In J. J. Arnett (Ed.), *Encyclopedia of children, adolescents, and the media* (pp. 200–202). Thousand Oaks, CA: Sage.

King, L., & Gilbert, B. (1994). *How to talk to anyone, anytime, anywhere: The secrets of good communication*. New York, NY: Crown/Three Rivers Press/Random House.

Liepmann, L. (1984). *Winning connections: A program for on-target business communication.* Indianapolis, IN: Bobbs-Merrill Press.

LoCicero, J. (2007). *Business communication*. Cincinnati, OH: Adams Media (F+W).
Lucas, S. E. (1998). *The art of public speaking*. New York, NY: McGraw-Hill.
Merrier, P. (2006). *Business communication*. Cincinnati, OH: Thomson South-Western College Publishing.
O'Neil, S., Evans, J., & Bigley, H. (2007). Communications in business. In *Encyclopedia of business and finance* (2nd ed.). Farmington Hills, MI: Gale Cengage (Macmillan Reference).
Oberg, B. C. (2003). *Interpersonal communication: An introduction to human interaction*. Colorado Springs, CO: Meriwether.
Reardon, K., & Christopher, N. (2010). *Comebacks at work*. New York, NY: HarperBusiness.
Ross, R. (1983). *Speech communication: Fundamentals and practice*. Englewood Cliffs, NJ: Prentice-Hall.
Rothwell, J. D. (2009). *In mixed company: Communicating in small groups and teams* (7th ed.). Farmington Hills, MI: Gale Cengage (Thomson Wadsworth).
Simmons, A. (2007). *Whoever tells the best story wins*. New York, NY: Amacom Press.
Verderber, R. F., Verderber, K. S., & Sellnow, D. (2009). *Communicate!* (13th ed.). Retrieved from http://www.cengagebrain.com/shop/content/verderber36403_1439036403_01.01_toc.pdf
Windley, C., & Skinner, M. (2007). Selecting a topic. University of Idaho. Retrieved from http://www.class.uidaho.edu/comm101/chapters/selecting_topic/selecting_topic_printable.htm

CHAPTER 2

The Process of Human Perception

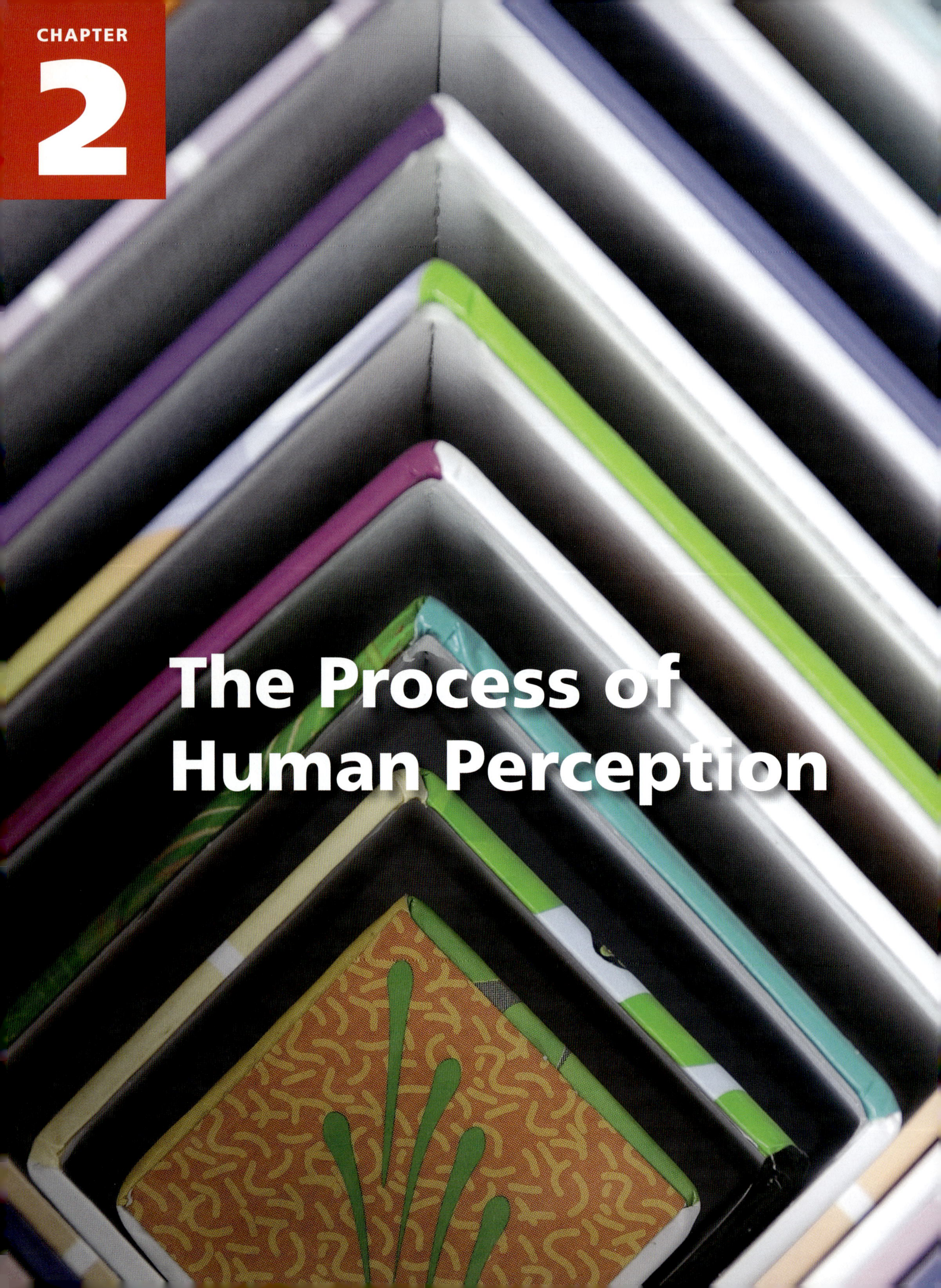

Marc is excited, but uneasy. He is about to walk into his new office. It is his first day working as a paralegal, and in fact, it is the first office job he has ever had! He worked hard to land this job—it has been two months since he graduated from college—but he knows that this job was worth waiting for.

The elevator opens into the hushed lobby of the law office where Marc will be working. Marc looks around nervously and smiles at the receptionist as he approaches the main desk. Several employees rush past, focused intently on their work. He wonders if they will be unfriendly, or if they are just too busy to take note of him now.

Before he introduces himself to the receptionist, Marc pauses to take it all in. Everything in the office lobby looks and smells expensive—the leather furniture, the wall of windows, and even the beautiful bouquet of lilies and roses on the receptionist's desk. The plush carpeting springs back with every step he takes. Marc immediately checks his reflection in the glass wall to make sure he does not look disheveled from his commute. Relieved that his hair is still in place and his appearance is neat and professional, Marc greets the receptionist. She smiles back, tells him she has been expecting him, and asks him to take a seat.

After a short wait, Marc at last sees the friendly face of Rita, the office manager who hired him. Once they exchange a warm handshake and greeting, Marc feels much more at ease. He follows Rita back into the main office, smiling a hello to each of his new coworkers as he passes by.

KEY CONCEPTS

1. Human perception begins with gathering information by using the five senses. See page 24.

2. Perception involves both internal and external processes. See page 24.

3. Human perception affects both internal and external communication. See page 25.

4. There are three stages of human perception: selecting, organizing, and interpreting stimuli. See page 24.

5. Cultural perceptions affect workplace communication. See page 28.

WHAT IS HUMAN PERCEPTION?

Marc is using **human perception** in an effort to make himself more comfortable in a nerve-wracking situation. He is gathering external information using his five senses (smell, touch, taste, sound, and sight) and using that information to make conclusions about his surroundings. Marc is in a new situation—he wants to make a good impression and to do well in his new position. Consider how Marc would use perception differently if he were making dinner in his own home or stranded late at night on a deserted stretch of road.

Perception is an ongoing activity that involves both external and internal processes. As Marc used his five main senses to interpret his surroundings, taking in the sights, sounds, and scents, he considered how the place made him feel. You can imagine how much the heightened sense of nervousness and anticipation that Marc felt when he first entered the office gradually lessened as he was reassured by what he saw (his neat reflection in the glass) and heard (warm greetings from the receptionist and Rita).

The information you receive from your senses is usually filtered by your personal experiences. A person who has had many jobs before and knows that those first-day jitters will soon pass would feel much more at ease in this situation than Marc did. Perception is a guide that informs every move you make.

Understanding the role of perception is key to learning about public speaking and communication. After all, you must come to a clear understanding of how you perceive others, and how others perceive you, if you are to become an effective speaker and also an effective listener.

Selecting Stimuli

There are three main stages in the process of human perception. The first has to do with **select stimuli**. Each individual is different, and only certain sensory details known as select stimuli will get a response that influences perception. Irrelevant sensory details will go unnoticed. As a nervous new employee, Marc quickly focused on perceiving the people around him as he entered the office but noticed few details of the office's décor other than the thick carpet, the glass wall, and the flowers on the receptionist's desk. His filters of perception ignored countless other pieces of information because they were not relevant to his needs, interests, and/or expectations.

This automatic selection of what stimuli are most relevant to you often depends on your *needs*. Sometimes, the needs are biological. If you are very hungry, it may be more difficult for you to focus on anything except food. These needs may also be psychological, as in Marc's case—he is focusing on feeling comfortable in his new job setting. Emotional needs also drive which stimuli you select. Maybe you had an exhausting week of final exams, so you decide to spend the evening with a good friend who makes you laugh. As you spend the evening with

that friend, you probably will not notice much about the setting and will instead focus on your friend's words and nonverbal communication.

A person's interests often determine what stimuli will be selected. Imagine that you are at a restaurant having dinner with two female friends. One is a huge sports fan and the other is completely uninterested in sports. As the three of you talk, the sports fan's eyes and attention will frequently drift from the discussion to the basketball game on the TV above the bar.

Select stimuli are also often based on expectations. If a vacation package from a travel agent assures you fun-filled days on sandy beaches in the sunshine, you will look for those expectations to be met while you are on your trip. You will be quite disappointed if you do not experience sun and fun.

Organizing Information

The second stage of perception involves how people *organize* the information obtained by their senses and filtered by the select stimuli in order to prepare to understand it. When you leave your home to drive to work, you probably always take the quickest and easiest route. The same is true of the process your brain undergoes as it organizes the information it receives from select stimuli. Your brain works very hard to simplify a scene in order to help filter out any unnecessary stimuli.

For instance, when sports fans enter a restaurant packed with wide-screen TVs, each of which is showing a different sporting event, their brains automatically process the scene and simplify it. In the example in which you are dining out with two friends, your friend who is a sports fan will likely exclude all the games that she is not interested in and focus solely on the game involving a team she roots for. On the other hand, non-fans simplify the scene by screening out the TVs altogether and focus instead on other stimuli—the food, conversation with dining partners, or the background music. Your non-fan friend may even choose to sit facing away from the TVs.

Closely connected to the organizational principle of simplification is the process of looking for **patterns** among all the incoming information from stimuli. In the restaurant example, even if all the televisions were tuned to commercials, the sports fan would likely be able to quickly deduce which games were playing on which TVs by scanning the groups of people clustered around them to see what colors or team jerseys they were wearing.

Constructivism

Constructivism, or the practice of organizing perceptions based on past experiences, is also something people naturally do to understand the world around them. Perhaps the friend who does not like sports is not interested because she was injured playing basketball at a young age and thus associates sports with pain and suffering. Perhaps the friend who likes sports became interested in games

because she is naturally shy and finds it much easier to talk to others about sports than about other issues. Each person has constructed a filter for interpreting select stimuli in order to understand her surroundings.

Interpreting Information

The third stage in the process of human perception is the *interpretation* of stimuli after it has been collected and organized. What do all these bits of information mean? How can these meanings be communicated internally and externally?

Assumptions

Most children like to color pictures. When they first learn to color, they grab whatever color pleases them at the moment. As they grow older and learn more about their environment, the stimuli they encounter help them organize certain concrete visual patterns: Leaves are green, bark is brown, and the sky is blue. Then they apply these patterns to their coloring books and make *assumptions* related to these repetitive stimuli. They use the color green for the leaves of trees, brown for bark, and blue for the sky.

Assumptions like these are often based more on feelings than fact, but if others reinforce assumptions, they may become processed as reality. Your perception of the colors of objects in nature have become locked in over time—you have a tendency to perceive leaves as green, bark as brown, and the sky as blue, despite the fact that leaves are often other colors than green (particularly in the fall), tree bark is just as likely to be gray as it is brown, and the sky is essentially a different color every moment of the day (and is quite a different color at night as well).

How are assumptions connected to perception and organizing information? Keep in mind that assumptions aid perception and help people to understand and communicate in their world. Assumptions can cause people to limit their perception of situations and of people, as in the case of stereotyping and bias.

Stereotyping as a Way to Filter Information

People tend to collect and organize information about those with whom they come into contact. They also collect and organize various stimuli as a way to interpret their surroundings. In other words, after reacting to the same sensory details and organizing them as a way to understand and interpret people, individuals often make assumptions about groups. This is known as **stereotyping**.

In the example of the friends dining out together, the sports fan might automatically stereotype the fans watching the game—the fans who liked the same team that she did as "good" and the fans that liked the opposing team as "bad." The friend who did not like sports might stereotype all the sports fans as being loud or obnoxious in general simply because they were cheering and enjoying the game.

There is a general perception that stereotyping is bad, but assumptive perceptions of people can have positive or negative results.

Positive and Negative Results from Stereotyping in Different Situations

People who tend to think alike or have certain common characteristics—for example, fans of the same basketball team—generally feel more comfortable around each other than people who do not share common characteristics. You can extend this example to include any group with similar characteristics—people who are looking for jobs, people who are studying the same subject in school, or people who like to read novels. In a group, these people with common characteristics can enjoy communicating about their shared interests and often feel as though they have common expectations and needs. They stereotype other members of the group as being "like" them, and this can lead to a sense of community and personal growth.

On the other hand, the results may be negative. Perhaps members of a group also draw the conclusion that people who do not share common characteristics with them are "different" and thus are "bad." These conclusions are largely groundless, of course, but stereotyping can be powerfully convincing.

In fact, some of the darkest days in human history began with negative stereotyping. Consider, for example, how racial stereotyping during World War II resulted in the deaths of millions of Jews, homosexuals, and disabled people, as well as many other people who were stereotyped as "different" and/or "bad." Furthermore, consider how following the events of September 11, 2001, racial profiling in the United States has resulted in persecution of some Americans of Arab and South Asian descent, as well as countless Americans who practice the Muslim faith. Clearly, negative stereotyping is unhealthy for everyone.

Stereotypes can be positive when they are used to encourage or motivate. Many families, for instance, stereotype their own members. If a father consistently reminds his children, "We Smiths are intelligent and hardworking," his children may learn to value and benefit from these attributes. Perhaps the Smith children will want to follow this example and will willingly self-identify as intelligent, hardworking Smiths.

Of course, the inverse may also be true. Some Smith children may resent their parents' desire to have them fit a mold. Imagine what might happen if one of the Smith children began to perform poorly on tests, perhaps because of an undiagnosed learning disability. He might begin to feel that he does not "belong" in his own family, because he perceives himself suddenly as less intelligent. He may begin to distance himself more from the rest of the family, perhaps even becoming an outsider in his own home.

Sometimes stereotypes can improve relationships among members of groups. For example, in a work setting where certain team members are not communicating well with one another because of cultural differences or expectations, diversity training may used to break down these barriers. This diversity training may involve confronting stereotypes and dismantling them. In these encounters, team members share their perceptions about how they have felt stereotyped and limited in their roles. As they use these stereotypes as a springboard for open discussion, these coworkers can come to a better understanding of one another and ultimately work together more efficiently and effectively.

The Media's Influence on Stereotypes

One of the most prevalent influences on our perceptions is the media, which includes both positive and negative results from stereotyping. Radio programs, TV shows, movies, advertisements, online postings, and every other source of news and information contains images and descriptions of people, places, and things. Each of these media messages has a specific target audience in mind, which helps reinforce stereotypes.

Imagine that a supermarket chain's management team discovered that a nonprofit senior citizens' organization provided free transportation for its members to and from their stores each Friday. The chain might decide to run an advertisement in the local newspaper each Thursday featuring happy senior citizens shopping at the store and a mention of the nonprofit organization's free transport. It may even decide to partially underwrite the cost of the transportation. This positive use of stereotyping leads to a win for all parties: The nonprofit organization will hopefully gain more use and funding for its service, more seniors will become aware of the available assistance, and the store will make more money as more seniors visit the store.

On the other hand, media influence often reinforces negative stereotypes. In the early days of television, for example, many advertisements and TV shows that featured family situations depicted men in the role of breadwinner and women in the role of homemaker. This perpetuated a stereotype that fathers are never primary caregivers for their children and that mothers should not work outside the home. Today, the responsibilities of childcare and housekeeping are shared in most two-parent households, but the media has been slow to change. This continued stereotype has ramifications in the family court system (as mothers are often given preference in child-custody arrangements), in the workforce (as men are often paid more than women for the same work), and in other areas of society. Once stereotypes are ingrained, they can be very difficult to purge from a culture and its communication channels.

Bias

Negative forms of stereotyping can lead to **bias**, or preferential treatment of one group over another. For example, because men are often stereotyped as financial providers for, but not primary caregivers of, children, mothers are more likely to be given preferential treatment in a child-custody arrangement, and fathers are more likely to be required by a court to provide child support.

Historically, women have always been a part of the workforce, but bias still exists in some areas. For example, many women find that a "glass ceiling" exists in their workplace—that they are unable to advance above a certain level because of their

CAREER PERSPECTIVES

In many cases, a potential employer makes a decision about a job candidate within the first few moments of an interview entirely based on initial perceptions of the individual. In some situations (for example, a job fair), you may only have a few minutes to talk. Since these initial perceptions can make all the difference to some employers, you should remember to dress well; be neat and well groomed; and keep your communication direct, friendly, and confident. Make and keep eye contact with your interviewer. Firmly shake your interviewer's hand and introduce yourself. Be prepared to answer any questions you may be asked and provide concrete examples of your skills. Research the company first so you can ask questions about the role and the company's culture that demonstrate both your strong interest in and knowledge of the organization. Make yourself memorable.

gender. Many assign these limitations on advancement to stereotype-based concerns that a woman would be more likely to put the needs of her family before her job, or that a woman would be less invested in her work because she could rely on a male wage-earner to support her if she wished.

Bias is everywhere, but you can and should make an effort to eliminate it from your communication with others. Terms should be kept gender-neutral unless there is clear logic behind referring to only one gender. Try using plural instead of singular, so "he" and "she" become "they," or "single mother" and "single father" become "single parents."

Assigning Attributes

Of course, gender is only one area where bias occurs. Bias is as limitless as the variety of attributes that can be assigned to humanity—ethnicity, religion, economic status, education level, sexuality, and so on. How people perceive the attributes of the people around them, and how they assign labels to these people, affects their communication.

Have you ever heard the advice not to shop for groceries when you are hungry? The idea is that you will buy much more food than you would otherwise. Research has shown that the emotions a person is feeling at the time of an incident have strong bearing on the way that person perceives a situation and the people within it—and also on how that person will behave in the situation. This behavior also includes communication related to the event. Event-related biases like this may end up being extended to other attributes, like ethnicity or faith.

Imagine that you are in your office working. You accidentally shut your desk drawer on your finger just as your boss walks in to ask you a question about something you have done. How will the pain you feel physically influence your thoughts about your boss's comments? You may—at least initially—transfer the annoying pain to your boss. Suddenly, your boss, and the information your boss is sharing with you, will be labeled in your mind as annoying, and you may end up communicating that annoyance back to your boss encoded in your response.

Now imagine that the person who enters your office just as you slam the drawer on your finger is a friend coming to share a funny story. You both laugh

off the incident. You may assign a pleasant attribute to this situation, sharing the humor in your clumsiness with this friend rather than annoyance.

Influences on Perception

In addition to the influence that a person's attributes may have on your perception of that person, there are other external influences on those perceptions and the communication you share. These *environmental influences* on perception include not only the current environment, but also past experiences.

Environment

Have you ever heard of the booming industry of home staging? Home staging involves adding to, removing from, or embellishing the furnishings and décor of a home for sale in order to make it more attractive to potential buyers. What do home staging experts typically do? First, they declutter and depersonalize the home, removing toys, knick-knacks, and family photos. They make quick and relatively inexpensive updates to the existing home, including neutralizing the décor (for example, this includes repainting boldly colored walls in a softer tone). Last, they give consideration to the senses other than vision, including adding comfortable seating, warm and inviting fabrics, scented candles, or soft music.

Staging does not make a home bigger. It cannot make a home's negative points—a location on a busy street, for example, or a lack of closet space—go away. Instead, the goal of staging is to help buyers perceive that the house could be their new home. Since no one else's clutter or photos are present, the décor is current and neutral, and the house is filled with welcoming scents, buyers are more likely to be able to see themselves living there. On the other hand, a potential buyer may not respond positively to staging. A staged house may seem sterile and uninviting. Perhaps they do not like the apple pie scent of the candle, or the staging is too obvious and seems like a ploy.

Keep this example in mind as you consider how your past environment and your present environment may be affecting how you communicate with others. If you grew up in an environment or culture that discouraged asking questions of anyone in authority, for example, how might that affect your communication in the workplace? Although you may be able to overcome this environmental tendency, it may not be easy to learn to ask questions. Environmental influences on perception and communication are difficult to overcome without consistent effort.

DID YOU KNOW?

Stereotypes can have a negative effect on job searches. Many researchers have explored whether people with "ethnic-sounding" names are stereotyped, and thus discriminated against, when they are being considered for jobs. Known as the "ethnic penalty," the practice of assigning negative attributes to a job candidate has long been suspected; many immigrants change their name when they come to a new country and culture in order to avoid the ethnic penalty. A candidate with a name that can be connected to a particular ethnic group may be perceived as someone who is not well assimilated into the prevailing culture, for example. A recruiter may make an assumption that the candidate may not understand the language spoken in the workplace or may not "fit in" with the corporate culture—after only a quick glance at the person's name.

COMMUNICATION ACROSS CULTURES

Communicating in a workplace that includes people from a variety of different cultures can be challenging. You must give consideration to how members of each cultural group perceive and process various situations, especially within the work environment. For example, many workers from Western societies focus on their individuality, while workers from some Eastern cultures focus more on being part of a team, and making sure the team is successful as a whole. People from some cultures take a daily break each afternoon to rest and relax before returning to work—a practice that may be misunderstood by people from other cultures. Familiarizing yourself with the cultural practices and perceptions of all your coworkers can help you collaborate and communicate more effectively with them.

SUMMARY

- Human perception—how people interpret the world around them—has a strong influence on communication.
- Perception not only influences external communication with others, it also affects how people think and respond to the world.
- There are three main stages to human perception: selecting, organizing, and interpreting select stimuli.
- Accurate and bias-free perception and communication requires cultural sensitivity and balance.

CHAPTER

3

The Self and the Communication Process

KEY CONCEPTS

1. The message sender has the responsibility for creating the message and presenting it in a way that the receiver can easily understand. See page 34.

2. Self-understanding is necessary to becoming an effective public speaker. See page 39.

3. The identity circle and Johari window are excellent tools to help you better understand yourself. See page 41.

On the first day of class, instructor Victoria Chisholm announced to her students that their first speech assignment would be to create a presentation about their hometown. Aiesha chose to focus on the physical and geographic aspects of her hometown. Jake chose to talk about his friends from his hometown, and Andre decided to do a speech about his hometown's restaurants and places for entertainment.

After each member of the class delivered his or her speech, Victoria asked the students to consider why each focused on a different aspect. To help get them started, she explained that each student has a unique set of experiences and that the speeches' content and message was based on those experiences.

THE IDENTITY CIRCLE

In order for communication to take place, there needs to be a speaker or sender, a message, an audience or receiver, and feedback. A speaker not only delivers the speech, but also determines the exact message or messages for the audience to receive. How are those messages selected? What makes a speaker decide on one message instead of another?

Imagine that you are a speaker. As you are researching, preparing, and presenting your speech, remember that you must also identify and decide what message the audience is going to receive. You are the one who must decide how best to present that message. As the speaker, you need to ask yourself important questions before preparing your speech. For example, ask yourself: What is your message? Who is your audience? How do you want your audience to respond to your message?

As the speaker, the messages you send and the way that you send them are unique to you. This is why it is important for you to have a clear understanding of yourself and why you make the decisions you do in regard to the messages you send. Your identity is matched and made up of your individual set of life experiences. We each have our own thoughts and opinions on a variety of subjects that have been created and defined by those experiences.

For example, imagine you are going to a birthday party and are asked to take pictures of the events at the party. How do you decide which pictures to take? As the photographer, you are the person behind the camera making the decisions.

What influences the decisions that you make in terms of the pictures that you take at the birthday party? In this example, the role of the photographer is similar to the role that you have as a speaker when you are preparing and giving a speech. Just as the photographer has to decide on what pictures to shoot, you are the person who must decide the message for your speech. You must do the research and determine what content to use to support your message. You must learn about your audience and determine the best way to present the content so the audience can understand your message. Finally, you must decide what type of feedback you are seeking from your audience. What do you want the audience to do with the information? What do you want the guests at the birthday party to remember about the event?

One of the best tools to help you understand yourself and how you communicate is the identity circle (see Figure 3.1). Consider yourself as the hub, the center of the circle. In any wheel, of course, the strength of the wheel depends on the center.

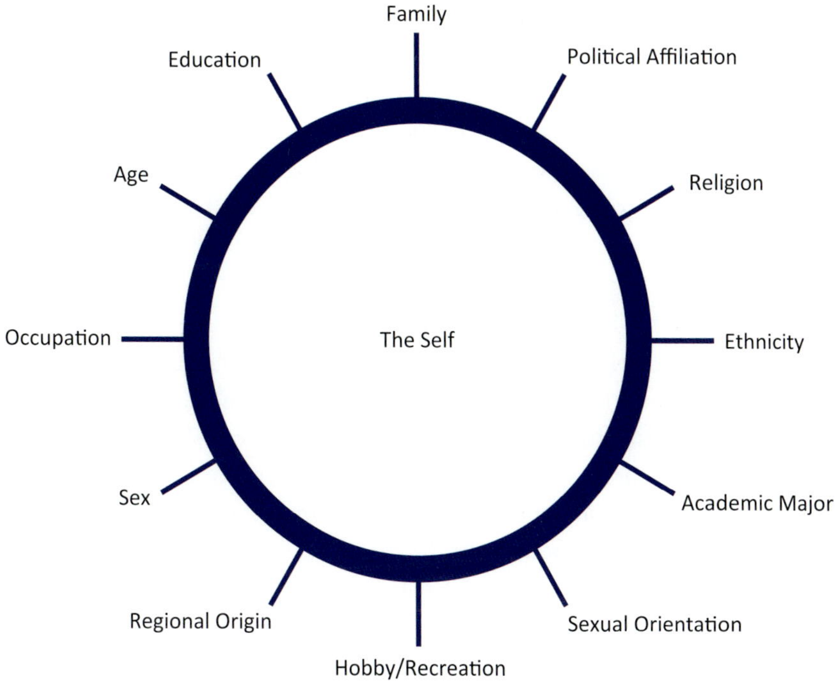

FIGURE 3.1 **Identity Circle**

Around the identity circle, place the many unique individual characteristics you have acquired that help define who you are.

By making yourself the hub and putting your life experiences around the circle, you create an identity circle for yourself. Have you thought about the various ways in which you can identify yourself? Knowing who you are, and having specific awareness of your characteristics is an advantage as a public speaker. This self-understanding means you will have the ability to think critically about who you are as a speaker, how your audience may perceive you, and what adjustments you might make to your communication to bridge any gaps between you and the audience. Remember that the audience also comes to your speech with their own identity and set of experiences, culture, and values. The identity circle includes 12 areas to consider. As you read the upcoming discussion of each part of the identity circle, make notes about yourself in each of these key areas.

Roles of Identity

Gender Roles

Gender, including how you define your gender role as a male or female, is central to your identity, and it may influence how you communicate. There are stereotypical gender roles for men that include a macho, strong personality; a competent, confident personality; and a stoic presence. Men are not supposed to cry—at least not in the typical American culture. In Latin America, on the other hand, men also are part of a macho culture but are often more expressive emotionally than in the United States—complete with tears, hugs, and kisses.

What are typical gender roles for women in U.S. culture? How might these roles affect your communication with an audience of women only? What might you need to be aware of when communicating, to avoid stereotyping men (breadwinners) and women (caretakers and mothers)?

Family

Family has many definitions. For some people, a family consists of a married man and woman and their children. A family could also be two married people with no children. A family might also be a grandmother who is raising her grandson by herself. Or a family can be two women who are bringing up an adopted child, or a single father raising his son. How do you define a family? What does this say about your identity?

Field of Study

Your field of study can be an indicator of your interests and goals. This can have an influence on how you think and how you speak. For example, if you are studying to be an oral hygienist and you are preparing to give a speech about this, you might use technical terms such as bicuspid, canine, or incisors. Unless your audience is made up of other dental students, they might not understand the terminology, and therefore will not receive your message.

Religion

Do you practice a particular religion? If you are the speaker or sender of a message, it is important to be aware of your own views on religion and to understand that not everyone will share your perspective. Be cognizant of whether there is anything in your speech that suggests religious material, and if so, how this will affect your audience. Is it your intention to bring religion into the message? If not, reword your speech to avoid any misconceptions or perhaps offending someone in your audience.

Education

Education is a key that frequently opens the door to a better job or a better living situation for you or your family. Having knowledge and skills can better prepare you for the work world as well as living an informed life. Making the commitment to improve your education while taking the time to make that happen can take a great deal of work. How has your education made a difference in how you see yourself? In what ways does education make a difference in how you think about and discuss a subject?

Age

It is natural to make assumptions based on age. If another person is your age, you might assume that he or she better knows and understands what you are saying or your point of view than someone from a different generation. Often, people of the same age share similar experiences with music and culture. Be aware of your audience if you are making a reference, for example, to a television show from 1980 but you are speaking to a group of teenagers who will not be familiar with the reference. If a person is younger or older than your target audience, he or she might not understand your message or point of view. How will you speak to an audience of different ages? What unique life experiences can you share with a person who is older or younger?

Regional Orientation

In the United States, there are many geographic similarities and differences. The United States is largely an English-speaking nation, but as it becomes more diverse, Spanish and many other languages are spoken more frequently.

As in other nations, there are also regional differences across the United States. What is called "soda" in one part of the country is referred to as "pop" in other areas. In Pittsburgh, Pennsylvania, some locals say "younz" when referring to a group; the same meaning is conferred to the term "y'all" in the southern U.S.

Weather differences influence foods that are grown, industry, and the clothes that we wear. Some of these regional differences can take place within a city or neighborhood as well. What is your regional orientation? Are others in your class from the same city or town? Do others in your class know some of the more popular locations in your town, or do you need to explain these favorite places to others? How might this affect choices you make when speaking to an audience who is from another part of the country?

Hobby/Recreation

Hobbies and recreational activities are another part of identity. What do you enjoy doing most? Do others enjoy the same activity, or will you need to explain your hobby at length in the hopes of getting others to either participate or understand why you enjoy it? If you are speaking to a group and need an example, sometimes talking about a hobby or recreational activity works well—especially if your audience is familiar with it. Remember, if you know this activity well but your audience does not, you may want to choose another example, or be sure to explain any information they will need to receive your message accurately.

Occupation

When you are getting to know someone, often one of the first questions you ask is, "What do you do?" A person's work is important in many cultures and can impact how people respond to them. Do you place more value on someone who is a physician than someone who works the phones at a telemarketing company? Do you treat people differently when you know what they do for work? How do people respond to your education or work experience?

Be aware of these responses and understand the effect on you and others when you are communicating to a group. Do you speak to people with whom you work differently than with those who are your close friends? What do you have in common with people at work? What do you have in common with your friends? All of this information is good self-knowledge and serves to make you a better communicator.

Sexual Orientation

Whether someone identifies themselves as heterosexual, homosexual, bisexual, or transgendered, this element is a personal part of identity. Knowing and accepting your own and others' sexual identities are critical to communicating without prejudice. Be aware of whether issues or biases associated with sexual orientation enter into your communication, whether it is subtle or overt. Remember, people cannot see sexuality to notice a characteristic in the same way that they can see skin color. Also, for some, sexuality is a private part of life, and disclosure may not happen right away

Imagine that you have been asked to make a speech advocating for gay marriage. Imagine how different your speech would be if the audience consisted of the following three options: men and women who are gay rights activists, men and women who are opposed to gay marriage, or a group of parents of gay teenagers. How would you change your message depending on the audience? What questions might you expect from the audience?

Ethnicity

Ethnicity refers to people who share a common background; they may be of the same race, nationality, religion, or cultural heritage. For example, your family's heritage might be Hungarian; if so, you might particularly enjoy the foods of Eastern Europe that your grandmother cooked. If your parents immigrated from Argentina,

DID YOU KNOW?

Gender Roles

Why are girls supposed to wear pink, and boys supposed to wear blue? This tradition in the United States is part of many social constructions about gender. In the late 19th century, male babies wore dresses until they had their first haircut, and after that they wore pants or shorts. Before the early 20th century, women wore dresses and men wore pants exclusively. Today, of course, women wear pants as well, but men do not typically wear dresses. These cultural gender roles are ingrained, but they do vary from culture to culture.

Women in the United States fought for and passed the 19th Amendment to the United States Constitution, which gave women the right to vote. Today, more women are in the workforce than ever before. It is now part of the American culture that women take a more active role in speaking up and speaking out about their thoughts and ideas. How would you speak about women's rights issues to a group of women who were either born or have lived in the United States for a long period of time? How would you speak about women's rights in the United States to a group of women who are new to this country and may be from a culture where women are required to defer to men?

you might have fond memories of your parents dancing the tango at parties. Or perhaps you are Cuban American—or any other cultural background that you and your family identify with and are part of in a community. The experiences that you have growing up can be framed by your ethnicity.

As you begin to think about the categories on the identity circle, consider which categories have had the most impact in terms of your life. How have your life experiences influenced how you perceive situations or decide to think about a topic or subject? Have you thought about other categories that you can place on the identity circle that would help you to better describe or identify yourself?

The identity circle is an excellent tool to help you think about the unique experiences in your life. It is also a good tool to help you determine the identity of your audience and how to address your audience on certain topics.

DEFINING YOUR SELF-IMAGE

The identity circle is a first step in helping you to understand your self-image, who you are, and how you can define who you are using your own unique set of experiences.

Self-Awareness

The second step to defining your self-image in more detail is asking yourself questions about how you see, think, and feel about yourself. How do you see yourself? How you see yourself is known as self-awareness. How do you think about yourself? How you think about yourself is known as your self-concept. How do you feel about yourself? How you feel about yourself is known as self-esteem.

When you go clothes shopping and look in the mirror, do you ever find yourself saying, "Is that me? Do I really look like this?" Just as the actual mirror can give you either the real you or a distorted picture of the physical you, the same can happen when you are defining your self-image. Are you seeing yourself clearly? Is your level of self-awareness accurate?

How you see yourself, what you think about yourself, and how you feel about yourself all contribute to your self-image. Defining your self-image takes time, patience, and a willingness to take a close look at yourself. Being open, honest, and clear in how you see yourself adds to your level of self-awareness. **Self-awareness** relates to how much you know about yourself and the role that you play in your work, home, and school. You can reflect on the elements in the identity circle to increase your self-awareness.

Self-Concept

How you think about yourself is known as your **self-concept**. As you become more self-aware, begin considering how you think about yourself. Do you have a mental image of yourself? What is your self-concept? If you think of yourself as a responsible employee, what are the characteristics that you need to have? In most cases, a responsible employee will be on time to work, know exactly what is expected of in terms of the job, perform work well, and establish an excellent relationship with the manager. Do you think of yourself as having those characteristics? Do you have an accurate self-concept?

How you think of yourself is framed by a variety of factors. Your friends help you form and define how you think about yourself by how they behave around you and what they say to you. The same is true for your relatives and family. How did your friends and family respond when you told them you were going to pursue a degree? Did they give you words of encouragement? Did they offer to help you? What did you think about their responses? How did this make a difference in how you think about yourself? Did these responses help you to change how you think about yourself?

Self-Esteem

Now that you have increased your level of self-awareness and can better describe your self-concept, the next challenge is assessing how you feel about yourself, which is often referred to as your **self-esteem**.

In the classic children's book *The Wizard of Oz*, the character of the cowardly lion does not like himself. Lions are expected to have courage, but this particular lion does not feel as though he had any. He is sad and disappointed in himself. What positive characteristics do you have that you like? Do you have a strong level of self-esteem?

Think about a person you know with high self-esteem. How does he or she dress, walk, and talk? Often, a person with good self-esteem seems confident and bold. Self-confident people stand tall, speak directly and with strength, and in general approach life with a very positive attitude. They also have a great deal of self-satisfaction.

How do you feel about yourself? Do you like yourself? Is there a feeling about yourself that you would like to change?

Identity Scripts

An **identity script** is a set of information that you repeat to yourself until it becomes part of your identity. For example, if you tell yourself that you are very good with people and that they tend to listen to what you say, you are enforcing an identity of yourself as a confident speaker.

Of course, the opposite is also true. If instead you reinforce negative messages, such as, "I will never become the musician I wanted to be. I am just not good enough," you will likely fulfill this prophecy.

Attachment Style

How do you respond to various communication experiences? Do you respond with self-doubt or anxiety if someone disagrees with your opinion? Or do you confidently explain your point of view? How you respond to communication experiences is known as your **attachment style**. There are four types of attachment styles:

- Secure
- Fearful or unlovable
- Rejecting or dismissive
- Anxious

Attachment styles are ways people respond based on how they were raised in childhood. These factors relate directly to how those who are caregivers communicate with and treat the children under their care.

- Caregivers who are kind, loving, and consistent with their messages raise children who are secure. Offering positive words with strong meaning to a child helps the child grow into a person who communicates with confidence and self-assurance.
- Caregivers who are constantly criticizing a child or suggesting that the child is unlikeable will raise fearful and possibly disturbed children with low self-esteem. How might a person communicate who does not feel lovable or worthwhile?
- Caregivers who are dismissive raise angry children who feel rejected. Think about a child who is constantly being told to be quiet or go sit down and watch television. This child begins to feel unimportant. The child will feel rejected and may grow up to reject others and behave in the same dismissive way as well.
- Caregivers who are inconsistent raise children who are anxious. Imagine what it would be like to be a child whose caregiver was inconsistent in treating a child. One day the caregiver is kind and loving, and the next day the caregiver is moody, critical, and rejecting. Before long, the child will become confused and will never know what to expect. He or she will anxiously and nervously try to anticipate the mood of the caregiver on any given day. This child is likely to be anxious when communicating.

These attachment styles are guides to help you to understand yourself and others better. They are tools that help you to understand why you communicate the way that you do. They can also help you to define your self-image. What is your attachment style? How does your attachment style relate to how you communicate?

THE JOHARI WINDOW

Other tools, including the Johari window and Maslow's hierarchy of needs, also help you to understand yourself and how you communicate. These tools are helpful because they ask you to get feedback from others regarding how they see you.

Reflected Appraisal

Reflected appraisal refers to how you see yourself reflected through other people's eyes. The Johari window is a tool created by Joseph Luft and Harry Ingham in 1955 to help people understand how they communicate as well as how they relate to others. Here is how it works. First, read through the list of 56 adjectives in Figure 3.2. Select five that you think best describe you.

able	extroverted	mature	self-assertive
accepting	friendly	modest	self-conscious
adaptable	giving	nervous	sensible
bold	happy	observant	sentimental
brave	helpful	organized	shy
calm	idealistic	patient	silly
caring	independent	powerful	smart
cheerful	ingenious	proud	spontaneous
clever	intelligent	quiet	sympathetic
complex	introverted	reflective	tense
confident	kind	relaxed	trustworthy
dependable	knowledgeable	religious	warm
dignified	logical	responsive	wise
energetic	loving	searching	witty

FIGURE 3.2 **Adjectives for the Johari Window**

Next, share the same list with several friends, colleagues, or classmates and ask them to select the five adjectives that best describe you. Once you have assembled both sets of adjectives, place them into a grid as shown in Figure 3.3. This grid is known as the Johari house. Each of the four quadrants in the Johari house is considered a room.

- Room 1 contains those characteristics that we see in ourselves and others see in us as well.
- Room 2 is for those characteristics that others see in us, but that we do not see in ourselves.

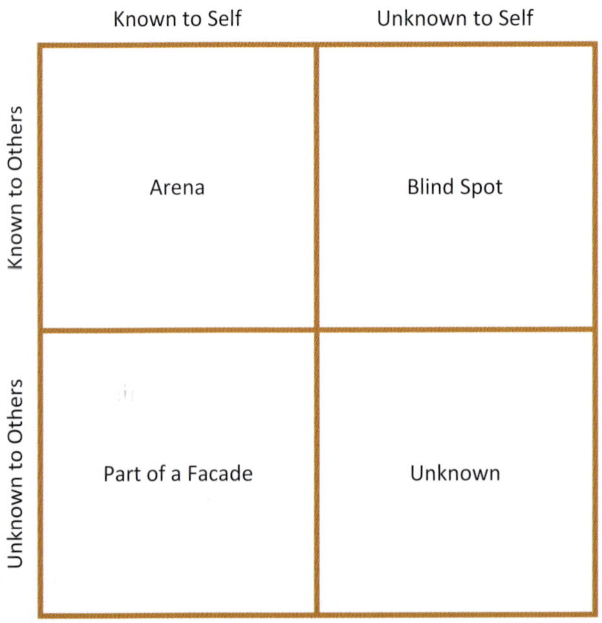

FIGURE 3.3 **Johari House**

- Room 3, the most complex, is where your unconscious characteristics, or parts that are not seen by anyone, including yourself, are placed.
- Room 4 contains those characteristics known only to yourself.

The rooms in the Johari house are arranged beginning with Room 1 in the upper left-hand corner. The rooms are then placed clockwise in order.

Once you have selected your five words, place each of them in the four grids. The same is true for the adjectives obtained from others.

- Adjectives that both you and others select regarding you get placed in Room 1. This is considered the open room. That is because those are characteristics that all see in you.
- Adjectives that are selected by others but not by you are placed in Room 2, which is often considered the blind spot. These are areas that you simply do not see in yourself.
- Adjectives that were not selected either by you or others are placed in Room 3. These are characteristics that might not necessarily be appropriate or apply to you, or they might be characteristics that you have, but they have not been acknowledged.
- Adjectives that are known to you, but not to others, are placed in Room 4. These are often referred to as hidden descriptions. There might be a valid reason why you hide these characteristics, or they might be characteristics you should allow others to see.

As you read through the adjectives and understand how to place the adjectives into the grid, you can begin to see the value in terms of understanding yourself—not only from your perspective, but from the perspective of others. By having a better understanding of yourself and how others perceive you, you can begin to better identify your self-image. Do you see yourself the same way that others see you? What do people see in you that you do not see in yourself?

Employers are reviewing social media websites prior to hiring, and others are using social networking sites like Facebook and LinkedIn as a means for finding potential employees. Whatever your situation, it is important to be very attentive to the messages that you are sending through social media. You never know when an employer or decision maker will be reviewing your site. Keep in mind the Johari window. Are you posting pictures or information on your site that support your self-concept, or are they pictures or information you would be hesitant to have others see? Is the information that you are posting today information that you might possibly regret?

It is critical to consider that the messages you send from through social media sites support your overall self-image. Is the message you send the message you want your audience today or potential audience in the future to have? When using social media, as when speaking with a group, keep in mind your self-image. What do you think about yourself? Are the messages you send the messages that you want others to receive?

The pyramid shown in Figure 3.4 is a model of Maslow's hierarchy of needs. The concept was first presented by Abraham Maslow in his 1943 paper "A Theory of Human Motivation." Rather than studying those who had problems and difficulties, Maslow studied the top 1 percent of the healthiest college students at that time. In addition, he studied people who were outstanding in their field of work, including Albert Einstein, Eleanor Roosevelt, and Jane Addams. (His entire study can be found in his book *Motivation and Personality*.) The book was published in 1954, but his pyramid is still used by many today to help understand basic human needs.

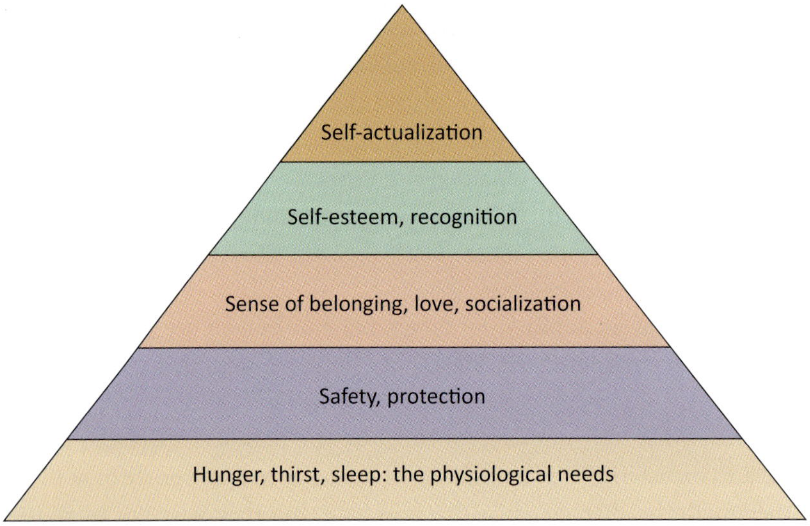

FIGURE 3.4 **Maslow's Hierarchy of Needs**

As you look at the pyramid, you can see that the base of the pyramid is where the most basic of human needs can be found. According to Maslow, the top of the pyramid is where you need to be to realize your full potential. Before you can reach your full potential, certain needs have to be met. The bottom four needs were termed by Maslow as deficiency needs (d-needs).

Maslow explained that people generally know when their basic physiological needs are not met. You know when it is difficult to breathe, for example, or when you are hungry. However, with the other deficiency needs, such as friendship, love, security, or esteem, a person might experience feelings of nervousness or tension when these are not met. Maslow believed that in order to reach one's highest potential, these lower-level needs must be met first.

In order to specifically understand Maslow's pyramid, review the needs listed and then think about the pyramid as it relates to your life. Are your needs being met? How might you best meet those lower-level needs?

Physiological Needs

At a very early age, you learn the basic human needs you must meet for survival. Those needs include food, clothing, shelter, air, and water. If these physiological needs are not met, it is difficult to address other things in life.

Oddly enough, the issue of physiological needs can arise in a speaking or communication situation. If the audience is listening to a speaker in the pouring rain, they might have a difficult time paying attention to the speech as they think more about finding shelter. If audience members are hungry, thirsty, or too cold or hot, they will likely find it hard to keep their attention focused on the message you are communicating. Always remember that your own basic physiological needs, and those of your audience, must be met for you to deliver your message effectively.

Safety Needs

After your basic physical needs are met, it is important to feel safe. There is a need to live in a world that allows people to feel safe not only in their own homes and neighborhoods, but in their world as well. It is natural to want job security, for example, and to know that the work you are doing is valued and appreciated. Security is a key need for all human beings.

Love and Belonging

It is human nature to love and to want to be loved. As you know, love has many definitions, and the same is true for relationships. There is romantic love, but there is also the love between parents and children, between friends, and between siblings.

Maslow's research suggested that all people need to feel a sense of belonging to something and a sense of being accepted. The feeling of belonging can take place in large social organizations, such as religious groups, clubs, professional organizations, teams, and of course at work. This sense of belonging can also come from family relationships, intimate partners, or close personal friends. When these relationships are absent or lacking, one may experience loneliness or even depression.

Esteem

Self-esteem and self-respect go hand in hand. Maslow found that humans have a strong need to be appreciated, accepted, and valued by others. The best way for people to gain self-respect is to have an activity in which they can excel or show leadership. Good self-esteem does not happen overnight. It comes from a series of experiences over time where you can begin to see yourself in a positive manner because you are involved in working toward or accomplishing goals that are valuable.

Self-Actualization

What is your goal? What is your dream? Is it to become a good parent? Is it to be successful in your career? Maslow's work suggested that in order to realize your full potential, you must first meet your physiological, safety, love and belonging, and esteem needs. Once you have those needs met, you will have a much better opportunity to realize your dreams and goals.

Understanding yourself and how you communicate requires a great deal of thought, analysis, time, and attention. The information in this chapter should encourage you to think more about yourself, to understand who you are, and to understand why you communicate the way you do. This chapter also examined the notion that others have thoughts and opinions about how you communicate. Whether your audience is a large group to whom you are delivering a speech, a friend, or a group with whom you are communicating online, it is important that you consider the messages you send and the people you are sending them to.

THE CULTURE OF BUSINESS ACROSS THE GLOBE

Internet access and communication varies across the globe. Depending on a region's culture and government, a country's citizens may use Internet communication in a variety of ways. This is important to know when you are communicating—perhaps when you are participating in a webinar with colleagues in China, for example.

It is important to be aware of cultural differences in terms of expectations and cultural norms when it comes to communicating via new media. For example, in China, all Internet users must register using their real names; there is no anonymous usage on the Internet. Requiring registration might keep businesses from contacting each other internationally.

In 2009, China banned Twitter, YouTube, Facebook, and a number of sites that host film downloads. Some Chinese users fought back and launched their own competing sites, which were quickly shut down. Have you ever wondered what business situations in the United States would be like without the Internet? Or if everyone had to use their real name when they posted information—no matter what the subject or forum? How would communicaltion be different? Think about how the possibility of anonymity affects the material that is posted. Just as in any form of communication, it is necessary to consider how use media and the issues of identity that different cultures attach to media.

SUMMARY

- As a sender of messages, you have a responsibility to your receiver or audience to present a clear, understandable message.
- How you assemble your messages for your receiver or audience is directly related to your thoughts and opinions.
- It is important for you to know yourself and know why you have the thoughts and opinions that you do.
- Your thoughts and opinions have been created by your unique set of experiences.
- A variety of tools exists to help you look at yourself and your unique set of experiences for better self-understanding. These tools include the identity circle, the Johari window, and Maslow's hierarchy of needs.

REFERENCE

Hornby, L., & Le, Y. (2009, December 22). China to require Internet domain name registration. Retrieved from http://www.reuters.com/article/2009/12/22/us-china-internet-idUSTRE5BL19620091222

CHAPTER

4

Verbal versus Nonverbal Communication

Kasey has a new job as a project leader at an advertising firm. She is meeting with two team members, Sara and Louise, for the first time. During the meeting, Kasey delivers a brief presentation about the company's new client, as Sara and Louise will be working under Kasey's direction to service the client. As Kasey gives her presentation, she notices that Sara sits up straight in her chair, meets Kasey's eyes regularly, and nods in response to each major point Kasey makes. Louise, on the other hand, is seated at the opposite end of the conference table from the other two women. For most of Kasey's presentation, Louise looks down at her lap or out the window.

By the end of the meeting, Kasey finds herself feeling much more confident about delegating responsibilities to Sara than Louise. The wordless reactions of the two women have communicated a great deal to her about their willingness to engage in the project. She leaves the meeting pondering the power of nonverbal communication in the workplace.

KEY CONCEPTS

1. Nonverbal communication is just as important as verbal communication. See page 50.

2. Nonverbal communication is communication made without using words, such as body language, facial expressions, gestures, physical appearance, tone, and inflection. See page 50.

3. One type of nonverbal communication involves personal space and the distance between you and those you are communicating with. See page 51.

4. Paralinguistics refers to how you use your voice to communicate. See page 53.

5. Deception can be detected by closely attending to the nonverbal communication of a speaker. See page 56.

THE FUNCTIONS OF NONVERBAL COMMUNICATION

You are involved with the spoken word when you are speaking in person with a friend, chatting on the phone, listening to the radio, watching television, streaming video on the Internet, participating in a webinar, or listening to a book on tape. While obviously a great deal of emphasis is placed on verbal communication, we are all greatly impacted by nonverbal communication as well.

What is nonverbal communication? Simply put, **nonverbal communication** is how you communicate without using words to help convey to others your understanding, thought, or emotion. Nonverbal communication can also give a receiver unintended information that a sender might not want to send. Think about the times in your life that you have understood what someone wanted or needed and they did not have to speak. Perhaps while having dinner with a friend, you noticed her dislike for her meal without her saying a word about it. You probably read her feelings simply by studying the look on her face—or did you? You might have misunderstood that nonverbal communication, and perhaps the distaste your friend showed was for you and not her meal.

Researchers estimate that 93 percent of all communication is nonverbal. This makes nonverbal communication a very strong and powerful factor to consider as you are speaking to others formally—both in class and on the job—or informally, when you are with friends and family. What nonverbal messages are you sending and what nonverbal messages are you receiving from others?

CAREER PERSPECTIVES: INTERVIEWING SMART

When you are interviewing for a job, your body language is just as important as your verbal communication. Your body language sends powerful messages to the interviewer. Interviewers are trained to notice details about your body language—eye contact, tone and inflection of voice, posture, and clothing style—and interpret those details into facts about you as a person.

When you are preparing for a job interview, brush up on your verbal skills as well as your body language! If you know a friend or professional who has interviewing experience, ask him or her to do a mock (practice) interview with you. Ask your "interviewer" to give you feedback on both your verbal and nonverbal communication styles.

TYPES OF NONVERBAL COMMUNICATION

There are many types of nonverbal communication, including facial expression, eye contact, hand gestures, tone of voice, touch, and clothing styles. Nonverbal communication also includes the distance between people when they are communicating with one another. This is referred to as **personal space**, or the space that you consider to be your own. How do you feel when a person you have never met before stands too close to you? It is common to feel uncomfortable in a situation like this. You might decide to step back or move away to a distance that feels more comfortable.

In 1966, anthropologist Edward T. Hall researched the distance between people when they are communicating with one another. He introduced the word **proxemics** to describe his study of the measurement of distances between people as they communicate and interact.

Imagine you are in the center of a circle surrounded by the four zones: intimate space, personal space, social space, and public space. Family members or romantic partners commonly stand close to one another. This closeness of space is known as the **intimate distance** or intimate zone, which includes everything from an embrace to standing one and a half feet away from each other. When standing this close, you might be hugging, touching, or whispering. Intimate distance is the distance of physical involvement of love or affection between romantic partners and close family members.

Good friends and relatives interact with one another in personal space, a distance of between one and a half and four feet away from each other. Think about how close you stand to your good friends or acquaintances when you are talking. Do you sometimes find yourself standing or sitting too close or too far away? You might find yourself automatically adjusting the distance by sitting closer or sitting back a little farther in order to make you feel more comfortable.

Social space is reserved for impersonal business or casual social interactions. Think about being in a meeting with your boss, at a party where you only know a few people, or standing in line at the post office. How close to these people do you stand or sit? Researcher Edward Hall's research has shown that you are likely to be standing or sitting between 4 and 12 feet away from the person with whom you are speaking.

Presenting a speech occurs in a more formal setting, and there is a sense of detachment or separation between you and the audience. This is called the **public space**, which is generally considered to be between 12 and 25 feet.

Territoriality

Social space varies from country to country. In countries that are more densely populated, such as India or China, social space might be closer to four feet, and in less densely populated countries, such as the United States, it is closer to 12 feet. Social space in the United States is very similar to that in England, Germany, Sweden, and other Scandinavian countries. This can possibly be attributed to similar cultural values among these countries. However, one cannot generalize about the desired personal space of all people from a particular country. You may have a German friend who always kisses you on both cheeks when she sees you. Perhaps you have a Chinese friend who is comfortable with more social distance than the average American.

Prior to Hall's study, little was known about how people used personal space in communication. Today, proxemics is used extensively in the design of business environments to improve the comfort level of employees. For example, meeting rooms are typically designed to allow 4 to 12 feet of social distance among staff.

COMMUNICATION ACROSS CULTURES: PERSONAL SPACE DIFFERENCES IN THE UNITED STATES AND SPAIN

In the United States, the leader of a group typically takes a seat at the head of the table during a business meeting, and the participants generally sit fairly far apart. However, in Spain, the leadership location is not at the head of the table—instead, the leader of the meeting typically sits at the center of one of the table's sides. This center position is considered the place of leadership, power, or honor. The communication distance between the leader and those in attendance in Spain is also closer than that in the United States.

Paralinguistics

Paralinguistics, which is also known as paralanguage, refers to the various qualities of speech that involve your voice—how loudly you speak, whether you take long pauses, and so on. Each person's voice has its own individual set of qualities. These qualities include pitch, volume, inflection, articulation, rate, pauses, and vocal variety. You recognize a friend's voice on your voicemail because of his paralinguistics—the unique qualities of your friend's voice.

You can generally tell if people are happy or upset by the tone of their voice. Your tone of voice helps to convey your message not only in terms of the words that you use, but the emotional message that you convey. Sometimes, people who are speaking can make a subject interesting simply by modulating their voice to show their enthusiasm. Tone of voice includes variations, such as pitch, volume, inflection, articulation, rate, pauses, and vocal variety. Each of these elements of tone of voice is examined in the following sections.

Pitch

Pitch is directly related to the vibration of vocal cords. The more a vocal cord vibrates, the higher the pitch of one's voice. The natural rate of vibration is directly related to the length and thickness of one's vocal cords, which explains why women have higher pitched voices—in general, women's vocal cords are shorter than men's. This is why it is usually easy to distinguish between a man's and a woman's voice. However, there are individual differences in the pitch of vocal cords based on physical size and structure.

Have you ever noticed that your voice can change if you are happy, sad, or angry? When you get excited, your vocal cords can become tense and create a higher vibration. This change is also noticed by others who hear your voice, and they will often base their responses to you not only on what you say, but on how your voice sounds.

Volume

Often, a loud voice is associated with anger or being upset, but is it also appropriate at an athletic event or a music concert? Loud voices can convey a message of information, joy, or enthusiasm as well as anger or frustration. Of course, softer voices are appropriate in a wider variety of settings. For example, a parent trying to put a child to sleep probably will speak in a very soft voice. It simply depends on the situation and the message that is being conveyed.

Inflection

Inflection also has an effect on voice. **Inflection** refers to the raising and lowering of one's pitch, either consciously or unconsciously. For example, if a friend asked, "How are you?" with no inflection or change in pitch, you might interpret that your friend was just asking the question to be nice or to pass the time. If, however, your friend asked the question and placed a higher pitch on the word *you,* you are more likely to think that your friend is actually interested in how you are.

Articulation

Articulation, another component of voice, refers to the clear pronunciation of words. Have you ever listened to people who do not pronounce their words very well? It is difficult to understand what they are saying; after a short period of time, you will likely stop listening.

Think about how you might respond to a person who says, "I want to show you our latest product"—a clear declarative statement. Now, think about a person who says, "I wanna show you our latest product." Taking shortcuts with words in a business environment sends a message that the person is unprofessional.

Rate

The **rate**, or the speed, at which you speak has an effect on how people receive your messages. Consider listening to a person who is happy and excited about a situation and wants to tell you all about it. She will likely speak quickly; by the time she has finished telling the story, you may be confused about what she was talking about.

Vocal Variety

Think about a person who speaks very slowly and deliberately. He gives you every detail and takes long pauses between sentences to think about what he is going to say. He may be speaking very slowly in order to ensure you understand his message. However, if he speaks too slowly and in too much detail, you may become bored and stop listening.

Your voice can be a very powerful tool in communicating a message. Your pitch, volume, inflection, articulation, and rate all send messages along with the words you are using. Be aware of these factors, and practice variations in voice to improve your skills in delivering your message.

Facial Affect

Facial affect, a powerful nonverbal source of communication, refers to observable expressions of emotion on a person's face. Babies cannot speak, so how do you know if they are happy? They smile, squeal, and appear bright-eyed. How might you interpret a friend's blank stare when you are speaking with her? Is she responding to you or thinking about something else?

Kinesics

In the 1950s, anthropologist Ray Birdwhistell studied how humans communicate through nonverbal body movement. He coined the term *kinesics*, which is the interpretation of nonverbal body movement. **Facial expression** and other physical gestures have been characterized by the study of kinesics. Nonverbal communication via body movement is studied for a variety of reasons. Salespeople, lawyers, teachers, and customer service representatives use nonverbal communication and body movement to send and receive messages that are crucial to their job performance.

Hand movements or gestures are often interpreted as a form of nonverbal communication. For example, if you see a person with clenched hands, you might conclude that the person is under pressure. Rubbing the back of the head or forehead can indicate frustration.

Chronemics: The Perception of Time

Have you ever arrived very late to a meeting? In the United States, arriving on time for meetings is important. If you are late, your boss may interpret it as disrespect or disinterest—a form of nonverbal communication. You are sending a strong message about your ability to be prompt and respectful and show your commitment. In the business world, Americans are expected to arrive on time for business-related events. However, Americans find it acceptable to arrive late to parties and dances. Whether you are on time or arrive late for a meeting or a party communicates information about you to the people you are with.

The perception of time is called **chronemics**; it includes promptness and willingness to wait. Researcher Lyle Sussaman has found that when men in the United States interact with women, they generally control the situation, including frequently interrupting and spending more of the time talking than women do.

In the United States and many European countries, a value is placed on time and promptness. Business meetings are set to a specific time, and employees are expected to start at the appointed hour—in general, being late is not an accepted practice. However, in other countries, including some in Latin America and Africa, it is common to set a meeting for the afternoon with no specific time stipulated—it is simply understood that the meeting will take place sometime in the afternoon.

Artifacts and Physical Appearance

Dress is another form of nonverbal communication. Do you dress the same for work in an office as you would if you were going out with your friends? Depending on your office setting, you likely wear dressier clothes for work and more casual clothes at home.

Artifacts are tangible items that communicate something. They can include jewelry, clothing, pictures, and other items that communicate something about you, your lifestyle, or status that cannot be expressed in words. How you decorate your cubicle at work is a form of nonverbal communication—but the primary artifact is the way you dress.

What do your clothes say about you? Think about what you might wear to a job interview. Most human resources professionals recommend that you should dress for the position that you are seeking—or perhaps even a position above it. Dressing in appropriate attire sends a message that you truly want the position and understand the culture of the company. So if you do not know for certain, find out the dress code before the interview by directly asking the person who is scheduling you for the meeting.

Haptics: The Study of Touch

The study of touch is known as **haptics**. One of the most common forms of touch is the handshake, but a kiss, a high five, and a pat on the arm or back are other examples of touch. Touch is dependent on the people involved, the environment or culture, and the exact situation. In many European cultures, for example, it is common to greet or say good-bye with a kiss on both cheeks. Touch can communicate that you are listening, or that you are showing compassion. A pat on the back might communicate that a job was well done. Be aware that the acceptance of touch varies culture to culture, and even from person to person.

DECEPTION

Some people use nonverbal communication as a means to be deceptive in their communication. It is very important to be aware of the fact that people who understand the impact of nonverbal communication can and do use this information to mislead others.

Have you heard the term *poker face*—the complete absence of expression on one's face? High stakes poker players do not want to give away any feelings about the cards that they hold in their hands, so they carefully practice showing no emotion. Displaying a poker face is actually a device of deception.

However, there are other ways to use body language to determine whether someone is deceiving you. When people are being deceptive, their bodies will often be stiff, and they will make very few hand or arm movements. (If any hand or arm movements are made, they generally will be toward themselves rather than gesturing to others.) Deceivers generally make limited eye contact and frequently touch their face, throat, or mouth, or even cover their mouth. They also might be likely to scratch their nose or behind their ear, or flutter their eyelids rapidly. How people smile is often an indicator of deception. When a facial expression only involves movement of the mouth, the emotion is likely not genuine. Look for consistency between what people say and the expressions on their face. Have you ever been in a situation where a friend opens a gift and exclaims, "I love it!" but her expression says otherwise?

Now that you have explored nonverbal communication in detail, you can see why it is so important to match your nonverbal communication to your verbal communication. Otherwise, the way you communicate nonverbally through your facial expression, tone of voice, dress, hand gestures, and other factors may undermine your verbal messages.

DID YOU KNOW?

Differences in Hand Gestures

A hand gesture that means one thing to you might mean something quite different to someone on the other side of the world. President George Herbert Walker Bush found that out in Australia in 1992, when he made a "V" sign with his palm facing inward to a crowd from his limousine. The "V" gesture was popularized during World War II when Winston Churchill made it to signify the Allies' victory—but Churchill did so with his palm facing outward. Bush did not realize it, but he was actually making a very offensive hand gesture to the Australians gathered to see him.

In the United States and Europe, the "OK" gesture is made by holding the thumb and index finger together and spreading the rest of the fingers. However, in France and some South American countries, it is considered an insult. Similarly, the "thumbs-up" sign is widely accepted in European countries, but some Asian and Muslim cultures consider it to be an insult.

VERBAL COMMUNICATION

Verbal communication is an opportunity to put thoughts, ideas, dreams, feelings, and emotions into words that can be understood by yourself and others. How you speak and the words that you use, however, can vary depending on a variety of factors, including your environment, regional location, and cultural background.

Language

Think about *how* you speak. Do you vary your speech depending on whom you are with? Is there a difference in how you speak depending on the situation? Is there a difference in how you speak depending on your mood or feelings about the subject? During press conferences, most political leaders speak formally, including using a teleprompter to deliver the message. The words used in the speech, the length of the speech, and the speed at which the speech is given are all intricately planned, organized, and controlled. Now think about the question-and-answer sessions that often follow a speech. Does the speaker behave differently then, including pausing frequently to think of answers?

Standard Vocabulary

Think of the words you use in your everyday life. Are there words that most people know and accept? For example, when you are at work or in class, there is an accepted group of words that are used. These words are often referred to as **standard vocabulary**. They are words that are universally understood. However, there also might be words in your vocabulary that you might not use in class or at work. They might be words that you use very informally with your friends. These words are considered non-standard.

DID YOU KNOW?

Sign Language Is Verbal Communication

It might seem counterintuitive, but American Sign Language (ASL) is actually verbal communication. While it does not involve speaking, ASL is very much a language, and any language is verbal communication. ASL is a visual language because it has its own grammar and vocabulary. ASL incorporates hand positions, movements, and hand shapes with gestures and facial expressions. All of these techniques are used to form words. Despite the fact that ASL "speakers" do not use their voices, they are able to convey inflections and other variations that might be conveyed by the voice in a spoken language through facial expressions and gestures.

ASL is not the same as English. It is a distinct language with its own grammar, punctuation, and sentence order. One interesting example of its many differences from English is how a question is indicated in ASL. Speakers raise their eyebrows, widen their eyes, and slightly lean their bodies forward to indicate that they are looking for answer.

Code

Code refers to types of nonstandard language, such as slang or jargon, or words with arbitrary meanings, arranged by the rules of syntax and used to communicate. A **slang** word that has been used for a number of years is the word *cool*. Slang is a way of expressing an idea, image, or symbol to others in a unique verbal manner. For example, when used as slang, *cool* is a term that suggests that something or someone is very good or positive, but the standard definition of *cool* is related to temperature.

Words that are commonly used in certain regions are known as **colloquialisms**. For example, in the Midwestern United States, soft drinks are frequently referred to as *pop*. However, on the East Coast of the United States, soft drinks are generally referred to as *soda*.

Most professions have vocabulary that is specific to their particular line of work. Words that are specific to your work or profession are known as **jargon**. For example, in an office environment in the United States, the expression "I put that in the circular file" is jargon that means "I threw that in the wastebasket." If you are in nursing, law enforcement, information technology, or virtually any another profession, you will find yourself using words that are specific to your profession, and others who are not in your profession might not know or understand these words. In the television and radio business, a common piece of jargon is the term *sound bite*, which refers to snippets of an interview. The words "sound" and "bite," if taken literally, do not make sense together, but to a television producer, they signify useful material from an interview.

Throughout the United States, accents can vary dramatically. Even though the common language—English—is shared, there are regional differences, or **regionalisms**, that can quickly reveal where a person is from. Consider the speaking voice of former U.S. presidents Bill Clinton and George Walker Bush. Their accents give away their Southern heritage. Now consider the speaking voice of John F. Kennedy. His inflections revealed his Massachusetts upbringing.

Ethics: How Verbal Communication Can Be Used to Deceive

It is possible to use the spoken word to mislead or deceive others. Sometimes, people lie directly, using words and messages that can be confirmed as untrue. Some use language to **doublespeak**, or deliberately distort or manipulate the meaning of the words that they are using. People also sometimes *sugarcoat* the truth with expressions known as **euphemisms**. For example, a company who is firing employees for economic reasons might use a word like *downsizing* instead of *layoffs*—simply because it seems less harsh. However, it is important to draw a distinction between using euphemisms and intentional deceit.

There are many ways in which doublespeak enters your life. Think about advertisements for cars. Instead of saying *used car,* dealers prefer terms like *preowned* and *executive-driven*. The supermarket is full of doublespeak as well. Most processed foods that advertise their low fat content also contain a high sugar content—usually not prominently displayed on the front label.

Every communication you have is a new opportunity to share thoughts, feelings, ideas, and emotions with others. A natural relationship exists between verbal and nonverbal communication, and the two are equally important. It is valuable to understand your own verbal and nonverbal communication as well as that of others, and to make wise and responsible choices for both.

ETHICS: DOUBLESPEAKING

It is not surprising that a government might want to lessen the horror of a war by communicating a softer, gentler message to its citizens. Doublespeak is a convenient way to do so, by deliberately hiding the real meaning of words from a frightened population. This brings to bear a significant ethical question—is it acceptable for a government or media outlet to soften the blow by using jargon or euphemisms that suggest a war is not as bloody or destructive as it actually is? Here are a few phrases that make the point:

- A *casualty* is a person killed or injured in a war.
- *Denying the enemy* means bombing a military target.
- The term *assets* generally refers to bombs or other weapons of destruction.
- *Collateral damage* refers to death or injury among civilians during bombings or firefights.

Can you think of other doublespeak terms or euphemisms that you have heard on the news or in the media that are diminishing the real truth of a situation?

SUMMARY

- Nonverbal communication is a very powerful and important factor in the communication process.
- Ninety-three percent of communication is nonverbal.
- Nonverbal communication includes a very broad spectrum of categories, including body language, facial affect, artifacts, and haptics.
- While speaking, it is important to be constantly aware of your nonverbal body language.

REFERENCES

Center for Media Literacy. (2002–2011). Military doublespeak: How jargon turns gore into glory. Retrieved from http://www.medialit.org/reading-room/military-doublespeak-how-jargon-turns-gore-glory

National Institute on Deafness and Other Communication Disorders. (2011, July 5). Retrieved from http://www.nidcd.nih.gov/health/hearing/asl.html

Sussman, L. (n.d.). Effective communication. Retrieved from http://cobweb2.louisville.edu/faculty/regbruce/bruce//mgmtwebs/commun_f98/chronemics.htm

CHAPTER

5

Communicating Across Cultures

During a cultural diversity workshop at work, Jasmine and 30 of her fellow employees are asked to split themselves into different cultural groups: married, single, and divorced; male and female; and native or non-native speakers of English. Next, the students were asked to group themselves by ethnicity.

The first thing Jasmine noticed during this activity was that culture was not easily defined; at times, some of the participants were not sure which group to join. In some instances, Jasmine and some of the other participants said that they felt they belonged to more than one group. They also expressed confusion about the connections between groups, particularly the issues related to ethnicity. All of the participants had been born in the United States, so were they all Americans, or did their heritage (the group included people of Brazilian, Latvian, and Russian heritage, for example) somehow fit into the mix?

KEY CONCEPTS

1. The term *culture* is often used—but rarely fully understood. See page 64.

2. Culture refers to any group of people who share a common identity and function. See page 64.

3. People can belong to more than one culture and/or subculture. See page 65.

4. The largest subcultures within each culture tend to dominate and define it. See page 65.

5. All communication is intercultural. See page 66.

6. There are at least six main characteristics that help define culture. See page 68.

7. As cultures interact, members must be open to differences. See page 72.

8. The various aspects of a culture tend to spread to other groups and places. See page 72.

THE DEFINITION OF CULTURE

The term *culture* is used frequently; however, even experts struggle to define it. **Ethnicity** refers to a social group that shares a common national or cultural tradition—for example, Ashkenazi Jews, Arab Americans, the Amish, Navajos, Romanians, or Yorubas. The best approach is perhaps to define **culture** in broad terms, as a group that shares a breadth of experiences that ultimately lead to a shared understanding. Culture includes marital status, nationality, gender, and race, but adds much more to these specifications. It is not surprising that Jasmine was confused when faced with choosing only one group. She was born a female to an American family of native English speakers of Turkish descent. She had also recently split from her husband, which changed her culture from "married" to "divorced."

Remember that in addition to providing a way to categorize and understand groups of people, cultures are living entities with specific functions and purposes. Because they consist of people, cultures reflect the human experience. For example, although Jasmine's family had lived in the United States for two generations, they still maintained many of their Turkish customs. Jasmine grew up with her grandparents living in the same home with her, her parents, and her siblings, and almost all of her extended family still lives within a short walk of one another's homes. These living arrangements derive from the belief in Turkish culture that extended family must be readily available to one another to help in times of need and to maintain the strong bond of family and culture.

Likewise, a cultural group evolves over time in relation to how its members perceive themselves. For example, because of Jasmine's family's Turkish heritage, they defined themselves in part by their belief that family is most important. Most Turkish people marry at a young age, and they tend to stay married. Jasmine herself was married at the age of 18, and she was encouraged to have children as soon as possible. Members of a cultural group also pass down the artifacts of their group, leaving behind a material record that becomes associated with them. Jasmine's family maintains some family heirlooms from her great-grandparents, who lived in Turkey. Now that they also see themselves as American, Jasmine's family has evolved into a new cultural group of Turkish Americans.

Culture allows people to feel that they are part of a group and less isolated; they derive a sense of belonging to a larger entity because they share a collective identity. People who believe they are a part of a larger group feel more safe, secure, and comfortable. For instance, when Jasmine steps out of her front door, she can see her parents' house next door; she can hear others speaking Turkish; and she can often smell Turkish coffee brewing. All of this makes her feel a connection to her family and her heritage; despite the fact that she now lives alone since her recent divorce, she does not *feel* alone.

Finally, keep in mind that cultures are often defined by what they are not, and that within each cultural group, differences may make someone feel more of an affinity with another group. Jasmine's more assimilated neighbors may consider her family to be part of their neighborhood culture; however, they may also understand that Jasmine's family has a different culture than their own group. Also, because divorce is rare in Turkish culture and fairly common in American culture, Jasmine may at times feel more a part of American culture than of Turkish culture.

Co-culture

Just as Jasmine may have been confused about which group to stand with during the workshop activity, others may feel very strongly that they are part of more than one culture. In addition to feeling a sense of belonging to both the American and Turkish cultures, for instance, Jasmine may also feel as though she could fit in with either the single or married groups, because at different times she has been part of each one.

The term **co-culture** reflects the fact that people can be part of more than one culture, and in communication the term also denotes a subculture within a larger group. In the previous example, Jasmine's Turkish-American culture is a subculture within the larger group of American culture; her status as a divorced Turkish woman also places her within a subgroup of a larger group of married Turkish women. As one of only two females in the icebreaker activity who enjoyed sports, she helped to form a subculture within a nearly all-male group of sports enthusiasts.

Co-cultures are sometimes viewed negatively. For example, the culture of married Turkish women may frown upon the co-culture of divorced Turkish women. One of the aspects of culture that is so fascinating is that its complexity reflects the complexity of individuals. Each person has more than one connection to a cultural group; and these are additionally tempered by each person's own experiences, which shape their perceptions and communication. Even though Jasmine sees herself as a part of Turkish culture, her identification with American culture and her personal experience of having gone through a divorce may lead her to view divorced women in a different way than many other Turkish women might view them.

Dominant Culture

Within any given culture, there is a dominant culture—that is, the largest subgroup within the culture—and it tends to dictate the norm for the entire culture. Given its geographical position and size, the culture of the Midwest in the United States often dictates the way American English is spoken in its standard form, and depictions of life in the United States tend to show the Midwestern way of life as more typically American than that of a California surfer or a New York stockbroker.

It is also possible that a large dominant group may expand into the territory of other cultures, thus becoming the dominant culture. Both the European immigrants who settled in the United States and the Turks of the Ottoman Empire who dramatically expanded their own cultural boundaries incorporated other cultures into their own.

Such situations continue naturally into the present. For instance, while Caucasians historically have been the largest cultural group in the United States, making up about three-quarters of the population, the Hispanic population is rapidly increasing and recently surpassed the size of the African-American population, which had been the second-largest group. While the non-Hispanic U.S. population rose just 2 percent between 2000 and 2004, the number of Hispanics in the United States rose 14 percent. This indicates the potential for a future shift in the dominant culture of the United States.

ALL COMMUNICATION IS INTERCULTURAL

People often say, "It's a small world," and in many ways, the rise of the Internet and the globalization of business have made the world seem even smaller. This trend has created a need to communicate differently than in the past. An important part of this change is realizing that all communication is intercultural.

When you consider Jasmine's situation, you can see the variety of cultures of which she is a part. You can also easily assume she belongs to other cultures, perhaps based on her age, income, position with her company, and so on. Now, if you multiply this by the other 29 employees in the activity, each with his or her own cultural affiliations, modified by individual experiences and perceptions, it is not hard to see how all communication is intercultural and how easily misunderstandings may occur even with the use of effective communication techniques.

Researchers Marcelle E. DuPraw and Marya Axner delineate six fundamental patterns of cultural differences and how each should be considered if intercultural communication is to be successful. The six patterns are differences in

- communication styles,
- attitudes toward conflict,
- approaches to completing tasks,
- decision-making styles,
- attitudes toward disclosure, and
- approaches to knowing.

First, people communicate differently. A more straightforward example of this is the different ways people use spoken language. For example, both Americans and Britons speak English, but what Americans call a lawyer, the British call a solicitor; in turn, the word *solicitor* brings a salesperson to the mind of the American English speaker. Another part of language usage is nonverbal communication, which involves gestures, personal distance, expressions, and other factors.

In American business culture, typically the leader will sit at the head of a conference table; the chairs will be evenly but not too closely spaced around the table; and the meeting will proceed with the goal of addressing a particular task in the time allotted. In other cultures, the perception of a "head of the table" seat may not exist, and time may be devoted to getting to know each member of the team prior to discussing the day's business.

A second pattern of cultural differences involves a culture's attitude toward conflict. American businesspeople expect to conduct meetings in a civil manner, maybe even in accordance with a classic convention such as Robert's Rules of Order, and they expect to deal with disagreements openly. In other nations, expressing conflict in an open environment may be considered humiliating. In such cultures, arguments are usually settled one on one, in writing, or in a similar quiet environment. Good communicators will be sensitive to the attitudes other cultures have regarding disagreements.

How do different cultures approach the completion of tasks? Europeans and Americans tend to be very focused on each task, getting acquainted with one another as they work on a project, whereas Asian and Hispanic cultures place more value on getting acquainted first before focusing on a project. It is not hard to imagine the potential for annoyance or even offense that each group may feel in dealing with the other's approach.

- The first three considerations may be grouped together under the umbrella of information handling. This includes such issues as: Do supervisors make the decisions, or do they delegate decision making to middle managers? Should supervisors or employees disclose personal information and feelings to one another, or should those feelings be kept private and out of the workplace? How is information obtained? Do the cultures involved in the project rely on and accept as valid information collected through objective study and research, cultural imagery and lessons, and/or divine inspiration?
- The fourth pattern for cultural communication involves how decisions are made. In the United States, decisions are often delegated. For example, a supervisor might give a task that involves selecting among a variety of choices to someone on his staff. However, in Latin America and some European countries, the supervisor takes responsibility for making decisions.
- The fifth pattern involves attitudes toward disclosure. Americans tend to disclose more information about relationships and conflicts in general, but this approach can be viewed as inappropriate in other cultures.
- The sixth and final pattern examines different approaches to knowing. In most European cultures and the dominant culture in the United States, information comes from thought, research, and measuring. Others, such as Native American or African cultures, rely more on feelings and symbols to understand the world around them.

COMMUNICATION ACROSS CULTURES

One of the mistakes people most frequently make is to assume—especially when those around them speak the same language and share the same general appearance—that their different cultures communicate in the same way. A large part of intercultural business etiquette is to realize the importance of adapting communication to various cultures rather than presuming that one's own is standard and that others should adapt. It is worth familiarizing yourself with some of the intercultural communication considerations of the groups you will most likely encounter in your community and profession. When in doubt, do not hesitate to ask questions. It may actually be a relief if you politely ask a question like "How do you typically conduct meetings in your culture?" Polite consideration quickly wins others over.

COLLECTIVE SYSTEM OF MEANING

In addition to communicating with people of other cultures, individuals must learn to communicate effectively within their own cultures. First, the **collective system of meaning** within a culture must be considered. This means considering your own culture's values, expectations, perceptions, communication styles, history, and the like. Then, for the most effective communication, this norm should be matched.

For example, Jasmine clearly knows how to communicate effectively within her Turkish heritage. She understands the Turkish language; she married young; and she lives near her extended family. As is typical of Turkish culture, she has not left the group. Likewise, she meets the expectations of American culture by being an independent woman, speaking American English, and managing a career. In these aspects of her life, Jasmine demonstrates an understanding of the collective system of meaning within at least two of her cultures.

Jasmine also understands some of the symbolic and visual communication of each group: She knows that the color red in a *kilim* (a Turkish rug) represents prosperity, and she would automatically rise to her feet for the American national anthem at a baseball game and place her right hand over her heart.

Fluency within this collective system of meaning is key to effective communication within a culture. Psychologist Geert Hofstede referred to this phenomenon as knowing "the unwritten rules of the social game." Those who know the rules well stand a better chance of succeeding socially within this cultural group.

On the other hand, people who are part of a group but who do not seem to understand the collective system of meaning, and those who deliberately communicate contrary to it, run the risk of becoming disenfranchised or ostracized from the group. For example, in American culture, men were historically expected to be the breadwinners and financially support their families, while their wives stayed home to raise the children, cook, and clean the house. In recent decades, women entered the workforce in great numbers. Today, the collective system of meaning dictates that the average American family is a two-income family. Both men and women are expected to have successful careers outside the home. Due to this expectation, a decision for either the father or the mother to stay home to raise their children is a potentially disenfranchising choice. Although this is rapidly changing, there remains some stigma toward a father who wants to stay home to care for his children, and a mother who chooses this role is sometimes viewed as selling herself short.

There are potential advantages and disadvantages to becoming fluent in the collective system of meaning of another culture. Imagine that you are traveling to Turkey for business. You would appear to be more of an insider in a culture if you showed an understanding of it, such as knowing that a *kilim* is a traditional Turkish textile rug with designs and motifs that often include symbolism like a horse representing freedom and a camel symbolizing wealth and fortune. Likewise, during a business meeting in a South American country, if you know to enjoy getting acquainted with your new business colleagues before working on the meeting's agenda, you may become a part of the culture more readily. This should lead to better communication and a more comfortable and successful business trip.

What might the negative effects of not fully understanding or adapting to the collective system of meaning of a culture be? Perhaps you might unintentionally offend someone or be viewed as too much of an outsider.

TECHNOLOGY: CULTURAL CHALLENGES

It is a mistake to assume that all cultures take full advantage of the communication technology that is available and commonplace in the United States. Most workplaces in the United States use e-mail, cell phones, webcasts, and other communication technology to conduct business. However, in other cultures, this is not always possible or desired. The economic situation of a culture may prohibit people in that group from affording the latest technology; also the infrastructure needed to support technology may be limited, unstable, or simply unavailable within the culture. In Nepal in 2011, for example, due to a shortage of electricity in the country, the electricity was on for only 12 hours each day. A situation like this can severely limit the use of technology that requires electricity.

People from cultures that prefer getting to know someone before working on a project with him or her may be resistant to using technology to get acquainted. Additionally, in some cultures technology is seen as pretentious or stress inducing; individuals in these cultures may be happy to have computers at the office, but they don't want them in their homes. For the best intercultural communication, it is wise to check into the preferences of participants as early in the relationship as possible.

Process of Social Interaction among Groups

With the increase in technology, advancements in travel, and the globalization of business, it is rare for individuals not to encounter people who belong to other cultures. Consider the different cultures in your own community, where you may find people of different occupations, religious views, and ages. How do these groups connect to one another?

Social interaction refers to the way groups or cultures interact or influence one another. Often the hope is that these interactions will be cordial, cooperative, and helpful. There may be a simple objective in mind. For example, Jasmine's neighborhood might decide to sponsor a block party. In an effort to make sure that everyone feels welcome, the neighborhood association might invite Jasmine's family to prepare authentic Turkish foods for the event. Occasionally the interaction between cultures is competitive. Jasmine's neighborhood association might decide to sponsor a friendly ethnic pastry contest. On the other hand, sometimes the competition can be less friendly. Almost every day there is a news report about conflict in the Middle East or between countries and cultures fighting for limited land or resources. The resulting social interaction may become extremely negative and result in open, even armed, conflict.

Cultural Types

Roles of identity are cultural types—sex, family, academic major, and so on. To take this beyond personal identity and personal culture, consider cultural types that occur on a global, national, regional, or local level (see Figure 5.1). Think about how some co-cultures may interact positively and/or negatively. For example, how might a Canadian female (co-culture of "gender") animal rights activist (co-culture of "occupation") interact with people from Ghana who attend an annual deer-hunting festival? What might be some positive interactions? Some negative interactions?

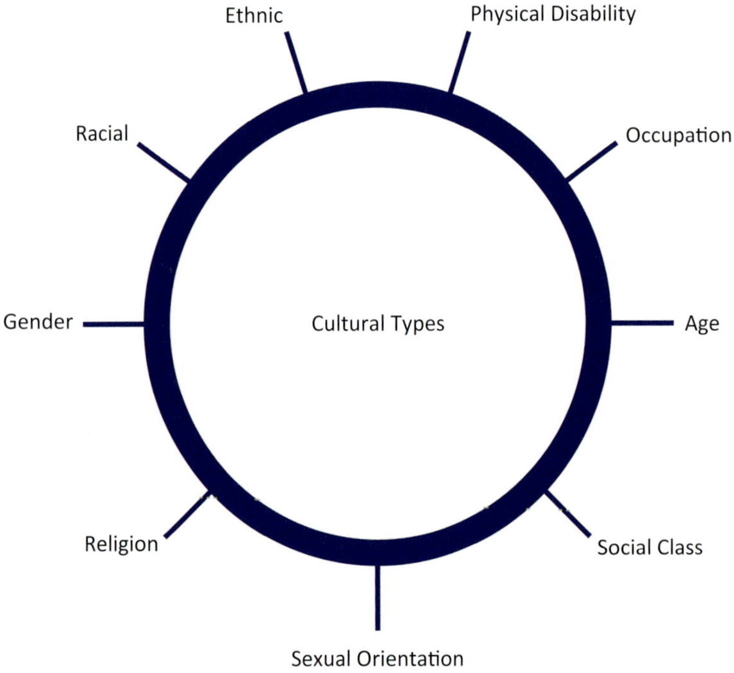

FIGURE 5.1 **Cultural Types**

Cultural Identity

Culture influences how individuals define themselves. Within the constraints of her Turkish culture, Jasmine may feel embarrassed about her divorce; however, as part of American culture, she may feel empowered for taking charge of her life. People may also identify against a cultural identity. Jasmine may define herself as an American woman only, not a Turkish one—especially given that she was born in the United States.

Uncertainty Avoidance

Think of how unsettling it is to lose a job. People like to feel safe and secure and do not like when the unexpected happens. People tend to handle unexpected situations with varying degrees of tolerance: Some remain grounded no matter what comes along in life; after losing a job, a person like this will simply regroup and find another one. In contrast, others may become so derailed that friends have to step in to help them move forward.

A culture also provides structure and a safety net so that its members can avoid uncertainty and receive support in the normal ups and downs of life. A culture may create folklore to teach its members how to avoid uncertainty. Cultures may create laws to guide behavior, and they may establish programs like Social Security to provide for their members in their old age or if the unexpected happens.

Power Distance

It is a challenge for even the smallest group to distribute power evenly all the time; therefore, the members of a culture must accept that power is distributed unevenly. Certain groups within a culture may even have to accept that gaining power is unlikely. For instance, children in a family must accept that their parents are the ones who typically hold the most power in the home. The mother and father are the providers, decision makers, disciplinarians, protectors, and teachers. Just as the children in a family usually accept and even (at least until the teenage years) happily endorse being distant from the power within the family, members of cultural groups tend to support the power structures within their own cultures.

Cultural Norms

Throughout time each culture develops **cultural norms**, or certain belief systems, practices, and teachings that become an agreed-upon method of operation. Cultural norms are the accepted and recommended ways in a particular culture of perceiving and coming to terms with the good and the bad things in life. For instance, cultures may teach their members to refrain from open confrontation because they believe it leads directly to war; their myths, legends, religion, and laws may be unified in this approach.

Norms provide more than guidelines for handling the extremes of life. They also provide accepted models and stable guidelines for daily living. In most cultures, parents are expected to care for their children, who are in turn expected to grow up, marry, and become caring parents themselves. The norm of a culture may dictate that its members practice a certain religion, dress a certain way, or behave a certain way. If the members adhere to these norms, the culture will flourish.

Cultural Universals

When norms become the standard for most cultures, they become known as **cultural universals**. These are the practices that most cultures share, accept, and endorse. For example, most, if not all, cultures share universal concerns for children. The young must be protected, provided for, and raised in secure, happy, and healthy environments. Most cultures take care of their own, providing firm structures of management (whether they are governments, neighborhood associations, or company boards of directors) that will facilitate the successful operation of the group. Cultural universals can become powerful communication tools for groups that are potentially or historically in conflict.

CAREER PERSPECTIVES: CROSS-CULTURAL CONSIDERATIONS IN BUSINESS

Although it can be quite intimidating to communicate with people from other cultures, don't be afraid to try. Remember that the people with whom you are interacting may be nervous about communicating with you, too, so make the effort to make others comfortable by being open and friendly. Here are some quick tips to meet accepted behaviors in other countries:

- Avoid using a firm, American-style handshake.
- Realize that your concepts of time may be different.
- Keep your voice down.
- Do not disclose too much personal information.
- Smile and be friendly.

Finally, keep in mind that the best thing to do when interacting with people from another culture is to research the expected behavior for that region or country. This will decrease the chances that you will make a mistake.

CULTURAL RELATIVISM

As members of different cultures communicate with one another, individuals must acknowledge and be open to the fact that cultures typically have their own communication expectations and social norms. In order for intercultural communication to be successful, people must be open to these differences and accept the members of other cultures for who they are. This is known as **cultural relativism**.

For example, visitors to a Catholic or Orthodox Christian cathedral will be expected to dress in a particular way: Women should wear skirts or dresses and cover their heads with light scarves or veils; men should wear suits with neckties. It is best to avoid wearing flip-flops and clothing with bright colors or designs and carrying electronic devices into these churches. Visitors are entering the territory of another culture; therefore, for the time period of the visit, guests should be respectful of the cultural norms that are in place.

The reverse is also true. Although Catholic and Orthodox Christians would likely appreciate gestures of respect for their culture, they also probably would not remove you from the premises if you showed up wearing open-toed sandals or carrying a cell phone.

CULTURAL DIFFUSION

Given that people may belong to more than one culture, that cultures often share spaces, and that cultures interact with one another (usually for their mutual benefit), it is not surprising to find out that cultures may share their characteristics and materials with one another. Jasmine's neighbors may enjoy the

Turkish pastries she and her family share with them so much that they ask for recipes or even cooking lessons. The neighbors may then share the recipes with other friends and family and help the Turkish pastries to become a common part of the local culture. On a larger scale, American companies like McDonald's and Coca-Cola are a part of cultures around the world. Conversely, the United States has adopted foods from other cultures, such as Italian wines, Mexican food, and French croissants.

Cultural diffusion goes beyond personal taste. Various cultures adopt the same outlook on government, for example, to form larger political groups like the European Union and the United Nations. Migration also results in cultural diffusion. This was evident when the British colonists settled in America and expanded their culture into the existing territory, which was then inhabited by Native Americans, who had their own culture.

Unfortunately, cultural diffusion may occur in unpleasant ways. For example, a natural or human-made disaster may leave a region open for a new culture to expand into it, or one culture may conquer another and force its inhabitants to change their culture.

DID YOU KNOW?

Geert Hofstede, a Dutch psychologist and anthropologist known for his pioneering work on cultures and intercultural relations, is perhaps best known for developing the Hofstede dimensions of national culture. The conceit of Hofstede's dimensions of national culture is that cultures may be characterized by the way problem areas are handled: power distance, uncertainty avoidance, individualism, and masculinity. Later he added other dimensions and assigned scores to cultures.

SUMMARY

- The term *culture* may be understood as the shared identity of a group and all of its material objects.
- People belong to more than one culture, as cultures reflect the complexity of human beings.
- All communication is intercultural communication.
- Cultures have characteristic functions like establishing collective systems of meaning, uncertainty avoidance, power distance, and norms.
- Individuals should be open to the fact that there are differences between cultures.
- Cultures naturally spread their characteristics and materials through interaction with other groups.

REFERENCES

Demographics of the United States. Retrieved from https://www.cia.gov/library/publications/the-world-factbook/geos/us.html

DuPraw, M. E., & Axner, M. (2003–2007). Working on common cross-cultural communication challenges. Retrieved from http://www.pbs.org/ampu/crosscult.html

Willcoxson, L., & Millett, B. (2000). The management of organisational culture. *Australian Journal of Management and Organisational Behaviour, 3*(2), 91–99.

CHAPTER 6

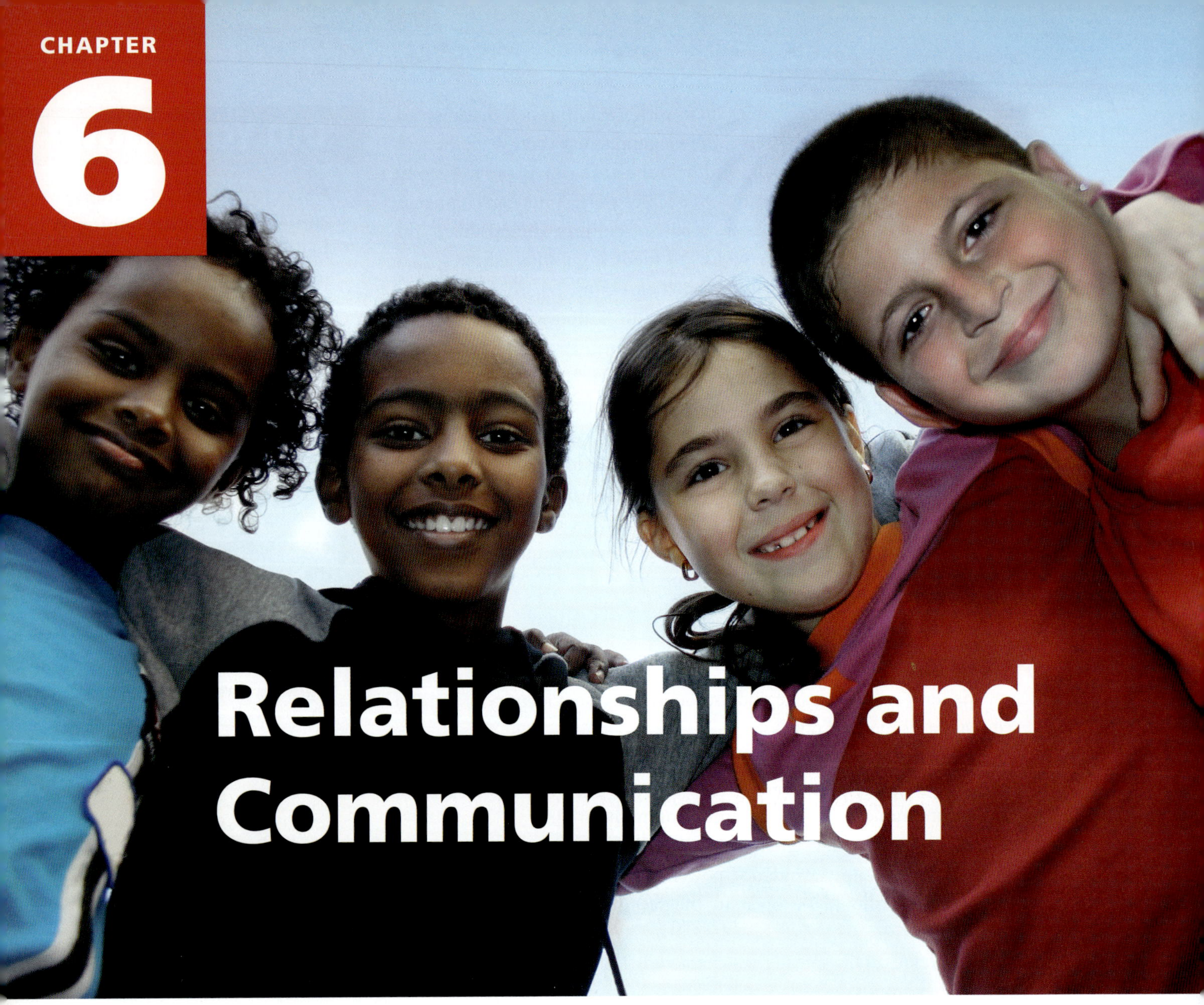

Relationships and Communication

On the first day of class, high school journalism teacher Mrs. Kalember asks the seniors in her class what they plan to do after graduation. Most of Mrs. Kalember's students have no definite plans yet, but a few speak up with their plans. Leisha remarks that she is planning to work for her father's auto sales business. Sam plans to attend a local college to study water resource management, and Jane wants to get married and start a family. Robert wants to attend a college with online courses so he can pursue a degree in criminal justice and keep a full-time job as a security guard.

Mrs. Kalember asks her students to consider Leisha, Sam, Jane, and Robert's real-life goals and link them to advice columns they find online in newspapers, magazines, or Web sites. Her assignment is for the students to read various lifestyle and career advice columns to find out what types of questions were asked about these career options and what type of advice was given.

Sam is the first to lodge a complaint. "Why do we have to read advice columns? All they do is tell losers how to resolve problems with their girlfriends or boyfriends or how to deal with clueless parents!"

Mrs. Kalember takes advantage of Sam's complaint to pose a pointed question. "What do all of the questions for the advice columns have in common and why?"

The students answer with a variety of responses. "Everyone has problems?" "No one can make a decision?" "People are confused?"

"Yes, all of those things are true," Mrs. Kalember answers. "But what is common to all of those situations?"

Suddenly, Sam begins to understand. Sheepishly, he says, "All advice columns are essentially about dealing with situations that happen among people."

"Yes!" Mrs. Kalember says. "People are often seeking answers to problems that happen in relationships between two or more people. After all, your relationships are based on how you connect with another person. Part of that connection has to do with how you think, feel, speak, and behave toward that person. It is about how you communicate verbally and nonverbally!"

KEY CONCEPTS

1. Relationships begin with making acquaintances; they then build up, continue, and may de-escalate. See page 77.

2. The law of attraction, social penetration, and social exchange theories focus on how relationships develop. See page 81.

3. All relationships have conflict that can be managed and resolved. See page 87.

TYPES OF RELATIONSHIPS

A **relationship** can be defined simply as how two or more people are connected. What is the role of relationships in your life? What do you do when you face conflict in a relationship? Do you have different types of relationships?

Relationships, depending on their level of emotional involvement, can have a variety of meanings. Life without relationships would be very limited. With whom would you share experiences or your thoughts and feelings? Who could you depend on if you became ill or needed help? The answers to many of these questions depend on relationships.

Romantic Relationships

Frequently, people will ask you, "Are you in a relationship?" The broadest answer to that question is "yes," because in fact you are certain to have a number of relationships. Of course, what the question really means is, "Are you in a *romantic* relationship?"

Romantic relationships can be very enjoyable, but they also can be complicated. When a relationship is new, the couple feels an emotional connection and a physical attraction. Things are usually very happy, joyful, and full of promise.

Think about yourself being in a new romantic relationship. You would probably find yourself excitedly planning dates and calling or messaging your new romantic partner constantly. You will escalate your communication in order to be in more frequent contact with one another. As you build your relationship, you get to know one another through this communication, enjoying all of the fun aspects of the newness of the relationship. You will talk about what you like to do together, the foods you both like or dislike, and the movies you enjoy.

TECHNOLOGY AND SOCIAL RELATIONSHIPS

Technology has brought the world to your fingertips. YouTube, Facebook, Twitter, LinkedIn, and many other social media sites allow you to network with friends and business associates from all over the world. Information can be exchanged instantly, but the vast majority of all communication is nonverbal, and without the verbal aspects of communication, a great deal of content and meaning is lost.

For that reason, it is necessary when communicating on social media sites to write in a very clear and understandable manner, and to be very careful with your words. You are building relationships through communication, and these relationships are dependent in part on your ability to effectively send your message. Think about what you say, and how you say it. Use your words to develop trust, and avoid divisive or argumentative comments. You never know who might be able to see your comments and what they will think of what you have written.

In a new romantic relationship, each person is busy sending and receiving messages, and the feedback is generally in agreement and matches the other's excitement and acceptance. What the couple chooses to communicate helps to define the relationship as romantic and creates intimacy between the two.

Social Relationships

There are, of course, many other types of relationships in addition to romantic relationships. Think about the ways that you connect or come together with another person. You can have relationships built simply on friendship, relationships with family members, relationships based on religious affiliation or organization membership, or relationships related to your work.

Next, think about how you have built social relationships at the acquaintance level into closer relationships, such as friendships. Did you find that you have a great deal in common? As in a romantic relationship, a connection or something in common between you and the person whom you are beginning to consider your friend is key in getting things started. You may have found that you enjoyed similar activities, knew the same people, or had similar upbringings. Relationships are dependent on how and what you communicate to each other, as your shared communication forms the bond and type of relationship you will have.

STAGES OF RELATIONSHIPS

Just like most living things, relationships also have a lifespan. A relationship has a beginning, grows and matures, and at some point, ends. Many models for the development of relationships have been created, but one of the most commonly used and understood models is that of psychologist George Levinger. Levinger initially created his relationship stage model to describe romantic relationships between men and women, but it has been used for other types of relationships, too. The model has five stages:

1. Acquaintance
2. Build-up
3. Continuation
4. Deterioration
5. Termination

Beginning Relationships

The term **acquaintance** denotes a relationship between two people who know each other only slightly. Acquaintance is usually based on a commonality between two people, such as how close they live or work to one another. Acquaintances communicate on a less intimate level than deeper friendships or relationships. They are likely not to progress beyond talking about the weather, the schools their children attend, or similar small-talk topics. Levinger found that acquaintances can be sustained over a long period of time, but if people begin to like one another and find that they have something in common, that the relationship can advance to the next stage.

During the **build-up** phase, acquaintances begin to know more about each other and develop a trust and confidence in one another. This is where common characteristics, such as goals, activities, or background, can influence how often people continue to see one another. Communication during this phase might consist of making plans to engage in activities together or having conversations about common experiences or goals.

Maintaining Relationships

Continuation is the phase in which participants realize that they want to stay in the relationship. The relationship continues to grow, and the participants are very happy spending time with each other. They can each expect that the relationship will be stable and will continue. Trust is a factor as well, serving as an anchor for the relationship. Communication during the continuation stage is likely to be more intimate and to include discussion of values and personal feelings.

De-escalation and Ending Relationships

In the **deterioration** phase, the relationship begins to unravel. Of course, not all relationships deteriorate—some are lifelong. When a relationship *does* deteriorate, the participants become bored or unhappy. Trust, which was once a cornerstone of the relationship, is lost. The participants will likely shut down emotionally and communicate less and less. It is possible at this stage for people to acknowledge that they have problems and find a way to solve them, but if not, the relationship likely will end.

At the **termination** phase, the relationship ends. Even a healthy relationship terminates upon the death of one of the participants. Termination can also refer to a breakup or divorce, or even a dispute that leads friends to never see one another again.

CASE STUDY: FORGING A FRIENDSHIP

Paralegals Sharon and Rudi forged a strong friendship despite significant differences, as they chose instead to focus on their similarities. Some found it surprising that they were such good friends. Sharon was the cheerleader of the two, a person who was always lively and upbeat. She was carefree—so much so, in fact, that sometimes her work suffered as a result. Rudi, on the other hand, was much more serious. Rudi often worked late just to get her projects completed and was always offering her help to others. Both women worked in law firms as paralegals.

Sharon and Rudi initially met when the lawyers they worked with were collaborating on the same case. Sharon and Rudi generally found themselves exchanging the information needed to be shared between the attorneys. During these frequent communications, their talk gradually drifted from business topics to personal ones. The women learned that they had graduated from the same college, which led them to talk about many happy shared memories with one another.

They decided to meet in person and immediately found that they liked one another. After that, they met for lunch at least once a month. As time passed, Sharon and Rudi learned more about one another and began socializing together after work. They both found that they were mutually interested in fashion and trying new restaurants.

More time passed, and with each conversation and each meeting, they moved from being acquaintances to becoming very close friends. Each woman met the other's family and children. Their friendship became anchored in trust; deep, mutual respect; and admiration. Sharon, Rudi, and their respective families began to share more time with one another.

Five years into the relationship, Rudi's husband was transferred out of state. Sharon and Rudi were unsure what would happen to their friendship as a result. Of course, they thought, they could continue to share news and conversations over the phone or via social networking sites, but would that be enough to let the relationship continue? Both women, along with their families, decided that they would make every effort to continue their relationship—and in fact would attempt to grow the relationship.

Three years later, Sharon and Rudi's relationship remains strong. They communicate and visit one another regularly, but the regularity is not what has cemented the relationship. Sharon and Rudi are dedicated to knowing what is going on in one another's life—the fun parts and the difficult parts alike. The women made a commitment to not allow the relationship to deteriorate. Instead, the physical changes that took place—Rudi's move—helped make the relationship even stronger.

One of the key elements throughout Sharon and Rudi's relationship was communication. In the beginning, they got to know one another and learned about their common experiences and interests through communication. As time went on, they became closer by learning more about one another, and from this learning came respect and confidence. The relationship moved from acquaintance to friendship—again, courtesy of communication.

Sharon and Rudi's friendship was cemented over time because of the experiences their families enjoyed together. They each became a part of one another's lives. When Rudi's move took place, both families agreed to remain in contact and communicate frequently with one another. They accepted their commitment to the relationship and assumed responsibility for maintaining the necessary level of intimacy and contact.

Have you ever had a friendship that was put to the test by change, like Sharon and Rudi's? How did you handle the situation? Did you talk through the change

in your relationship? Did you communicate your thoughts and feelings in a way that helped keep the relationship together? Or did you drift apart?

The relationship between Sharon and Rudi is just one type of friendship. Friendships can exist between women and men, men and men, people of the same age, or between people of very different ages. Relationships of any type that are particularly close are called *intimate* relationships. Intimate relationships can exist between any two people with an emotional attachment. An intimate relationship can be a friendship, a dating relationship, a family relationship, or a marital relationship. Many people automatically assume that an intimate relationship is sexual, but it can be completely platonic. Intimate relationships are often divided into two categories—emotional intimacy and physical intimacy. Intimate relationships can include a sexual component, but it is not necessary for a relationship to include a sexual component to be considered intimate.

STAGES OF LOVE

Think about the difference between an acquaintance relationship and a more intimate relationship. What makes an intimate relationship more fulfilling? Like all humans, you have a need to belong and feel accepted and loved. An intimate relationship fulfills this basic human need of belonging.

Intimacy and Sex

The study of intimate relationships is a new discipline and falls under the research and study within the area of social psychology. Of course, sex is a natural desire, but physically and emotionally intimate relationships require a different level of maintenance than exclusively emotionally intimate ones. How can you keep a physically intimate relationship vibrant and healthy? What do you need to do to keep the connection going? Key factors for a successful physically intimate relationship include sexual compatibility and an emotional bond. This emotional bond is established by communicating with disclosure and honesty. In addition, you must work to let your guard down and strive to set a balance of equal partnership in the relationship.

Repairing a Relationship

Relationships can suffer from violating trust and expectations. This can occur if one person in a marriage or love relationship has an affair, or if a close friend violates the trust of the other by talking about something they both agreed would be a secret. How can these and other types of damage to a relationship be repaired? One approach is to quickly offer a sincere apology. It is particularly effective if the apology is voluntary. The person should promise not to violate the relationship again. Both people should agree to reaffirm their commitment to the relationship and its values. It is useful to talk about ways to avoid similar problems in the future.

Coping with a Loss of a Relationship

Everyone must cope with the loss of a relationship at some point in their lives, but it is never easy. You must allow yourself to feel the anger, fear, or sadness that naturally accompanies such a loss, and to acknowledge how important the relationship was in your life.

When dealing with the loss of a relationship, consider increasing the contact you have with other friends and family to help you remember that there are other people in your life who care about you. Ask them for the specific type of support that would be most helpful to you during this time.

It takes time to heal from the loss of a relationship, so be patient. This is not the right time to make major life decisions. Instead, take care of your health and maintain a routine. Use the time to reevaluate your life and priorities or perhaps to try out a new interest. Helping others can be a great way to heal from the pain of the loss. Recognize that guilt, self-blame, and bargaining can be defenses against the natural feelings of a loss of control. If you are unable to work or go to school, remain depressed for a long period of time, or otherwise simply cannot seem to recover from the loss, consider seeing a physician or a specialist, like a psychologist or qualified counselor.

Theories of Relationship Development

No two intimate relationships are alike. What is common, however, is that successful relationships are developed over time between people who know and understand themselves very well. Different theories exist about how relationships develop, and the following sections will examine a few of these theories.

The Law of Attraction

The law of attraction, which essentially suggests that like attracts like, considers the factors that draw people together or push them apart. Such factors as physical appearance, nonverbal body language, personal scents, and environmental factors all contribute to whether people are attracted to or put off by one another.

Social Penetration Theory

The **social penetration theory** suggests that as people get to know one another in intimate personal relationships, they learn more and more about each other's personal and private lives because they have learned to trust one another. Social penetration theory includes the following phases:

1. Orientation. During this phase, people begin to get to know one another using small talk.
2. Exploratory affect. During the exploratory affect stage, people begin to tell each other more about themselves, including sharing some (but not all) of their thoughts, feelings, and emotions. This is the stage when people decide whether they want to go further with the relationship and develop trust.

3. Affective. During the affective stage, the relationship moves from casual to intimate. The participants begin to share some of their private thoughts and feelings. In the affective stage, people become more sensitive to the responses of their partner; as a result, disagreements can happen. In such cases, the participants must work together to resolve the issues and difficulties.
4. Stability. During this stage, people become comfortable with one another. Understanding and trust develop between the people in the relationship.
5. De-penetration. If the relationship starts to have problems and those involved are not willing to work through the difficulty, then the relationship is likely to end.

Social Exchange Theory

The law of attraction and social penetration theories are based on measuring how each participant in the relationship thinks, feels, and responds to a variety of situations. The **social exchange theory** is quite different, as it is based on economics, psychology, and sociology.

The theory suggests that all relationships are based on a cost–benefit analysis that each person intrinsically makes. Simply stated, each person has needs and wants when it comes to relationships. According to the social exchange theory, each person's level of satisfaction in the relationship will determine its outcome. However, the social exchange theory also suggests that a comparison among the level of satisfaction that one has in the relationship in question and any alternative relationships makes the real difference.

For example, consider a couple that has been married for more than 30 years. They are unhappy and dissatisfied, but it would be wrong to automatically assume the couple will divorce simply because they are unhappy. Other factors can make a difference. For example, perhaps there are children or grandchildren involved. A divorce can be costly, as well. The couple may also maintain other relationships with friends or family—or perhaps extramarital physically intimate relationships—that allow them to remain together.

As you can conclude from these three theories about relationships, there is no one right way to look at a relationship. Relationships are about how two people connect, the level at which they connect, the time it takes to get to know one another, and whether the participants are committed to making the relationship work.

At the core of each of these theories is the need for affective communication. Relationships do not just happen. They require people who are in them to send, receive, and give feedback to messages in the form of thoughts, feelings,

HOW TO IMPROVE COMMUNICATION IN RELATIONSHIPS

Just as there are rules at work, on the road, or when playing sports, there are rules to follow when you are having a disagreement with your significant other or an intimate friend. When you are speaking, you want to be heard, so when your partner or friend is speaking, you must listen as well. Note that listening does not include thinking about what you are going to say next while your partner is speaking.

Just as you care about your partner, your partner cares about you. If you did not care about one another, your feelings would not be as intense. An argument is just that, an argument—you are not at war with your partner. The objective of any argument is to reach a solution together. Try not to judge your partner. Remember that arguments or disagreements come about because two or more people think differently, yet just as strongly, about a situation. Listen to what is being said, and then put yourself in your partner's place.

Once your partner has finished speaking, repeat what he or she said in your own words in order to emphasize that you heard and understood the message. After you have done so, you can share your thoughts and opinions. Remember to stay focused on coming up with a decision or response that works for both of you.

Too often, people in relationships feel the need to win at any cost, and this can certainly damage a relationship. An argument should be treated fairly by both participants and should not end until a solution has been reached that works for both. "Winning" through personal attacks or demanding to be proven right does not lend itself to a more acceptable outcome.

or behavior. When communication breaks down, arguments or disagreements are the likely result. Words—perhaps hostile ones—will be exchanged, and depending on how each person in the relationship responds, those words can be very hurtful and cause damage to the relationship. It is important to argue and disagree fairly.

Relationships That Need Improvement: Codependency

Just as in most situations, there are relationships that are healthy and those that are not. There are those relationships where one of the people in the relationship is very involved and committed to the relationship and the other person is not. How can you determine if a relationship needs to be improved on?

The term **codependent** refers to an unhealthy relationship in which one participant is trying much harder than the other participant. Codependency is also used to refer to relationships in which one or both of the participants has a substance abuse problem, an addictive personality, or difficulty controlling certain urges, such as needing to have attention focused on oneself at all times. If, for example, you consider the relationship you are in right now to be more important than you are to yourself, you are likely in a codependent relationship.

Think about that for a moment. Have you ever been in a relationship where you worked harder to salvage or maintain the relationship than your partner? Were you the one always thinking of ways to get together, making all of the phone calls, and constantly helping your partner? In such a relationship, your own personal needs are likely neglected while you remain preoccupied with your partner's needs. Was your partner demanding of your time? Did your partner expect you to do most of the heavy lifting in the relationship? Was your partner emotionally demanding?

Codependency can also occur when one partner is very self-absorbed or seems uninterested in the relationship. This disinterested type of person frequently attracts a codependent personality. Ironically, these relationships can be mutually satisfying. Self-absorbed people are satisfied because their needs will be totally met. Codependent people are satisfied because their self-absorbed counterparts present a problem for them, thus offering the codependent a sense of control over a person who is out of control. Codependent people often define themselves as being strong and able to deal with the issue when in fact they almost completely sublimate themselves and their needs to their partner.

Organizations like Al-Anon, a group dedicated to helping the loved ones of substance abusers cope, have been formed to help people repair codependent relationships and change them to healthy relationships. At Al-Anon meetings, every participant shares a story, and all are treated as equals. No one member of the group is in a position to give advice or direction to any other member. Everyone at the meeting has experienced a problem with someone else's drinking. In organizations like Al-Anon, relationships sometimes form among members connected by their common interests, needs, and shared past experiences.

Emotional Intelligence

Do you have emotional intelligence? One of the cornerstones of developing intimate relationships is learning how to be a good and active listener and learning how to establish an understanding and developing trust in others. People who understand their own emotions and the emotions of others—and also know how to manage their emotions—are said to have emotional intelligence.

Researchers Peter Salovey and John Mayer have conducted a great body of research on emotional intelligence over the years. Salovey and Mayer's research has suggested that people vary in their ability to understand and manage emotion, and the two created a model that lists four types of abilities when considering emotional intelligence.

1. Perception of emotions. The first ability of emotional intelligence is an area where nonverbal communication is extremely helpful. At this stage, you can read emotions in faces, pictures, and voices. This means you can understand your own emotions, too. You need to have the ability to perceive emotions in order to experience the other three abilities.

2. Using emotions. Do you have changing moods? Do you understand your moods and use them to accomplish different goals? For example, perhaps you need to be in a particular mood to get your homework or housework done. This is what it means to use your emotions. If you are capable of doing so, you clearly understand yourself and the nature of your moods.
3. Understanding emotions. If you understand the emotions of others and how the various emotions relate to the thoughts, feelings, and behaviors of others, you are more likely to be successful in relationships. Do you understand your own emotions? Do you know what you are feeling? Are you aware of how your emotions become more defined over time?
4. Managing emotions. This is perhaps the most difficult of the four abilities. In order to successfully manage your emotions, you must know what to do with your emotions once you are able to identify, use, and understand them. How can you personally use your emotions to help you have a more active, productive life and ensure that you are able to set and accomplish your goals?

Now that you know more *about* emotional intelligence, reconsider this section's opening question. Do you have emotional intelligence? Can you think of others in your life who do not? How can emotional intelligence help you develop healthier relationships?

Maintaining Relationships with Emotional Intelligence

Relationships develop in stages. It takes time to get to know one another and to develop trust in one another. At the same time, trust is based on understanding one another, so having emotional intelligence clearly plays a role in the development of relationships. When you understand the emotions of others and yourself and you can manage these emotions, relationships are more likely to develop with ease and last, as they will be reinforced with trust.

Over the period of a semester, what relationships do you develop with your fellow classmates and instructor? In a public speaking class, for example, the first day may be filled with waiting and wondering what is going to happen in class. If you are like most people, you probably have reservations about the class because of a reluctance to get up in front of a group and speak.

As the class progresses, everyone has an opportunity to get to know one another. Over the semester, you will have the opportunity to communicate directly with some, if not all, of your classmates and will get to hear what they have to say. You may even begin to anticipate how some classmates will behave; by the end of the class, you will likely have a new level of respect and understanding for some of your classmates that comes from a combination of time, understanding, and anticipating what might happen. What emotional intelligence ability is likely to play a role in the development of these relationships?

As the class comes to an end, you and your classmates may want to keep up your relationships or at least stay in touch with one another. Have you experienced this personally in any of your classes? What have you found to be the common ground that keeps these relationships strong and growing?

DID YOU KNOW?

Nonverbal Greetings

Nonverbal greetings differ from culture to culture. As an example, in the United States, and other Western countries, it is common for men and women to greet one another with a handshake. People shake with their right hand, and you are judged by the firmness of the handshake and whether you make direct eye contact when you shake a person's hand. In Muslim cultures a man will shake a woman's hand only if she extends her hand first.

The custom when greeting others in many Eastern cultures is quite different. Bowing is the expected greeting practice China, Japan, and other Asian countries. There is a great deal of tradition in these countries. Elders are to be respected, and the bow is a strong sign of respect. It is disrespectful to look a person in the eye when bowing.

Generally, the most important factor in maintaining a connection between yourself and others is the ability to communicate with one another both verbally and nonverbally. As you know, the communication model shows that effective communication needs a speaker, a message, a receiver, and feedback. Without any one of these four elements, interpersonal communication cannot take place. You will simply have people who are talking but not communicating.

Are you an effective communicator or simply a talker? What do you need to do to improve your communication skills? Do you need to become a better listener? Do you need to present your messages more clearly? Can you understand your emotions and the emotions of others?

Think of the many situations in which being a strong communicator can make a difference in your life. Will it make a difference for you as far as your job is concerned? Is there an impact on your friendships and other social relationships?

No matter how successful you are in terms of communicating, there is always room to evaluate yourself and look for improvement. Figuring out what you do well and areas where you can improve is always a useful activity. Following are key ways you can check yourself and determine how effective you are as a communicator.

The first step is to know yourself. Are you comfortable in social situations, or are you self-conscious? Do you value your family? Is education important to you? Have you thought about how your past experiences affect your thoughts and decisions? Often, the thoughts and feelings you carry from past experiences can influence how you respond to situations. Sometimes these responses are positive, and sometimes they are not.

For example, there are many recent news stories about children getting bullied by their classmates. If you have been bullied before, you might be more or less likely, depending on your experience, to be willing to speak publicly about being bullied. But imagine the power of your message to someone else in your audience to is currently being bullied—if you were to acknowledge to yourself and others that you had experience being bullied, you would offer that person your first-hand experience and may help him or her deal with the problem.

The second step in learning how to maintain a relationship is to be open to learning more about others. As you get to know people and advance from the acquaintance stage to the intimate stage in your relationships, you learn more about the thoughts and feelings of your fellow relationship participants. You will learn more about what they like to do, how they think, and, in some cases, how they feel.

As you have more practice being open with others, you will understand why people do what they do, think what they think, and feel what they feel. As a result, you will get to know the receiver on the communication model much better. In the end, your message will receive a warmer reception from receivers, and you will begin getting the feedback you want.

Think about this concept for a moment. When you are speaking with someone, how much of your conversation is intentional and how much of the conversation is simply noise, or talking for the sake of talking? How many times over the course of a conversation do you speak and not pay attention to what you are saying? How many times to do you speak with a specific message in mind?

Having a specific message is expected when you are giving a speech. There is a deliberate reason for giving any speech. There is an intended audience and an intended message. Perhaps there are other situations in your life where you should speak with intention but occasionally forget to do so. When you are speaking with a supervisor, for example, you should consistently speak in a business context and avoid treating him or her as you would a friend. One of the best ways to maintain your relationship with your boss is to remember that business is business. The messages that you send at work need to be grounded in business etiquette. Even if your relationship with your boss is more casual, you and the messages you send to him or her will get more respect if you remain ever mindful that you are in a business environment.

Business relationships are very important to your overall well-being and security. They need to be developed and maintained in order to have a satisfying work experience. In addition to your boss, it is quite important to consider your relationships with your coworkers. How do you communicate with them? Do you get to know them and understand how they communicate? Can you determine the emotions of a coworker? Your emotional intelligence can make a big difference in the workplace. If you ask a coworker to share how she is feeling or express patience with communicating with her during a difficult time, you will send strong messages that you respect and understand her—and she will reciprocate by showing you respect and understanding.

Now think about your more intimate relationships, those with a significant other, a family member, or a very close friend. When you speak to people with whom you share close, intimate relationships, do you talk in the same manner no matter what the situation is, or do you change your communication based on the situation and the message that you are seeking to send?

By modifying your style of communication and your body language, you allow others to know when you are serious and when you are in a more casual or informal mood. Just as it is important for you to understand the thoughts, moods, feelings, and emotions of others, it is important for you to give others the opportunity to understand you better.

CONFLICT

Whenever two people are in a relationship, disagreements and conflict can and will arise. Conflict is often disliked and feared by many people, as it can make some people very uncomfortable and in some cases lead them to completely avoid certain situations likely to create conflict. In fact, conflict is a part of healthy and unhealthy relationships alike, and avoiding it only causes more problems.

Causes of Conflict

The causes of conflict can vary, but it is generally agreed that conflict is caused when two people with varying ideas, each of which is workable by itself, come together. In a conflict situation, these ideas are not in sync, and may even directly contradict

one another. This is often referred to as **dialectical tension**, and all relationships experience dialectical tension.

Dialectical Tension

Three contradictions occur in episodes of dialectical tension. The first is a contradiction between **autonomy** and connectedness, or the issues related to balancing a need to be connected to another as a partner and a need to be independent. This is a contradiction that all people experience; however, the degree to which each person encounters this conflict is dependent on many factors, including personality and disposition.

The second contradiction is between openness and closedness, or expression and privacy. This is best described as balancing the need to be open and talk about yourself with a need to remain closed and private about yourself and your thoughts. Some people are naturally more open than others, so as before, people are affected by this contradiction in varying degrees.

The last contradiction is between predictability and novelty, or stability versus change. Do you ever find yourself caught between a desire to keep stability in your life and wanting to simply do what you want when you want? Some might consider this simply becoming more spontaneous. In any relationship, you must balance the need for predictability with the desire for spontaneity.

Values of Conflict

Conflict *can* be positive. It can provide opportunities for people with differing ideas to come together, discuss their ideas, and perhaps come up with a better solution than any one person could come up with on his or her own.

In relationships, participants often vie for control or to have power in the relationship. The balance of power in any relationship may be constant, with one participant always calling the shots, or it can shift depending on the situation. Conflict can assist in balancing or shifting the power in a relationship.

For example, imagine that you and a classmate are asked by your instructor to prepare a presentation for the class. As you are working with your partner, you begin to direct your partner about what she should do, and you tell her what you are going to do. Your partner gets upset and frustrated because you are controlling the situation. In order to resolve the conflict, you will both need to analyze and discuss the situation. In this situation, with this particular partner, you may be displaying too much power and domination of your partner, and you may need to share control of the project. A different partner might be perfectly happy to let you run the show.

Think about your own relationships. Are you always the one who is in control? Or are your relationship partners always in control? Or does the power switch from one to the other depending on the situation? Would you rather have your relationships be more equal, that is, in better balance?

Conflict can also help establish better boundaries between participants in a relationship. If a conflict is caused by one person overstepping the boundaries of acceptable behavior of the other, both parties can discuss the issues and come to a clearer understanding of what will be acceptable in the future.

Another outcome of conflict is that it encourages those in the conflict to talk about their wants and their needs. To return to the example of the presentation project, if you and your partner begin to have differing opinions about how the project should be approached, you should have an open discussion to resolve the conflict. You should both discuss in detail why you have come to the decisions you have reached, followed by an equally in-depth discussion of what you each want and need to accomplish by the end of the project. Once you both have aired out your reasons and your goals, you should be able to reach agreement on a plan of action.

Finally, as you work through and complete the project, you have created a wealth of understanding about one another. You have learned what each of you needs in order to be happy and successful in your working relationship, and should the opportunity present itself in the future to work together, you will know and understand how best to accomplish that goal. You have created a history together.

Theorist Luis Pondy has indicated that project-related conflict typically proceeds through four separate stages:

- Stage 1: Latent. In this stage, two or more people are required to cooperate with one another to complete a project or objective, so there is a possibility of conflict. Latent conflict happens when a change occurs in the existing arrangement for accomplishing the project. This can include a change in the organization, added responsibilities given to one or more of the participants, or a change in a personal goal for one or more of the participants.
- Stage 2: Perceived. In this stage, people who are involved in the project or activity begin to sense and be aware that a problem might exist, even if they are not aware of where it might come from. It is at this point that tensions can begin.
- Stage 3: Felt. During this stage, all parties begin to want to identify the perceived problem and focus on the conflict. People begin to build walls around their positions and dig in their heels in support of their side of the issue.
- Stage 4: Manifest. During this stage, people are more overt with their thoughts and opinions, and it becomes very apparent that conflict exits. At this point, it is important for each party to work to resolve the conflict as quickly as possible. The longer the issue simmers, the more difficult it becomes to resolve.

Conflict Resolution

You might be asking yourself, "Well, I can see that understanding conflict is important, but what can I do to resolve it?" Your interpersonal communication and emotional intelligence skills can make a major difference in managing the outcome of any conflict.

- First, it is important for you to determine the nature of the conflict. Does it relate to any of the three contradictions associated with dialectical tension? What is the source or nature of the conflict?
- Second, it is helpful to understand the needs, wants, and communication style of the person with whom you are having the conflict. Do you understand the other participant emotionally, as well as his or her needs? Consider whether you are able to speak directly with the other participant or whether you should be less direct and more subtle when discussing the conflict.

■ Third, when managing conflict, always consider the intentions. At some point, you have probably heard the term *win-win*. In such a situation, all parties faced with conflict walk away from the conflict feeling happy and satisfied with its outcome. In a win-lose situation, one person or group wins the conflict and the other loses. The third intention, of course, is a lose-lose situation—where no one wins, and everyone loses.

Managing Conflict

There are certain ways that people deal with or manage conflict, including accommodation, avoidance, domination, negotiation, and collaboration.

- Avoidance, of course, is a strategy chosen instinctively by many people. Avoidance is fed by the misconception that ignoring a problem might make it go away.
- Some who are looking to make a problem go away choose to accommodate their counterpart in the conflict by simply giving in instead of working through the conflict. Saying, "Fine. We will do it your way," does not resolve a conflict. In fact, it can create even more conflict, as resentment will likely follow.
- In the case of a work conflict, a supervisor might resolve the issue by making a decision without consulting those directly involved in the conflict. Domination can result in a quick resolution, of course, but this type of behavior also can lead to resentment.

- Negotiation is another strategy for managing conflict. Negotiation can lead to a situation where the conflict is managed but neither side is satisfied with the outcome.
- Collaboration is a more involved strategy for managing conflict. It requires those involved to spend time directly speaking with one another about the situation until they resolve the conflict.

Defensive versus Supportive Communication

Some key behaviors will help you work through and decide the best way to resolve conflict. They will help you see the value in conflict and disagreements, and that solutions can be resolved without a great deal of pain or upset to those involved.

CAREER PERSPECTIVES: CONFLICT MANAGEMENT

Among the best strategies to manage any conflict is to make a conscious effort to begin any sentences that could be construed as confrontational with the word "I" rather than the word "you." Consider a situation in which an opponent in a conflict says to you, "You are wrong!" Next, consider the same opponent saying instead, "I disagree with what you are saying." See how much more palatable that message—which says exactly the same thing—seems? Using "I" to introduce such a statement shows a sincere desire to work through a problem and suggests to your partner in the conflict that you are being sincere and nonjudgmental.

First, it is helpful to be open. By stating your thoughts and feelings honestly and directly, you are giving others involved the opportunity to see that you are committed to resolving the conflict. It is important at this stage to use *I* statements. "*I* think that *we* are making a mistake" will be received with much more warmth than "*You* are making a big mistake." *You* statements put your counterpart on the defensive instead of keeping the conversation open for discussion.

It is critical to always exhibit empathy—here, your emotional intelligence can make a real difference. Making an effort to understand and listen to all comments helps others see that you are interested in resolving the conflict. Use statements like, "I understand what you are saying," I agree with what you have to say," or "I was thinking about what you said, and I think it is a good idea."

ETHICS: THE RULES OF ARGUING

When engaged in an argument or disagreement, always be sure that everyone involved plays by the rules. The first step is to make sure that all involved know exactly what the issues are by carefully explaining and defining them. Next, focus on solutions to the disagreement, making sure that each participant offers at least one option. Finally, decide on the best solution or resolution for the issue.

For example, imagine that you are in an argument with a loved one about a vacation destination—you would like to go to the beach, and your significant other wants to go to the mountains. First, you can work together to determine if the vacation destination is really the root of the argument, or if instead the argument is actually about something else—perhaps the timing of the trip or a desire to stop off at a family member's home for a few days. After you have determined that the argument really is just about the destination, you can move on to working together to find solutions—for example, a destination like southern California, which offers both beaches and mountain peaks. Once you have determined a set of solutions, you can select the right one together.

Stay away from personal attacks—they will only prolong and intensify the disagreement. An argument is a time to look at the issues, discuss options for solutions, and agree on a solution.

Being supportive and letting others know what you have difficulty understanding or accepting will help to guide the conflict to a more speedy solution. Keeping others in the dark or guessing your thoughts will only slow down the process. At the same time, identify any areas in which you agree with your counterpart in the conflict. There is almost always some common ground in every disagreement. Also, make sure that you enter any negotiation treating everyone involved as equals. Be sure to listen to all comments that are being made and offer thoughtful feedback.

Conflict can arise any time two or more people are in a relationship. Conflict is human and natural. It is important to consider your goal for the outcome of the conflict, and to work toward that goal using the information that you have learned in this chapter.

SUMMARY

- Relationships are an important part of everyone's daily life.
- Effective interpersonal communications are critical to creating and maintaining relationships of all kinds.
- All relationships are subject to conflict and disagreement.
- Resolving conflict takes time and dedication.

REFERENCES

Lewicki, R. J., & Tomlinson, E. C. (2003, December). Trust and trust building. Retrieved from http://www.beyondintractability.org/essay/trust_building/

University of Texas at Dallas Counseling Center. (2011, January 19). Self-help: Coping with a breakup. Retrieved from http://www.utdallas.edu/counseling/breakup/

CHAPTER 7

Listening

Roberto, a professor of dance, enters his classroom, greets his students, and turns on the video projector. A tape of dancers performing a show begins to play.

Roberto says, "You'll all be able to view the tape again later, but I want you to pay close attention to this first viewing."

Roberto's students have been studying the history of this dance group and learning to analyze of the quality of its choreography. As the students watch the tape, some take notes, including writing the time elapsed on the tape so they can return to that exact point later. Other students sit back and ignore the tape, thinking that they will be able to watch it again later if necessary.

By the time the tape ends, one of the students who was not paying attention has fallen asleep. Fortunately, a good friend sitting next to him elbows him to wake up again.

"Very good," says Roberto. "Thank you for your attention. Please take out some paper and a pen and write a two-page reflective response on the dance you have just seen. Please analyze whether the music and the movement went together, and what patterns of energy flow the choreographer used. Your writing will count as a quiz."

As Roberto turns toward the whiteboard, many students begin to groan. Roberto spins around. "Of course it's fair. I told you a week ago we would have an in-class quiz on the materials we have been discussing. This is your chance to show me how well you paid attention. You have 20 minutes."

KEY CONCEPTS

1. The steps to effective listening are defined in six distinct goals. See page 96.

2. There are two main types of listening: active listening and passive listening. See page 99.

3. Paralanguage refers to a speaker's rate, volume, tone, pitch, and pauses. See page 103.

4. Personal space is important to effective listening. See page 105.

5. Listening is a process involving several steps. See page 105.

6. Effective listening can be learned and practiced. See page 109.

THE GOALS OF LISTENING

You must keep six distinct goals in mind in order to ensure effective listening:

1. Prepare yourself to listen.
2. Know what deserves your attention most during a communicative interaction.
3. Try to overcome barriers to effective communication.
4. Learn how to provide appropriate feedback.
5. Safeguard your hearing.
6. Learn strategies for improving memory.

Listening is extremely important to communication, but many people are often disinterested in listening or overlook its significance. Few people are formally trained in listening, but many people are completely unprepared to listen effectively.

Getting Ready to Listen

How can you prepare yourself to listen? The first steps are being willing to listen and equipping yourself with prior knowledge about the subject. Also, you should familiarize yourself with the speaker and the content that will be presented prior to the interaction.

For example, if you are planning to attend an important presentation about e-mail etiquette in the workplace, you would first research the topic a few days prior to the date. If you are unfamiliar with the presentation speaker, you might consider learning more about the person as well. On the day of the presentation, you can take more steps to prepare yourself to listen better, including getting plenty of sleep the night before, arriving early for the presentation, taking notes, and sitting up instead of slouching.

What Should You Listen For?

Just before the presentation begins, you should take a few moments to think about what you will need to listen for. It is difficult, if not impossible, to retain all of the information you will hear, so instead you should focus on the discussion's main points, which are its most important pieces of information.

See if you can identify the presentation's main points by analyzing the speaker's introductory statements. Main points are essential topics that help organize information into categories. Knowledgeable speakers generally focus a presentation on three to five main points, as too many main points may confuse listeners.

Overcoming the Barriers

As you listen to a presentation, you may encounter physical, physiological, and psychological barriers to effective communication.

- Two people in the row behind you may begin whispering to each other about a fellow coworker.

- Your cell phone may begin to vibrate in your pocket, which could lead you to wonder about the voicemails and e-mails that have arrived while you have been away from your desk.
- You may feel sleepy or have difficulty concentrating.
- You may find it hard to hear from your seat in the back of the room.
- You may find the speaker either unattractive or very attractive, both of which can be quite distracting.

How can you recognize and overcome these barriers? First, alleviate all physical distractions that impede your ability to listen. Turn off your cell phone. Ignore those side conversations.

If you do not feel well, you will not be able to listen well—a physiological barrier—so take good care of yourself and get plenty of sleep. Another physiological barrier is impaired hearing, so make sure you are close enough to the speaker to hear every word.

Psychological barriers include any misconceptions or biases you have against the speaker or his or her message. Forget about the physical characteristics of the speaker and focus intently on the speaker's message instead. After all, appearance is meaningless—it is the message that matters.

Put the Focus on Feedback

Next, consider what types of feedback are appropriate for the situation. Feedback is an integral component in active listening, and successful listeners are always aware of the feedback they are sending. For instance, maintaining eye contact is a simple yet effective way to stay engaged and demonstrate that you are listening. Nodding your head in agreement will signal that you are being attentive and agree. Asking questions and paraphrasing are useful responses.

There are many forms of feedback. The most common form is **paraphrasing**, a method of active listening that summarizes or serves as an interpretation of a message. Paraphrasing requires a listener to communicate a summary or interpretation back to the communicator. For example, a woman might say to her husband, "Let's watch 'The Exorcist' instead of that movie about the FBI chasing down a double agent." Her husband could paraphrase and say, "In other words, you want to see a scary movie instead of an action movie." The husband paraphrases his wife's message to ensure that the message was received correctly.

Other forms of feedback include note taking, eye contact, and other variations of nonverbal communication. Eye contact is important in active listening because it lets the speaker know that the listener is truly engaged. A listener may also nod her head or reciprocate with an appropriate facial expression. Active listeners may also verbally respond—for example, they may say "mmmhmmm" or "uh huh"—to convey that they are listening and comprehending the message.

Asking questions may help avoid misunderstandings, and paraphrasing will help you understand the information. One final note about feedback: avoid inappropriate feedback such as yawning or sleeping during an important presentation.

To Really Listen, You Must First Be Able to Hear

Of course, to be a good listener you must first be able to hear well. Always select a seat close to the speaker in order to make sure that you can hear every word clearly. Also, distance yourself from any external noise sources—for example, away from any windows or noisy machines.

Have you ever had your hearing checked? Consider doing so if you have difficulty hearing a conversation in a busy restaurant with other background noise, or if you often find yourself frequently asking others to repeat what they say. To maintain your hearing, avoid loud noises as much as possible or wear ear protection. People who work in noisy environments, such as drilling or construction sites or at loud rock concerts, are more likely to lose their hearing at an earlier age.

Listening and Memory

Finally, memory is an important part of the listening process. **Mnemonics**, a strategy to improve memory, uses rhymes, memory aids, and other devices to help remember important information. For example, if you need remember how to spell "arithmetic" correctly, you might recall that "A Rat In The House May Eat The Ice Cream." Phrases like these designed to help you remember key terms or ideas are called mnemonics. Learn as many memory retention strategies as you can and discover which ones work best for you.

THE LISTENING PROCESS IN ACTION

Maya, a college student, wakes up early for an important lecture in her biology class. Her instructor, Dr. Collins, will be delivering a lecture on a crucial process that will be the focus of the upcoming midterm examination. The night before, Maya read the course packet of articles and the textbook chapter relating to the lecture. She is prepared to use this prior knowledge to help her process today's information.

Maya arrives early, eliminates distractions by turning off her cell phone, and chooses an aisle seat close to the podium in the lecture hall. As she places her backpack in the seat next to her, Maya feels completely ready to listen to the lecture.

Two of her classmates, Sam and Nigel, are sitting directly behind her and start talking about the party they attended the night before. Maya finds this distracting, so she politely asks them to be quiet.

The lecture begins, and Maya diligently begins to take notes. Unfortunately, about 10 minutes into the lecture, Dr. Collins describes a process that directly contradicts a section of the course packet Maya read the night before. Nonetheless, she continues to take notes, even though she is still confused. She writes down her question for later and continues to focus on Dr. Collins's message, maintaining eye contact with her for the entire time.

Maya understands much of the information in Dr. Collins's lecture because she read the class materials and attended all of the classes this semester. She eventually wants to be a veterinarian, so the information is interesting and important to her.

When Dr. Collins wraps up the presentation and asks the students if they have any questions, Maya raises her hand and asks her question about the misunderstanding she had earlier. She carefully paraphrases for Dr. Collins what she heard during the lecture and then paraphrases what she read in the course packet. Dr. Collins quickly clears up the source of her confusion, and Maya realizes she had misinterpreted the information and now understands the point that confused her.

ACTIVE LISTENING VERSUS PASSIVE LISTENING

Infants can hear, but they cannot engage in listening: while they can hear sounds, they have not yet learned to listen. Listening and hearing are not the same. There are two ways in which to listen—actively and passively. You might be truly involved in listening or just passively following along. Active listening involves responding with feedback, and passive listening does not require feedback or interaction. If you can differentiate between active and passive listening, you will become more a competent listener and communicator.

Active listening involves focusing on what the other person is saying, and active listeners demonstrate an understanding of the content of the message and the feelings underlying the message. Active listening requires effort on the listener's part. Many people think that listening is a passive activity, and the responsibility of the communicative interaction should rely on the speaker. Yet active listening is a method of reiterating another person's message back to him or her. As an active listener, you will be rewarded for engaging in communication because you will absorb more information than passive or apathetic listeners.

In addition, the interpersonal relationship between you, the listener, and the speaker may improve. Speakers like to be heard, and listeners who are visibly uninterested in the speaker's message seem rude or impolite. Students who engage in active listening are more likely to succeed in classroom settings than students who are passive or apathetic. Think of a time when you were an active listener, and a time when you were a passive listener. Which communicative endeavor do you recall more accurately?

Imagine that you are again sitting in the e-mail etiquette presentation. Survey your fellow listeners in the crowded lecture hall and estimate how many of them are engaged in active listening. Are the listeners taking notes, asking questions, or demonstrating that they are listening through some other means of feedback?

Active listening requires feedback, or some response to the message. Feedback, which might include evaluating, analyzing, interpreting, reassuring, supporting, questioning, paraphrasing, and understanding, is crucial to communicative interaction between speakers and listeners because it demonstrates that a message was effectively sent and received. Even clapping is a form of feedback.

Listeners who engage in active listening are more likely to understand the

speaker's message. Language can be ambiguous or unclear, so active listeners strive to ensure that they thoroughly understand the message. Many do so by taking notes or asking questions.

You are much more likely to be an active listener if a message is personally important to you or when you think a message is vital to your success. Remember Maya, the college student who dreamed of becoming a veterinarian? The biology lecture was important to her future success, so it was of primary interest to her.

Paraphrasing, mentioned earlier, is an important tool for receiving messages more accurately. You may also paraphrase online communication. You probably use e-mail and text messaging frequently, but how can you guarantee that the meanings of your messages are accurately conveyed? How can you let the sender know that you interpreted their message accurately? Communication may be ambiguous, and online communication is susceptible to being received inaccurately. Use paraphrasing to help you with face-to-face and online communicative encounters.

Passive listening is the opposite of active listening. Most people are usually passive listeners in everyday conversations. It may be tempting to become a passive listener if a message is important to you, but not so crucial that you must listen to every minute detail. For example, listening to a CD in your car is a form of passive listening. You do not focus on every word in the song lyrics because your attention is on the road in front of you. No one can actively listen to everything they hear, and it is never necessary to focus on every word that is said.

Mindful Listening

Mindful listening means being aware in the present moment. A mindful listener is attentive, nonjudgmental, and involved in the acts of receiving and responding. Since you are bombarded with innumerable messages every day, you probably find it impossible to mindfully listen to everything that you hear. Instead, you develop

COMMUNICATION ACROSS CULTURES

Many Native American tribes rely on oral traditions to pass on their customs, beliefs, spirituality, and values to later generations. Only the most revered tribal elders were selected to pass oral traditions to future generations. Originally, many Native American tribes did not have written languages, so they instead relied on—and still practice today—strong listening skills. Many Native American tribes also relied on nonverbal communication skills to communicate messages. For example, members of some tribes tend to talk more softly, minimize eye contact (especially with elders), and show less emotion.

Today, for example, many members of the Navajo nation farm and live off of the land, as their ancestors had done for generations before them. The Navajo oral tradition is still alive and well among these people. At a very young age, children are taught to revere and respect their elders, and their listening skills are instilled early on. Listeners are required to sit and listen to traditional stories in total silence.

a sense of what messages are worthy of mindful listening. For example, you listen closely as your manager tells you that your annual work evaluation is next week, but you might tune out a good bit of a colleague's discussion of what he had for lunch. In other words, you choose what is important to listen to. Also, if someone you care about—your parent, your child, your friend, or a significant other—is talking about an important issue, you are more likely to pay close attention to him or her than you would a stranger.

Mindfulness is a choice—an ethical commitment—to pay close attention to others. No techniques will make you a good listener if you don't choose to be mindful. Your choice of whether to be mindful is the foundation of how you listen—or how you fail to listen.

Attitudinal Obstacles

Anything that interferes with a message is called **noise**. Noise can take many forms—an audible sound that detracts from a message, side conversations during a lecture, illness, or a lack of sleep. Learning to ignore noise can be a significant challenge to practicing active listening.

Pseudolistening and cognitive dissonance are attitudinal obstacles that can prevent effective listening. Have you ever pretended to listen to an uninteresting conversation or lecture? Everyone is guilty of pretending to listen at one time or another. A listener may appear to be actively listening by nodding and maintaining eye contact, but in reality is actually thinking about something else. Mindless listening is usually harmless, but pseudolistening involves deceiving another person. Pseudolisteners appear to be paying attention and reinforce this impression by supplying nonverbal communication like head nods and smiles.

Think of times when you have engaged in pseudolistening. Not every instructor is a dynamic speaker; some have contrived or monotone methods of delivery. Many business meetings are not particularly entertaining. You may consciously engage in psuedolistening to save face during these instances. Do you know a person who rambles on and on? It is easier to tune him or her out, but you because you do not want to seem rude, you might nod and pretend to listen.

Pretending to listen obviously creates a barrier to effective listening because the receiver is not listening to the message. You may miss important details or messages when pseudolistening. Many college students attend lectures without actively listening to the information given—a total waste of the instructor's and the students' time. Missing critical instruction may affect your grade. You might damage interpersonal relationships by not actively engaging in listening to your friends and family.

Pseudolistening is deceptive in nature, and most people furthermore find it impolite. It is risky to willingly deceive others because they may perceive you as untrustworthy or lacking adequate social skills—and in the end, you lose the most. Communication is important to all interpersonal relationships, and using deceptive techniques like pseudolistening may cause negative emotions.

Cognitive dissonance, another attitudinal obstacle to effective listening, is a discrepancy between what a person believes, knows, and values, and persuasive information that calls these beliefs into question. You may experience cognitive dissonance in any communicative situation.

For example, you may think of pit bulls as dangerous dogs based on numerous media messages you have received about people being attacked by them. But what if you then hear a persuasive speech about how pit bulls are not dangerous and actually make wonderful pets? You may have trouble listening without judgment because of your prior belief that pit bulls are dangerous. If you listen actively and with an open mind, you may end up feeling conflicted because you now hold two very different views of pit bulls.

Cognitive dissonance affects how people receive certain messages. It is often more difficult to actively listen when you have a previous viewpoint that differs from the new information you are listening to. Human beings are complex creatures with intricate brain functions, and each person has a unique set of **schema**, or files stored in the brain. People file their experiences and what they hear into these schema and then rely on them to help process new information.

If your schema includes a perception of pit bulls as dangerous, what will you do with the new information about pit bulls? Simply deleting the previous files, or information, is not possible. Instead, you have to negotiate new information based on your cognitive schema, which requires a more complex type of listening.

The Consequences of *Hearing* Instead of *Listening*

Hearing, a natural response to stimuli, involves receiving sound, but not necessarily processing it. *Listening* involves processing received information. You must rely on your personal experiences and linguistic abilities to successfully process the information that reaches your ears. Listening is a complex activity that requires your brain to categorize and organize stimuli or sounds.

Hearing and listening are not synonymous, and simply hearing rather than listening has its consequences. For example, it may lead to misunderstanding a speaker's message. Misunderstandings are natural and commonplace, but you are more susceptible to misunderstanding a message if you do not truly listen to it.

Think of a time when you heard an important message instead of listening to it. For example, imagine that during an appointment with your doctor, a nurse gives you instructions about taking the medication the doctor has prescribed. You assume that the instructions will also be included on the packaging information when you pick up the prescription, so you do not listen closely to the instructions and instead just hear them. You are then surprised to see that the instructions on the prescription are incomplete. The instructions tell you to take the medication twice daily, but you cannot remember if the nurse told you to take the medication immediately after waking up or after you have been up for a while. Now what do you do?

Many students bring their computers or cell phones to class and e-mail or send text messages instead of actively listening to their instructor. These students are simply hearing the instructor's message. They will certainly be missing crucial information because they are hearing but not listening.

Hearing another person is not listening. Strong relationships are the result of strong communication. Can you recall a recent experience when somebody was simply hearing you rather than listening? How did that make you feel? How did you know the person was not listening? Such encounters may make you feel that your ideas and feelings are not important to that person. This can cause negative emotions and can hurt the relationship. Quality interpersonal relationships require each person involved to use effective listening skills. Empathy, or walking in another person's shoes, is instrumental to relationships and requires true listening and understanding of the other person's message.

PARALANGUAGE

Think of how a common phrase can mean different things based on the way it is said. For example, the phrase "I'm fine" may have different meanings based on whether the speaker says it politely or harshly. **Paralanguage** refers to *how* something is said, not *what* is said. Paralanguage often reveals a person's true feelings, which may contradict the message. There are five types of paralanguage:

- Rate
- Volume
- Tone
- Pitch
- Pauses

The **rate** is simply how fast or slowly you speak. Speakers should strive to achieve a comfortable rate that listeners can understand. Speaking too slowly may seem condescending, and listeners may think that the speaker is talking down to them. Speaking too quickly can confuse listeners and will likely lead them to miss valuable information. You have a natural rate of speech, but it is important to adapt this to diverse audiences. Good speakers analyze their audience and adjust their speaking rate to meet that particular audience's needs.

Have you ever had to ask a speaker to speak up? **Volume** refers to how loud a speaker voices a message. Volume is similar to rate, because speakers must learn to adjust, or modulate, their voices to accommodate specific situations. A loud speaker may intimidate or annoy an audience, whereas being soft-spoken can make it more difficult for an audience to hear you—and *listen* to you—effectively. The audience may not hear important segments of the speech or presentation. If you are asked to speak up, you are probably speaking too quietly.

Your **tone** of voice is an indication of your mood and your attitude about the audience and the topic. Somebody who is monotone may seem dull, while a speaker who uses abrupt speech may seem gruff and angry. As a responsible communicator, consider using appropriate tones of voice. Tone of voice is dependent upon the message's content, and unique and diverse audiences may read your tone differently. Since you cannot hear your own voice objectively, it is often best to rely on the feedback of others to help you set the right tone.

Experts define **pitch** as a characteristic of sound that fluctuates with the changes of vibration in a human's vocal chords. Speakers who have a high pitch to their voices may sound strained and may unintentionally indicate nervousness or excitement. A low pitch, on the other hand, may suggest to an audience that the speaker is sad.

When you are in stressful situations, you may find that your pitch will change. Pay attention to how you speak when you are nervous, sad, or excited. If your voice stays at the same pitch without varying, that is your **monotone**. In some cases, a monotone is a helpful pitch level—for example, if you wish to convey a sense of calm or to help overly excited peers steady themselves. But in other situations, a monotone may convey a lack of interest in your subject matter.

It is also harder to listen when a speaker's words do not change in pitch, or have **inflection**. By noticing when your voice moves up and down the scale naturally, and simply putting more breath and energy behind it in those moments when it is higher or lower, you can develop your speaking voice in a way that sounds natural and enhances your listeners' ability to hear you and share an interest in what you are saying.

Pauses, which are moments of silence between thoughts or main points, are an important part of paralanguage. Think of a pause as the start of a new paragraph or idea. Speakers use pauses to catch their breath and set up the next idea. They are natural and should be used appropriately; for example, pauses indicate a transition, or the end of a particular main point. However, sporadic pauses may distract listeners. Nervous speakers tend to pause more frequently. Also, too many pauses may suggest to your listeners that you are unsure about your message or not an authority on the topic.

Rate, volume, and pitch, as well as rhythm, pronunciation, and articulation, are all elements of voice quality. The rhythm of your voice suggests quite a bit about the meaning of what you have to say. If your voice has an easy rhythm, you are comfortable about the statements you are making. If it takes on a staccato rhythm, you may be suggesting a relative lack of comfort with your message. Your pronunciation also says a lot about you—if you are unable to pronounce words correctly, you suggest to your audience that you lack authority on the topic. If your articulation is poor, you may slur your words together or clip the endings off words. As with pronunciation, poor articulation may suggest that you are not an authority on the topic at hand.

Paralanguage is just as important as the words you speak. You may contradict your message with the paralanguage that accompanies it, so always remember to be aware of *how* you say things. Listeners have an advantage over you because they actually hear your paralanguage, so record yourself and listen to your own voice. How do you think you sound? What is your paralanguage like? This simple step can help reveal a lot about your speaking style and paralanguage.

PERSONAL SPACE

Proxemics is the study of personal space, and use of space is instrumental to the act of listening. Communicators who are engaged in intimate conversations stand close to one another. They are engaged in face-to-face communication, and their audience consists of a small group of people. It is acceptable to use an intimate level of personal space in these situations. Public speakers, on the other hand, generally stand a significant distance away from their audiences and have to engage many people at the same time.

As an experiment, think about how to challenge these norms by standing 10 feet away from a friend and try to conduct an intimate conversation. How did your friend react to your use of personal space? Did your friend try to move closer to you?

If you are addressing a larger group, imagine closing the distance between you and your audience. How might your audience react to this potential violation of personal space? Would the audience members in the front row be uncomfortable with your use of personal space?

Some people enjoy being close, while others wish to maintain a respectful distance. Speakers and listeners have different levels of comfort when it comes to personal space. Observe your listeners' nonverbal communication, as their cues will help you determine how far you should stand or sit from them.

Keep in mind that personal space is also affected by cultural norms. Personal space also depends on whether the context is public or personal—whether you are at home with someone close to you or in a public setting with an acquaintance, and whether you are with friends or people you have never met before.

THE LISTENING PROCESS

You are continuously bombarded with sounds every day. You may listen to a classroom lecture in the morning and attend an extremely loud rock concert that same night. As you experience all this sound, you selectively choose to focus on particular stimuli while ignoring other stimuli. What you choose to *listen* to, rather than *hear*, involves the listening process. There are four steps in the listening process:

- Attending
- Understanding
- Remembering
- Responding

Attending

The first step in the listening process is *attending* to specific messages. Attending means devoting your concentration to a given speaker or another verbal or visual resource. Because you hear so many messages each day, you must choose which messages are worth attending to. For example, students pay more attention to lectures that they know contain material they will be tested on.

People are more attentive to messages delivered by people they consider important. Usually, you will attend more closely to messages from friends, family, and others close to you. If information is not attended to, it is more difficult to interpret, understand, or actively respond to it.

In the course of a day, you receive many more messages than you can possibly attend to, a situation known as message overload. You choose to attend to certain messages based on personal choices and other factors, including physiological influences, expectations, cognitive structures, social roles, and cultural and social communities.

For example, college students focus on their instructors' messages, and the most conscientious students take diligent notes. Taking good notes is a skill that must be mastered in order to ensure academic success, because it directly enhances the listening process.

Professionals must also learn to attend to specific messages. Depending on your vocation, you will probably need to demonstrate your listening proficiency each day. Most jobs require employees to attend to numerous messages every day, but some vocations are more demanding than others. For example, a doctor must carefully listen to each patient—apathetic listening could be disastrous in most doctor–patient situations. An incorrect diagnosis could jeopardize a patient's life.

No matter what your profession, a visible lack of interest or care can jeopardize any social interaction. Every vocation requires listening, and learning to attend to important messages is the first stop in this crucial process.

Loud and boisterous communicators are difficult to avoid, but quiet, shy, and demure communicators have a difficult time being heard. Quiet speakers are often told they need to speak louder. They may feel ignored when listeners fail to grasp their main points. You can adapt your listening styles to attend to messages you consider important, but you are more likely to listen to loud, strange, and extraordinary messages.

DID YOU KNOW?

Do people listen more than they speak? Listening often takes a back seat to speech because most people do not realize how much listening needs to be done on the job. Some careers require more listening than others, but it is important to realize that much of the day is spent listening. Here are some noteworthy statistics about listening:

- **Corporate employees listen about 60 percent of the time on the job.**
- **Listening consumes more than 60 percent of an executive's workday.**
- **More than 60 percent of an executive's salary is paid for time spent listening.**

Active listening in corporate America is an important key to success. Employees are responsible for listening to their superiors and their colleagues. Mistakes caused by a failure to listen could result in loss of revenue—and even jobs. Companies should incorporate more training in listening, as the intrinsic value of listening skills is often overlooked.

Understanding

The next step in the listening process involves *understanding.* **Understanding** refers to decoding a message to determine its meaning. Understanding is an integral component of the listening process because there is little you can do with a message you do not understand. Pick up a book written in a language that you are not familiar with, or try watching a foreign language movie without subtitles. You will hear the messages, but you will certainly not understand them. You understand a message when are first able to make sense of it. You can hear and attend to a message without truly understanding it, and it is also possible to misunderstand the meaning of a message.

You have your own unique past experiences and knowledge, and you use this cognitive information to process any new incoming information. Learning language is a crucial component of culture, and language is required to understand complex communication.

Prior experience also helps you understand messages—for example, you know that fire will burn you and cause pain. Your understanding of pain and fire can help you understand messages that pertain to both. In order to understand another person's message, you must be able to compare new information to your past knowledge.

In order to create understanding, you must use both your short-term and long-term memory. New information is stored in short-term memory. You recall relevant information from long-term memory, where permanent information is stored. The two are coupled in the understanding process.

Misunderstanding a message is always possible if you do not have prior knowledge about or sufficient language skills to understand a message. What happens when a student or a professional misunderstands a project or deadline? A student could receive a failing grade; a professional could lose his or her job. Think of some instances when you were involved in a misunderstanding. What happened? Was the outcome favorable or negative for you?

Remembering

Human memory is a complex process that has been studied for decades. It is impossible to *remember* everything that you hear and see because you receive so many messages every day. Unfortunately, people forget much of what they hear. Within a few minutes of hearing a message, you probably remember only about half of it. On average, within eight hours of receiving a message, people are able to remember only about 35 percent of their interpretation and understanding of the message, and after a few days, they recall perhaps 25 percent of the message.

It is extremely difficult to retain information during long messages, such as lectures or presentations. Consider the childhood game of "telephone." The game involves one player being told a message. Next, that player must pass on what he or she remembers about the message to the next player—a process that is repeated until the message is received by the last player. In the final act of the game, the last player verbally states what he or she remembers of the message, and that memory is compared to the original message. Usually, the final message delivered is changed substantially from the original message.

Your ability to recall what you hear varies is based on certain factors. Some people recall vast amounts of information without much training. However, many people have to work very hard to remember what they hear. This is why it is extremely important to alleviate distractions when you are trying to focus on a message.

How much you remember depends on how much you value the message. Professionals should focus on remembering messages that will directly impact their job security. When your task involves pure memorization, it is easier to have a high level of recall. When interpretation is involved, recall can be diminished.

Responding

Responding to a message may alleviate misunderstandings. Responses, or feedback, signify to a message's sender that the information was successfully received. Consider responding to a speaker by expressing interest, asking questions, offering your ideas on the topic, and showing general attentiveness.

Effective communicators express attentiveness by providing appropriate feedback. A good listener provides multiple forms of feedback. Instructors know their students are listening when students nod, ask questions, take notes, and maintain eye contact. Professionals demonstrate similar listening behaviors in crucial meetings and one-on-one conversations with supervisors. When you provide appropriate responses to a speaker, the speaker will know that the message was successfully received. Providing feedback may also alleviate misunderstandings.

Active listeners engage in appropriate feedback constantly as a message is delivered and received. Speakers will easily become frustrated with an inattentive audience—imagine how you would feel if you were facing a group of listeners who were failing to make eye contact with you, yawning, or even sleeping. Such negative nonverbal communication distracts and discourages a speaker. Actively listening involves more than attending and understanding—it also involves demonstrating that you understand the message by providing clear, positive, and constructive feedback.

Feedback must be observable, or the speaker will not know that you as a listener are actively paying attention. Feedback must also be appropriate; for example, laughing at a speaker who is telling a serious story is clearly inappropriate. Adjust your responses to the speaker's emotions and the type of message being conveyed. A good listener will learn to read and respond to speakers in a wide variety of diverse situations.

You can offer both positive and negative feedback. As an active participant in the listening process, you should always strive to adapt your feedback appropriately to different situations. Some examples of positive feedback include maintaining eye contact, nodding, paraphrasing, asking appropriate questions, and providing vocal responses—even those as simple as "mmhmm" and "okay." Negative feedback includes yawning, falling asleep, laughing at inopportune times, and not maintaining appropriate eye contact. Sometimes negative feedback is appropriate—but the careful listener is very selective about when to use it.

HOW TO IMPROVE YOUR LISTENING SKILLS

There are no simple remedies for poor listening skills, as listening is an art rather than an inherent behavior. You are born hearing stimuli, but you learn how to listen through experience and education. Listening is a very important part of human communication, and it is crucial to take advantage of all of the listening strategies available to you. Communication experts and researchers have proposed numerous strategies to improve listening skills, and you will probably try quite a few of them before you decide what works best for you in each specific listening situation. The following nine strategies can help you improve your listening skills:

- Keep an open mind.
- Do not prejudge speakers or situations.
- Listen carefully for main ideas.
- Avoid becoming distracted by nonverbal messages.
- Hone your listening skills by spending time listening to skilled, veteran speakers.
- Work hard to understand complex messages.
- Use empathy to better relate to and understand the message's sender.
- Provide constructive feedback to the message's sender.
- Practice, practice, practice!

Listeners must enter listening situations with an open mind. All human beings have biases and prejudices, and it can be very difficult to prevent them from interfering with successful communication. You may mistrust certain people because of your past experiences with them, or with people who share some of their characteristics. You may consider certain topics to be forbidden, and listening to a discussion of them may challenge your morals or values—for example, listening to a presentation about religion or politics may make some people uncomfortable, so instead of feeling uncomfortable, some listeners may avoid the presentation altogether.

Effective listeners do not prejudge a speaker, because successful communication cannot occur without reciprocal interactions. Prejudging a speaker may distract listeners from the message or cause them to avoid the speaker altogether. For example, some students may avoid certain classes taught by instructors who may have reputations as being particularly harsh or boring. As a result, these students may miss out on positive experiences. Everyone has biases and prejudices, but yours should not discourage you from experiencing opportunities.

Successful listeners listen for main ideas, which are the skeletal system of a speech. They hold the entire speech together, serving as a road map for listeners. An effective speaker will likely have no fewer than three and no more than five main points, as too few main points suggest a lack of authority and too many main points may lead to confusion. A presentation with an overabundance of main points will likely seem unorganized or even chaotic. Indicators of main points include any statements the speaker emphasizes and restates during the introduction and conclusion or that are led by transitional words like *first, second, before, after, next,* etc.

It is possible to become distracted by a speaker's nonverbal communication. Nonverbal communication includes dress, gestures, paralanguage, and physical appearance. A monotone speaker, for example, may quickly lose your attention, while you may find a loud and boisterous speaker annoying. A speaker's inappropriate dress may also distract you from his or her message.

Seek well-informed, knowledgeable speakers to hone your listening skills. For example, instructors are experts in their fields of study, so college students have an advantage because they have access to countless specialists and experts. Take advantage of lectures given at college campuses and in your community. By attending these lectures and listening carefully to the presentations, you will learn what it takes to be an effective public speaker *and* an effective listener—and at the same time, you will certainly learn new things.

Never let a seemingly complicated lecture or presentation discourage you from enhancing your listening skills. Attend a lecture about something completely foreign to you, because you just may learn something about the topic and your capacity to listen. You should always to listen to difficult messages that may be beyond your immediate comprehension. Doing so will encourage you to use effective listening strategies in order to process the information received. College students also have an advantage in this area because most students are required to pass general education requirements. For example, imagine that Max, an English major, is required to take an advanced math course and history course in the same semester, despite the fact that math and history are Max's weakest subjects. Being compelled to take the two classes simultaneously will likely help Max become a more effective listener.

Empathy, or the ability to look at something from another person's perspective, is a wonderful tool in an effective listener's arsenal. Empathy is not sympathy, however. Sympathy involves feeling remorse or sadness for another person, whereas empathy involves relating to another person's experiences or perspective.

Provide feedback during and after a speech or presentation. Asking questions will help you clear up any misunderstandings, and paraphrasing will ensure that you comprehend the message. Maintaining eye contact will help you focus on the speaker and the message. The speaker will also know that you are interested. How do you feel when people are not looking at you when you speak? Do you think that these individuals are ignoring you or bored? Nodding your head in agreement will indicate that you are engaged. However, use appropriate feedback judiciously.

Practice makes perfect when it comes to listening, for listening is a skill that can be learned and mastered. You can to train yourself to become a better and more efficient listener. To do so, you must hone your skills in real-life situations. Learn what strategies work best for you, and practice these as much as possible. You cannot expect to become a strong listener in one day.

SUMMARY

- Learn specific listening goals.
- Effective listeners use active and mindful listening and avoid passive listening.
- Paralanguage and the use of personal space are important factors to consider.
- Following the listening process is key to understanding a speaker's message.
- There are numerous strategies to improve listening skills.

REFERENCES

Adler, R. B., & Proctor, R. F. (2007). *Looking out, looking in* (12th ed.). Belmont, CA: Thomson Wadsworth.

Canary, D. J., Cody, M. J., & Manusov, V. L. (2008). *Interpersonal communication: A goals-based approach* (4th ed.). Boston, MA: Bedford/St. Martin's Press.

Hybels, S., & Weaver, R. L. (2009). *Communicating effectively* (9th ed.). New York, NY: McGraw-Hill.

McCornack, S. (2007). *Reflect and relate: An introduction to interpersonal communication.* Boston, MA: Bedford/St. Martin's Press.

Wolff, F. I., & Marsnik, N. C. (1993). *Perceptive listening* (2nd ed.). Fort Worth, TX: Harcourt Brace.

Wood, J. T. (2010). *Communication mosaics: An introduction to the field of communication* (6th ed.). Belmont, CA: Thomson Wadsworth.

CHAPTER 8

Virtual Communication

Katya has just enrolled in a college that offers classes both online and in a hybrid, or a mixture of classroom and online, format. She is thrilled about having the option to have both types of classes, because she is a single mother and works full-time. Katya can take classes at night from home by just logging into her computer, but she also has the option of attending classroom courses if her schedule allows for it. At her previous school, Katya was forced to attend night classes in person and had to pay for a babysitter, which was quite expensive.

There is one issue—Katya has only a very basic laptop computer and does not spend very much time on it. She is not confident that she will know how to use the technology she needs to take courses, communicate with her classmates, and retrieve class materials from online sources. Worse yet, Katya's advisor has mentioned that some of the classes involve blogging—Katya has never done that before, and is quite intimidated by the idea of it. Virtual communication has taken center stage in Katya's life, and she is unsure about how to take the first steps.

KEY CONCEPTS

1. Virtual communication is becoming increasingly common in schools and in the workplace. See page 114.

2. Types of virtual communication used in the workplace include conference calls, e-mails, and webinars. See page 114.

3. Practicing professionalism in virtual communication means communicating in a thoughtful and more formal way at work and school. See page 117.

4. When communicating across cultures, you must be aware of cultural differences and vigilant about avoiding misunderstandings. See page 120.

5. Remote teamwork has its advantages and disadvantages. See page 121.

TYPES OF VIRTUAL COMMUNICATION

In the fall of 2009, 5.6 million students were taking at least one of their classes online. In that same year, the number of employees working remotely reached 45 million in the United States alone. Even if working remotely is not an option for you (for example, if you plan to be a scientist working in a laboratory) or if you simply prefer working in a traditional office setting, it is very likely that you will use virtual communication in school or on the job.

Knowing how to work well with others when communicating through a variety of electronic and virtual communication methods, such as e-mail, teleconferences, and social networking, will be vital to your future success. The types of virtual communication you will need to master are nearly as numerous as the types of people you will work with.

Conference Calls

One of the oldest and most frequent types of virtual communication is the conference call. Typically, a call's host provides you with a telephone number and access code, and you dial in at a certain date and time. If you are not located in the same time zone as a call's host, you must check carefully to make sure of the time of the meeting in your own time zone—so you do not miss the meeting altogether. You must also make sure you can be in a quiet location for the duration of the call, and if you are using a cell phone, ensure that you are in a location where your connection is strong. The best choice for a conference call is generally a landline, as cell phone connections are much less stable and much more likely to have static or other noise issues.

If you are hosting a conference call and will be discussing any materials, send them to participants to be read in advance. Sending a meeting agenda ahead of time is also wise. The host should also sign in to the call five or ten minutes before the appointed time. As the host, you will have to enter a special code to open the line. Think of this as unlocking the door to a meeting room, turning on the lights, and making sure that anything else needed for a successful meeting is ready.

When participants sign into the call, you will be notified by a special alert tone. It is helpful to greet everyone as they enter the call as you would in a face-to-face meeting. Identify yourself as soon as each caller joins and then give the other participants in the call a chance to identify themselves. If the alert tones signifying callers joining go off in rapid succession, wait a few moments until they stop before initiating the greetings.

Finally, after it seems that most of the requested attendees have joined the call, check to see who is present by saying: "Welcome everyone! Thank you for joining the call today. Let me go down my list of attendees to confirm who is on the call." You should always verify that all participants are present before you begin. Some participants may have difficulty joining the call, so it is often helpful to have a secondary method of contact (either a cell phone or e-mail access) so they may reach you or you can reach them.

If you are a participant in an upcoming conference call, record the meeting dial-in information both in writing (e.g., in a pocket calendar) and virtually (e.g., store the number on your cell phone). When you dial in, make sure that no one else is speaking before you speak (as conference calls often mute any other speakers who talk when someone else is already speaking) and that no alert tones are sounding. Once you hear a period of silence, greet everyone and give your name, and then wait for direction from the host.

Although it is fine to chat with your team prior to the start of the meeting, once the meeting time arrives, stop any informal chatter and focus on the agenda and the guidance provided by the host. It is helpful for everyone involved in the meeting to place their telephones on "mute" when they are not speaking, as doing so reduces background noise and static on the call. When you do wish to speak, state your name before speaking each time. It is important to never put a conference call on hold, because background music will potentially interrupt the session.

As the conference call comes to a close, briefly recap the action points of the call, including asking for any needed information to be sent to you or offering to send any materials that may be of use to the other participants. Whether you are the host or a participant, thank everyone for their time and contribution and close with a clear valediction to signal the end of the call, such as, "Thank you, everyone. Have a great afternoon!"

E-mail

Most people are familiar with e-mail as a form of virtual communication; however, electronic mail within academic and work contexts should be considered more formal than informal. Generally speaking, a professional e-mail should be composed much like a short memo or business letter. Begin with a greeting and always use **standard English** (English that uses correct spelling, punctuation, and grammar). Do not use **emoticons**, which are representations of facial expressions or shapes created via characters, or abbreviations frequently used in text messaging, such as *TTYL* (*talk to you later*). These are too informal for use in academic and business environments.

Before you even begin composing an e-mail, keep in mind that some people receive hundreds of e-mails each day. First, take a moment to consider whether the e-mail is really necessary (see Figure 8.1). Because e-mail is so convenient—and free—many e-mails are sent needlessly.

Always be sure you have typed in the correct name in the "To:" box. The only people who should be included in the message are those who need to know. Using "bcc," or blind-copy addressing, is typically considered unprofessional, as it suggests that you are not being honest with the person to whom you are sending the message. When replying to a message, do not select "reply to all" unless everyone who received the original message needs to read your response.

Finally, make good use of the subject line to show professional consideration for the recipient. It is acceptable to use standard e-mail notifications in the subject line, such as FYI (for your information), NNR (no need to reply), or Action Item. Most e-mail systems also allow you to apply a label to an e-mail—for example, you can label a message as being of "high importance," but use this setting sparingly and only when absolutely necessary.

Appropriate
Dear Mr. Blake,
I appreciate the time you spent reviewing my job application. Please notify me when you have made a decision about scheduling an interview. I look forward to discussing with you what I can offer to InfoSystems.
Sincerely,
Joshua Haskell

Inappropriate
Thanks for the chat!
Josh

Too Informal for School or Work
Hey Dave,
Great interview. Hope we can make this happen. TTYL!
Josh ☺

FIGURE 8.1 **Sample E-mails**

In any e-mail message, focus on concisely expressing your points. E-mails that are unnecessarily long are usually not read thoroughly. If you need to share more information than a small paragraph, or if the issue is complicated, a telephone call or face-to-face conversation is recommended.

Next, be aware of the timing and delivery of your e-mails. Make sure after you hit "send" that your e-mail did indeed send. Occasionally, if your e-mail storage reaches its limit, your e-mail may become lodged in your outbox and will not be delivered. The results can be disastrous if a time-sensitive message does not reach its recipient on time. Allow your message recipients 24 hours to respond to an e-mail during the week and 48 hours over weekends or holidays before following up. Before sending an e-mail, double check that all attachments are correct.

If you will be unavailable via e-mail for a day or more, set up an out-of-office automatic message to be sent to anyone who sends you a message. Your message should thank the sender for contacting you and provide a clearly stated expectation of when you will get back to them. For example, your message could say: "Thank you for contacting me. I will be out of the office through the end of this week with limited access to e-mail. I will respond to you as soon as possible." It is also helpful to provide an alternate person to contact (including his or her contact information) if the sender needs immediate assistance.

Finally, whether you are using e-mail at your college or workplace, always review your organization's electronic communication policy and adhere to it carefully. E-mail is never private at institutions.

PROFESSIONALISM

Think before you hit send! Always take a moment to read every message before you send it—in particular, think about how a total stranger would react to the message. Review and edit the message for tone and professionalism.

Tone refers to the way your e-mail sounds when it is read; it is the attitude you project toward the subject and your reader. In a stressful academic or job situation, it is easy to react emotionally and fire off an angry message—but always think carefully before sending an e-mail. Your message will live on forever and can be forwarded to literally anyone with an e-mail account. Particularly if a situation is stressful and heated, wait at least 24 hours before sending your response. Read it several times and ensure that the tone is unfailingly polite, respectful, and professional—just as if you were speaking to the recipient in person.

Retain the format of a business memo or letter in your mind as you draft a professional e-mail message. Your message should formally greet its recipient, be clear and concise, and close with a standard valediction (e.g., "Best regards"). Make any requests in a very polite form, and express your appreciation at the close of the message.

Every message you send or receive can be intercepted and read by others. Use these e-mail accounts only for school or business-related communication, and never write anything in a message that you would be embarrassed to share with others.

Webinars

As another type of virtual communication, the **webinar**—a combination of the words *web* and *seminar*—combines the voice capabilities of a telephone conference with a shared view of a computer screen and an instant-message written "chat" feature. A webinar host chooses to deliver a presentation or hold a meeting via an online address so that all participants can also see what is on the host's computer screen. Often, the host can share the screen and speaking capability with participants.

A webinar host generally sends the meeting's URL (the Internet location) as a link in the invitation message, along with any additional instructions (for example, to have your headset with microphone ready) or an agenda in advance of the meeting. Participants click the link and perhaps provide a user name and password to log into the webinar. When participants sign into the webinar, they are asked to provide their name; participants should always provide both a first and last name in order to avoid confusion.

Many of the guidelines for a telephone conference and e-mail apply to webinars as well, but there are a few differences that facilitate and improve communication in this format. Hosts can **moderate** a meeting, which means (among other things) that they are able to view a participant's post before it is published to the group and decide whether to accept or reject it. This can be helpful in keeping a conversation on topic. Similarly, hosts may set up a meeting to be held by invitation only, so participants are required to ask for permission to join. This reduces the potential for uninvited attendees.

Internet-Based Meetings

Although a webinar is perhaps the most popular form of online meeting, there are other ways a team may communicate online. For example, a college may offer an **asynchronous course**, which means that the students may enter the class whenever it is convenient for them to complete a task, rather than at an appointed time. Similarly, a company may have an **intranet** (an internal website available only to employees) site where employees can get together asynchronously to post comments, share documents, ask questions, and so on.

Blogs

Another type of virtual communication is a *blog*, a term derived from the words *web* and *log*. A **blog** is an Internet site where hosts post information and updates related to a particular theme. For example, a college may host a student activities blog that shares information and updates about upcoming events. A company may host a blog to share information and updates about its products or services. You might decide to create your own blog to broadcast your thoughts on everything from laundry to world politics. Participants who subscribe to blog posts are able to respond to messages, whether the response is intended solely for the host or also for any other visitor to the blog.

Blogs are typically informal, but always carefully consider the context. As an employee of a company, for example, it would not be a good idea to post a negative message on the company's blog. You should also think carefully before posting anything controversial or hurtful on your own blog (or as a response or post to someone else's blog). Blog postings live on forever and are always accessible, even after deletion.

Texting

Texting is a type of virtual communication conducted by using the keypad of a cell phone to send written messages. Words and common expressions are often abbreviated into acronyms, and words are frequently misspelled for convenience (for example, *u* instead of *you*).

Text messages are a perfectly acceptable type of virtual communication to use in informal situations, such as with friends and family. It can be helpful when needed to communicate with someone in an environment where a telephone conversation would be inappropriate or undesirable. Cell phone users can set up their phones to silently receive text messages so as not to disturb or alert those around them. Texting can provide a quick, silent, and efficient way to send quick messages, such as a reminder to a friend to meet you at noon or a link to directions to a meeting place.

However, texting is a very informal method of virtual communication that can be misunderstood easily. It is not advisable to use text messages in academic or work situations. Unless it is absolutely necessary to do so, text messages should not be used to communicate within formal contexts, such as with your instructor, your classmates, or coworkers. Many instructors are concerned about issues related to texting in a school setting. Students have been known to text during class, use text messages to cheat during tests, use text-message shorthand like "LOL" in formal papers, and so on.

Social Networking

For thousands of years, humankind has engaged in social networking—for example, one person introducing two acquaintances to each other, or a person setting up a place and time for several people to gather in order to achieve some mutual benefit. For example, people have used social networking to facilitate travel (e.g., staying with the friend of a friend in another town) and trade (e.g., trading produce for pottery) since ancient times.

Recently, social networking has expanded into the virtual world. There are sites, for example, where people can connect with family and friends informally, sites where job seekers can meet potential employers, and where members of a profession can communicate with others in that same profession. The benefit is that members can then network by extending their connections to include the colleagues of other job seekers, potential employers, and members of their professional community who they may not have had the chance to meet face-to-face. The potential to meet people around the globe via social networking sites is nearly limitless.

This advantage brings with it certain precautions in regard to virtual communication:

- First, these are public sites. Even if privacy settings are in place, these sites may be viewable by people with whom a participant may not want to network.
- Second, participants should be careful about mixing contexts. For example, you may not want to have friends, family, coworkers, potential employers, and so on all networking with you on the same site.
- Third, be careful about what information you share. For instance, you may want to set up a special e-mail address only for use with a specific social networking site. This can safeguard your physical address or full name and still allow for e-mail contact. Never post any compromising photos of yourself (or others) on the Internet. Remember that a future employer could search for your name and find these photos.

DID YOU KNOW?

Sixdegrees.com is considered to be one of the first social networking sites. Founder Andrew Weinreich, who started the site in the mid-1990s, based it on the concept of "six degrees of separation"—that each person in the world can be connected to one another by at most six individuals. Weinreich's hope was that the site would connect everyone virtually, as participants' friends and family would introduce them to others they knew. Sixdegrees.com is available now by invitation only, but perhaps you have heard of another site named Facebook?

Instant Messaging (IM)

Instant messaging (IM) is used in many virtual environments. If you are working remotely, for example, and you have a quick question for a coworker, you can send an instant message that will instantly pop up on

your coworker's computer screen. This allows employees to communicate almost as quickly as texting—with somewhat less potential for misunderstanding.

Many instant messaging programs often come with the ability to sign in with a status (for example, "available," "busy," or "do not disturb"). You should make sure your status is accurately set and that you respect the status settings of others. As with e-mail and some other types of virtual communication, IM may be set to send an audio alert that someone is sending an instant message. This feature is often referred to as "pinging" someone.

Last, always remember that most instant message systems save a record of the conversation unless you specify otherwise (and sometimes even if you do specify otherwise). Observe the same restraint you do with e-mail when communicating via instant message. Make sure nothing you write can come back to haunt you.

TECHNOLOGY

Imagine that a company in Poland that is developing a new part that will help airplanes fly faster announces that the part will be ready for manufacture within two months. A team that builds airplanes in China hears about the part and decides to include it in its new aircraft set to debut in six months. The Chinese company confirms its plans to specify the Polish company's part in an e-mail message to the company's president—but unfortunately, the company's name is misspelled in the To: line of the e-mail and the message never reaches the Polish company. It does not take a degree in aerospace engineering to know that a delay in the production of that single part would put the airplane's schedule in jeopardy as well.

It is easy to miscommunicate—or fail to communicate—when using virtual communication. When should you use virtual communication, and when should you use other more direct types of communication? When communicating virtually, global teams must provide concrete expectations and directives, such as deadlines to their members and confirmations of plans sent in various forms, including by regular mail. Cultural differences must also be kept in mind. At times, however, a meeting in person is preferable. When a project is extraordinarily complicated, for example, a face-to-face meeting often works better. Calling a group together to meet in person can quickly bring the team's goals back into perspective and strengthen the team.

VIRTUAL TEAMS

A **virtual team** is a group of coworkers who are not located in the same office building. The team of individuals works from various geographical locations, and is sometimes called a **geographically dispersed team (GDT).** People in such teams use communication technology as a link that strengthens their work.

Functioning Well on a Multinational Team

One of the obvious reasons why institutions make use of virtual communication is its unmatched ability to develop and support multinational teams instantly, effectively, and inexpensively. Virtual communication can quite literally extend the reach of an institution to include any other region of the world. As an employee of a company in the United States, for example, you may often find yourself working virtually with colleagues who are on the other side of the world.

Advantages of Communicating with Remote Teams

There are many advantages to working with and communicating virtually with remote teams. Imagine that you are in an art history class studying the Pantheon in Rome. Through the miracle of virtual communication, a tour guide actually in the Pantheon can give you a walking tour of the building—without the expense of international travel.

Next, imagine that you work for a company with a critical product that contains a part assembled in another country. After the country that makes the part suffers a major natural disaster, you and your colleagues can set up a virtual meeting to speak directly to the part manufacturer's management team. At the meeting, you can find out whether the part's manufacture will be delayed and what types of disaster planning strategies the manufacturer has in place. If a face-to-face meeting with the manufacturer's management team is necessary, but it is simply not cost-effective or possible to send everyone overseas, your company could send carefully chosen representatives for the face-to-face meeting and then hold a virtual conference for other team members to attend.

Consider the advantage that virtual communication holds for news organizations. They can coordinate with other news teams—or even private citizens who happen to have cameras or video recorders at the ready during a breaking news event on the other side of the globe—to share eyewitness reports with their viewers. As an increasing number of business organizations become global enterprises, rapid communication with suppliers, distributors, buyers, and other stakeholders is critical for success.

Challenges of Communication with Remote Teams

Working with remote teams does have its challenges. Technology is not readily available or reliable in all parts of the world, for example. Cell phone and Internet service are not necessarily available at every location. Other considerations for working internationally include having the correct electrical outlet converter to charge and use a computer or cell phone, or even ensuring that electrical service is reliable and available.

Another disadvantage of remote communication is the delay that can result from speaking over a satellite transmission. You have probably noticed this effect when watching live broadcasts from reporters speaking via satellite. When a reporter is asked a question by the anchor in the newsroom during a satellite transmission, it may take a few moments for the reporter to hear and respond. Imagine the same situation during a conference call with multiple participants around the world.

Other forms of disturbance may interfere with virtual communication. Satellite transmissions may be interrupted by severe weather events or solar flares. In turn, these same events may interfere with, slow down, or halt completely telephone and Internet connections. Although most users take connectivity for granted, it is wise to have a backup plan for a virtual meeting (e.g., a conference call to back up a video chat) in case your first choice for the mode of technology fails.

Additional Difficulties of Communicating Remotely with Other Cultures

Consider how important it is to be aware of the belief systems, values, mores, and traditions of members of other cultures when you work with them on a team. For the purpose of good communication, you must always be aware of and sensitive to these differences. Many workplaces hold diversity training sessions to help employees learn about the cultures their coworkers hail from.

Even if your business uses American English enterprise-wide, for example, colleagues who come from other cultures or nations may not comprehend English at the same level of proficiency. As a result, you may have to speak more slowly or listen more carefully to understand these colleagues. You may also encounter British, rather than American, spellings of common words in written communication (e.g., colour instead of color). As a matter of fact, in British English, some words even have a different meaning than they do in American English; you may be aware of some of these (e.g., the word *football* in much of the world refers to the game that is known as soccer in the United States).

What is considered acceptable in terms of humor also varies from culture to culture. A remark that is considered funny and completely appropriate in one culture could be insulting in another. Similarly, be careful when communicating with video, as something behind or near you, or even your style of dress, could be considered offensive to participants from other cultures.

It is always a good idea to learn as much as possible about the cultures your colleagues, suppliers, and clients come from. Always be conservative, respectful, and welcoming when communicating with people from other cultures, and they

TECHNOLOGY

A successful online presentation begins with extensive preparation and setup, not with the first word spoken. It is important to know the software used to deliver the presentation inside and out before scheduling your first meeting. Take advantage of any free training opportunities that may exist. These may be offered virtually—a double bonus, since you will learn about technology at the same time you are practicing participating in virtual communication.

There are also many websites that can help you learn about technology and prepare to communicate virtually. A quick search of YouTube, for example, produces quite a few instructional videos that show how to set up and conduct a webinar using Microsoft PowerPoint®.

Finally, be sure to practice. If your company uses a program like Adobe Connect to hold meetings, set up a dry run of the meeting with a coworker you know well. During the practice session, use all of the same features of the software you plan to use during your presentation. Once the meeting begins for real, you will be glad you rehearsed.

will treat you with the same regard. Taking time to understand your teammates' perspectives will help everyone communicate better and work well together.

SUMMARY

- The advantages and ease of use continue to increase the presence of virtual communication in colleges and in the workplace.
- Students and employees must become comfortable with using the common types of virtual communication.
- Students and employees should become aware of best practices in the use of virtual communication.
- Special considerations should be taken into account when communicating virtually with people in other nations or from other cultures.

REFERENCES

Allen, E., & Seaman, J. (2010, November). *Class differences: Online education in the United States, 2010.* Retrieved from http://sloanconsortium.org/sites/default/files/class_differences.pdf

Boyd, D. M., & Ellison, N. B. (2007). Social network sites: Definition, history, and scholarship. *Journal of Computer-Mediated Communication, 13*(1), article 11. Retrieved from http://jcmc.indiana.edu/vol13/issue1/boyd.ellison.html

Brown, J. E. (2010). An empirical look at the relationship between personality type and the challenges of telecommuting (Doctoral dissertation). Retrieved from Proquest. (Publication No. 3415608)

Part II: Public Speaking and Speech Presentations

CHAPTER

9

The Contemporary Communication Process in Public Speaking Situations

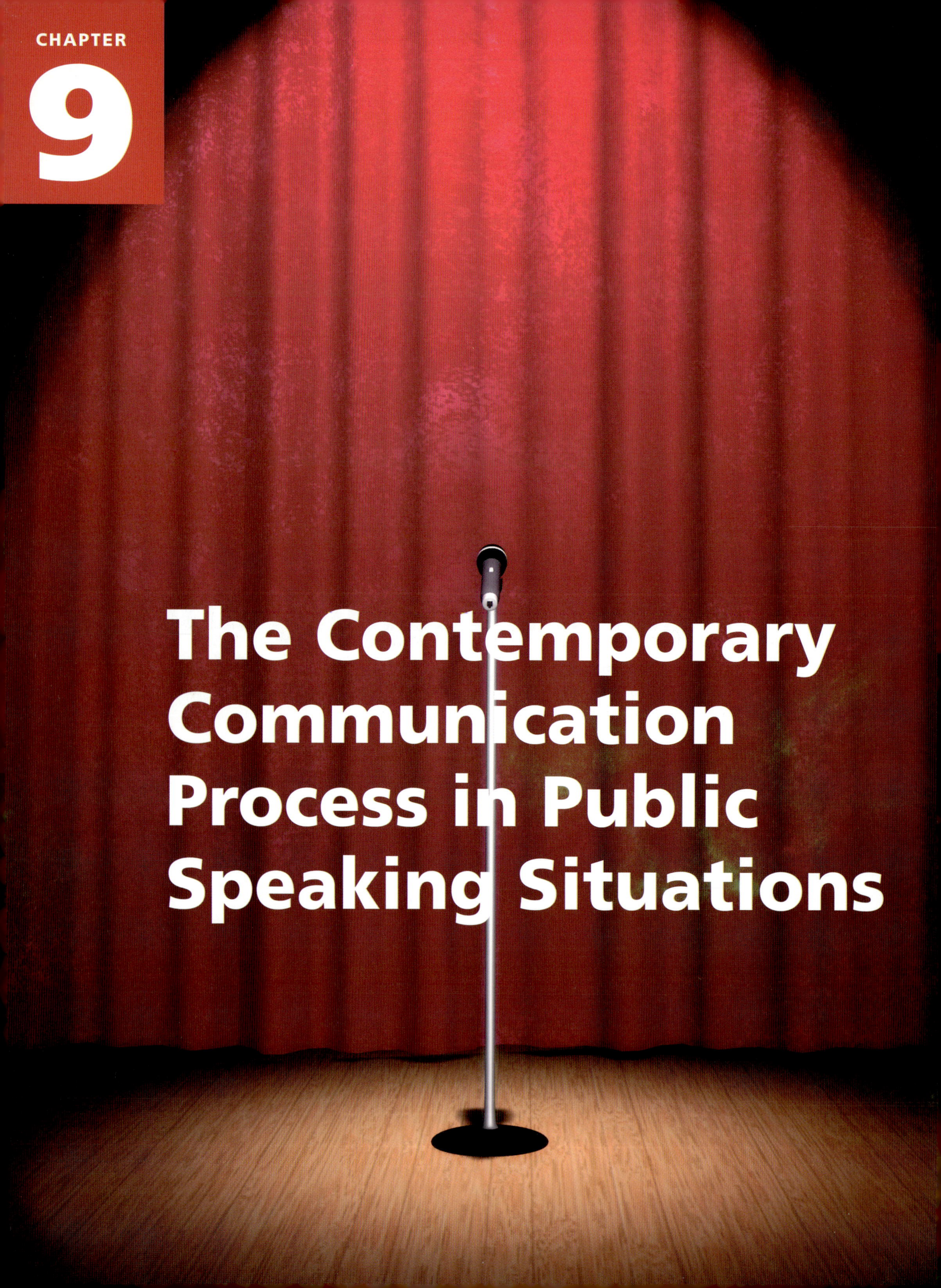

KEY CONCEPTS

1. The speech communication process includes the speaker, message, channel, listener, feedback, interference, and situation. See page 128.

2. Ethical speakers keep the audience in mind and are respectful to their listeners. See page 129.

3. Never mislead an audience. See page 130.

4. The feedback loop is the mechanism by which one-way communication becomes two-way communication or a dialogue or conversation—true communication. See page 132.

5. The sender is the initiator of the message (the speaker) and the receiver is the audience. See page 134.

Raisa Clark is giving a presentation at her local library about how to use the library's resources to find and apply for jobs. How can Raisa make sure that her audience, a group of 30 library patrons, knows what is expected of them? Should Raisa provide the audience with a written outline of her presentation before she begins? Should she give a brief overview before the presentation begins? Or should she use a combination of these communication options?

Even if Raisa provides both a written outline and a verbal overview of her presentation, how can she be sure that these two devices will make everything clear to her audience? How can she be certain that her audience will get her message?

THE CONTEMPORARY COMMUNICATION MODEL

Most people agree—public speaking can be quite intimidating. Since **public speaking** is typically defined as any speaking engagement before an audience of 20 or more listeners, the stakes are high. A public speaker risks embarrassment or a a negative reaction. Public speaking is usually the most formal environment for communication, with clear delineation between the speaker and his or her audience.

The communication process has many moving parts working in a coordinated

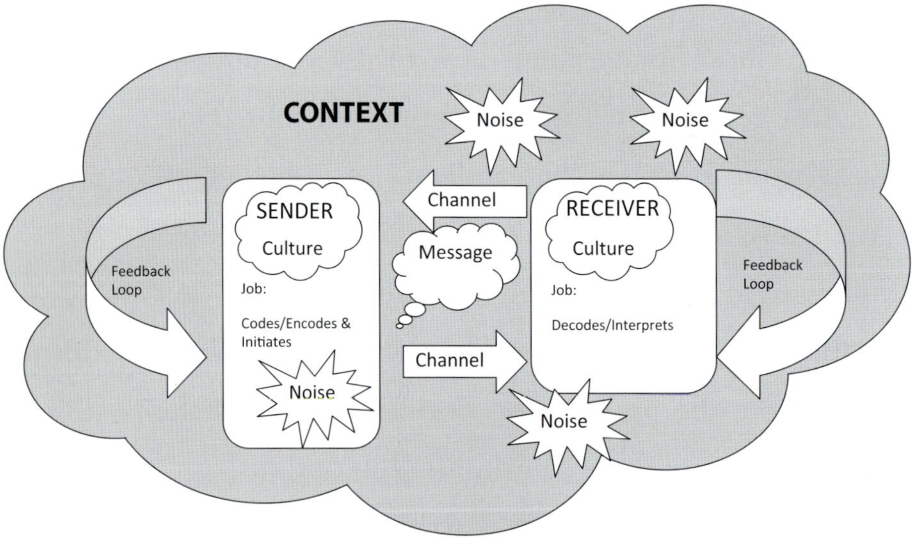

FIGURE 9.1 Contemporary Communication Model

and interdependent effort. What is occurring between the speaker and audience in a public communication setting? First of all, the presenter is making a commitment to the audience. The presenter is working to prove a point that will either win the support of the audience or generate action—or both. Second, the audience is making judgments about the presenter. *Do I really trust this person? Does this information make any sense to me? Is it being adequately explained? Are the facts presented accurately?*

The components of the speech communication process include some familiar and some new concepts, including:

- Speaker
- Message
- Channel
- Listener
- Feedback
- Interference
- Situation

So how does this relate to the model shown in Figure 9.1? The speaker is the sender and initiator, and is responsible for coding or encoding the message. The listener is the receiver and interpreter, and is responsible for decoding the message. Interference is the same thing as noise. The situation is the context in which you are expected to deliver your speech—in the example of Raisa's speech, the situation is the library and its forum on finding jobs. In your own experience, public speaking situations could include a speech that is a final class project, a presentation to a client, or an announcement to a group of peers and supervisors at work.

No matter what the speaking situation may be—informal or formal and public—certain common goals remain, including influencing, persuading, and entertaining others. In work and school settings, informing and persuading are generally the foremost goals of a speech. Of course, in a public speaking setting, those goals can take a back seat to fear management. And what are the best ways to cancel out that fear? Preparation, plain and simple, and a single-minded focus on four critical points:

- Who you are, and how your message represents you
- What you want to achieve by delivering your message
- Who the members of your audience are
- What your audience wants, and how your message will affect them

ETHICS AND COMMUNICATION

You may never have thought about the ethics of communication. But if you stop for a moment, you may be able to come up with more than a few examples of unethical communication. Has a President of the United States ever lied to the American public? If so, that certainly would be an unethical communication. You can probably think of additional examples—telling a lie on the witness stand at a court trial, or even misleading an audience who is placing their trust in you. A car salesman may try to convince you that a car is a better deal than it is. How would you interact with such a salesperson? If you do not believe she is credible, it is unlikely you will buy a car from her. And so it goes with any communication—if you do not engender the trust of your audience, it is unlikely that they will listen or believe your message.

What guidelines can you follow to ensure that your communications are ethical? In *Communicate!*, Verderber, Verderber, and Sellnow list five standards for keeping communication ethical and forthright:

- Be truthful and honest.
- Have integrity, which means that you will do what you say you will do.
- Be fair. Give equal time to all sides of an issue. Do not take sides.
- Be respectful. Communication means that communicators will not always arrive at mutual understanding; should this happen, respect others' interpretations.
- Be responsible. The messages you encode and decode may have meanings you did not intend or anticipate. Be accountable for how your messages may be received.

Ethical speakers begin by always keeping their audience and the backdrop of the message in mind. They attempt to shape and match their message in order to accommodate the audience, the situation in which the message will transpire, and the context of the communication. In order to achieve this match, ethical senders must study their receivers carefully and pay close attention to how the message is being received. Failure to do so could create confusion, or, worse yet, inadvertent or intentional fraud.

Communicating with Civility

The message is not all that matters. How it is delivered can be just as important. A message that is rudely delivered may not be heard at all. Instead, the receiver may hear only the rudeness and completely discount the meaning of the message. A civil speaker is well mannered, appropriate, courteous, gracious, and considerate. If you are thoughtful not only in the coding of the message but also in its delivery, you are doing all you can to ensure successful communication.

Effective speakers follow rules of **etiquette,** which are the ground rules of polite, civil communication. Rules of etiquette include how to start, sustain, and stop communication—the sender(s) and the receiver(s) taking turns and working together in order to effectively transfer information. Effective use of etiquette can help you navigate difficult situations, including communicating with a diverse audience or in diverse contexts.

The cooperative nature of civil communication means that as conversations go on, all the parties involved build their own respective understanding together, and not separately. Rather than involving an active party—the sender—and a passive party—the receiver—a conversation actively engages both parties at all times. Senders and receivers engage in a constant negotiation of understanding.

Never Mislead an Audience

Speeches can and do affect their audiences, and this effect can be either positive or negative. Speakers are responsible for the effects of their messages on their audience, and they must carefully prepare in order to ensure that the messages do not contain wrong information or bad (or easily misconstrued) advice.

Speakers and audiences enter a basic contract during the communication process. It is a contract of mutual understanding. If the communicator is honest and has goodwill towards the audience, the communicator is likely to receive trust and goodwill from the audience. Receivers assemble an idea of a sender's credibility early on in this contract. If credibility is established and maintained, the sender can count on the audience's acceptance of the message. After all, if an audience thinks a speaker is an authority on a topic, the audience will invest trust in that speaker. The audience will believe the speaker to be very knowledgeable about the issue at hand, and will believe that the message is accurate and earnest.

Preparation

When cautioning speakers about the importance of preparation, talk show host Larry King remarked that an audience is always "worthy of your best effort." Of course, this does not necessarily mean that you can only talk about topics that you are an expert about—King himself could not possibly have known all there was to know about all the topics his show covered. A speaker must instill some sense of expert credibility with his or her audience, and the quickest route to doing so is to thoroughly prepare for the communication. An ethical speaker respects two important phases of preparation: research and personalization.

Research, no matter how thorough or light, will show when you communicate a message. Doing your homework before speaking is key to creating a sense of authority. If you spend time learning details about a topic and honing your presentation, your audience will be far more likely to listen to you and trust your message. Research involves reading and learning about what others have had to say about a particular topic, so the second part of ethical preparation involves processing the research—the thoughts of others—and then coming up with your own interpretations and opinions about the topic.

The Contemporary Communication Process

During communication, a message is sent through a channel, the route by which it travels from sender to receiver. Communication is any means by which living things send information to one another. It is a process composed of the following components:

- Models of sender and receiver (affected by culture)
- Noise
- Feedback loop
- Channels
- Message
- Coding (encoding) and decoding messages
- Initiator
- Context

In addition to considering Figure 9.1, which shows the relationship of these components to one another, it may help to study each component individually.

The Models of Sender and Receiver

Figure 9.1 shows that the communication process begins with the sender, the individual who sends or initiates a **message.** The message, which is the physical product of the communication process (for example, an e-mail or a lecture), is sent to the receiver, who is also sometimes known as the interpreter.

Senders and receivers are the communicators shown in Figure 9.1. The sender begins the communication process with creating a message by thinking about how to approach the receiver with a message they can understand. This is called "encoding" the message. In the previous example, Raisa, the presenter of the lecture at the library, is the message's sender and the receivers are the job seekers.

Early models of communication envisioned the sender and receiver as distinct and separate entities, but today the communication process is considered to be interactive, dynamic, and interdependent. When they communicate, senders and receivers are practicing both expressive and receptive skills, both of which are related and complementary. Senders use expressive skills like speaking and writing, and receivers use receptive skills like listening and reading. Keep in mind that culture plays a major role in sending and receiving messages. The sender may come from a different cultural background than the receiver. This can affect how the receiver decodes and interprets the message. See Figure 9.2.

SENDER		RECEIVER	
Encoder	Initiator	Decoder	Interpreter

FIGURE 9.2 Sender and Receiver

You may think that the communication model in Figure 9.1 suggests that messages are simply and easily transmitted from sender to receiver; however, most messages are not received exactly as they are delivered. The receiver receives a message through the channel(s) in spite of the interference or noise. Noise is anything that interferes with the message's delivery (cell phones ringing during a lecture, for

DID YOU KNOW?

You Can Listen Faster Than You Can Speak

The average person speaks at a rate of 100 to 200 words per minute, but an average listener can process 400 words per minute. You would think that this fact would mean that listeners would be equipped to fully understand any message sent their way, but in fact, the opposite is true. Because the listener is able to process so much more input than a speaker can deliver, the listener is likely to use that capacity in other ways: predicting what the speaker is about to say, zeroing in on one of the speaker's points and going off on a mental tangent on it, engaging in other types of daydreaming, focusing on some of the noise present in the communication space, and so on. In short, this excess capacity results in a higher likelihood of a listener "tuning out" a sender. Communication is inevitable, and so is noise. Communicators must develop skills to successfully push their messages through this inevitable noise.

example). Given that noise has nothing to do with the message and is only an unnecessary by-product of the communication process, noise may affect the receiver's ability to decode or interpret the message. When the receiver decodes or interprets the message, the receiver determines what the message means—and noise may well play a role in the receiver's interpretation of that message.

Noise

Noise refers to the distractions, the unwanted background input, the interference, or any other barriers that may cause complications or distort a message for both sender and receiver. **Internal noise** includes psychological distractions—such as thoughts, feelings, or reactions—that interfere with the communication process. Suppose that during a professor's lecture, you begin to worry about a fight you had with a friend earlier in the day. If you are so distracted by your thoughts and feelings about the fight that you fail to hear the professor's message, you are experiencing internal noise.

External noise, which is sometimes called "physical noise," includes environmental factors—such as sounds and visual stimuli—that distract from the intended message. Imagine trying to have a conversation with a friend while exposed to the external noise of a car alarm. It would be very difficult to send and receive messages. Both internal and external noise hamper an individual's ability to concentrate on the message and understand it. The sender may have to work to code (choose the language needed for) the message so that the meaning will not be altered by the noise.

Similarly, the receiver may have to work to ensure that decoding is not affected by the noise. In a classroom, this noise may include external noise, such as the students' chatter, the odor of popcorn coming from a neighboring office, the rustle of backpacks and papers, or the roar of a lawnmower outside. Noise is not just unwanted sound—it also may include the foggy haze induced by a cold and the medicines you might take to treat its symptoms. After all, illness definitely has the ability to distort the coding and decoding process.

Feedback Loop

The **feedback loop** is the space in which the sender adjusts the message based on responses from the receiver. It is the mechanism by which one-way communication becomes two-way communication—a **dialogue** or conversation. The receiver may respond to the sender through the feedback loop with a new message, but at the very least, the receiver should always confirm his or her interpretation of the message with the sender.

The sender may respond to the receiver through the feedback loop as well. Once the sender has passed along the information to the receiver, the process becomes two-way, as shown in Figure 9.1. In the figure, the channel arrows point in both directions, reflecting the fluid, continual nature of the feedback loop.

The feedback loop in the example about making a presentation at the library is actually much more dynamic than Figure 9.1 suggests. Imagine that Raisa, the presenter at the library, announces that she has a surprise guest. The audience will provide feedback right away by whispering about who they think the guest is. In doing so, they will assume the roles of sender and receiver as needed. Decoding,

coding, and feedback loop continue as communication occurs. The receivers (job seekers) are not only influenced by the sender (Raisa) but also by other audience members (other senders and receivers). Raisa must consider the totality of the environment where the communication is taking place.

The feedback loop also reveals the receiver's perception of the message. Perhaps a sender intended a message to be a joke, but instead, the receiver took offense to it. In the feedback loop, the receiver may not necessarily respond to the message the sender intended—instead, the receiver will respond to an interpretation of it.

Messages and Channels

A **message** is any piece of information passed along from a sender to a receiver; the sender's goal is to convey this piece of information to the receiver. A sender sends a message through the appropriate **communication channels,** which are the means, methods, vehicles, modes, and techniques used to send messages. Some communication channels include oral or verbal communication (including face-to-face conversations or meetings, or perhaps virtual or otherwise technologically facilitated communication, such as videoconferencing), nonverbal communication, written communication (including e-mail and online communication means such as chat/instant messages or postings on discussion boards), and mass communication (television, radio, magazines, or newspapers, for example).

In the library presentation example, Raisa's channels might include verbal (voice), written (handouts or whiteboard notes), and nonverbal (perhaps a cold glare at an audience member whose cell phone rings) elements. Channels are usually categorized by determining each channel's strengths and weaknesses. For instance, among the strengths of e-mail as a communication channel are its speed and convenience. However, e-mail communication does not allow communicators to hear each other's tone of voice or see facial expressions and body language. Accordingly, e-mail users have developed an elaborate system of **emoticons** designed to stand in for common face-to-face communication markers.

Do you think the message is more important than the channel? Or vice versa? The debate over whether message and channel are equally important, or if one is more important than the other, has raged for some time. **Media richness theory** categorizes communication channels and ranks them according to their "richness." The richest channel, such as a face-to-face conversation, allows for a variety of signals and feeds multiple senses. The least rich channels would include brochures, Web pages, or letters and e-mail messages. Typically, the richer the channel, the more likely it is that the message will be received and interpreted as it was intended.

Coding and Decoding Messages

Although coding and decoding are complementary processes, the differences between them lies in the ownership or the origin of the message. The sender is typically the one who codes and initiates the message, and the receiver is typically the one who must decipher, or decode, another's message.

Imagine that you are about to deliver an important message to a group of employees about their team's upcoming performance evaluation. You must decide first how to properly code your message. Your coding choices include options like including the date for the evaluation and deciding whether to call it an "evaluation," a "performance assessment," or a "performance feedback session." In the end, your coded message is as follows: "Your team's performance evaluations will take place at 10 a.m. on April 28th."

Of course, coding is also dependent on channel. If you decide to write the message in the form of an e-mail, you may opt for even fewer words—perhaps nothing more than sending a meeting request with the subject line "Performance Evaluation" for 10 a.m. on the 28th of April.

The coding and decoding process may also be complicated by channel. Have you ever had to replay a voicemail several times before fully understanding it? Did your decoding of the message change as you listened to the message several times over? Are letters and e-mails more difficult to decode that verbal messages because of the lack of nonverbal cues? When coding messages, are you more careful when you write or when you speak? Why?

Sender and Receiver

The sender is the **initiator** and begins the communication process by coding the message. Noise (cell phones ringing, traffic noise, and so on) may impact the receiver's ability to decode the message or determine what the message means. After all, it is not simply a matter of decoding the message; the receiver also must decode the *intention behind* the sender's message. The sender, through thoughtful coding, tries to influence how the receiver will perceive the intention.

Perception is the primary reason why the communication process is so complex. Perception is ever changing and continual, as sending and receiving the message affects the perceptions of both the sender and the receiver. Those perceptions change along with the ongoing communication. In the library presentation example, the receivers are the job-seeking audience members. However, as the communication continues and naturally grows, the audience members interchangeably assume the roles of sender and receiver, as they talk with each other about the presentation.

In the process of perception, the receiver applies meaning borrowed from past experiences to make sense of the present message. Since the sender and receiver do not have identical past experiences, identical meaning will not flow from sender to receiver. Have you ever interpreted a piece of art—a painting, perhaps, or a poem—with a friend and each of you come away with different interpretations of the art's meaning? Most likely, you and your friend did not "see" the same thing. Interpretation is highly subjective and dependent on many different internal and external components.

SUMMARY

- The contemporary communication model includes the sender and receiver, noise, the feedback loop, channels, message, coding and decoding of the message, and context.
- Ethical communication means assessing communication goals and communicating with civility. An ethical communicator would never mislead an audience.
- Preparing for communication is vital to ethical communication. An audience's time must never be wasted or misused with an ill-prepared or inaccurate speech or other communication.
- The communication process is interactive, dynamic, and interdependent.
- The feedback loop is the space in which the sender adjusts the message based on responses from the receiver, and one-way communication becomes two-way communication.

REFERENCES

Beebe, S., Beebe, S., & Ivy, D. K. (2009). *Communication: Principles for a lifetime: Vol. 4. Presentational speaking* (portable ed.). Needham Heights, MA: Allyn & Bacon/Pearson Education.

Brenner, D. M. (2007). *Move the world: Persuade your audience, change minds, and achieve goals.* New York, NY: John Wiley & Sons.

Brignall, M. (2007). Describing the transactional communications model. Retrieved from http://www.wisc-online.com/objects/ViewObject.aspx?ID=oic100

Capp, G., Capp, C., & Capp, G. R. (1990). *Basic oral communication* (5th ed.). Englewood Cliffs, NJ: Prentice-Hall.

Cherney, L. R. (2005). Communication. In G. Albecht (Ed.), *Encyclopedia of disability* (Vol. 1, pp. 279–282). Thousand Oaks, CA: Sage.

Christians, C. G. (2007). Communication ethics. In *Encyclopedia of science, technology and ethics.* Farmington Hills, MI: Gale Cengage (Macmillan Reference).

Communication; Nonverbal communication. (2008). In *International encyclopedia of the social sciences* (2nd ed.). Farmington Hills, MI: Gale Cengage (Macmillan Reference).

Communication channels; Speaking skills in business. (2007). In *Encyclopedia of business and finance* (2nd ed.). Farmington Hills, MI: Gale Cengage (Macmillan Reference).

Dellinger, S., & Deane, B. (1980). *Communicating effectively: A complete guide to better managing.* Radnor, PA: Chilton Book Company.

Duckworth, C., & Frost, R. (2008). Noise pollution. In *Gale encyclopedia of science* (Vol. 4). Farmington Hills, MI: Gale Cengage (Macmillan Reference).

Hargrave J. (2007). Listening skills in business. *Encyclopedia of Business and Finance* (2nd ed.). Farmington Hills, MI: Gale Cengage (Macmillan Reference).

Harris, T., & Sherblom, J. (2011). *Small group and team communication* (5th ed.). Needham Heights, MA: Allyn & Bacon/Pearson Education.

Headrick, D. (2005). Communication overview. In *Berkshire encyclopedia of world history.* Retrieved from http://www.scribd.com/doc/36159228/Ency-of-World-Hist

Hu, Y., & Sundar, S. (2007). Computer-mediated communication (CMC). In J. J. Arnett (Ed.), *Encyclopedia of children, adolescents, and the media* (pp. 200–202). Thousand Oaks, CA: Sage.

King, L., & Gilbert, B. (1994). *How to talk to anyone, anytime, anywhere: The secrets of good communication.* New York, NY: Crown/Three Rivers Press/Random House.

Liepmann, L. (1984). *Winning connections: A program for on-target business communication.* Indianapolis, IN: Bobbs-Merrill Press.

LoCicero, J. (2007). *Business communication.* Cincinnati, OH: Adams Media (F+W).

Lucas, S. E. (1998). *The art of public speaking.* New York, NY: McGraw-Hill.

Merrier, P. (2006). *Business communication.* Cincinnati, OH: Thomson South-Western College Publishing.

O'Neil, S., Evans, J., & Bigley, H. (2007). Communications in business. In *Encyclopedia of business and finance* (2nd ed.). Farmington Hills, MI: Gale Cengage (Macmillan Reference).

Oberg, B. C. (2003). *Interpersonal communication: An introduction to human interaction.* Colorado Springs, CO: Meriwether.

Reardon, K., & Christopher, N. (2010). *Comebacks at work.* New York, NY: HarperBusiness.

Ross, R. (1983). *Speech communication: Fundamentals and practice.* Englewood Cliffs, NJ: Prentice-Hall.

Rothwell, J. D. (2009). *In mixed company: Communicating in small groups and teams* (7th ed.). Farmington Hills, MI: Gale Cengage (Thomson Wadsworth).

Simmons, A. (2007). *Whoever tells the best story wins.* New York, NY: Amacom Press.

Verderber, R. F., Verderber, K. S., & Sellnow, D. (2009). *Communicate!* (13th ed.). Retrieved from http://www.cengagebrain.com/shop/content/verderber36403_1439036403_01.01_toc.pdf.

Windley, C., & Skinner, M. (2007). Selecting a topic. University of Idaho. Retrieved from http://www.class.uidaho.edu/comm101/chapters/selecting_topic/selecting_topic_printable.htm

CHAPTER

10

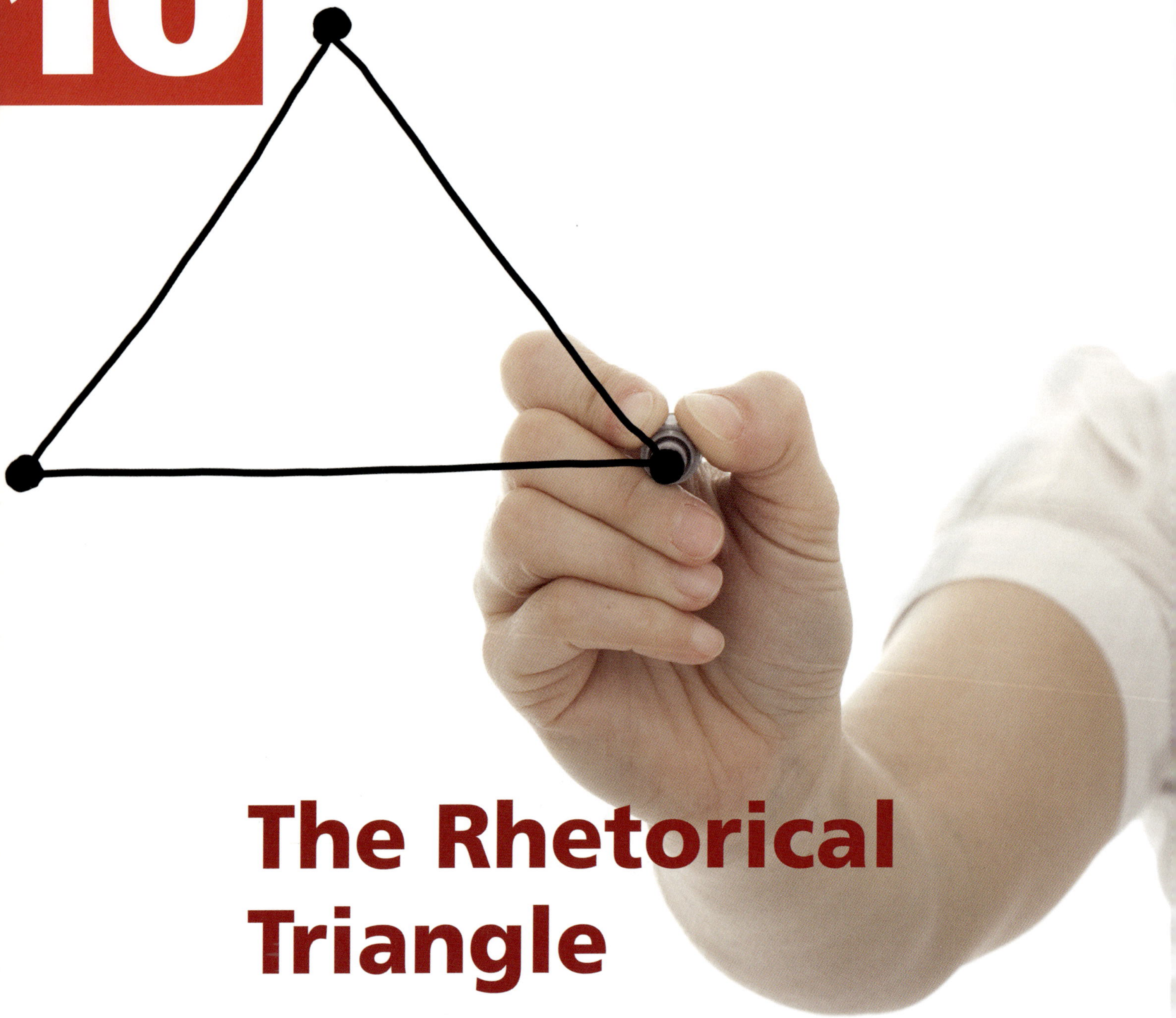

The Rhetorical Triangle

Joshua, a line supervisor for a manufacturer of men's shoes, has been asked to give a presentation about the company's new computer process for receiving and filling orders to the 16 employees he supervises. This is not good news—Joshua is terrified of speaking in front of anyone.

The moment his boss, Tasha, mentioned giving the speech, he was immediately reminded of an awful episode in high school. Joshua was supposed to present a counterpoint in a debate on extending the school day before all of his fellow junior class members. His opponent, Rosa, went first and delivered an excellent argument, beautifully illustrating her argument's three major points—more time for structured homework assistance, more resources for at-risk young people, and studies revealing that students who had longer school days were 50 percent more likely to graduate from college—and using several charts to support her statements.

Then it was Joshua's turn. He had figured it would be easy to argue against lengthening the school day—particularly in front of his classmates, who certainly had an interest in keeping the day short. Because of this advantage, which he thought was quite obvious, he had not prepared much. On his way to the auditorium, he had put together a few ideas in his mind—*the school day is already long enough! There won't be enough time for football practice!*—but he was far from ready to counter Rosa's well-planned, beautifully executed argument.

Joshua stepped up to the podium. Five hundred sixty pairs of eyes stared at him. The lights above the stage were blinding. He began to sweat and stammered a bit; the class jocks, who were all seated in the front row, began to laugh and several people started to chant "Joshua" in a mocking tone. Terrified, embarrassed, and totally unprepared, Joshua bolted from the stage.

And now Tasha wants him to do this all over again? *No way!* Joshua thinks.

KEY CONCEPTS

1. The rhetorical triangle shows the interdependence of the speaker, audience, and situation. See page 138.

2. The audience receives the message and communicates verbally and nonverbally with the speaker. See page 140.

3. The situation of the speech is the purpose as well as the setting and location. See page 142.

4. Ethos, logos, and pathos refer to three approaches to speaking. See page 143.

5. There are key differences between writer, reader, and purpose. See page 144.

THE SPEAKER: SOURCE OF THE MESSAGE

This chapter examines three elements of effective speaking and how they interact with each other:

- The speaker and the message
- The audience
- The situation (which includes both the physical setting and the purpose of the speech)

Think about the first time you gave a prepared speech, even a very informal one, in front of classmates or coworkers. How did it go? Did the results of that speech influence your feelings about any later speeches—no matter what the differences were between that first experience and the later experiences? Now think about the scenario you just read. What are the differences between the speech Tasha has asked Joshua to give and his painful high school speaking experience?

FIGURE 10.1 **The Rhetorical Triangle**

As the originator of a piece of communication, the **speaker** holds primary importance within the **rhetorical triangle**, which refers to the interdependence of the speaker, the situation, and the audience. As a speaker, you are charged to select a topic and decide how to focus or "code" it into a specific message for a specific group of listeners within a certain context. There is typically a purpose or goal in mind for the speech—perhaps you want to convince your coworkers and supervisor to help you lobby for a flex time policy with the company's upper management. Certainly, you hope your presentation will be well received, especially by your supervisor.

The Speaker and the Message

Being a speaker is like being a good host. It is the speaker's role to reach out and make a connection with the **audience**, which are the spectators, listeners, or viewers of the presentation. The speaker must somehow connect the content of the speech with the listeners. Speakers must also have a physical presence that commands the audience's attention. Try to make frequent eye contact with members of your audience, but do not fixate on one or two members, as the audience members will find this unnerving. Instead, look from one audience member to the next casually, while thinking of your speech as more of a one-on-one conversation with that particular person, at least for a moment. You may also choose to walk around a bit inside the space where you are standing, as movement suggests that you are comfortable and confident. You can also help yourself keep the audience's attention by varying the volume and pitch of your voice.

If you think back about really effective speakers you have heard in the past, consider what characteristics they share. You may even want to read or listen to other great speeches (see Figure 10.2). One of the first common characteristics you will likely notice about these particularly effective speakers is that they were all believable. Speakers must establish, and maintain, a sense of **credibility**, which is the ability of the speaker to elicit the audience's belief in his or her words and actions. Even if the speaker is a comedian whose sole purpose is to entertain the audience, this characteristic of believability must be present—otherwise the audience may reject the message altogether.

History.com's Famous Speeches in History	http://www.history.com/speeches
Say It Plain, Say It Loud: A Century of Great African American Speeches	http://americanradioworks.publicradio.org/features/blackspeech/
American Leaders Speak: Recordings from World War I and the 1920 Election	http://memory.loc.gov/ammem/nfhtml/
The National Jukebox: Historical Recordings from the Library of Congress	http://www.loc.gov/jukebox/

FIGURE 10.2 Historical Speeches

Credibility is even more relevant within academic and work environments. In these settings, a speaker is expected not only to be credible, but also to present with **authority,** which is the power to influence thought or behavior. Speaking with authority means that the speaker projects some special expertise, skill, or knowledge. If you are delivering a speech to your class, your classmates and instructor will expect you to be knowledgeable as you present your message. If you are delivering the speech in which you lobby for flex time schedules, your coworkers and supervisor will expect you to speak authoritatively on a topic of value to them in the workplace. Even a comedian's audience expects a level of expertise (e.g., that the comedian is an authority on making people laugh).

Speakers should also demonstrate **eloquence**, which means that they should have the ability to express themselves in a persuasive and powerful way. The way speakers express themselves should be very attractive to listeners. Imagine that you are planning a presentation and want to capture your audience's interest with your language. What particular words, phrases, and expressions will be most effective for getting

their attention? How can you use the sound of your voice alone to win their full engagement in your presentation? Like an artist creating a painting, how can you bring images before the imagination of your audience using only your words and your voice? As you begin to speak, pay close attention to what parts of your delivery get a positive, interested reaction from your audience. Be flexible and make adjustments in your delivery whenever you see hints of disinterest among audience members.

Finally, make your appearance appropriate for the setting of the presentation. Be a bit more formal with your attire than the norm. If business casual is the norm in your office, dress up on the day of your presentation. Be careful that you do not overdress (e.g., formal wear); instead, dress in such a way that gets you noticed and visually commands the attention of your audience. Even in a college classroom, you will notice that your peers will give you more respect and attention if you dress for success. Generally speaking, a conservative suit, moderate shoes, and minimal jewelry are recommended. Style your hair in a neat and professional way. Consider carrying any visual aids in a portfolio or briefcase.

The Audience: The Receivers of the Message

It goes without saying that the audience is expected to pay attention to the speaker, but the reverse is also true. The speaker must always pay close—perhaps even closer—attention to the audience. Consider a few situations in which you were part of an audience. Examples could include a lecture in a college classroom, a training session related to your job, or a news broadcast you watched on television. Compare and contrast the different speakers you encountered. Did they make you feel a connection with them and their topic? Did the speakers seem credible to you? Did they dress for success? What did you like, and dislike, about their speaking style and presentations?

Prior to your speech, think carefully about your listeners. Consider their **demographics**, or the statistical data about a particular population's makeup. Will you be speaking mostly to men or to women? Young people or older people? Highly educated people or people with limited levels of education?

Take a moment to think about how you will adjust the content and delivery of your speech based on this demographic information about your audience. For example, you would probably adjust the content of a speech about princesses significantly if your audience were suddenly switched from a group of five-year-old girls to a group of teenage boys. How would you adjust the topic further to suit the needs of a college-level Introduction to Psychology class? For a group of toy buyers at a convention who are interested in your company's princess dolls?

Next, go beyond these two considerations. Think about what your audience already knows about the topic. What do they want, and what do they need, to know about it? Can you think of any preconceived notions, mistaken beliefs, attitudes, or values that you should consider, and how those issues could affect their interpretation of the information you plan to share? Has your audience had any experience with the topic of your discussion that you could use in some of your examples or to launch into the key points you will make? See Figure 10.3 for suggestions on how to assess your audience.

- Whenever possible, get to know your audience before your speech. Talk with members individually if you can. Find out their interests—and better yet, what they are *not* interested in.
- Evaluate the demographics of your audience: What are the gender, age, ethnicity, and education-level characteristics of the audience you will be appealing to? How might you change a speech about auto repair if you knew your audience was mostly married women aged 25 to 35?
- Is your audience required to attend your speech, or are they there voluntarily? A captive audience gives you the opportunity to really take on a challenge and persuade and inform a group with varying levels of interest in your topic.
- The beliefs and values of the audience play an important role in the speaker–audience relationship. Is the audience already in agreement with you, or will you need to convince them?
- Your audience probably includes a wide range of cultures and ethnicities. Keep in mind that some members of the audience may not understand slang. Be aware of cultural differences that should be addressed in your speech. Be sensitive to your audience.
- What does your audience already know about the topic? Naturally, you do not want to spend too much time discussing information your audience already knows.

FIGURE 10.3 **Factors to Consider When Assessing Your Audience**

Finally, do not ignore your audience during your speech. Just as a conversation partner would, audience members expect you to meet their gaze and pick up on their nonverbal cues. **Nonverbal cues** are information communicated through body language and other unspoken hints. If audience members sigh, yawn, or slump down in their chairs, they may be showing disinterest. React positively by working harder to engage them in your presentation. If your audience members are leaning toward you as they sit, following you with their eyes, and taking notes on what you are saying, you will know that you have their interest. Make sure you keep it.

Most members of an audience are sympathetic to a speaker's nervousness. If you make a mistake, the audience will be more likely to forgive you if you laugh off the error and move on to the next item. Your audience will remember you as a speaker who showed the courage to hang in there and finish the speech.

Situation: The Purpose, Setting, and Location of the Meeting

The third corner of the rhetorical triangle is the **situation**, or context, of the speech. Where and why have the speaker and audience come together? How does the situation affect the delivery of information? Remember, the situation is not just the place where the presentation is being held. It also includes the purpose of the presentation.

Imagine that you have a great time having dinner one Friday night with a group of friends. The next night, you tell a friend who could not attend all about it. What details would you share about the evening with the friend who could not be there? What is your **purpose** for sharing this story with your friend? Now imagine that the very next day, you have dinner with your parents, who also ask about your Friday evening. Will the details and delivery of your story change? What is your purpose for sharing the story with your parents?

This situation shows how a speaker makes rhetorical decisions based on the situation, or the purpose and location of the speech. In the first version of the story, you want to entertain your friend with the funny details of your Friday night out with friends, but you want to also be careful not to make your friend feel left out. The purpose changes with your parents, who would probably hear a pretty different version of the same story.

Now imagine that you are in an academic setting. What is the purpose of a presentation an instructor asks you to give to your classmates? Is the purpose of your presentation to entertain them? To inform them with more detail about a topic covered in the course? Imagine that you are asked to explain one effect of the Civil Rights Act of 1964 on U.S. history or society. Is the purpose of this presentation to persuade your classmates about a particular view you hold about civil rights? Or perhaps to inspire them to take action on a matter regarding civil rights?

The purpose of a speech often fits into one of three larger aims:

- Self-expression or entertainment
- Information
- Argument or persuasion

Thinking first about what category your presentation fits into can help you make some decisions about content and delivery.

As a speaker, you must give thoughtful consideration to the location part of the situation as well. If possible, visit the location ahead of time and check out the setup of any equipment you may be using (e.g., a computer and projector to show slides). Test the acoustics of the room and consider the layout. You may even want to consider adjusting the seating arrangement if possible. Taking all of this into consideration will help to ensure you are more comfortable giving your presentation and that it is successfully received by your audience.

The three components of the rhetorical triangle—speaker, audience, and situation—influence each other. If the audience is familiar to the speaker, then the speaker may adjust the speech accordingly. If the audience consists of a group the speaker has never met and has little information about, then the speaker will be challenged to respond to audience feedback and must make more choices about how to present the speech. Each of the three elements of the rhetorical triangle is dependent on the others.

Defining the Rhetorical Triangle by Specifying What It Is Not

You now know that the rhetorical triangle consists of three parts that influence each other. The Greek philosopher Aristotle, known as the father of rhetoric, identified ethos, logos, and pathos as three approaches a speaker can take in order to appeal to an audience. These are often confused with the rhetorical triangle, so it is important to clarify the difference.

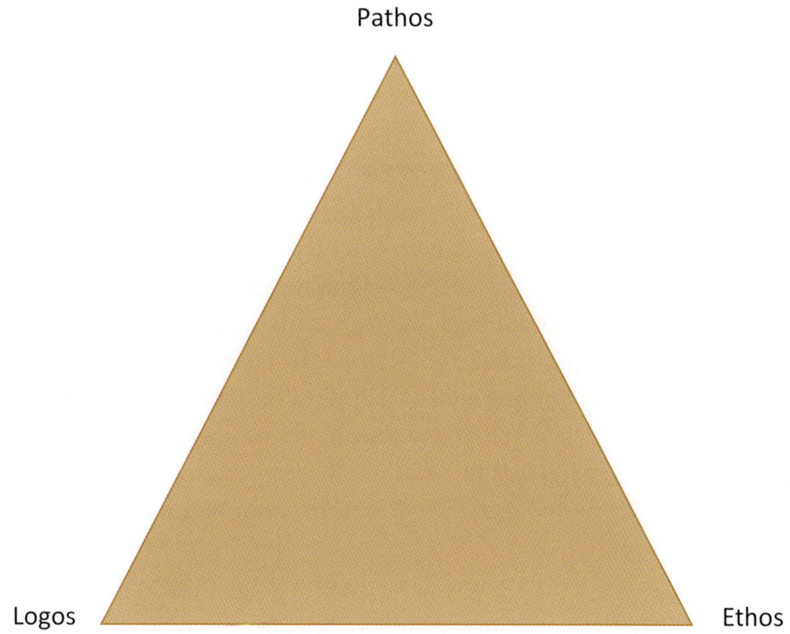

FIGURE 10.4 Three Approaches to Speaking

Ethos refers to the distinguishing beliefs or character of the speaker. Is the speaker credible? Knowledgeable? Authoritative and eloquent? Not trying to manipulate the audience? These characteristics are at the core of the characteristic of ethos. This element drives the appeal of the speech—the audience's belief in the speaker—but it does not necessarily mean that the topic of the speech, or the speech itself, is ethical. The speaker needs to instill in the audience a sense of ethos, or belief, in his or her character, but that sense of ethos is not the only way the speaker can influence an audience. Ethos refers to an approach to speech in which a speaker relies on his or her upstanding character to make an effective speech to the audience.

What ethos does not address, for example, is that a credible speaker is also affected by the audience and the situation. What if there are 100 people in the

DID YOU KNOW?

Audiences that are affected by appeals to emotion (pathos) usually do not stay persuaded. They usually revert to their original point of view when their initial emotional responses subside. Good reasons are required for lasting change, and those good reasons also must stand up to subsequent reflection.

For example, a young buyer looking for a new car may initially be excited about a particular sports car with all the latest features. However, as the time goes by, that rush of emotion subsides, and reason may take over. She will likely realize that she cannot afford the payments and insurance on such an impractical vehicle. Instead, she will look for something more sensible.

room ready to hear you speak and you have no microphone? You will be forced to make adjustments in order for the speech to be effective—an entirely different issue for the speaker than being a credible person. The ethos of a speaker is one piece, but not the entire picture, of what it means to be a speaker.

The characteristic of logos is sometimes defined as a rational appeal made by a speaker to an audience, but thinking of logos as a rational appeal can be misleading. **Logos** refers to evidence that is presented by a speaker and how that evidence is shared—in other words, "good reasons," as Aristotle described it. Speakers must support what they are saying, and this support needs to be organized in such a way that the audience can follow the reason and logic of the ideas.

The last term, pathos, is often defined as an emotional appeal that a speaker may use to persuade or influence an audience, but this, too, can be misleading. Speakers who use pathos do not necessarily make their audiences cry or feel angry about the injustices of the world. Instead, **pathos** is the act of *engaging* the audience in the presentation. A speaker who exhibits the characteristic of pathos commands the audience's attention, and may well inspire them. Pathos is a positive characteristic that produces positive emotions and actions.

Speaking/Listening versus Writing/Reading

Although there are some parallels between speaking and listening and writing and reading, the two are not identical. For example:

- Speakers and listeners meet for a specific purpose in a specific location at a specific time (although sometimes that meeting is a virtual one). Writers and their readers do not make the same type of connection.
- Speakers rely on the sound of their own voice to help deliver their message. Writers depend on grammar and mechanics.
- Speakers have the opportunity to be flexible in response to their audience. Writers are generally locked into their statements once they have composed and published their work.
- Many speakers receive an immediate reaction from their audience, whereas writers must often wait.
- Listeners may judge a speaker on appearance, while readers can typically only imagine what a writer may look like.
- Most people naturally learn to speak and listen; however, not everyone learns to read and write.

SUMMARY

- The rhetorical triangle includes the speaker, audience, and situation.
- The rhetorical triangle is a useful tool to help speakers succeed with their presentations.
- Speakers should carefully consider the importance of the audience and the situation.
- Speakers must be flexible in communicating with their audience.
- Nonverbal cues among the audience should be carefully observed and appropriately responded to by speakers.
- Ethos, logos, and pathos are characteristics of public speaking, but are often misunderstood.
- Speakers should keep in mind that speaking and listening are not the same as writing and reading.

REFERENCE

American Communication Association. (2011). *The ACA open knowledge guide to public speaking.* Retrieved from http://www.textcommons.org/node/2

CHAPTER

11

Audience Analysis

Katrina is a sales representative for Triple Z Textbooks and will be attending the company's sales meeting next week. At the conference, she is expected to give a speech about how to use the company's new software for market surveys, which she designed. She has scheduled her speech presentation for the last possible day of the sales conference—mostly because she is dreading it.

Katrina has spent hours preparing the presentation. She is a very good writer, but talking in front of a group of people terrifies her. She has worked at Triple Z for less than a year and does not know her colleagues—especially the ones working at regional offices—very well. She thinks, *Do my colleagues know anything at all about this software? How much computer experience do they have? Should I start the presentation with a joke about my first time using the software?*

Katrina is finding it frightening just to imagine facing a large audience. What if they become bored or laugh at her? What if her supervisor does not like the speech and interprets her trembling voice as incompetence and lack of authority?

KEY CONCEPTS

1. A speaker can analyze an audience's response and use the information to make adjustments to improve communication with the audience. See page 148.

2. Academic and professional audiences are specific audiences that are seeking particular gains from a presentation. See page 149.

3. Media outlets use a variety of techniques for audience analysis. See page 148.

4. An effective speaker establishes common ground with listeners. See page 151.

5. Communicating across cultures requires the speaker to make additional considerations for effectively getting a message across to a diverse audience. See page 151.

PUBLIC SPEAKING

Perhaps the biggest fear most people have about public speaking is focused on facing an audience. If you find the thought of giving a presentation to a class or to coworkers frightening, you are not alone. In fact, studies have shown that the fear of public speaking ranks number one among people in most cultures, which means that it is often feared more than death itself.

Most people who are fearful about public speaking express concerns about the audience and the fear of failure in front of an audience. For example, when you think about making a speech, you probably get nervous thinking about the audience being focused on you. The audience will be watching your every move and listening to every word you say. They will also be evaluating your performance. The audience may include a professor grading your speech, a boss observing your ability to share information with coworkers, or clients making a decision about whether to do business with your company. What if your audience becomes bored or disagrees with your presentation? What if you forget what you plan to say? It can all add up to a lot of pressure.

If any of these thoughts or feelings has ever crossed your mind, this chapter will help. One of the key solutions to the fear of public speaking is getting to know your audience. Even if you will not see the audience or know much about its members until the day of your speech, there are ways to analyze who your listeners will be so that you can better prepare and expect a favorable response to your presentation.

IDENTIFY AUDIENCE ANALYSIS INFORMATION NEEDS

Audience analysis involves taking a close look at who you will be speaking to, and evaluating their attitudes, opinions, needs, and wants. First, a speaker must identify a starting point: What does the audience already know about the topic of the speech? The audience is looking for a speaker to move beyond the common ground they share—perhaps a mention of a television show or movie with which they are all familiar—and teach something new and relevant. A wise speaker must identify the audience members' existing knowledge as the jumping-off point to explain what else they need to know.

Certainly stepping beyond the information base of the audience involves a bit of risk taking. Therefore, speakers must find common ground with their audience as early as possible in the presentation. If listeners see a speaker as being like-minded, they are often less hostile and therefore better able to be positively affected by the information shared.

It will most likely take more than one attempt, and more than one approach, to win an audience over. A **neutral** audience will need more information about the subject to be able to form an opinion; an **apathetic** audience is informed, but will need motivation to make them care; and a **resistant** audience will need to be shown that the speaker has a clear understanding of opposing views.

The level of persuasion usually should equal the level of resistance, so proceed carefully and sensitively with listeners. Successful persuasion means that an audience is persuaded to listen to opposing views. Different degrees of persuasion exist, so consider various approaches to persuasion and choose the one

DID YOU KNOW?

Surveying Media Audiences

Media outlets, including television networks, carefully survey and study their audiences. The most widely known study is the Nielsen ratings system, in which in-home viewers report the television programming they watch via electronic monitoring systems. Included in this data is a profile of the viewers, including age, income level, and other demographic information. This information is then shared with advertisers to help them decide which shows will help them reach a specific target audience.

that is most appropriate for your audience and the context of your speech.

GATHER AUDIENCE DATA

To analyze an audience effectively and increase your potential for success, you should gather as much information about your listeners as possible in order to guide the decisions you make about a presentation. Some of this information may be gathered informally, but you must think carefully about what you know about your audience. Asking yourself questions can be helpful. Consider the following examples:

- Who is my audience? Are they clients, customers, coworkers, or classmates?
- Will my audience consist of males, females, or a mixture of both?
- What is my audience's age range?
- What is my audience's level of education?
- How large will my audience be?

Asking questions such as these will help you determine what information, examples, level of language, and approach should or should not be used.

As a speaker, you will also need to consider the expectations, attitudes, and values of your audience. Is the group expecting you to teach them something, like how to use a new software application at work? Do they expect you to sell them a product? What are their attitudes toward the topic? Certainly, if the software or product is needed to perform their job duties successfully, your audience probably will be serious and engaged.

Finally, consider your audience's values. Do they value profit over product? Does your audience consist of members of a community organization who value service to those in need, or do they value profit?

Keep in mind that more formal research strategies may be needed. For example, public relations firms sometimes create **case studies**. These are more formal studies involving activities like in-depth interviews, polls, surveys, questionnaires, focus groups, observations, and the collection of additional relevant data. This information is carefully analyzed to make conclusions about the potential audience. These conclusions are then synthesized or integrated into a speaker's presentation to better meet the needs of the audience.

A case study made in preparation for a training session on a new piece of software, for example, may reveal that a target audience of coworkers is excited about the new software because they believe it will make their jobs easier. However, the case study could find that the audience is concerned about the learning curve involved in using it. It may also reveal that half the employees do not have the hardware necessary to run the software—which would certainly be a major consideration for a presentation. The value in a case study is that it often goes right to the source and makes unexpected discoveries.

VERBAL COMMUNICATION

The words you choose to convey your message are as important as the nonverbal communication you have with your audience. There are several elements to attend to when preparing the verbal communication of your speech, including using standard English and avoiding slang. Adapt your language for your audience, as there may be people from a variety of cultures in the audience. Be sensitive about how you use humor, remaining mindful it that may exclude some people or cultures. Use concrete details and avoid vocalizing pauses.

Language Use

The language of a speaker should closely reflect that of the situation and the audience for the speech. Consider a situation in which you are giving a presentation to a small social organization of which you are member. In this situation, more informal language is probably acceptable. You probably can feel comfortable using contractions, colloquialisms (informal phrases often used in ordinary conversation), and maybe even a bit of slang. Your sentences should be simple, with only moderate concern about good grammar and mechanics, and your diction (choice and use of words and phrases) should be commonly used by your audience in everyday speech.

On the other hand, if you are presenting in an academic or professional environment, more formal language is expected. You should use few, if any, contractions, colloquialisms, or slang. Good grammar is an expectation, and your sentences should be varied and complex. The diction of speakers in more formal contexts must be precise.

Keep in mind that your audience will expect you to use language confidently. Avoid many of the common weaknesses that occur in everyday spoken language. For instance, try not to begin sentences with weak expressions such as "I think" and "I feel."

Finally, remember the expression "make your words work." Each word you utter should support the goal of your presentation in some way. Particularly descriptive words do not make a speech memorable; instead, they may make it confusing, so choose adjectives and action verbs wisely. Place your ideas and their support in a framework of organization that will be effective for your listeners. Your audience should not have to work to figure out the point of your speech—your words should do the work for them.

Audience Adaptation

Adapt your speech based on what you know about your audience. Is it a tough crowd, or is the group on your side? Do they appreciate visual aids and a few jokes, or a short and serious presentation?

COMMUNICATION ACROSS CULTURES

Many of the techniques for assessing the audience can be applied to communicating across cultures. However, there are a few other techniques to keep in mind. Avoid using words and examples specific to your own culture. Ask the audience to repeat an important concept back to you in their own words, but do not do so in a derogatory way. If you find that your audience does not understand one of your points, find a different way of expressing the idea rather than continuing to repeat the same explanation. Always be respectful and sensitive to the values, views, and attitudes of the various cultures your audience represents.

Knowing Your Audience

How will you make a connection with your audience? Whatever you can think of that will help adapt your presentation to your audience should work well. Remember these primary guidelines for making sure you forge a bond with the group that is hearing your presentation.

- *Establish common ground.* "Since I am an employee who also had to learn how to use this new software, ..."
- *Share your feelings.* "Does the idea of learning about this new software make you feel as nervous as I did when I first confronted with it?"
- *Offer an amusing anecdote.* "Remember when we used those black floppy disks that were the size of Frisbees?"

Tailoring Examples for an Audience

Part of adapting your speech for your audience is using examples that are appropriate to the situation, supportive to the topic, and helpful to listeners. In the software presentation example, providing your audience with examples of how the software can be used to make their jobs easier will help the audience adapt to the information you are providing.

The examples should be carefully organized within the structure of the speech so that the audience can follow the message. It is often helpful to use manipulatives, props that the audience can perceive with their senses, to demonstrate examples. Giving the audience a chance to share their own examples is often helpful, too.

Rhetorical Sensitivity

When you are thinking about how to present your ideas to the audience, pay close attention to issues of **rhetorical sensitivity**, or how you choose language and present ideas to appeal to your audience. The range of rhetorical considerations includes issues of humor, stereotypes, profanity, culture, and stereotyping. Any of these could offend your listener and mentally turn them off to any message you give. In addition, be careful to use concrete details and avoid vocalized pauses. Taking the time to consider these points will ensure that your speech is effective and executed with professionalism (see the boxed item on professionalism).

Humor

One way to adapt your speech to your audience while accomplishing your purpose is through the use of humor—but only in a setting where doing so is appropriate.

Laughing makes people feel good, and it makes them receptive to new knowledge. Speakers sometimes feel they cannot use humor in a formal speech, but if you have performed a careful audience analysis, you have probably developed some ideas about what your audience will think is funny and what should be avoided.

Inclusive versus Exclusive Language

Avoid words and examples that may make your audience feel like outsiders, including singling out individuals based on gender, ethnicity, religion, physical traits, or any other factor. Always refrain from using implied stereotypes or derogatory remarks. Instead, focus on details that make everyone in the room an insider, a part of the group.

Use of Profanity

Always avoid using profanity in public speaking situations. A presentation is not a comedy routine, after all. In particular, speakers in academic and job settings should never curse or use vulgar terms.

Anything that may go against the "sacredness" of the situation can also be considered profane. For example, students giving a presentation to fellow students and faculty should not criticize the school, its classes, or its administration. Consider the situation in its context: A student who makes statements about how awful a course is during a presentation to her classmates and instructor will not be well received by her audience. Likewise, an employee addressing his coworkers about an upcoming project they will be collaborating on who complains about what an awful place the company is to work for will not be respected by his listeners. The context of a speech is generally sacred, and to violate it is a form of profanity.

Cultural Sensitivity

Speakers should treat listeners from all cultures with the same level of respect and empathy. No culture should be spoken of in a derogatory fashion, nor should anything in the presentation display a culture in a way that is stereotypical or demeaning. The different belief systems cultures hold should not be ridiculed or judged.

Also, always remember to be sensitive to the audience's personal space, eye contact, and other nonverbal customs. For example, in some cultures, people are not comfortable making eye contact, speaking in close situations, or speaking freely in response to a speaker.

Concrete Details versus Abstract Generalities

When communicating verbally, focus on using concrete details rather than abstract generalities. **Concrete details** are words and expressions that describe something that can be perceived by one of the five senses. If you use an image that the audience can see, touch, hear, smell, or even taste, it is a concrete detail. The more sensory details you use in your speech, the more engaged your listeners will become, and the more they will understand and remember the information you present.

Avoid **abstract generalities**, which are words and examples that cannot be readily understood by using the physical senses. In the software presentation example,

PROFESSIONALISM

Model a professional environment by:

- Knowing your audience
- Adapting your presentation to your audience
- Displaying rhetorical sensitivity
- Engaging in appropriate humor
- Using inclusive rather than exclusive language
- Avoiding profanity
- Displaying cultural sensitivity
- Using concrete rather than abstract language
- Avoiding vocalized pauses

consider how much more your coworkers could learn about the software if you show the software actually being used and have them engage in hands-on training during the speech, rather than spending the entire presentation discussing the technological theory behind the function of the software.

Avoiding Vocalized Pauses

A final consideration for verbal communication is to avoid **vocalized pauses**. These are the little fillers often used in everyday speech to keep the conversation going externally while a person tries to process the next idea to express in the conversation. They include meaningless words and expressions like "um" and "you know" or affirmation-seeking statements such as asking the audience, "Right?" Vocalized pauses can be very distracting to an audience, while nonvocalized pauses—moments of silence—give speakers the chance to collect their thoughts and their audience an opportunity to process the information they are hearing.

SUMMARY

- Overcome your fear of public speaking by thoroughly understanding and relating to your audience.
- Knowing your audience is one of the best ways to overcome fear and be a more effective speaker.
- Put your words to work in order to successfully share your message with your audience.
- Speakers should be rhetorically sensitive to the needs of their varied listeners, especially when communicating across cultures.
- Avoid using vocalized pauses in your presentation.
- Focus on providing your audience with concrete, relatable details.

REFERENCES

Fear of public speaking statistics. (2011, February 13). Retrieved from http://www.speech-topics-help.com/fear-of-public-speaking-statistics.html

Nielsen Company. (2011). *Nielsen: A world of insights.* Retrieved from http://www.nielsen.com

CHAPTER

12

Rhetorical Modes

Leah has recently moved back to Oregon after a five-year stint in New York City. For the past three months, she has been juggling pursuing a degree in education and looking for full-time work in child care. The interview process has been daunting for Leah, to say the least. Leah has found that during job interviews, her nerves cause her to become tongue-tied easily, and she even has trouble responding to simple queries like "Tell me a little bit about yourself."

Leah is well aware that in a job interview setting, she is trying to make herself stand out among all the other candidates. She wants to impress her interviewers and at least sound coherent, intelligent, and friendly. How should she respond when interviewers ask her pointed questions?

KEY CONCEPTS

1. There are three main rhetorical modes—self-introduction, information, and persuasion. See page 156.

2. Each rhetorical mode can be engaged successfully by using specific tips. See page 156.

3. Speakers should avoid misleading an audience. See page 163.

4. Speakers need to learn how to best handle controversial topics and audience reaction. See page 164.

5. Groups can learn to function together to give an effective presentation. See page 165.

THE RHETORICAL MODES

Rhetoric refers to the art of speaking or writing effectively. Many roads lead to effective speaking. This chapter covers three **rhetorical modes**—self-introduction, informative speech, and persuasive speech. Leah's job interview predicament is a self-introduction situation. Each of the rhetorical modes is explained in detail in this chapter.

Self-Introduction

Throughout your life, you will be in a position where you need to introduce yourself in front of a group many, many times. This might be in a school setting, at work, or as part of any group you belong to. Being comfortable introducing yourself to others is a key element of achieving success in work and life.

The Art of Self-Introduction

The most important and difficult part of a self-introduction is the self-assessment process you undergo before anyone ever asks, "Tell me a little about yourself." In order to be prepared to answer that question, you must think carefully about who you are, how you got where you are today, what your motivations have been, and how you can best define yourself. Reflecting on these points can help begin the process. Introspection is usually the hardest part of creating a self-introduction speech—the rest is easier.

Some find it helpful to ask friends to name five personal characteristics, or defining traits, that would apply. Often those who are closest to you can help provide good insight into who you are. Consider your friends' responses and then formulate your own list. The result could be a start for talking points about yourself.

Think also about the defining events and memories of your life. What are some funny things you remember? What were some mischievous things you did as a teenager? What was your most embarrassing moment—and how did you recover from it? Who has inspired you? How has that person's behavior and leadership influenced your own? All of these events have shaped you into the person that you are, and talking about them will help you connect with others in an audience.

Next, think about what makes you unique. You may have shared many similar experiences with the members of your potential audience, for almost everyone has gone to school, forgotten to study for a test, or undergone an awkward period during adolescence. Focus instead on what is unique about you—your life, your background, and your perspective. What can you say about yourself that no one else can claim? Do you have a unique or surprising hobby? Do you have an unusual goal, like becoming a stunt woman or a world-class distance runner? Anything of this sort will help you establish a connection with an audience, through sharing something interesting and unique about yourself.

After you have collected a set of ideas about yourself, remember that self-introduction speeches are typically quite brief. You only have a few minutes at most to impress your audience. Therefore, keep the classic elevator pitch model in mind, which refers to the idea that you have no more than the time spent in an elevator ride to capture a listener's attention. Grab your audience's attention by sharing a key idea or two, and then wrap up your self-introduction in a memorable way. *Be clever and concise.*

In a job interview, if you are asked to introduce yourself, give your name and a brief summary of your professional qualifications. Next, share something unique about yourself that you bring to the table. Your unique experience may be something you have already done (climbed to the top of Mt. Hood, for example) or something you hope to do (set the world record for bungee jumping). Consider adding an element that is creative, fun, or energetic to express yourself. Remember to keep your answer concise, too, and you might just get the job.

Consider Leah's predicament. She followed this advice and was prepared at the next job interview, this time at a large child care center. When she was asked to describe herself by the center's director, Leah gathered her wits and began to speak.

"Well, I'm here today because education chose me. When I first started thinking about what I wanted to be, back in high school, education never seemed like the right fit. My big career choice at that point was becoming a professional sky diver—now just a hobby, because there's not much of a future in that. After I graduated and moved away to New York, I struggled for more than a month to find a job. I was terrified that I would have to come home, defeated, and move back in with my parents.

Leah paused, and then continued dramatically, "After one particularly disastrous job interview, I went to a park nearby to collect my thoughts and sat on a bench by a playground. A mother sitting on the bench next to me struck up a conversation with me—and to my shock, within 15 minutes I'd found my first job, as a nanny. I'd had very little experience with young children before then, so it was a shock, to say the least. But once I got the hang of it, and saw how much of an effect I had on the children I cared for—well, something just clicked. I wanted to make a difference in the lives of children. I'm pursuing my bachelor's degree in elementary education now, but eventually, I plan to get a PhD in education, because I see a future for myself as an elementary school system administrator."

In a clever, concise way, Leah shared something memorable about herself with the child care center director. She told her interviewer about her past, her present, and her future. She shared goals and dreams. And she did it all in the same length of time as an elevator ride.

Amir, a 25-year-old student, sits in a college classroom. He is asked to introduce himself to the rest of the group. Amir walks to the front of the room and turns to face the audience.

"Hi, everyone. My name is Amir Sahid, and I am here today because I am a recovering fast-food restaurant manager." [Amir pauses briefly to give the audience a chance to react.]

"I was just out of high school when I got my first job. At first, it all seemed great—I could pay all my bills with what I earned at the restaurant, because I was still living at home with my parents. I felt that the job would be very low-stress, because it simply involved mastering a process and executing it, time and again. Gone were the days of studying hard for tests and staying up all night working on papers. This was a job where I could just show up, do the same thing for six to eight hours, and then go home and forget all about it.

"Unfortunately for me, I was really good at my job. I was so good that I was quickly promoted to night manager. Don't get me wrong, though. I really enjoyed the prestige of being a manager. I was good at it—I had no problems scheduling the other employees, encouraging them in their work, and training new hires. I spent 40 hours each week showing the new kids how to maintain quality and make the fries and burgers exactly the right way.

"Of course, there were negatives to the job as well. It was anything but low-stress! I was constantly settling arguments among employees, fixing broken equipment ... you name it. It was up to me, and me alone, to solve every problem on every shift."

"Then the franchise's owner asked me to stop in his office before my shift one day. I thought, 'Wow ! I must be about to get promoted to the day shift.'

"Imagine my surprise when he told me that he was letting me go. It was true that I was good at the scheduling, training, and leadership aspects of my job. What I wasn't good at, however, was the financial aspect of the work. I had inadvertently hired two employees at too high a pay rate because I paid too little attention to the details. Workers on my shift wasted at least 25 percent more food than those on any other shifts, which meant that I was an inefficient manager. I scheduled too many employees for the shifts I managed. In the end, the owner told me, my shifts were at most half as profitable as the other managers' shifts, and on many occasions, the restaurant actually lost money while I was in charge.

"So that is why I'm here today. I want to be a manager, and a leader, but I only know part of what I need to know to be a good one. I know that school is the answer, and here I will learn the remaining pieces I need to be successful. I'm scared, but I'm excited, too. I want to learn to be a manager of the highest character and skill, and I look forward to working with each of you this semester."

FIGURE 12.1 **A Sample Self-Introduction Speech**

Informative Speech

Informative speeches are typically divided into four types: speeches about objects, events, processes, or concepts. Each type of speech requires description; in fact, description is more or less the sole purpose of an informative speech. The next section details how you can make your descriptions more effective in informative speeches.

Description

When speakers describe something to an audience, they must paint an image with their words discussing how it looks, feels, tastes, smells, and sounds (or whichever of these are applicable to the subject at hand). One caveat—if the presenter has the object available for the audience to see, touch, and work with, then less description is needed in the speech.

When you present an informative speech, your challenge is to take your audience with you on a journey and to show them an object, concept, or place with clarity through the power of your words. As a speaker, you must entice your audience by summoning their five senses and using carefully chosen, powerful details. Because a description can be challenging to organize, **spatial organization** is often used. This means the speaker moves through the description section by section, according to space. For example, if you were giving a speech about a painting by Claude Monet, you could discuss the painting in quadrants. You could describe each quadrant of the painting in a clockwise fashion, from the upper right side of the painting to the upper left side, taking time to describe each section fully.

Another method of organization is to move from the most to least important information. In this case, the speaker would focus first on the large objects in the painting (e.g., a palace), and then draw the viewers' attention to smaller details, such as a peacock perched on a windowsill in the distance. Whatever method of organization speakers choose, they should do so only after carefully considering the speech's purpose and the needs of the audience.

Types of Informative Speeches

The subjects of informative speeches are typically divided into four types:

- Objects
- Events
- Processes
- Concepts

In a speech about objects, the speaker presents a product or item; the goal is to familiarize the audience with the item and interest them in it. Perhaps the item might be a new tool or type of software.

Speeches about events involve sharing a story with an audience about an event or events that happened at a particular point in time. These events may be global or local. No matter what the setting of the event might be, the speaker must use descriptive details effectively enough that listeners will feel as though they were in the place where the event occurred as it unfolded. The presenter must explore the five "Ws":

- Who? Who was involved in the event?
- When? When did the event occur?
- Where? Where did the event occur?
- What? What happened during the event?
- Why? Why did the event occur?

Speeches about concepts typically explain ideas to an audience—either a general interpretation of what the idea means or a personal interpretation that the speaker holds. For instance, as a supervisor, you may be asked to describe to your employees what professional development means. You could use the definition provided in your employee handbook, or you may decide to make a careful distinction between professional development and job training that you have come up with yourself.

Speeches about processes are demonstrations that explain *how* or *how to.* The *how to* process expects the audience members to be able to perform the demonstrated action, but the *how* presentation does not. For example, in a *how* demonstration, a doctor may explain to a group of patients how a surgical procedure removes tumors. On the other hand, after a speaker demonstrates how to use a new photocopier machine in a *how to* demonstration, the employees should know how to use it as well.

Even if you are presenting online or via webcam, most of the same rules apply. You will not be in the same room as your audience, but you must still carefully consider the information you are presenting and how you are presenting it. Really, the primary difference between presenting in person and presenting via webcam is that you cannot see (and thus read the body language of) your audience. Despite the fact that you cannot see them, they most certainly are there—and thus you must imagine them. In reality, this makes your job as the speaker a little harder. Many technologies exist to help you gather feedback from an online audience, such as chatting, "raising your hand," polling, and rating systems that allow students to interact with each other during and after student presentations.

The Demonstration Speech

A **demonstration speech** involves an active showing of its subject. Demonstrators engage the audience in the presentation as much as possible by using **manipulatives**—props that the audience can perceive with their senses—and by asking the audience questions. Finally, check with the audience at the end of the speech to make sure they learned something new. See Figure 12.2 for an example of a demonstration speech.

These speeches are also known as demonstrations, where the speaker, or demonstrator, shows the object to the audience in addition to describing it.

Raoul Hunford, a corporate trainer, stands before a group of five employees in a training room. Each of the employees sits in front of a long conference table.

"Welcome, everyone! Have you ever been in a social situation where you didn't know who to talk to, when to jump into the conversation, or what to say? My name is Raoul Hunford, and I'm going to put you into just that sort of situation so you can practice your teleconference skills.

"I'd like each of you to pick up the paper cup sitting in front of you. This is your telephone. Now, join me here at the front of the room. I want you all to stand in a circle facing outward so you cannot see the others on the call. I'll stand right here, in the middle of your circle.

"Does everyone have the telephone number and the access code? Good. Now dial in. I'll wait a minute so you can all gain access to the call.

"As the host, I know that there should be five of you on this call, so I am listening for five ringtones before I start the meeting. Okay, I've heard all five ringtones now. I'm going to start the meeting.

"Hello, everyone. This is Raoul. Thank you for joining us. Is John on the line? Hi, John. Josef, are you here? Great. Risa, are you on the line? Wonderful! Imara? Tony? Great! It looks like everyone is here, so let's begin.

"Now ... how does every one feel about having a conversation with a group of people you can't see?

[Raoul waits a moment for the participants' responses and reacts spontaneously to them, as if this is a real telephone conference. The group goes on to model a teleconference, including a polite signoff of all participants.]

"I appreciate your participation. You may all return to your seats—and it's okay to look at each other once again! Hopefully, this bit of practice made you realize that in spite of the initial awkwardness of not seeing one another for a meeting, standard business meeting practices and etiquette can work well on a telephone conference, too. Of course, the real beauty of the teleconference is that you can participate in your pajamas!"

FIGURE 12.2 A Demonstration Speech

Persuasive

You are now familiar with two of the three rhetorical modes: self-introduction and informative speeches. The third rhetorical mode is persuasive speeches.

The Goals of a Persuasive Speech

Persuasive speeches have a much more powerful purpose than personal expression (self-introduction) or informational speeches. The primary goal of persuasion is to change the audience's minds about a topic. Perhaps you are a salesperson speaking to a roomful of potential clients who are not sure if they want or need the product you represent. Maybe you are sitting before a hiring committee whose members are scrutinizing you to see if you are the right person for the job. Whatever the situation, the audience is being asked to change their minds.

The second goal of a persuasive speech involves getting a nonreceptive audience to do something. Many persuasive presentations advocate a particular plan of action. The salesperson might try to get the audience members to commit to purchase

the product before leaving the room by telling them that they are entitled to an introductory discount, for example, or the job candidate might tell the committee members that she is entertaining two other job offers, so they must act quickly if they wish to hire her.

As with these two examples, this goal implies the need for urgency. You have likely seen infomercials that insisted you would get two, or even three, of the item in question at no cost if you made a purchase within 10 or 15 minutes of viewing the commercial. Asking a potential employer, "When can I expect to hear from you?" at the end of an interview implies that you are a busy professional with several pending offers.

To persuade an audience to take action, you must first *align* yourself with the audience, thus establishing a sense of togetherness. The audience for a persuasive speech is not necessarily friendly and receptive, like most audiences for self-introduction speeches or most audiences motivated to learn from an informational speech. Rather, the audience for a persuasive speech may be **neutral** (having no preference one way or another about the topic), **apathetic** (not caring about the topic), or even **resistant** (not wanting to hear about the topic or even from someone representing it). Therefore, a speaker must immediately win over the audience by establishing common ground, shared interests, related values—anything that will create a sense of togetherness between speaker and audience, rather than an "us versus them" attitude.

Another technique for persuasive speaking is to establish authority. You probably can recall an instance where you were moved by a speech by a political candidate who really knew how to get a crowd excited—and then later, after a little reflection about the speech you heard, you realized that the candidate did not really say anything substantial. The speaker's authority was likely what moved you—the message was less important than the authority you conferred upon him or her.

Persuasive speeches are not necessarily about drastic change. A presenter may want to argue for the **status quo**, which means that the speech suggests that making a change or taking a certain action may be detrimental. For example, what if your company has a mandate to become more environmentally friendly, but after investigation, you discover that some of the planned measures will be far more expensive than originally thought and may endanger the financial health of the company? What if you find evidence that some jobs may be lost if the environmentally conscious measures are taken? You may want to argue for the status quo, or at least a somewhat more conservative step.

Persuasive Approaches

The three approaches to persuasion are as follows:

- Using emotion to persuade an audience
- Using one's reputation or charismatic appeal to persuade an audience
- Using an appeal to reason to persuade an audience

These approaches were first introduced by Aristotle and are respectively called **pathos** (based on emotion), **ethos** (the appeal or reputation of the speaker), and **logos** (appeal to logic). See Figure 12.3. Persuasive speeches can use any one of these three approaches, or a combination of the approaches. These approaches can be authentic, credible techniques to presenting a persuasive speech, but pathos, ethos, and logos also can be misused to guide listeners in ways that are not ethical. Speakers must be careful not to mislead the audience either deliberately or accidentally. In order to avoid doing so, you should always check carefully for uses of these three approaches, which could conceivably mislead an audience.

Although speakers always want to engage *pathos*, or a successful emotional appeal to an audience, they should be mindful not to do so in such a way that the audience is misled into believing something that may not be true, or in a way in which a side issue of no real consequence hides the real issue. The politician who excites the crowd but presents nothing substantial is a good example of misused pathos.

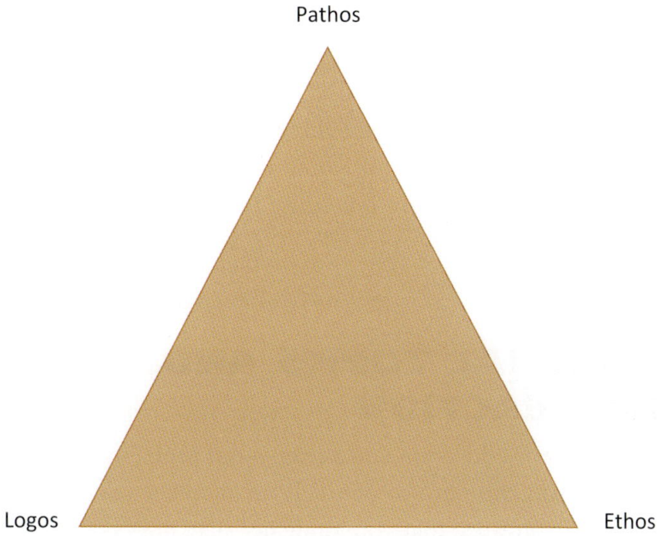

FIGURE 12.3 **Three Approaches to Speaking**

While speakers should present themselves as credible authorities to their audience—*ethos*—they must not exaggerate their level of expertise or claim authority that is not really their own. If the job candidate in the example wanted the committee's job offer so much that she claimed to have a college degree she did not actually earn, she would be creating a fallacy of ethos.

Logos can be split into two main types. Speakers must provide evidence that their claims are true, and they cannot exaggerate or fabricate this evidence. Imagine that you are the head of sales for a company that launched a new product last year. Unfortunately, you struggled to find a market for that new product, and only sold it to one person all year. If in the first quarter of the following year you manage to sell the product to two other people, that would represent a 200 percent increase in sales. That is in fact true, but to go to on advertise the product as "doubling in

CAREER PERSPECTIVES: SALES AND ETHICS

Speakers should always avoid intentionally misleading an audience for any reason. For example, imagine that you get a job selling time-shares of oceanfront apartments and come up with a strategy to sell people on the concept without fully disclosing that you are a salesperson for the company. Giving potential customers information about the apartment's floor plan, huge closets, lavish décor, and how much you personally enjoy sitting on the balcony of the time-share apartment and staring out at the ocean is fine if your aim is only to express yourself or to tell them about the terrific vacation you have had. But if your ultimate goal is to engage the audience in conversation only to suddenly ambush them with a sales pitch, doing so is a serious breach of ethics. Just imagine if you were the audience and this sales tactic were used on you. Would you feel betrayed? Would you feel angry?

demand" or some such claim when only three units of the product have actually been sold would be misleading and would be creating a fallacy of logos. To purposefully disorganize information to confuse the audience is a misleading use of logos.

CONTROVERSIAL TOPICS AND AUDIENCE REACTION

There will be times in your education and career—and probably even in your personal life, too—when you will need to persuade an audience about a controversial topic. You may know in advance that your audience may not take the information well. For example, imagine that you are the supervisor of a group of employees who work on an assembly line. One day, you learn that the recent downturn in the economy has had a catastrophic effect on your company's revenues. You must let your employees know that you and they must all take a pay cut, or the company will go under.

In such a situation, you must always remain up front with your audience, even though the news you have to deliver will be difficult for them to hear. A speaker should do whatever is possible to create a sense of togetherness. This may sound odd or impossible at first, but think about it. In the supervisor example, the employees know that the downturn in the economy has been bad for business. If you share with them the consequences of not taking a pay cut—e.g., the potential that they would lose their jobs altogether when the company closed its doors—you are being honest and also giving them a compelling reason to accept the news more readily. Although no one wants a pay cut, most people would prefer that to unemployment. Perhaps you should also share the fact that you, too, are making a sacrifice—accepting a pay cut—so your direct reports will know you are in the dilemma with them.

An audience listening to a controversial presentation will *not* want the speaker to avoid the issue. Even in the worst of circumstances, audiences tend to respect a speaker more if the speaker is honest. It would not be good to your direct reports to leave a meeting believing their pay had not been cut—only to see a much smaller amount on their next pay stub.

You may be fighting your natural reactions. Perhaps your pay cut is only half what your employees are facing—or perhaps it is twice as much. Perhaps you are so filled with dread at the idea of the company going under—and losing your job—that you might be tempted to lash out in anger at any employee who gives the slightest resistance to the news. Either way, your emotions will get in the way at some point. Whatever the circumstances, you must address your own emotions as part of your preparation process in order to keep them at bay during your presentation. Focus objectively on the facts and the issues, rather than the emotions. Depersonalize the situation as much as you possibly can.

THE GROUP PRESENTATION

One of the most rewarding—and challenging—forms of public speaking is participating in a presentation as part of a group. A group presentation by a collection of coworkers or teammates can involve much less of a fear factor—the built-in support goes a long way. Also, presenting as a group lessens the pressure on each person, as the burden of success is split among several people. When a group functions well together, its members also can build upon one another's energy and creativity; they can then infect an audience with this sense of excitement as they share the presentation.

The Stages of Group Dynamics

Next, consider the various challenges of group presentations. Sometimes groups do not mix well. Perhaps the group undergoes a power struggle as two members try to wrest leadership from one another. Perhaps certain members of the group try to turn teamwork into a rivalry. Perhaps the group lacks leadership and ends up aimless and unproductive. These challenges—and many more—may end up increasing, rather than decreasing, the level of pressure felt by individual members of the team, and can lead all to fear—and realize—failure. Understanding as much as possible about the stages of group dynamics can be helpful to anyone about to embark on a group presentation.

Forming

Group presentations are common at work and in college courses. The first step of putting together a group presentation is **forming** the group. An instructor may divide a class evenly into groups, with each giving a presentation on a particular legendary business leader. Other times, the choice of group members may be self-selected, or made by the team's members.

This first stage of group dynamics is exploratory. Exchanges between group members are generally cordial and guarded. As the group members get acquainted with one another, they begin to figure out how each will function individually within the group. Who will take the lead? Will certain members provide background knowledge or information, while others will lead development of the group's proposals? Does one or more of the group's members possess organizational or technical skills? Does any one have a special insight into the project?

Many of the considerations that speakers think about in preparing for a self-introduction presentation can be put to use during this stage of group development, as each member shares his or her unique story with the rest of the group. What does each member already know about the topic or focus of the group? What personal experiences about the topic can each convey? What does each member think the presentation's audience will want or need to know? As the group learns about one another, they can synthesize this information as they form a singular group dynamic.

At this stage, it is vital that all members be given a chance to communicate and share who they are and what they bring to the group and project. Efforts must be made to give equal time to all participants. Emotions may start to surface, and it is important to allow each member to share how he or she feels about the task at hand. As the group is just forming, there will probably be a tendency among its members to be more chatty and distracted than productive. With that in mind, all members should try to keep the group focused on becoming cohesive.

Storming

After all the members have had their say and have gotten acquainted with one another, the next stage—storming—begins. Typically, this is when the group's leader will emerge. This leader will likely have specific ideas about who should do what and how the presentation should be done, including both the process and the product itself. Often, one or more group members will disagree with these visions or will have a slightly different idea of certain aspects of the plan.

Still other members may be very reluctant to hold a leadership position but not at all reluctant to hold differing opinions about the situation and presentation. Rather than step up and speak out about their views, needs, or desires, these individuals may internalize their feelings and withdraw from the group. They may state their neutrality or apathy. All of this activity, including the disagreements and working through differences, is called **storming**.

As with any other relationship, group members in this stage must keep in mind their purpose for being together. They must try to find a way of approaching both the process and the product as a team. Defining roles and duties is essential and efficient, but it must also be accomplished in a way that brings the group closer together, not farther apart.

Many of the rhetorical techniques discussed previously can come into play during this stage. For example, the group's leader could use ethos to start a discussion about authority, asking members to share their knowledge about and experience with the subject of the presentation. The leader could appeal to pathos by motivating everyone to set aside their differences for the greater good. (If the presentation goes well, everyone will benefit.) Finally, an appeal to logos can unify the group, as the leader asks them all to set aside their emotions and squabbles in order to move forward and reach their collective goal.

Norming

Eventually, the group will settle into comfortable roles. Each member will embrace a clear role and function for the benefit of the group and the project's success—a stage called **norming**. An attitude of cooperation and congeniality prevails, helping the group become more efficient and effective. Real progress is made as the process moves forward.

The issues that arise at this stage are mostly operational. How will information be shared? How will it be analyzed? How could the pieces each member gathers be formed into a collective whole that can be presented later on to an audience? At this point, the group begins not only to tolerate their differences, but also truly embrace them, because they see the benefits of having multiple personality types, approaches, and perspectives working together in the group. The group is usually at its most creative during this stage.

Performing

At this stage, the group truly blossoms. During the **performing** stage, the group demonstrates innovation, dynamism, and success as it nears its goal. During this stage, the group usually first practices, and then delivers, the presentation. It is often best if each member of the group is responsible for a segment of the presentation—perhaps one member can provide background on the topic, another can explain the considerations undertaken, a third can share the research that went into the group's proposal, and a fourth can wrap up the presentation by stating its proposal. At this point, the dynamic is less about who will be the individual leader of the group internally, and more about how the group will function in unison as a leader within a larger community (e.g., the workplace).

Adjourning and Mourning

The presentation is complete! The group's purpose has been fulfilled, and now a need to function together no longer exists. The group may gradually disband and go their separate ways—the stage known as **adjourning**. (Restructuring and other external moves also may force the adjournment of a group.)

Of course, change is almost always difficult. For many, the end of a group's reason to be may lead to a sense of **mourning** for what has been lost. Once a group reaches the performing level, its members tend to become very comfortable working together and find that they are comforted by the presence of their teammates. Losing what they have become accustomed to and dependent upon may unsettle certain group members.

After the group gives its presentation and adjourns, there may be a period of mourning where the group members express the desire to get together or to work on another project. Perhaps they decide to present their work in another venue. Generally, however, the group will gradually realize that their time together has passed. Rather than mourn what is gone, it is best to see this final step as an opportunity. There are always more groups that can be formed, more creative projects to produce, and more venues in which to share ideas.

SUMMARY

- There are three main rhetorical modes: self-introduction, information, and persuasion.
- Each of these three rhetorical modes has distinct characteristics that can be learned in order to successfully reach an audience.
- Speakers should take special care not to mislead an audience.
- When topics are controversial, speakers should be open about the issue and foster a clear sense of togetherness to lessen the potential for a negative audience reaction.
- Groups have five main stages of development: forming, storming, norming, performing, and adjourning/mourning.

REFERENCES

Beebe, S., Beebe, S., & Ivy, D. K. (2009). *Communication: Principles for a lifetime: Vol. 4. Presentational speaking* (portable ed.). Needham Heights, MA: Allyn & Bacon/Pearson Education.

Brenner, D. M. (2007). *Move the world: Persuade your audience, change minds and achieve goals.* New York, NY: John Wiley & Sons.

Brignall, M. (2007). Describing the transactional communications model. Retrieved from http://www.wisc-online.com/objects/ViewObject.aspx?ID=oic100

Capp, G., Capp, C., & Capp, G. R. (1990). *Basic oral communication* (5th ed.). Englewood Cliffs, NJ: Prentice-Hall.

Cherney, L. R. (2005). Communication. In G. Albecht (Ed.), *Encyclopedia of disability* (Vol. 1, pp. 279–282). Thousand Oaks, CA: Sage.

Christians, C. G. (2007). Communication ethics. In *Encyclopedia of science, technology and ethics.* Farmington Hills, MI: Gale Cengage (Macmillan Reference).

Communication; Nonverbal communication. (2008). In *International encyclopedia of the social sciences* (2nd ed.). Farmington Hills, MI: Gale Cengage (Macmillan Reference).

Communication channels; Speaking skills in business. (2007). In *Encyclopedia of business and finance* (2nd ed.). Farmington Hills, MI: Gale Cengage (Macmillan Reference).

Dellinger, S., & Deane, B. (1980). *Communicating effectively: A complete guide to better managing.* Radnor, PA: Chilton Book Company.

Duckworth, C., & Frost, R. (2008). Noise pollution. In *Gale encyclopedia of science* (Vol. 4). Farmington Hills, MI: Gale Cengage (Macmillan Reference).

Hargrave, J. (2007). Listening skills in business. *Encyclopedia of business and finance* (2nd ed.). Farmington Hills, MI: Gale Cengage (Macmillan Reference).

Harris, T., & Sherblom, J. (2011). *Small group and team communication* (5th ed.). Needham Heights, MA: Allyn & Bacon/Pearson Education.

Headrick, D. (2005). Communication overview. In *Berkshire encyclopedia of world history.* Retrieved from http://www.scribd.com/doc/36159228/Ency-of-World-Hist

Hu Y., & Sundar, S. (2007). Computer-mediated communication (CMC). In J. J. Arnett (Ed.), *Encyclopedia of children, adolescents, and the media* (pp. 200–202). Thousand Oaks, CA: Sage.

King, L., & Gilbert, B. (1994). *How to talk to anyone, anytime, anywhere: The secrets of good communication.* New York, NY: Crown/Three Rivers Press/Random House.

Liepmann, L. (1984). *Winning connections: A program for on-target business communication.* Indianapolis, IN: Bobbs-Merrill Press.

LoCicero, J. (2007). *Business communication.* Cincinnati, OH: Adams Media (F+W).

Lucas, S. E. (1998). *The art of public speaking.* New York, NY: McGraw-Hill.

Merrier, P. (2006). *Business communication.* Cincinnati, OH: Thomson South-Western College Publishing.

O'Neil, S., Evans, J., & Bigley, H. (2007). Communications in business. In *Encyclopedia of business and finance* (2nd ed.). Farmington Hills, MI: Gale Cengage (Macmillan Reference).

Oberg, B.C. (2003). *Interpersonal communication: An introduction to human interaction.* Colorado Springs, CO: Meriwether.

Reardon, K., & Christopher, N. (2010). *Comebacks at work.* New York, NY: HarperBusiness.

Ross, R. (1983). *Speech communication: Fundamentals and practice.* Englewood Cliffs, NJ: Prentice-Hall.

Rothwell, J. D. (2009). *In mixed company: Communicating in small groups and teams* (7th ed.). Farmington Hills, MI: Gale Cengage (Thomson Wadsworth).

Simmons, A. (2007). *Whoever tells the best story wins.* New York, NY: Amacom Press.

Verderber, R., F., Verderber, K. S., & Sellnow, D. (2009). *Communicate!* (13th ed.). Retrieved from http://www.cengagebrain.com/shop/content/verderber36403_1439036403_01.01_toc.pdf

Windley, C., & Skinner, M. (2007). Selecting a topic. University of Idaho. Retrieved from http://www.class.uidaho.edu/comm101/chapters/selecting_topic/selecting_topic_printable.htm

CHAPTER

13

Topics and Research

Alberto is enrolled in a course about Africa. His instructor has assigned each student to create a hypothetical multinational textile manufacturing company and to choose the best countries in Africa to set up locations for the business. Alberto selects 15 African nations and collects information about population, natural resources, unemployment rates, literacy levels, languages spoken, access to airports, and primary energy sources for each of them.

Alberto researches professional journal articles about conducting business in Africa, reviews websites from non-profit organizations working in African nations, and consults recent books by experts in international business. He finds an article on the Internet about starting a business in Ghana, but quickly realizes that the site is only trying to sell a book—so he deletes that information from his notes.

Alberto wants to do a thorough job and impress his audience as well as the instructor, but Alberto quickly realizes that it will take at least an hour to present all of the information he gathered. He has only 15 minutes to speak.

He realizes that he has too much ground to cover; doing so would risk losing the interest of his audience. Alberto must narrow down his topic. He takes a second look through his list of countries and all of the information he has gathered. Ultimately, he decides to limit his discussion to the three best African countries for starting a multinational textile manufacturing corporation. He does this by comparing those countries with two other nations that would not be good choices.

His speech is now a much more manageable size and scope. It can be covered in the allotted time and will keep his audience focused and interested. Alberto also plans to ask the audience to add their own ideas in response to the information he presents as a method of involving them in his presentation.

KEY CONCEPTS

1. Speakers must carefully choose topics that will engage listeners. See page 172.

2. The setting for a speech can affect what topic a speaker should choose. See page 173.

3. Be aware of special considerations for choosing a topic in a cross-cultural situation. See page 176.

4. Brainstorming is one technique for finding a speech topic. See page 177.

5. Speakers must properly research outside sources of information and cite all sources used. See page 178.

DEVELOPING A TOPIC

Audience Analysis

Who will be in your audience? The answer to this question will help you determine what information to research and how to present your findings. The tone and focus of your speech may depend on, for example, whether your audience includes classmates, instructors, supervisors, or colleagues.

Your communication goals are also likely to be different if you are presenting to a coworker, a client, or a potential customer. The demographics of a group also may inform your preparations. What will the audience's age range and level of experience with the topic be? What values and attitudes should you consider in order to reach audience members successfully? Is English the first language of most of your audience members?

Giving thought to the needs of your audience will help you select your sources. Think carefully about what your listeners will consider to be credible evidence and what they may not consider to be valid. Which organizations and publications are most often referred to and used by the audience? For example, if you are presenting to a group of doctors about new innovations in treating a particular disease, they will likely expect you to use medical journals as your sources. If you are talking to a group of high school students about the same topic, they will likely have less rigorous standards.

Once you have given some thought to the makeup of your audience, you can use this information to make decisions about what to say and how to say it. A speaker must have a clear sense of whether the purpose of his or her presentation is self-expressive, informative, or persuasive. Has the audience gathered to hear you speak about your personal experiences in the workplace? Is the audience hoping to learn something of value? Are you hoping to change the mindset of your audience so that they take a certain action such as buying your product or joining an environmental foundation?

You analyze your audience ahead of time so you will know how to make your speech as effective as possible. Once the analysis is complete, you can figure out how to connect with your audience and establish common ground. The following are a few effective ways to keep an audience engaged and get your message across:

- Speaking the same language as your audience, which means keeping the discussion focused, relevant, and specifically aimed at the audience's level of understanding.
- Using the jargon of the field only if the audience is familiar with it (and avoiding jargon if it is not).

- Watching what you say, so listeners are not offended by your presentation.
- Involving your audience in the presentation.

Analyzing your audience will enable you to communicate effectively with your audience through the use of such elements as concrete scenarios, activities involving props, and role-playing scenarios. Without the perspective you will gain from audience analysis, these strategies may not be possible.

Situation Analysis

Situation analysis involves consideration of both the abstract situation and the physical conditions of the speech. Speakers should keep in mind why this group of people has come together and the **context**, or the circumstances, of the event. Is it a group of classmates or coworkers who have gathered to hear a presentation on something of internal interest to the group, or is it a group of strangers who are attending a professional conference with the goal of learning new information they can take back to their respective organizations?

Often, speakers forget the importance of considering the physical location of their presentation. If you are not familiar with the actual physical space you will be using, make arrangements to see it and familiarize yourself with it prior to the speech. You should practice using the technology that will be available to you (for example, an overhead projector) well before the presentation is actually held. You should also ask key questions of the person who has assigned the presentation, such as:

- "Who, if anyone, will be available to assist me with the presentation?"
- "Does the room have any audio equipment, such as a microphone and speakers?"
- "How long is the room reserved for?"
- "How soon will I be able to access the room before the presentation?"
- "Will I have some time after the presentation to either entertain questions or dismantle my setup?"

Once you are able to see the room, carefully observe the seating arrangement. Round tables are more conducive to group activities than straight rows of rectangular tables. Will you be restricted to a stage? Is there a podium? Do you want to stand before the audience, or would you prefer to walk among it? Will people in the back of the room be able to hear and see you clearly? All of this information will help you better prepare for your speech.

The end goal of familiarizing yourself with the setting of your presentation is to figure out how to use the surroundings to your advantage. You may want to consider greeting attendees as they walk into the room. Why not make a connection with your audience from the moment they set foot into your space? Getting a sense of the layout of the presentation space will allow you to plan this sort of strategy ahead of time.

Topics for Informative Speeches

The key to choosing a good **topic**, or subject, for an informative speech is to remember the basic purpose of this type of presentation: explaining something to audience members that they need or will want to know. Your topic is the broad area of information that your speech addresses. It is different from the speech's **theme**, or purpose. The theme explains to your audience what they need to know most about that topic. Your topic might be *recycling*, for example, but your theme might explain *how recycling programs can benefit a community*. The topic is the general area of information, and the theme is the message you wish to convey.

If you have the freedom to choose a subject for a presentation, start by listing the topics you know best. Consider jobs you have had, activities you enjoy, and any personal interests. As a secondary factor, take a second look at the list once it is finished and note how many of the items on it are unusual. While you are still responsible for making your speech engaging, no matter what the topic, unusual topics can help grab the attention of audience members. You may, for example, be very familiar with a social networking website that is not widely used by your colleagues. Your prior knowledge about this subject and the novelty of the topic to your coworkers are the foundation of a successful speech.

Along with your own **expertise**, or your skill or knowledge in a particular area, consider the interests, needs, values, and attitudes of your audience. Choosing a topic that you suspect will be useful and informational to your audience members is always a good idea. The most effective informational speakers find a way to access the prior knowledge of their audience and expand it through engaging and clear explanation.

Assessing the needs and attitudes of your audience provides you with information that can help you pick a prudent topic. To continue the previous example, imagine your coworkers do not use social networking because they do not understand its potential value as a marketing tool. By educating your audience about a topic that is unfamiliar to them and directly explaining how it can be useful to them, you are likely to get and hold their attention for the entire speech.

Before you select your final topic, also give some thought to the specific situation and setting of your presentation. You may have to adjust your topic depending on the length of time you are allotted, or you may need to adjust your approach depending on the layout of the room and what technology is available.

Choosing the most effective mode for relaying information to your audience is also a critical element to presenting your speech. The manner in which you present information about a new inventory process will likely be different from the manner in which you present information about a new corporate logo. The inventory process depends heavily on detailed steps, while the logo depends on visual images. The subject and the delivery of your speech should be related.

Topics for Persuasive Speeches

The process of preparing for a persuasive speech is similar to the process of preparing for an informative speech. The desired goal, however, is different: Instead of presenting information about a topic, you are trying to change your audience's

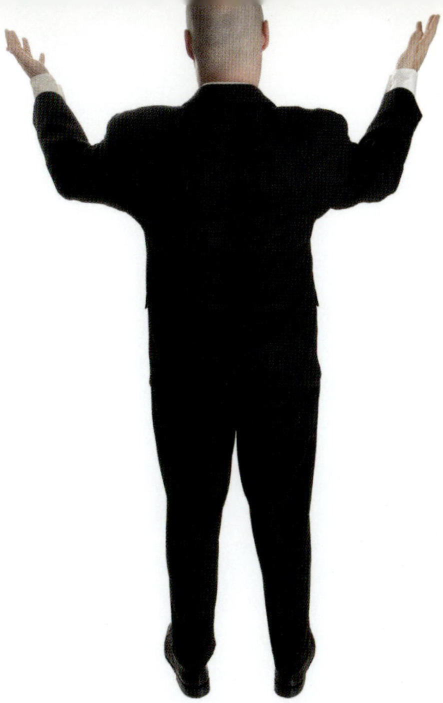

opinions or beliefs, and sometimes you are trying to motivate your audience to take action.

To generate a list of topic ideas, think carefully about what bothers you. Are you feeling frustrated that your coworkers worry about low sales while they also refuse to be innovative with technology or social networking? These critical feelings can be the catalyst for a good, persuasive speech. They can help you speak to your listeners with more sincerity and passion.

Persuasive speeches often address a problem in your workplace or community. A persuasive speech should describe the details of this problem, but the focus of your speech should be the ways to prevent or solve the issue at hand. The content should never focus entirely on problems, because it is difficult to persuade or motivate people with complaints or a negative tone. Emphasize the "this is what we need to do" portion of the presentation, which should include broad ideas, but should also clarify why your solution is achievable. People will pay attention to speeches that bring up creative and innovative solutions.

When choosing a topic, remember that the audience of a persuasive speech may respond differently than the audience of a self-expressive or informative speech. A speech about how new technologies like social networking can drive sales may be met with apathy or even resistance. Choose a topic and present it in such a way that will allow you to connect quickly with listeners. Do you think they share your same frustrations? An effective persuasive speech demands that you find some common ground with your audience. Keep in mind that you could choose a **status quo** topic, which would argue for the situation in question to stay the same.

Avoid a common pitfall with persuasive speeches: Do not try to persuade an audience about something that cannot be argued in a rational, defensible way. You cannot develop a good persuasive speech on a topic like "apples are better than pears." Such a topic is vague and a matter of personal preference. A more appropriate aim for a persuasive speech might be convincing an audience that the cafeteria should make organic fruit available. This topic brings up issues that can be reasoned and supported with arguments.

Occasions for persuasive speaking generally occur when people have differing opinions about how to solve a problem. This means that persuasive speeches are always confrontational, at least to some degree. Keep this in mind when you choose a topic for a speech. Speakers cannot shy away from confronting people, so choose a topic that you feel passionate enough about to defend it. Also, give some thought to what the other opinions about the issue are ahead of time and be ready to address them. You may even want to incorporate some of these counterpoint ideas into your own speech. Acknowledging different perspectives can help alleviate potential resistance from listeners.

Choosing a Topic That Is Familiar

Choosing a familiar topic for your speech has its advantages. You will feel more comfortable and confident if you are speaking about a familiar topic. If you are speaking about something that you already know a lot about, you will not need to worry about forgetting key information or the right words to discuss relevant ideas. You will also already have a wealth of experiences to draw on when listeners ask questions. If you select a topic that is also already somewhat familiar to your

audience, it will be easier to establish common ground with your listeners and get them invested in what you have to say.

Choosing a familiar topic also has its potential pitfalls. Often, people choose subjects for persuasive speeches because they have personal significance. It can be difficult to talk about something that brings up emotions—especially in front of a group of people. If your emotions get the better of you when you are giving a speech, the situation may be uncomfortable both for you and your audience. Worse yet, the addition of emotions may be counterproductive to your desired outcome. Even if you set aside your emotions for the speech, audience questions may trigger an unwanted emotional reaction.

By sticking to a topic that is familiar both to you and your audience, you also run the risk of failing to prepare and present an engaging speech. Most people do not want to listen to a speech that presents information that they already know. Novelty appeals to audiences—whether the novelty is in the topic, the perspective on the topic, or some other type of twist. A speaker who plays it too safe with a familiar topic runs the risk of boring the audience—never an effective means of persuasion.

In the end, the best approach is to choose a familiar topic that you are comfortable with and to take it in a new and interesting direction. Look at the topic from a different perspective and share that new perspective with your audience, or invite your audience to consider some cutting-edge research about the topic.

While you are preparing your speech, remember that your audience may have different background knowledge about a subject from your knowledge or research. What is familiar to you may not be familiar to your audience. But if you find something interesting and you present it with passion and thoughtfulness, your audience will likely find the information interesting and valuable as well.

Once you have a plan in place and your speech is written (see the section on research and citing sources later in this chapter), practice your speech by imagining that you are your own audience. Will you learn something new and valuable from what you share? What questions might the audience have?

COMMUNICATION ACROSS CULTURES

Cultural differences present additional considerations when choosing a speech topic. Many cultures, for example, consider horse meat to be a delicacy. The consumption of horse meat in Europe and Asia might be a perfectly fine topic for someone who hails from one of these cultures, but if the presentation is given to audience members from the United States, several audience adaptation issues will likely arise. Likewise, Americans might be surprised to learn that some other cultures believe that individualism is divisive and deters a sense of community. Knowing this, a speaker could build common ground by pointing out the shared values between the two cultures to encourage acknowledgement and acceptance of the differences and what each has to offer. This may open the door for learning more about each culture's unique perspective.

Pre-speech Strategies

How do speakers find engaging topics that their audiences will appreciate? Some use prewriting strategies designed to help them tap into their creativity to find original ideas and approaches. The key to all of these strategies is to let your thoughts flow onto paper so that none of your ideas are lost.

Avoid the temptation to evaluate or judge your ideas as you jot them down. Do not worry about structure, grammar, or mechanics. Just create and have fun, and you will be amazed at what you come up with. Finally, if one technique does not work for you, try another.

Brainstorming

During a brainstorming session, a speaker jots down anything—absolutely anything—that comes to mind. Brainstorming involves making a spontaneous list of ideas without evaluating them at all. Try brainstorming a list of ideas for your next speech by writing each idea down on an index card that can then be stacked and sorted in different arrangements, or on sticky notes that can be attached to a wall and rearranged in various sequences. This method can help you easily arrange the ideas and material for your speech.

Mindmapping

Mindmapping is a similar, but less organized, technique. A speaker jots down an idea in a circle in the center of a piece of paper, on a white board, or again on index cards or sticky notes. The goal is to add ideas to these ideas spontaneously, branching out in every direction, like a spider web, until the speaker can think of nothing else to add.

Once the ideas stop flowing, the speaker revisits the map he or she has made. At this point, it is time to sort the ideas out and choose the most creative topic, the best supporting points, and a preliminary arrangement of the discussion.

The Imaginary Dialogue Technique

In this technique, the speaker imagines having a dialogue with someone else in order to come up with ideas for speeches. Imagine a dialogue with a historical figure you will be speaking about for a history class, or a dialogue with your boss or coworkers. Imagining the speech will help you discover their wants, needs, and concerns in regard to the topic of your speech and the way you present it. Imagining a conversation with your audience is a great way to practice and to think of questions that your audience may have. This technique helps you to be better prepared and more confident.

Outlining

Once ideas have been generated, it is time to move the ideas to a more structured plan. Keep in mind that both informal and formal outlines may be useful, depending on your needs and preferences.

An informal outline may consist of the main point or message of your speech followed by a rough breakdown of the main supporting arguments. The main idea of a speech is the equivalent to a thesis statement for an academic paper. To generate the main supporting arguments of your speech, it is useful to ask yourself questions about your main idea, such as, "Why is this important?" or "What does this mean in the long term?" By asking yourself questions to outline a speech, you will be thinking in the same way that your listeners will be during the actual speech. It is a helpful method to think about your topic from different perspectives.

A formal outline (see Figure 13.1) consists of major sections (like paragraphs in an essay) indicated by Roman numerals (e.g., I, II, III, etc.), capital letters (A, B, C), Arabic numerals (1, 2, 3), and finally lower-case letters (a, b, c), each indicating the organization of the speech into main points, supporting statements, and supporting details. At each level, the outline should be indented, double-spaced, and written in complete sentences.

It is best to include two items or more on each level—if there is an *A*, there must be a *B*; if there is a *1*, then there must be a *2*, and so on. The logic behind this is that you are gradually breaking down a single idea into smaller, easier-to-understand pieces for your audience.

Topic: Climbing Mt. Hood
I. Why I chose to climb Mt. Hood
II. Background information about Mt. Hood
    A. Location of Mt. Hood
    B. Geography of the immediate area around Mt. Hood
    C. Facts about Mt. Hood
        1. Mt. Hood's height
        2. How Mt. Hood got its name
            a. Native American origin
            b. The origin of its current name
III. Mt. Hood and the local community
    A. Climbing accidents
    B. Hiking
    C. Economic effects
IV. Conclusion

FIGURE 13.1 **Sample Outline**

Outlines are useful for planning your speech and for guiding the creation of a Microsoft PowerPoint® presentation or other visual aids. An outline will keep your speech on track, too. Be sure you practice your speech enough so that you only need to glance at your outline—that way, you can keep your eyes focused on engaging your audience.

RESEARCH

Remember that especially in an academic or job-related situation, your audience will expect the information you present to be thorough, accurate, and credible. When the purpose of a speech is informational or persuasive, the research and sources you use to support your claims become vital to securing your audience's faith in your message. Conduct research carefully, using reliable, high-quality sources.

Ethics

Speakers must conduct and present research in a way that is ethical. **Ethics** refers to the moral principles that guide a person's conduct. It would be unethical, for example, to select and reference sources that only present one side of an issue. A responsible speech also includes sources that present alternative opinions, as opposing views must be analyzed and addressed in order to properly defend the speech's argument.

Likewise, research for any speech must be conducted ethically in order to avoid bias, which attentive audiences will be able to detect. When an audience does suspect that a presentation has bias or is based on irresponsible research, the speaker's credibility is compromised. Audience members will doubt all of the presentation's statements, no matter how true they may be.

Furthermore, credible sources must be used and cited. Speakers have the responsibility to weed through all sources to make sure that each one that is cited is well respected and legitimate. Imagine that you are preparing a speech on bile duct cancer research and find a website that says the cure has been found for this particular type of cancer. Before you cite the source, you must first establish its validity. If further investigation reveals that the site is selling a nutritional supplement that has shown no real evidence of curing the illness, the site is unreliable.

In addition to evaluating the credibility of a source, you have ethical obligations when it comes to citations. Careless decisions involving references can have serious implications on your professional career. Do not, for example, fabricate data or evidence, such as claiming that you interviewed someone you never met or that you read a resource you never actually investigated. As a rule of thumb, be truthful with your audience.

Carelessness should be avoided at all costs. Check and recheck that any direct quotations from a secondary source are reproduced exactly and faithfully. It is also unethical to omit key words from a source to manipulate the original meaning. For example, consider how the speaker's version below distorts the original source:

"This product is not the best on the market for the money." [Original source]

"This product is...the best on the market for the money." [Speaker's version]

One last note regarding sources: Always attribute credit where credit is due. Make sure you cite your sources accurately (see "Citing Sources" later in the chapter). If you obtain information from an interview or from unpublished notes, make sure to honor any requests that your sources make. For example:

- If a source identifies some information as being "off the record," honor that request and do not include the relevant details in your speech.
- Always be sure to treat your sources in a respectful manner, even if you do not agree with them.
- If someone helps you prepare your presentation, it is always appropriate to express your gratitude and acknowledge your thanks during your speech.

Your relationship with your audience depends directly on how you vet the references you use to prepare your presentation, how you cite the information you collect and share, and how you represent the information.

Selecting Sources

The Internet allows people all over the world to post and exchange information with one another rapidly. One result is an explosion of information available for easy access on any computer or mobile Internet-enabled device. Easy access is wonderful—but it means that responsible researchers must be vigilant, focused, and thoughtful.

It is very easy to search, find, download, and save newspaper and journal articles from the Internet; however, more sources do not automatically create a better speech. Resist the temptation to collect as many sources as possible, because a source will be useful only if you take the time to read it thoroughly and understand what you read. A few quality sources are much more valuable than many hastily collected ones. Consider the following strategies for successful research:

- Come up with a set of questions after completing the prewriting activities and planning your speech. Then, you can think of your research phase as a quest to find the answers to these questions. This will focus your research and keep you on track to give a thorough and supported speech.
- If you begin your search on the Internet, narrow your method of source research. There are many databases, such as ProQuest or EBSCO, that weed out sources that lack credibility. Databases are a bit like having a personal research assistant who has spent years sorting and organizing valuable academic sources into electronic file cabinets. If your speech examines new cancer research, for example, you can narrow a database search to include only articles published in medical journals during the last year—thus providing you with the latest, and most thoroughly vetted, information.

There are two general categories of sources: primary and secondary. **Primary sources** are original documents that were created by the person or people you are researching, or are directly about the topic. These include government records, interviews, journal articles, and other documentary artifacts. **Secondary sources** offer commentary or evaluation of the material from a primary source. These include encyclopedias, biographies, or magazine articles. A letter written by Thomas Jefferson is an example of a primary source; a biography about Thomas Jefferson is a secondary source.

It is always wise to choose a variety of sources. Different types of sources can lend different types of credibility to your speech. A book goes into more depth than an article in a professional journal, but books take longer to publish and distribute than journals, so a journal article will most likely be much more current. A personal interview with a cancer researcher or patient will yield even more current information and original insights than either a book or an article. Using a breadth of credible sources will strengthen your speech.

TECHNOLOGY AND RESEARCH

Technology should be used with care in the selection of scholarly sources. Consider using a specialized database such as EBSCO, which contains countless peer-reviewed journal articles that were written and reviewed by experts. Scholarly databases also offer users a variety of options to narrow and focus their search.

Evaluating Websites

Although all sources should be checked carefully for credibility, websites in particular should be thoroughly vetted. Anyone can post information on the Internet, whether it is true or not. Some websites even give the illusion of being credible but actually are not.

The last three letters of a **URL** (uniform resource locator) can be a good place to begin your evaluation of the legitimacy of a website. For example:

- Sites that end in *.com* or *.net* are commercial sites, and thus they typically should be avoided as sources for a presentation. Personal blogs, for example, fit into this category. Even if these websites post accurate information, they have not established credibility and are not worthwhile sources.
- Many *.edu* (education) sites contain accurate, well-documented information. However, many also contain materials that are not intended to be used as sources, such as blogs, class projects, informal discussions, and so on. They may be used with caution.
- Sites ending in *.org* are run by nonprofit organizations. They should be used with great caution.
- U.S. government sites with addresses ending in *.gov* (government) are considered credible. Although government sites are not always easy to navigate, the information they present is generally valuable and valid.

Regardless of the ending of its web address, you must carefully evaluate any Internet source. When considering a source, ask yourself the following questions:

- Can you find the names of those responsible for the site?
- What are their credentials?
- Are you able to contact them for more information?
- Is the contact information real?
- Do you see these names referenced in other sources?
- Has the site been updated recently?
- Does the site provide a comprehensive list of resources?

If you are able to answer all of these questions satisfactorily, the site is likely a worthy reference. Paying close attention to the credibility of all sources—especially websites—will improve the credibility of your own presentations.

Citing Sources

Whenever information is integrated into a speech that comes from a source other than the presenter's head, that information must be correctly cited. Lifting intellectual property from someone else's work without citing it adequately is immoral, unethical, and, in all cases, wrong.

Imagine that you worked for years on a significant finding, and after much effort and many obstacles, you finally were able to publish an article about your research. In that context, the mere thought of someone else claiming your work as his or her own is sure to bother you. Stealing wording or ideas from sources is called **plagiarism,** and it is a serious offense that can have profound academic and/or professional consequences.

Although it may seem tedious to document sources, doing so is expected in academic and professional communities. Sources act as support for your own arguments and beliefs. Imagine walking into the office of the president of your company and asking for a raise. Next, imagine walking into her office again—this time, with your immediate supervisor, who is ready to explain to the president why you deserve a raise. The supervisor in this case is serving the same purpose as a cited source in a speech: Having an authority on your side strengthens your message.

Your audience must be able to clearly see that you conducted ethical, unbiased research and that you fully considered all views and perspectives before settling upon your own. Knowing this will help them understand that just as you were fair to your sources, you will be fair to the audience. In addition, your audience may be interested enough in your speech to look up the full sources you used. The **citations** provide listeners with information of interest and a location where a source may be found.

Finally, sources may be documented using whichever style your organization prefers. Some style guides commonly used by schools include the Modern Language Association (MLA) and the American Psychological Association (APA). Regardless of the specific style, sources must be cited in the text where the information has been integrated into your speech, as well as at the end of the presentation on a *Works Cited* or *References* page. This last page should include the full citation for the work; the in-text citation is an abbreviated form of this showing the name or title (whichever comes first in the full citation) and the location of the information (for example, a page number). You can learn specifically how to format these in-text and bibliographical citations by using MLA or APA style guides, which can be found online or in a printed book.

slide 1

Format Picture ; Size ; Lock Aspect ratio

SUMMARY

- Analyzing the audience, situation, and purpose of a presentation can aid a speaker in choosing an effective topic that will engage listeners.
- Speakers should consider both the situation and the physical setting of a speech.
- Cross-cultural sensitivities should be considered when choosing a topic.
- Pre-speaking strategies can be useful for tapping into one's creativity.
- Information from outside sources must be properly found, shared with, and documented for listeners.

CHAPTER

14

Outlining

Alejandro has been in college for only a month, and his public speaking class instructor has just asked him to make an informative presentation in two weeks. Alejandro has dreaded this assignment. Already deeply afraid of getting up in front of others, he is also confused about how to organize his presentation.

KEY CONCEPTS

1. Outlining is an important part of planning a presentation. See page 186.

2. There are different types of outlines for different purposes. See page 190.

3. The patterns of organization can serve as formulas for arranging information in a speech. See page 186.

4. The principle of coordination and principle of subordination help keep information logically organized. See page 191.

Alejandro has chosen the topic of homelessness because as a teenager, he was homeless for more than a year. Alejandro wonders if he should explain how he became homeless first and then discuss how, with the help of some social services in his community, he started on the road to recovery. It took a lot of work and concentration, but eventually he found a job, a small and inexpensive apartment, and a grant for his education.

Alejandro also wonders if he should explain the wide variety of reasons why people find themselves homeless and discuss some of these programs that helped him. Because he is passionate about helping the homeless, Alejandro also considers the possibility of sharing some of the shortcomings of these programs.

As he sits back and considers all the ideas he has for his presentation, he feels that he does not know where to begin. How should all these points be organized? Should all of them be included in the presentation? Alejandro also wonders about how research fits into all of this. Isn't the presentation supposed to be about how *he* feels about homelessness, rather than about what other people think and feel about the topic?

ORGANIZING A PRESENTATION

Many people experience concerns similar to Alejandro's when faced with giving a presentation. Learning to plan effectively is one of the best ways to reduce the anxiety. Did you know there are some common formulas or **patterns of organization** to organize your speech effectively?

Patterns of Organization

There are four basic approaches to organizing the material for a speech:

- Definition
- Process
- Most to least important, least to most important
- General to specific or specific to general

Definition

One way for Alejandro to organize his presentation is by defining what it means to be homeless. It is easy to see how presenting a **definition**, a brief statement of what something is, can be an effective organizational pattern.

As he began to really think about organizing his presentation, Alejandro realized he should first clarify what it means to be homeless. Originally, he had thought that a homeless person was any person who was living in the streets with no place to go and no resources for help. However, after extensively researching the problem of homelessness, Alejandro discovered that the term *homeless* applies to anyone who does not have a permanent place to live. A person would be considered homeless even if he had a roof over his head every night, sleeping on a friend's couch or in the extra room at a relative's house.

Process

A speech based on a **process** tells the receivers *how* to do something. Alejandro might consider organizing his speech around the process of getting out of the situation of being homeless. He could begin his presentation with the low point in his experience—living on the streets. Then, he could explain how fear drove him to seek out a shelter. The next part of his presentation could explain the process of finding sources of food, clothing, and medical attention. Finally, Alejandro might discuss how he discovered a job retraining program that provided him with an income and place to live. Organizing a speech around a process means explaining the steps involved in how to do something.

Most to Least Important; Least to Most Important

Moving the discussion from the **most to least important** points is another viable organizational pattern. Alejandro would like his speech to include information about the demographics of homelessness. While researching the demographics on the Internet, Alejandro found a pie chart that showed most homeless people are single men, approximately a third are families with children, and a much smaller contingent are single women. An article he read discussed how many shelters only accepted women and children, and not men—even if a man was with his wife and children and there was no issue of abuse. As a result, some families choose to stay on the streets together to avoid being separated. Alejandro may decide to focus his discussion first on the largest group of homeless people, single men, and then move to the second largest group, and so on.

Later in his research, Alejandro also learned that the second largest group of homeless people included children and that the smallest group of homeless people was made up only of children. Although statistically speaking children made up less than a third of the homeless population, Alejandro could also organize his speech from **least to most important** because children are more vulnerable than adults and need the most help.

General to Specific; Specific to General

The information in a presentation can also be organized from general to specific or from specific to general. For example, Alejandro knows that people who are homeless often have issues with mental health, substance abuse, and employment. His research showed that approximately one-third of people who are homeless have problems with substance abuse, almost a full quarter of the homeless are mentally ill, and many other homeless people can only find extremely low-paying part- or full-time jobs—in fact, the pay is too low for them to afford housing.

Alejandro could share these statistics with his audience and then offer general conclusions about homelessness. He also considers that he could make the general statement first, and then back it up with the specific data.

Cause and Effect

Cause and effect is another excellent choice for organizing a presentation. Alejandro is of course curious about the causes of homelessness. He has learned during his research that the two most common causes of homelessness are a lack of affordable housing and low-paying jobs. Therefore, he reasons, the result, or effect, of homelessness most often stems from two causes: a lack of affordable housing and low-paying jobs. Alejandro believes his audience will be very interested in learning the hows and whys of homelessness.

Classification

Another common way to organize a speech is by classification. This means that the information is categorized, or classified, into groups that are logical. Alejandro might consider organizing his talk around groups of homeless people, such as those with mental health issues, those who are unemployed, or those who are single mothers. Then, he might discuss other groups, such as those who have substance abuse issues. The discussion of each of these categories of people who are homeless may shed light on the bigger problem of homelessness and how to address it.

Compare/Contrast

Alejandro wondered about some of the discrepancies in the information he found during his research. When he compared single men and women who were homeless, for example, he noticed a major discrepancy—there were more than twice as many single men who were homeless as single women. Alejandro thought this was an important finding. He wanted to compare the situations of men and women to

see how they were alike. Then he could contrast, or show how their situations were different. Alejandro wondered how the services for the homeless were the same for men and women and how they were different.

Any of the organizational patterns that Alejandro is considering could work well for an informational presentation, depending on the interests of his audience and his own interests.

The Attention-Getter

Perhaps you have heard the expression, "You never get a second chance to make a first impression." The first sentences you speak during a presentation should immediately engage your audience and guide them toward the main point of your presentation.

There are several approaches to consider. For example, you could start your speech with a short anecdote or story that illustrates the topic. If possible, you can refer to the anecdote or story later, at an appropriate point in your presentation.

Another technique that can be effective for engaging an audience is starting off with a question. Your audience members will naturally become involved in the presentation as they are challenged to think about an answer to the question or to share their answer aloud. Starting the speech with a question also helps the speaker focus on the topic.

Speakers must answer the questions they pose, of course, so the question-and-answer format can nicely bookend the content. For example, if you are giving a presentation on natural disasters, you might ask: Do you know what type of natural disaster is responsible for displacing the largest number of people from their homes around the world each year?

You might like to open your speech with some surprising information that your audience is unlikely to know but would be very interested to learn. For example, Alejandro found an article by researcher Eric Janszen that revealed the following facts:

- 15 percent of homeless people have full-time or part-time jobs.
- 88 percent of homeless people have been turned away from shelters at least once because the shelters do not have enough resources.

These are surprising statistics that will draw an audience's attention. If you locate statistics and information that surprise you, chances are good that your audience also will be surprised. You might consider opening your presentation with some humor. However, humor should be used carefully. Most people enjoy humor, so starting with something funny may be a good way to engage your audience members and relax them.

Finally, these techniques for getting the audience's attention may be combined. Alejandro could begin his presentation with a big smile and ask, "How many of you grew up dreaming of being homeless?" He could then follow that up with a lead into his own story: "Neither did I, but nonetheless I became homeless at the tender age of sixteen."

Introduction

In addition to an attention-getter, the beginning of a speech should include an introduction to the topic and also an introduction to the presenter. Alejandro, for example, may decide to share his own story as part of the attention-getter, and he may decide to narrow his presentation to the lack of resources available for people who are homeless—not only because a lack of resources is among the largest causes of homelessness, but also because it was his primary frustration when he was homeless. This device gives him instant credibility as someone who has first-hand experience with the topic.

The introduction should also preview the main points of the speech. For example, Alejandro learned that there are three main reasons for a lack of resources for people who are homeless:

- Lack of funding
- Lack of centralization of resources
- Lack of information about what resources exist in the community

Alejandro makes sure that he includes this brief list in the introduction.

Body

In the body of the presentation, the speaker expands the topic. The three main reasons Alejandro found for homelessness, for example, should be explained in more depth to the audience during the body of his presentation. One important note: A speaker should always follow the same order in the body of the presentation that is previewed in the introduction.

Distinguishing Main Points from Subpoints

In your presentation, you must be sure to identify several main points. Then, locate information that supports each main point. In other words, a clear distinction must be made between the three main points listed above and the supporting points or subpoints that help to prove them. For example, if Alejandro showed a map of where resources to help the homeless are scattered throughout the city, he would have this visual aid and discussion clearly located under his second main point: "lack of centralization of resources."

Support and Evidence

Although Alejandro's personal experience with homelessness is valid as a source, it must not stand alone. In an academic or professional context, an audience will expect more than just personal experience. They expect to see a variety of credible sources and evidence to support the main points.

Conclusion

To leave an audience with the feeling that they have truly benefited from a presentation, a speaker must ensure that he or she has ended the presentation effectively.

Some options include adding a clincher, referring to the attention-getter, or making a strong final statement as a takeaway.

Clincher

Speakers should try to insert a **clincher** at the end of a presentation. This is a statement, often factual, that definitively closes the topic. For Alejandro, an obvious clincher could be that homeless people could be helped by better facilitation of existing resources.

Reference to Attention-Getter

A good closing should also refer the audience to the attention-getter. The interest the attention-getter sparks in the beginning of the presentation should continue throughout the presentation. Tying the attention-getter back to the ending also completes the circle of information, thus providing an effective closing to the speech.

Strong Final Statement That the Audience Can Take Away with Them

Often, the clincher provides the strong closing statement; however, sometimes speakers will provide a last statement that is aimed directly at the audience. Alejandro, for example, might end his presentation by challenging his classmates to make donations to or volunteer their time at a local homeless shelter.

THE FORMAL OUTLINE

An **outline** is a summation of the parts of the speech that focuses on its structure rather than writing out word-for-word what the presenter intends to say. Outlines are often compared to maps because they are useful in helping speakers know where they are going. Outlines are also often considered to be the skeleton or structure upon which the body of a speech is built because they show the relationships among the main ideas and supporting details.

The first section of an outline provides the introduction, which includes a statement of the goal or purpose of the speech. It can be helpful to review the directions and expectations for an assignment if the speech is for a class. First, you should identify whether you are being asked to give an informative or a persuasive speech. Then, include a statement about the goal or purpose of the speech that indicates the speech is informative (or persuasive). For example, a persuasive speech might have the purpose of persuading your audience to buy the latest hybrid car from your company. Or an informative speech may have the purpose of educating the audience about hybrid cars. Including the purpose statement in the outline within the introduction will help you stay focused as you continue to develop the presentation.

Similarly, the context and audience should be carefully considered and noted in the purpose statement. The **context** refers both to the physical location (for example, a classroom or conference room) as well as to the feeling that exists or that the speaker wants to exist in the space. For example, classrooms and conference rooms can often be uninviting in their physical appearance. Can you create a statement in the introduction of your outline that will indicate how you will reverse this, fostering an inviting, friendly context? An additional statement in the

outline about who your audience is and what they need from the presentation also may be helpful.

The introduction section of the outline should include a statement about how you will lead into your presentation. What will the attention-getter be? How will you make that good first impression and set the presentation off in the right direction?

Finally, the introduction of the outline should contain its thesis statement. A **thesis statement** is a directly stated topic, typically containing a preview of the main points. Imagine that you are preparing a speech about the achievement gap between low-income and affluent students in the public education system of the United States. Your thesis statement might be, "There are three reasons students in low-income areas achieve lower test scores than students in affluent communities:

- teacher effectiveness,
- the quality and training of administrators, and
- family investment in student success."

This sentence directly states the topic (problems that cause an achievement gap between two different communities) and a preview of how this will be supported in the presentation (the three main issues).

After the introduction section, each of the main points should be outlined in its own section. In the outline for your speech about student success, each of the three main issues should be outlined in complete sentences including a **topic sentence** that summarizes and previews the main point of the section; **supporting sentences** that help provide proof or further explanation; and the **supporting details** that include the facts, statistics, and other pieces of evidence mostly from outside sources.

Finally, the outline should provide the structure of the conclusion. In a sentence, what will the clincher be? What will the final statement be? How will the audience be referred to the attention-getter?

Coordination in an Outline

When creating an outline, keep in mind the **principle of coordination**. This means that each main point is equal to the others in significance, breadth, and depth. Another way to think of this is to imagine balancing the main points. In your outline about school performance, each of the three main problems you identify—ineffective teachers, ineffective administrators, and uninvolved families—are equally important. Each point in the outline should also receive the same level of numbering or lettering (e.g., I., II., III.) to show visually that they are of equal importance.

Each Main Point Must Be Equal in Development and Importance

As each of these main points is explained in detail and evidence is added, each point must be developed equally and shown to be of equal importance. Your speech will not be as strong if it highlights one main point but does not adequately develop the others.

If, for example, you were to devote the majority of your speech about schools to a discussion of the problems that stem from families that are not invested in student learning, you would be sending a message to your audience that this factor is more important than the other two issues. By treating them all equally, however, your speech will be more balanced and will more effectively convey the complexity of the situation.

Subordination

As the content of the outline is developed with source information and more detailed explanations, the subpoints must be clearly indicated by labels (*A*, *B*, *1*, *2*, *a*, *b*, etc.) and indentation that demonstrate visually their subordinate, or lesser, position in the content. This is known as the **principle of subordination**. When used correctly, a reader will easily see that points *A* and *B* are subordinate to *I*; that *1* and *2* are subordinate to *B*; and that *a* and *b* are subordinate to *1* (See the sample outline in Figure 14.2.)

Use the Outline to Shorten or Lengthen a Presentation

One of the benefits to creating an outline for a presentation is that an outline allows you to calibrate the content with the length of time allotted for speaking. For example, it is possible you will have only ten minutes to give a presentation on a large topic, such as homelessness. Obviously, you cannot cover everything about this issue in ten minutes, so the outline can be helpful in narrowing the focus to fit the length. Consider using the outline to rehearse your presentation in front of a practice audience (perhaps a few family members or friends) to see how long it takes you to present the entire speech.

If your outline is too long for the time allotted, shorten it by choosing one of the main points, making it your topic, and expanding it into a full outline. You may also simply remove a main point and its subordinate points. Imagine that you are preparing a speech about Internet marketing. After preparing an outline for a speech that would be too long, you could focus on one specific main point, such as marketing using social media networks, and make that your topic. Finally, check the supporting details to see if any of those could be removed or reduced without harming the effectiveness of the speech.

The reverse is also true. Many people fear not having enough information for a presentation and that they will be standing in front of an audience with nothing to say. Keep in mind that the outline structure allows presenters to quickly recognize this weakness so they can add in another main point and expand it with subpoints, or include additional subpoints if a main point needs more support.

One good tip is to remember that in terms of logic, anytime something is broken, the break causes there to be at least two pieces of the thing. For example, if

you break your pencil, you will be holding at least two pieces. The same holds true for breaking down the ideas in an outline. For instance, suppose your speech about marketing with social media has three main points. Each of these should be broken down into at least two supporting sentences, which are in turn broken down into at least two supporting details. In an outline, if there is a Roman numeral "*I*," there must be a Roman numeral "*II*" If there is a capital letter "*A*," there must be a capital letter "*B*," and so on.

Each outline marker is followed by a single, grammatically correct sentence rather than a word, a phrase, a fragment, or a paragraph. For a full, formal outline, complete, grammatically correct sentences should be used. There should be no single words, phrases, or fragments. At the other extreme, there should not be any paragraphs, as the outline is not intended to represent word-for-word what a speaker intends to say to his or her audience.

Include sources, source citations, and a reference page. In addition to complete sentences, correct citations according to either MLA or APA style should be inserted into the outline whenever ideas borrowed from outside sources are included, regardless of whether the information is quoted directly. Figure 14.1 shows an MLA and an APA version from Alejandro's developing outline for his speech about homelessness.

MLA

"In 88 percent of the survey cities, emergency shelters may have turned away homeless families due to a lack of resources" (Janszen).

WORKS CITED

Janszen, Eric. "Ten Surprising Facts about the Homeless in the U.S." *iTulip.com*. iTulip, Inc. 7 July 2007. Web. 14 May 2011.

APA

Homeless shelters may not have been able to provide a place to stay for nearly 90% of the families who requested assistance (Janszen).

REFERENCES

Janszen, E. (2007, 7 July). Ten surprising facts about the homeless in the U.S. *iTulip.com*. Retrieved from http://www.itulip.com/forums/showthread.php/1672-Ten-Surprising-Facts-about-the-Homeless-in-the-US.

FIGURE 14.1 MLA and APA Citation Styles

THE BRIEF TOPIC OUTLINE

A formal outline is not the only type of outline that may be helpful. Often, a brief topic outline can be helpful, especially in the initial stages of planning for a speech when you are just trying to get your general ideas in place. The brief outline differs from the formal outline because it does not require complete sentences or the insertion of source information and documentation. The use of single words, phrases, and clauses is acceptable. See Figure 14.2.

The brief outline basically follows this format:

1. Tell them what you are going to say (introduction/preview).
2. Tell them (main points/share the information).
3. Tell them what you just said (conclusion/review).

I. Introduction: There may be three main issues with available resources to help the homeless: (1) lack of funding, (2) lack of centralization of resources, and (3) lack of information about what resources exist in the community.

II. Body

 A. Lack of funding

 B. Lack of centralization of resources

 C. Lack of information about what resources exist in the community

III. Conclusion: If local resources received better funding, were more centrally located, and were better publicized to those in need, homelessness could be greatly reduced locally.

FIGURE 14.2 A Brief Outline Example

Note that in Figure 14.2, Alejandro has expressed and organized his initial thoughts to help him solidify his topic more. If a speaker is feeling overwhelmed with planning a presentation, this is a helpful way to begin the process of planning. In fact, it is often recommended that speakers begin by jotting down what they already know about a topic and how the topic may be focused in an original way for the audience; then speakers should find the secondary source information to back up their ideas. This helps presenters from getting lost in their sources.

THE SPEAKER'S OUTLINE

Another type of helpful outline is known as the **speaker's outline**. This is an expansion of the brief outline above; however, it is designed to help the speaker remember some of the key aspects not only of the content, but also of the delivery. It can be similar to the stage directions given to actors within their scripts, reminding them what to do as they deliver their lines.

Figure 14.3 shows the basic outline Alejandro developed in Figure 14.2 modified into a speaker's outline. Armed with the outline shown in Figure 14.3, Alejandro probably will not forget anything, and he will most likely have a successful presentation.

I. [Check to make sure the presentation is showing up on the screen and that I am able to move through the slides. Be sure to smile and make eye contact with everyone in the room as the initial question is asked: "How many of you dream about being homeless?"]

Briefly explain how I became homeless and how finding and getting to the available resources was a hindrance to my getting out of this terrible situation. Define 'homeless.'

[Change to the first slide.]

Introduction: There may be three main reasons that there are issues with available resources to help the homeless: (1) lack of funding, (2) lack of centralization of resources, and (3) lack of information about what resources exist in the community.

[Change to the next slide.]

II. Body

A. Lack of funding

1. Clarify the types of funding/in-kind gifts.
2. [Change to the next slide.] Discuss the needs vs. available funds chart.
3. [Change to the next slide.] Explain the effects on the local homeless.
4. [Change to the next slide.] Share my experience and how it felt to be turned away from a shelter.
5. [Change to the next slide.] Explain the ways classmates can help.
6. [Change to the next slide.] Emphasize the point on this slide that homelessness can be ended in our local community if everyone pitches in a little.

[Pause here to see if there are any questions. Make eye contact with everyone briefly.]
[Change to the next slide.]

B. Lack of centralization of resources

1. Show the locations of various existing support services in our community on the map. Be sure to ask a few people how they would get from one place to the other without money or transportation. Discuss how a family with kids would do this.
2. [Change to the next slide.] Show the map of nearby Anytown and explain how all the resources to help those in need are centrally located. Connect to my story and how much easier it would have been had I lived in Anytown.

[Pause here to see if there are any questions. Make eye contact with everyone briefly.]
[Change to the next slide.]

C. Lack of information about what resources exist in the community

1. Go through the questions about where to find resources for specific needs to see if the audience knows where to find them and how to apply.
2. [Change to the next slide.] Explain how with 20/20 hindsight, I would know where to go and how to apply now and how much more quickly I could have gotten the help I needed.
3. [Change to the next slide.] Discuss the slide data and comments from a few other homeless people regarding the need for better publicity for resources.

III. Conclusion: If local resources received better funding, were more centrally located, and were better publicized to those in need, homelessness could be greatly reduced locally. [Pause to see if there are any questions. Make eye contact and pass out the flyers with information on how and where they may help out or find services if needed. Be sure to thank everyone.]

FIGURE 14.3 **Speaker's Outline Example**

THE ROUGH OUTLINE

A rough outline is a type of brainstorming activity to help you get the ideas in your head onto your paper. In addition to the main sections of telling your audience what you are going to tell them, telling them, and reviewing what you just told them in the introduction, body, and conclusion, you would also think about possible supporting ideas, your audience, purpose, and context. Alejandro's rough outline might resemble the one shown in Figure 14.4.

Audience: Public speaking classmates and professor, probably sympathetic to homelessness though they may not have experienced it.

Purpose: The purpose is to inform the class that the homeless could be helped by people sharing unused or underutilized stuff they have around their houses, by people sharing talents they may have that could help the homeless (for example, resume writing), and by publicizing the available resources and making them more accessible to the homeless.

Context: The classroom. There will be an overhead to show my slideshow from my laptop using the college's wireless network, but I should test this in advance and have a backup plan in case the wireless Internet or my slideshow doesn't work.

I. Introduction: Three reasons that there are issues with available resources to help the homeless: lack of funding, lack of centralization of resources, and lack of information about what resources exist in the community. Not sure if this is the right order. Consider reversing the order of the main points.

II. Body
   A. Lack of funding
   B. Lack of centralization of resources
   C. Lack of information about what resources exist in the community

III. Conclusion: If local resources received better funding, were more centrally located, and were better publicized to those in need, homelessness could be greatly reduced.

FIGURE 14.4 Rough Outline Example

THE SENTENCE OUTLINE

In a sentence outline, each heading and subheading is expressed as a complete sentence. This type of outline is usually more fully developed than a brief topic outline or a rough outline; however, you can use these outlines as the basis for a sentence outline. Alejandro's sentence outline might resemble the one shown in Figure 14.5.

I. Introduction: There are three main issues with available resources to help the homeless: a lack of funding, a lack of centralization of resources, and a lack of information about what resources exist in the community.
II. Body
   A. The current lack of funding has a significant impact on the local homeless community.
   B. Support services need to be centrally located to increase accessibility to the local homeless community.
   C. Information about what resources are available in the community needs to be made readily available.
III. Conclusion: If local resources received better funding, were more centrally located, and were better publicized to those in need, homelessness could be greatly reduced locally.

FIGURE 14.5 Sentence Outline Example

Note that in Figure 14.5, Alejandro has expressed all of his main points and supporting details as complete sentences.

SUMMARY

- Various types of outlines exist to help presenters create, plan, review, and deliver a presentation.
- Presenters can make use of existing patterns of organization to effectively and efficiently arrange content.
- The principle of coordination and the principle of subordination not only can help keep information organized, they also can be used to help identify strengths and weaknesses in content.

REFERENCE

Janszen, E. (2007, July 7). Ten surprising facts about the homeless in the U.S. Retrieved from http://www.itulip.com/forums/showthread.php/1672-Ten-Surprising-Facts-about-the-Homeless-in-the-US

CHAPTER

15

Visual Aids

KEY CONCEPTS

1. Graphics and images may enhance presentations. See page 200.

2. Whiteboards can be used to create visual presentations. See page 205.

3. Style is important when creating visual aids. See page 206.

4. There are important rules to follow when using materials that were written or created by someone else. Choose an appropriate type of alternative presentation software to use when creating visual aids. See page 204.

Beatrix recently finished an internship as a teacher's aide at an elementary school. On her last day, the teacher she worked with asked her to create a presentation about her internship for the next group of incoming aides. Of course, Beatrix wants the presentation to be interesting, but just thinking about giving a presentation makes Beatrix nervous.

She is worried because of the outcome of the last speech she gave. Back in high school, she did a presentation about a foundation dedicated to protecting whales. It did not go well. Even her friends in the audience giggled when she realized—midway through the presentation—that she had forgotten to bring the photos of whales and printouts of charts showing whale populations around the world.

This time, she has resolved to be prepared. First, Beatrix writes the main points of her speech on a whiteboard. She also brings along her laptop, onto which she has placed many photos of her working with the children in her class. She has also used software to label each photo with a caption that draws attention to the most important elements of each picture. Last, she visits the teacher the day before the presentation to receive training on using the projector that she can hook up to her laptop to show the photos.

GRAPHICS AND IMAGES

Charts

Enter just about any classroom or a conference room, and you are likely to see charts. **Charts** are graphics that visually convey information to an audience. Whether displayed on a poster board, an overhead projector, or a computer, they have the potential to communicate a lot of information in a concise and effective manner. Charts can come in a variety of shapes and sizes, but all charts should be clearly labeled and easy to read. Some common uses include clarifying a process and explaining difficult terminology.

There are different types of charts. One type is the **organizational chart**, which shows the structure of a company or organization. It reveals the hierarchy of the staff and it shows who reports to whom. An organization chart for a large company, for example, might indicate the relationships among the president and high-level staff, the board of directors, the different divisions, managerial levels, and all branches of the company. In addition to corporate organizational charts, there can be similar charts for divisions of government, volunteer groups, or student organizations and committees. An organizational chart is an effective way to succinctly show how all the parts that make up the whole of an organization relate to one another. Describing all of this information verbally might prove complicated, so displaying the information visually in a chart can be helpful for your audience.

Imagine a student who is planning a speech about college athletic conferences. In one part of her speech, the student wishes to discuss how some universities have belonged to different conferences at different times. A well-crafted organizational chart would help the audience visualize the makeup of the different conferences.

A **flip chart** is a visual aid that is useful for showing a series of pictures, words, or diagrams that need to be shown in order, one visual at a time. Flip charts are usually large pads of paper that can be set up on an easel. They are practical because they do not require electricity, they are portable, and they can be set up ahead of time. A flip chart can be helpful if you have a complicated subject requiring several illustrations, or if you want to emphasize one point at a time. This keeps the audience focused and helps them follow along with your verbal presentation. During your presentation, you can easily add information to the flip chart as it comes up, or you can color code information on the flip chart to make it even more accessible for your audience. Be cautious, however, as the flip chart requires the greatest amount of hands-on interaction for the speaker. Manipulating a flip chart can occupy too much of a speaker's attention, diverting away from the audience.

As with all visual aids, flip charts do have some qualities that pose potential problems. Flipping through numerous pages can be distracting, and you should be mindful of how many charts you create. Charts can be powerful tools for a speaker, but unless they are thoughtful and purposeful, they will detract from your message.

Simplicity is a necessary quality for an effective chart. Speakers often make the mistake of including too much information in a chart or presenting the information in such a way that is not readily intuitive or helpful for the audience. Technical information, such as medical data, has the potential to display especially well in charts, but always exercise caution—too much data on charts may become more of a hindrance than an aid.

Always take time to ensure your charts are user friendly. Weigh the advantages and disadvantages of using charts, and keep in mind that there are other visual aid options that will suit your needs if you decide charts may not be the right way to go. Once you have completed your charts, consult a coworker or a friend to get a second opinion about them. Practice talking about your charts before actually displaying them during your presentation.

Any time a presentation involves particularly complicated information, remember that not all audience members have the same amount of background knowledge on your topic. It is often useful to provide some brief context for your audience, so every person listening has the same minimum amount of prior knowledge. Charts also can meet this need.

Imagine that you are a financial aid counselor at a university. You are speaking to a group of high school students who are thinking about attending your school. You have assumed that the entire group is fairly familiar with the various types of financial aid that are available, but it does not occur to you that many of the students present have incorrectly figured that they are not qualified to receive financial aid. Those students tune out the presentation because they have always assumed that financial aid is not available for them. If you had led the presentation with a flip chart that showed each of the levels of family or individual income that do qualify for aid, and what types of aid are available for each of the levels, those students would have paid much more attention to the presentation.

Graphs

Graphs present numerical data in a visual form that helps audience members see similarities, differences, relationships, and trends. Like charts, graphs are only as helpful as they are well designed. Speakers must thoroughly understand their material and must think critically about the way to present relevant information.

There are three main types of graphs that speakers commonly use in presentations: line graphs, bar graphs, and pie or circle graphs. These different types of graphs each have qualities that make them useful for particular situations. **Line graphs** work well when you need to display developments, trends, or variances over time. For example, imagine that you are planning to deliver a speech about rising unemployment rates at a city council meeting. While practicing your speech, you decide that reading unemployment statistics aloud is not as effective as depicting them as an image. Therefore, you decide to use a line graph to explain how unemployment has risen during the past 20 years. Your graph would represent the past two decades with *years* on the horizontal axis and *unemployment percentages* on the vertical axis. Using such a graphic would make the rising rates of unemployment undeniably clear and would make your speech that much more effective.

A second type of graph, a **bar graph**, is used to compare amounts and quantities. The direct comparison of values is the principal purpose for bar graphs. Imagine that you are giving a speech about nutrition and you want to use a bar graph to demonstrate how different foods have different caloric levels. You will need to decide what foods to highlight and your graph will need a vertical and horizontal axis, along with a key. Calories will be on the vertical axis, and the foods you select will be listed on the horizontal axis. The graph's bars will each represent a different food's average caloric level, and the difference in the heights of the bars will demonstrate the relative differences in calorie content. Your audience members will be able to easily determine whether their perceptions of calorie content for different foods are accurate.

A **pie** or **circle graph** is helpful to show the relative proportions of parts of a whole. Imagine that you are giving a presentation about how much time a select group of your fellow students devote to studying, sitting in class, working at a job, or sleeping each day. You quickly find that the group you have surveyed spends quite a bit of time studying each day. You create a pie graph that shows the results of your research. Each piece of the pie—each activity— is assigned a different color. The pie chart emphasizes the amount of time students devote daily to studying in relation to their other activities.

Tables

Tables are columns of figures arranged in an order that helps audience members pick out specific information. Computer software, such as Microsoft Excel©, makes creating tables a straightforward task, but orderly, hand-drawn tables on a white-board, poster board, or transparency will also serve the same purpose.

As with any other visual aid, statistics and information in a table must be accurate and well organized. Statistics in particular can be easily misinterpreted. For this reason, you must always double-check the accuracy of any data in your table and make sure the statistics come from reputable sources.

Imagine that you are giving a presentation about the financial challenges of being a full-time student with a full-time job. You have only a few hours to create a visual aid for your speech, so you decide to break down your own monthly budget into a table and label each item. You add each dollar amount next to the name of the expense ("Rent, $700") and total all of the expenses at the bottom of the table. This table will make it possible for your audience to see what your expenses are, how much you spend on each of them, and what your total monthly costs are. Despite its simplicity, this table will be a powerful and useful tool for your presentation.

Diagrams and Maps

Diagrams are a specific type of graphics that show how the parts of a whole fit together or the order of steps you must follow to accomplish something. Diagrams vary in complexity; they may be simple organizational charts or complex illustrations of three-dimensional objects, such as the human heart. They can be created on a poster board or a transparency, but they are easiest to create on a computer. A visual aid should always enhance your presentation, so avoid including diagrams that are too complicated—they can distract audience members instead of helping them.

The goal of using a diagram is to help your audience understand pertinent information and to offer a visual in addition to your words. Some members of your audience may be able to pick up the important details of your speech just by listening, but others may appreciate a diagram, as it caters more to a visual learning style. Generally, you should use a diagram only to simplify and clarify your oral presentation. If it takes more than a few seconds to explain your diagram to your audience, then it may not be serving a useful purpose. Remember, clarity is always the most important goal when it comes to visual aids.

Visual aids are most effective when they convey information that is difficult to express verbally. Geographic information in particular is difficult to describe using words alone—a problem that makes **maps** ideal visual aids when the occasion for them arises. Maps come in a variety of formats, so spend some time thinking about what style will best serve your needs.

You can bring an actual map with you to the presentation, or you can quickly access a map on the Internet with the use of a computer. However, as with any other external source, you must follow fair use guidelines (see the Fair Use section later in the chapter) and cite your map thoroughly. It is unethical to copy a map from a website without providing adequate citation, so make sure that you follow all guidelines before transferring a map to a computer or transparency.

Imagine that you have been asked to give a presentation about a particular region in southern India. You want to discuss some of the geography associated with this region, so you decide to include a map as a visual aid. As you practice delivering his presentation, however, you realize that the map is too small for all of the students to see. You decide to figure out how large the map needs to be in order to allow students in the back of the room to easily see it and ask the college print shop to enlarge the map for you. (Because you have prepared your presentation well in advance, you are able to wait a couple of days for the map to be ready.) The map will allow your classmates to develop a better appreciation of the geography in southern India.

Photographs

Photographs naturally command an audience's attention. They are excellent visual aids when you want your audience to see exactly what you are verbally discussing. One of the challenges of including photographs in a presentation, however, is making them available for everyone to see. You can either enlarge the photograph or use a computer screen to project them, but it is generally *not* a good idea to bring a photograph to pass around to the audience. This can cause a real distraction both for you as the speaker and for the other members of the audience as the photo is passed from one person to the next. Print

or copy stores offer many helpful services for displaying images to groups, from creating an enlargement to producing slides that can be projected using an overhead projector. You can also include photos in a slideshow presentation using software such as Microsoft PowerPoint®. Whatever option you choose, make sure you use a photograph that is large enough for your entire audience to see. If it is too small, the visual aid will cause more trouble than it is worth. You must also make sure you follow fair use guidelines with photographs, just as you would with maps.

Imagine that you are giving a speech about adopting pets from animal shelters. You believe that showing pictures of pets in confinement may motivate your audience to adopt pets or volunteer at local shelters. You talk to the director of a local shelter and receive permission to use its website, which contains many photos of dogs and cats in their pens at the shelter, during the presentation. You project the photos directly from the website during the presentation so everyone can see.

Just as with any other presentation aid, there are certain drawbacks to using photos. You do not want to overwhelm your audience with too many pictures, but you want your audience to grasp the full effect. Remember: Sometimes, less is more. Many times, the speaking situation and topic will dictate how many pictures you should use during your presentation. You must also be sure that you have permission to use a specific picture, or that you cite where you found the picture. Copyright infringement and plagiarism are serious issues, and you are better off safe than sorry.

ENRICHING PRESENTATIONS WITH TECHNOLOGY

An audience can easily become overwhelmed by visual aids like diagrams, charts, and photographs. It is your responsibility to identify the needs of your audience members—and the best way to do it is by paying careful attention to their feedback. Does your audience seem bored or confused? Members of your audience may yawn or seem complacent. At other times, audience members may signal frustration through facial expressions and gestures—a signal that things are not going well. Successful speakers will adjust their speeches based on audience feedback. Focus on the necessary visual aids, and be prepared to skip some of them based on audience feedback or time limitations.

Visual Integrity

The following are several basic rules to follow when using visual aids:

- The focus should be on you, not the visual aid.
- Do not use any color or font that will be distracting (see the section "Visual Aid Style" for recommended styles).
- Use visual aids that will catch and hold your audience's attention, but make sure they are appropriate for your particular audience.
- Avoid using a visual aid that may be distasteful or offensive to your audience. If you plan on using nudity or graphic images, be prepared for the consequences of your judgment. If you have any concern that a visual aid may upset audience members, notify them prior to showing it.
- The visual aid must always clearly and concisely emphasize the topic.

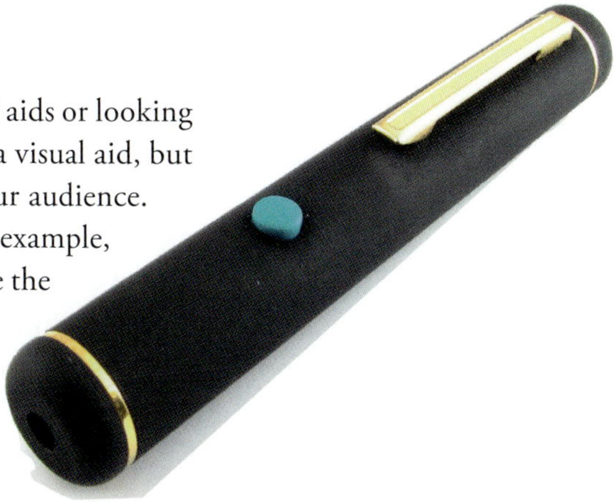

Many speakers make the mistake of reading from their visual aids or looking directly at them—a very bad habit. You can certainly glance at a visual aid, but do not stay focused on it at the expense of eye contact with your audience.

However, there are contexts where the opposite is true. For example, in sales and business environments, the visual is more likely to be the focus. Imagine the presentation of a new vehicle to the media, for example. The car itself will be the principal focus of the event.

In all presentations, however, you should maintain eye contact with the audience and speak directly to your listeners. Laser pointers can be especially effective when directing your audience's attention to a visual aid.

It is also your responsibility as a speaker to make sure that everyone in your audience can easily access the information provided in a visual aid. Perhaps some audience members have obstructed views or are seated in the back of the room. Therefore, it is very helpful to read aloud any captions on photos and graphs and generally describe each visual as you show it. Most rooms equipped with a projector are designed to allow all audience members to clearly see the screen, but do not assume everyone can.

A few additional tips to make the most of your visual aids:

- Make sure to conceal a visual aid until you are ready to use it. Many presenters do not conceal their visual aids when they are not referring to them, which can be distracting. The audience members should focus on your visual aid only when it is pertinent to the discussion. However, there are times when a visual may be available for viewing throughout your speech. For example, an outline of your main points written on a whiteboard may help the audience follow along as you speak.
- A visual aid should feature in a speech only if it serves a distinct purpose. Unless a visual aid is helping your audience in a meaningful way, it does not belong.
- There should be no elements of your visual aid that are not necessary to helping your audience access the relevant information. In other words, visual aids should be as simple as possible. Avoid cramming too much information into any one visual aid because this can take away from the core message you are attempting to communicate.
- Always be prepared for problems and have a backup plan. Any speaker can tell you about glitches experienced while presenting. Have you ever left your notes for a speech at home or on the bus? You may forget your visual aid on a speech day, or the technology in the room could malfunction. Consider bringing transparencies just in case the computer in the room is not working. Make sure that you leave your visual aid in a place you will not forget. Careful preparation will help you avoid any malfunctions that may occur during your presentation.

WHITEBOARDS

Teachers frequently use chalkboards and whiteboards because they are accessible and efficient. All you need is chalk or dry erase markers to create countless visuals for your audience. Whiteboards and chalkboards work particularly well for writing key phrases, drawing simple diagrams, or listing websites.

There are some disadvantages to using chalkboards or whiteboards, however. Writing or drawing on a whiteboard takes time during your speech, and writing on one generally means that your back will be turned to your audience—not ideal for engaging your listeners. The amount of time allotted for a presentation may thus suggest a more limited use of chalkboards or whiteboards.

Additionally, you should only write on chalkboards or whiteboards when you are comfortable writing legibly on a vertical surface. If your handwriting is difficult to read, consider using different visual aids.

VISUAL AID STYLE

Now that you are familiar with the types of visual support for presentations, it is time to consider the most effective ways of preparing these different types of visual aids. What is the best way to style a graph, a PowerPoint presentation, or a list of key points on a whiteboard? In order to make effective choices of style, you will need to make choices about typeface, color, and size.

Fonts

Ease of reading should be the ultimate goal of your typeface selection. Use strong, clean fonts, such as Arial, Helvetica, and Times New Roman. Ornate fonts are more difficult to read. Limit the number of fonts you use because too many types and varieties of fonts are distracting. Also use fonts that are large enough for all members of your audience to see. By adhering to these guidelines, you will create a professional-looking presentation that meets the needs of all of your audience.

Color and Contrast

Color makes graphics more attractive for the audience and makes it more likely for the listeners to retain information from the visual aid. Effective color organization can also make the subject matter easier to interpret.

Following are some useful guidelines to follow when using color in your visual aids:

- Choose colors that are professional and simple, and limit the number of colors you use in your presentation.
- When making a graph or chart, use as few colors as possible to avoid confusion and distraction.

- Colors should be clearly discernable and should contrast markedly with the colors next to them.
- Certain colors that are difficult to see (e.g., light yellow) should be avoided altogether, and similar colors (e.g., dark blue and black) should not be employed close to one another.

Color, like all other features of visual aids, should help your audience understand your message, and it is your responsibility as a presenter to make sure that the colors used in your visual aids do just that.

Size

Bigger is usually better when you are designing presentational aids. All of the members of your audience must be able to see the visual. Perform a test: Stand in the back of the room and look at the visual aid—can you see it clearly? If not, adjust the size of the type or the graphic.

White Space and Balance

White space is the area on a page or image that does not contain graphics, images, or writing. You may not think much about the white space on a page, but take a look at any book or magazine. Some pages will appear crowded and hard to read, other pages may feel clean and open with only a few lines of type or a simple graphic. The latter are easier to read and follow.

Clutter will distract your audience, so strive to make clean and balanced visuals. Center the graphic so that there are adequate margins surrounding it and refrain from including too much information in any one visual aid.

Simplicity

Keep It Simple, Students!—remember the acronym K.I.S.S. when you are creating visual aids. It will be easier for you to plan simple visuals, and your audience is less likely to get confused or distracted. Simplicity can go a long way to support your message and retain your audience's attention by making it easier to follow your presentation.

Consistency

Consider using one form of visual aid only—either a whiteboard, a flip chart, or computerized graphics. This will create a sense of continuity for the audience, and there will be fewer items for you to adjust during your presentation.

Also, try to keep the graphics themselves consistent. Use the same styling for titles, for example. All photographs should be close to the same size. Charts, graphs, and diagrams should be presented in a consistent way.

CAREER PERSPECTIVES

Will you need to use visual aids in your career? Many jobs require you to prepare visual presentations of some kind. It might be as simple as presenting your supervisor with a table that lists each of your projects, what has been accomplished, and the due dates for upcoming work.

Even when creating a simple graphic for a supervisor, keep it simple, consistent, and accurate. It is unlikely that a supervisor of clerks at a home goods store will expect the clerks to turn in multicolored tables with five different fonts that detail a weekly work schedule. Simple is best. A visual aid should enhance your presentation without becoming a distraction.

Many careers will require you to present material to peers or clients. Perhaps you are a sales manager and need to make a presentation to your salespeople about sales figures using a bar graph or a line graph. Or you might be a marketing assistant who needs to tell your manager how you plan to market the company's new product. In either case, be prepared to capture and hold your audience's attention. You might consider using a slideshow presentation, with each slide having the same background color and the title of your presentation, with no more than two main points per slide, in a font that is easy to read.

FAIR USE RULES

Fair use is a concept relating to copyright and the ownership of intellectual property. Every organization writes its own policy about fair use, including universities, colleges, and community colleges. Almost every organization has strict policies about plagiarism and copyright infringement. Students and employees must be familiar with the fair use rules that apply to them. Failure to adhere to fair use policies can have serious effects on your academic and professional careers.

Plagiarism is taking credit for someone else's work or stealing someone's intellectual property. As a responsible member of academia and the business world, you must document the sources you use and provide proper citation to anyone who reads or listens to your presentation. Your citations must be complete and thorough so your listeners can look up the information you consulted on their own.

In academic settings, the consequences for plagiarism range from a failing grade to expulsion. Direct quotations, no matter how short, as well as paraphrases from other sources must be cited and documented.

Never use copyrighted material without express consent. If you are ever not sure about the copyright status of a source, seek advice from someone else who might know—an instructor or supervisor, for example. If that is not an option, do not use the source. By adhering to a high standard of citing sources, you protect yourself against copyright infringement and you also bring more credibility to your presentation.

Your audience should be able to access the sources you use on their own based on the citation information you provide. For example, if you consult a website, provide the URL for the website as well as the date that you accessed the page. For print materials, provide author and title information, publication information (publisher's name, year, and place of publication), and page numbers.

Never use photos, movie clips, television show clips, songs, illustrations, or streaming online videos you find on the Internet during your presentations—these are copyrighted materials, and you will need permission to use them. Check with a knowledgeable person before you use any graphics or pictures.

ETHICS

You must be cautious about what you use as visual aids. You may, of course, use any personal photographs and diagrams or charts you create yourself. If you want to include a photograph from a book or magazine, you must obtain permission from the publisher or author to use it in your presentation, and you must state the source of the photograph either verbally or in the visual aid where the photo appears.

Providing source information also lets your audience know where they can access your information if they want to explore the topic further. Never show movie clips, play copyrighted music, or use television segments. The best advice is to not use something as a visual aid unless you are absolutely certain you have permission to do so.

ALTERNATIVE PRESENTATION SOFTWARE OPTIONS

Microsoft PowerPoint is probably the most common presentation software option available. You have probably seen PowerPoint presentations in your classes or at work; perhaps you have even created a PowerPoint presentation yourself. Presenters in workplaces frequently make use of this program to give speeches, and you will probably need to know how to create a PowerPoint presentation for your job.

As with any visual aid, there is a right way and a wrong way to use PowerPoint. Remember the primary guidelines of this chapter:

- Use large and clean fonts.
- Pay attention to color and contrast.
- Make no more than two primary points per slide.
- Make sure your presentation maintains the same level of consistency throughout.
- Avoid decorative clip art if it does not help the audience to understand the facts being discussed.

Other types of presentation software are discussed in the next sections.

SlideRocket

SlideRocket is an online presentation software package that allows users to import presentations or create their own. It is possible to import PowerPoint presentations into SlideRocket, but users should check compatibility with other presentation software.

You can use SlideRocket to make traditional slides, tables, charts, and diagrams, or use your own images and videos. SlideRocket is available online, so other people can also access it via the Internet and work on your presentation remotely, and you can monitor who has seen the presentation.

Google Docs

Google Docs, a free web-based service that is practical for students and professionals, works on both the PC and Macintosh platforms with the following browsers: Google Chrome, Safari, Firefox, and Internet Explorer© 8 and 9. It is similar to other alternative presentation software packages, but it is more economical since its features are free.

You can use Google Docs to create and store word processing documents, spreadsheets, and presentations. This web-based program allows users to edit Microsoft Office documents and share them. It is possible to work on the same document as another person remotely. For example, several members of the same group can work on the same presentation, regardless of their physical location. This is useful for collaborative projects, online courses, telecommuters, and companies where employees work from a variety of locations.

Prezi

Prezi differs from other web-based presentation software because its approach is different from PowerPoint. Prezi's creators wanted to design a presentation tool that illustrates their guiding philosophy: presentations should not be linear. Prezi offers a limited free service, but users must pay for additional options.

This Adobe Flash-based application allows users to zoom in and out, permitting them to emphasize certain areas of a presentation. Users can easily import images, text, videos, and other files. For example, if a student wants to use a map for her presentation about China, Prezi allows the student to display a clear visual map of China, and manipulate the map to emphasize the locations she is discussing (once she secures permission to use that map, of course). She can zoom in and out easily. In addition, the student can incorporate brief Adobe Flash files to enhance the presentation.

Captivate

Captivate is primarily useful for instructors and professionals who need to create e-learning content. However, it is less user-friendly than some of the other presentation software options—students may prefer Google Docs, SlideRocket, or Prezi, which were created for more mainstream use.

It is easy to create training and educational tools with Captivate, including demonstrations and interactive simulations. A teacher can create, store, and make course material public or private, all without needing to learn complex programming.

SUMMARY

- You should understand the different types of visual aids and how to use them.
- Style should be a consideration when designing and using visual aids.
- Fair use rules should never be violated. You must learn your institution's fair use guidelines.
- Presentation software packages can be very useful in planning and delivering effective presentations.

REFERENCES

Adobe Systems Incorporated. (2011). Adobe Captivate 5.5. Retrieved from http://www.adobe.com/products/captivate/

GoogleDocs. (n.d.). Retrieved from https://docs.google.com/

Grice, G. L., & Skinner, J. F. (2009). *Mastering public speaking* (7th ed.). Boston, MA: Allyn and Bacon.

Hybels, S., & Weaver, R. (2011). *Communicating effectively* (10th ed.). Boston, MA: McGraw-Hill.

Prezi. Retrieved from http://prezi.com/

SlideRocket. Retrieved from http://www.sliderocket.com/

CHAPTER

16

Productivity Software: Presentations

THE POWER OF PRESENTATIONS

Business professionals use presentation software to communicate data and information to an audience. Presentation software applications such as **Microsoft PowerPoint®** create attractive electronic slide shows of text, charts, and graphics.

An onscreen presentation visually echoes spoken information to clarify and reinforce concepts for an audience. That does not mean, of course, that the screen should be used as a teleprompter for the presenter to read aloud. Effective presentations capture an audience's attention and highlight important information. Effective presenters often use color, sound, video, and animation to do so.

PowerPoint slide shows are also popular because they can be shared electronically with those who cannot attend a presentation in person. In addition, PowerPoint includes features that allow the presentation to be printed and distributed as handouts. This way, the audience can follow along as the presenter talks about each section, including making their notes on the handouts and asking questions at the appropriate time.

Presentations can be timed to run automatically—for example, each time a CD is launched. They can be advanced with a remote control so that a presenter can move around during the presentation. They can even be set to repeat automatically on a continuous loop in a booth or kiosk location.

COMMON BUSINESS TASKS THAT USE POWERPOINT

PowerPoint is used in a variety of businesses where professionals need to present and share information. It is rare to attend a conference or a large meeting that does not include a presentation as an electronic representation of the speaker's main points.

PowerPoint is an important component of courtroom technology used by attorneys to present evidence to jurors during trials. Presentations help communicate technical evidence with charts and graphs in a format that is easy for jurors to understand. Law enforcement professionals might use PowerPoint for community programs, public safety education, or security training.

Health care providers might use PowerPoint for compliance training or for patient health education. Fashion designers might use PowerPoint to present their project plans to potential investors. IT professionals use PowerPoint to present training sessions to staff members usually intimidated by learning new software and concepts.

Business professionals use PowerPoint in many areas. Sales representatives and marketing and advertising professionals can present new product information to customers, company management can share company data and information with employees, and financial professionals use PowerPoint to present numerical data in meetings with company shareholders or clients.

PowerPoint is also popular outside the business world. For example, churches use it to present the music and lyrics of hymns to congregations. Videographers use it to add captions and music to picture slide shows.

As the saying goes, "A picture is worth a thousand words." The ability to reinforce a spoken presentation with appropriate, engaging visuals is a valuable skill anywhere your work takes you.

KEY CONCEPTS

1. The Power of Presentations
2. Common Business Tasks That Use PowerPoint
3. A Brief History of Presentation Application Software
4. PowerPoint Basics
5. Advanced Topics in PowerPoint

A BRIEF HISTORY OF PRESENTATION APPLICATION SOFTWARE

Before presentation software, pictures used in business presentations were often displayed with a slide projector or an overhead projector. Slide projectors held individual slides, each photographically developed and then manually sorted, arranged, and slotted into the projector. Typed or handwritten text and hand-drawn images were often projected with clear plastic sheets, called transparencies, laid on the lighted glass of an overhead projector.

The earliest presentation software was used by large graphics service companies to automate the production of slides—quite an expensive process. As PCs became more common and the popularity of PowerPoint grew, users began to develop their own presentations. Nonetheless, they still often relied on service companies for output, sending their PowerPoint files to be converted and returned as high-quality slides for a slide projector. Users with overhead projectors and access to laser printers printed their presentations directly to overhead transparency sheets.

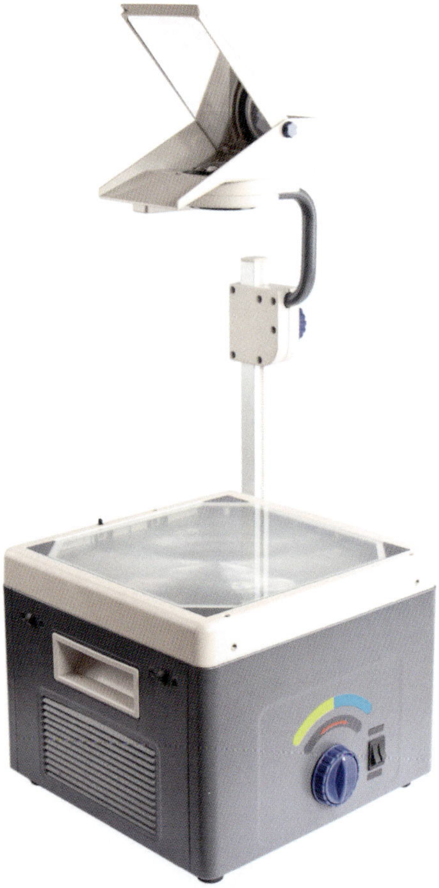

As video delivery technology evolved, slide and overhead projectors gave way to flat, LCD-based screens that were placed on overhead projectors as a replacement for transparency sheets. PowerPoint slide shows could then run directly from the application. These screens were eventually replaced by the sharper, more vivid display of video projectors, which were originally very expensive but gradually became more affordable.

The PowerPoint application as it exists today evolved from a software package called Presenter, which was developed in the mid-1980s, acquired by Microsoft in the late 1980s, and renamed and released for Windows in 1990. PowerPoint 2010, the most recent version of PowerPoint, was used to illustrate the concepts of presentation software in this chapter.

POWERPOINT BASICS

Planning a Presentation

Before creating a presentation in PowerPoint, consider the purpose of the presentation and the intended audience. Being clear about your target audience sets the tone and feel of the presentation and makes it easier to decide what visual elements and effects (sound, graphics, **animation, transitions,** and so on) to use. Next, identify the key points of the presentation and outline those on a sheet of paper. For example, if a college student named Marisa Abrogar makes a speech about becoming a lawyer, her information outline of this presentation might look something like Figure 16.1.

Title of speech: How to Become a Lawyer

Audience: College students who are interested in a law career

Main points:

Types of lawyers

- corporate
- entertainment
- matrimonial (marriage)
- criminal

What qualifications do you need to be a lawyer?

- law degree
- good research skills
- good analytical skills
- good communication skills
- personal traits (determination, persistence)

What is the process of becoming a lawyer?

- get into law school (make good grades, take the LSAT)
- get through law school (study hard, make good grades)
- pass the bar exam
- find a job

FIGURE 16.1 **Information Outline**

When you design a presentation, often called a **slide deck,** in PowerPoint, you must break up the information into manageable chunks for your audience. In the previous example, Marisa could choose to break up her outline so that each section appears as a page, or slide, to display for the audience. See Figure 16.2; the title slide is shown in the main frame, and on the left side, you can clearly see the other three slides that make up Marisa's presentation.

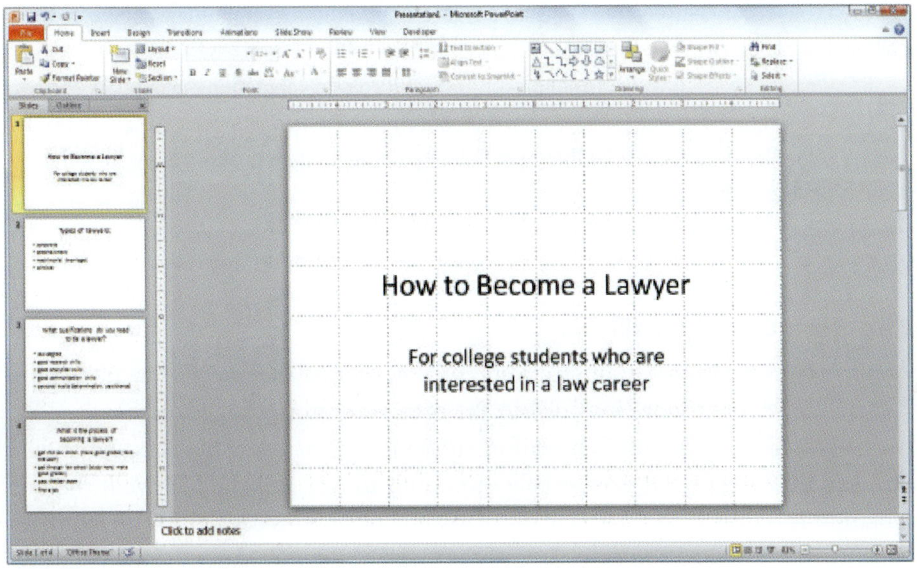

FIGURE 16.2

Design Guidelines

When you design visual presentations for an audience, certain design considerations will help you create successful presentations every time. The goal is to create a consistent, organized, and attractive presentation that audiences find pleasing and informative. The following are some conventional tips for designing visual presentations:

- **Minimize the number of different fonts used.** Typical presentations have one or two different fonts—a font for headings and a font for the body text. Use text enhancements, such as bold and italics, to emphasize other text.
- **Avoid font sizes smaller than 30 points.** Your audience members will not all sit in the front row. Smaller fonts are hard to see from a distance.
- **Use fewer than six bullets on each slide.** If you include more than six bullets on a slide, it will be too long and dense, and you may risk losing the audience. Pages are wider than they are long, so more than six bullets also makes the slide crowded and unappealing.
- **Avoid using paragraphs and long sentences.** Break information into a numbered or bulleted list, a few short phrases, or lists of key words. This is the best way to highlight important information for your audience without losing their attention while they try to read a slide.

INTERACTION DIVERSITY: IMPROVING READABILITY

One of the most significant benefits of PowerPoint is its ability to supplement the spoken word. One estimate suggests that one of every nine people in the U.S. workforce has some degree of hearing loss. By providing information in written form as well as the spoken word, you can help ensure that hearing-impaired listeners will not misunderstand or miss your point completely.

To improve the readability of a presentation for all members of your audience, make sure the font is large enough for even those with less-than-perfect eyesight to see from the farthest corner of the room. Choose simple and clear fonts, and avoid novelty fonts with excessive ornamentation.

Reserve the use of uppercase letters for short lines of just a few words, as research has shown a connection between reading speed and recognizing the overall shapes of words that contain both uppercase and lowercase letters used together.

Be sure your slides provide maximum contrast with color combinations, using dark shades on a light background or light shades on a dark background. When you are selecting background colors, be sure to consider the room lighting—light on dark is only successful if the room is dark as well.

File Size Considerations

Another consideration for an electronic presentation is the overall size of the file. Generally, the more slides included in the presentation, the larger the file size. The use of graphics, sound, and animation substantially increases file size and should be taken into account. It is especially important to consider the file size if the presentation is transmitted via e-mail, as many e-mail systems restrict file attachments larger than a specified size as a security feature. And, if you plan to show your presentation directly from a web location, larger files are slower to load and display.

Creating a New Presentation

You already know how to launch Windows applications. When you launch Microsoft PowerPoint, it opens with a new blank presentation on the screen. The blank presentation includes one slide with two centered text boxes—one for a title and one for a subtitle. See Figure 16.3.

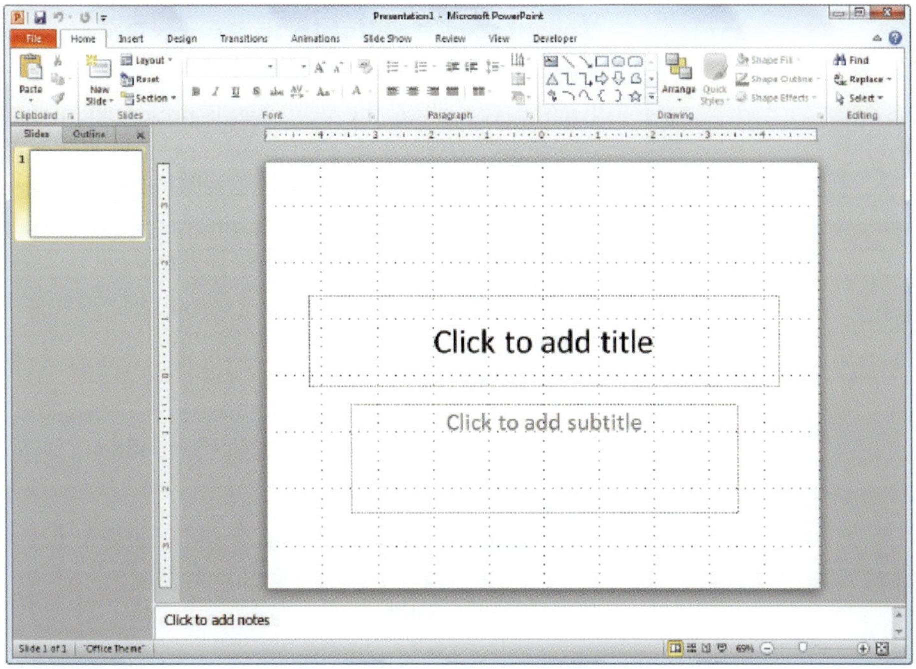

FIGURE 16.3

How to Use Help in PowerPoint

Chances are that you will have questions about working in PowerPoint that will not be covered in this book. Doing some of your own research to find the answers to your questions, using either the Help feature in PowerPoint or general web research, is an important component of success with PowerPoint.

On the top right of the PowerPoint window is a question mark icon. Click here to look for help on a topic using the Help function (or press the **F1** function key on your keyboard as a shortcut). See Figure 16.4.

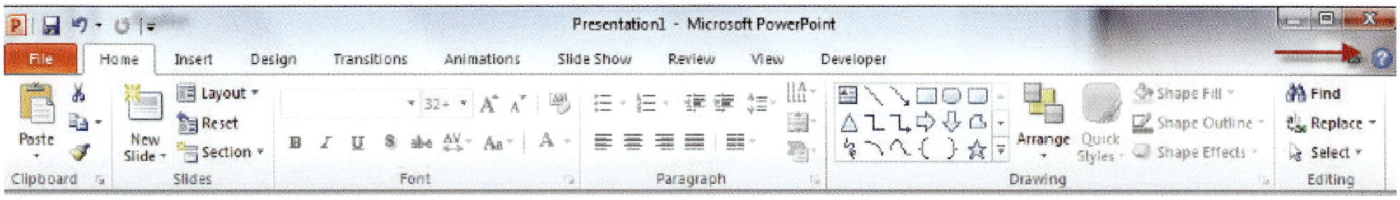

FIGURE 16.4

A list of Help topics appears in a pop-up window. If your computer is connected to the Internet, topics from Office.com are listed. If your computer is not connected to the Internet, topics from the built-in Help are displayed. To find out more about a PowerPoint feature, click in the search box at the top of the Help dialog box, enter a keyword to identify what you are searching for, and then press

FIGURE 16.5

the **Enter** key. If you do not know what the feature you are interested in is called, click on the topics listed to browse them. When you finish with the Help feature, click the **close** button in its top right corner to close the window and return to your slides. See Figure 16.5.

Templates Available in PowerPoint and on Microsoft Online

Even if you close the new, blank presentation that opens when you launch PowerPoint, you can still create a new one at any time. PowerPoint has a variety of preset templates available within the program itself and in the Microsoft online library. Templates include suggestions for slide content and design, so you might choose to close the blank presentation and create a new one based on a template to save time.

To create a new presentation based on a template:

1. Click the *File* tab.
2. Click *New* (see Figure 16.6).
3. Under Available Templates and Themes, click a presentation icon (see Figure 16.7).
4. Click **Create.**

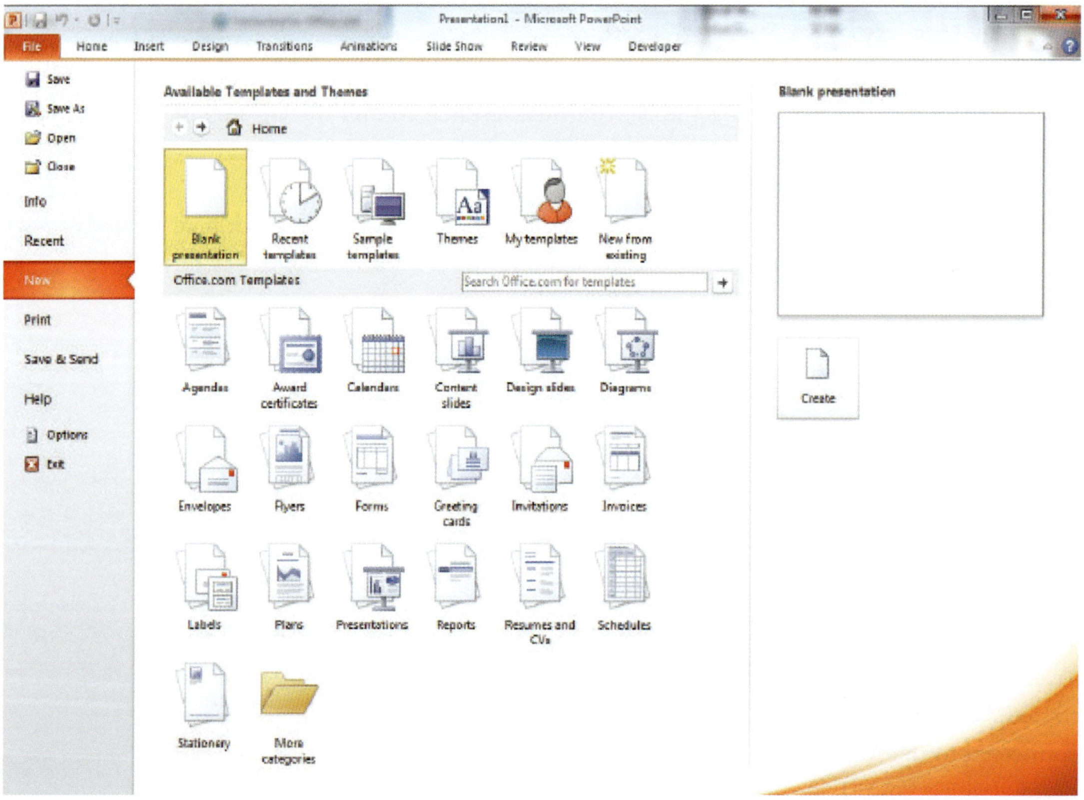

FIGURE 16.6

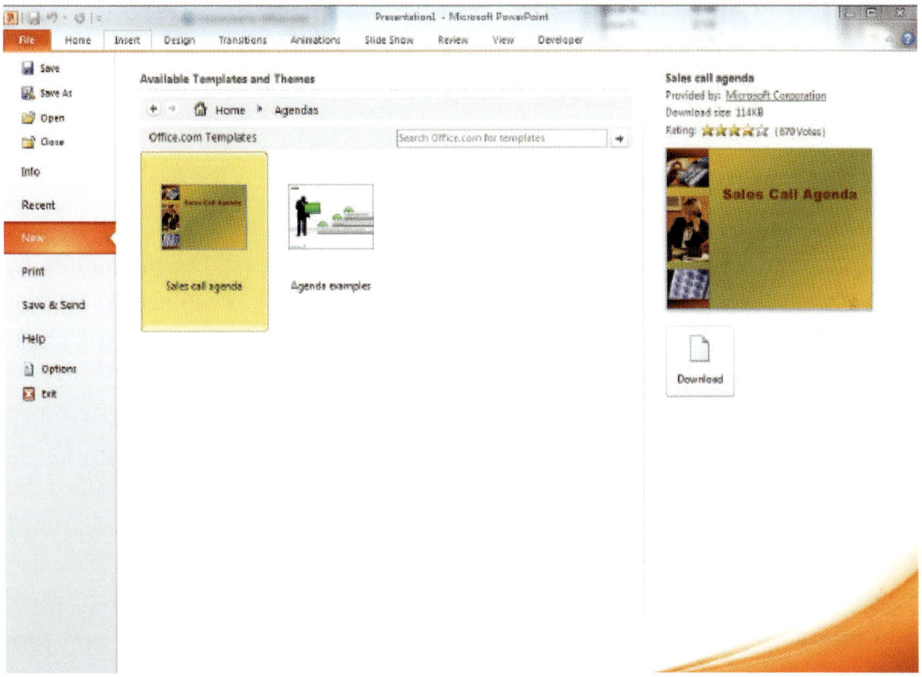

FIGURE 16.7

Choosing a Document Theme

Themes in PowerPoint are preset combinations of colors and fonts designed to produce professional, consistent presentations. PowerPoint 2010 has 40 built-in themes. You might choose to create a new presentation based on a theme, although you will see later in this chapter that you can apply a theme at any time.

To create a new presentation based on a theme (see Figure 16.8):

1. Click the *File* tab.
2. Click *New*.

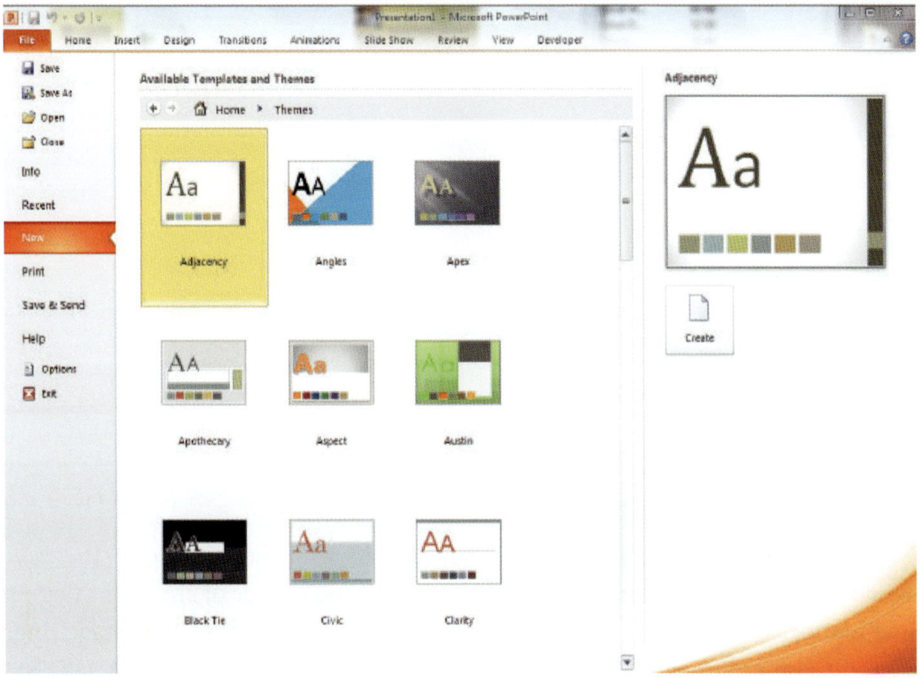

FIGURE 16.8

3. Under Available Templates and Themes, click a theme icon.
4. Click **Create.** You will notice that your slide(s) will all change to the theme background, font, and color choices.

The PowerPoint Window

The Ribbon at the top of the window contains the set of commands for working in a presentation. It is organized into tabs labeled *File, Home, Insert, Design, Transitions, Animations, Slide Show, Review,* and *View*. Other tabs appear as you need them. For example, it is possible to add charts to a presentation. When you click in a chart, *Design, Layout*, and *Format Chart Tool* tabs automatically appear.

Click a tab to display buttons for features organized by groups. For example, under the *Home* tab, the *Clipboard* group contains buttons for **Cut, Copy, Paste,** and **Format Painter.** Some groups have a small arrow at the bottom right called the dialog box launcher. Click the dialog box launcher to find settings for additional features related to the group.

Click the *File* tab to access the Backstage View. The Backstage View is where you manage your presentation. As you know, you click *New* to create a new presentation. *Open* lets you retrieve an existing presentation. You also save, send, and print documents from the Backstage View. To return to your presentation from the Backstage View, click the *Home* tab or press the **Esc** (escape) key on the keyboard. See Figure 16.9.

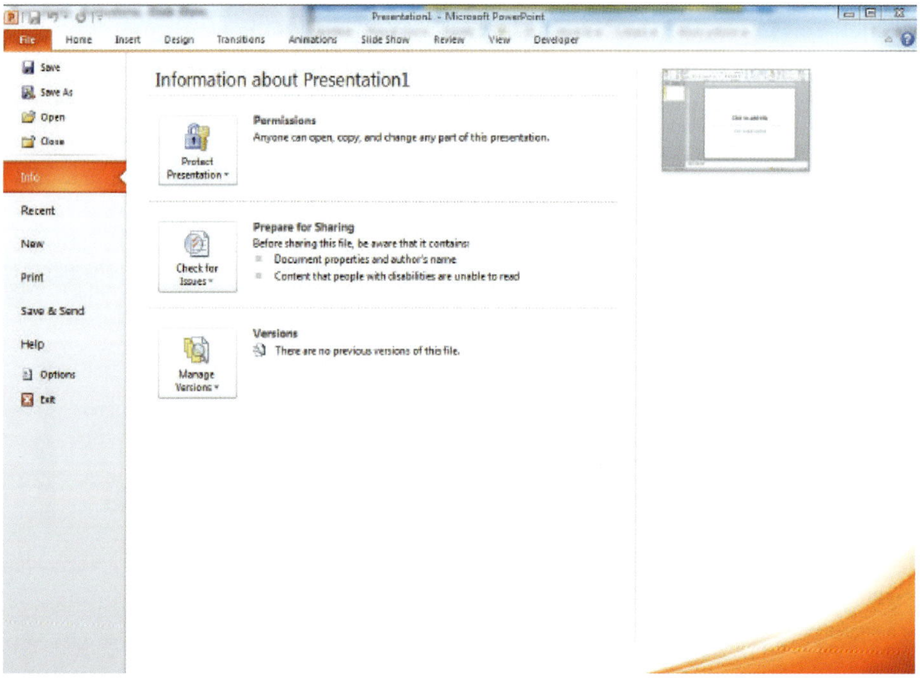

FIGURE 16.9

Create new slides and change their appearance from the *Home* tab. The *Font* group, for example, contains buttons to change the appearance of characters (letters and numbers) in the slides, such as the size of the text, boldfacing, and italicizing. You can also group and arrange graphic objects on your slide from this tab. See Figure 16.10.

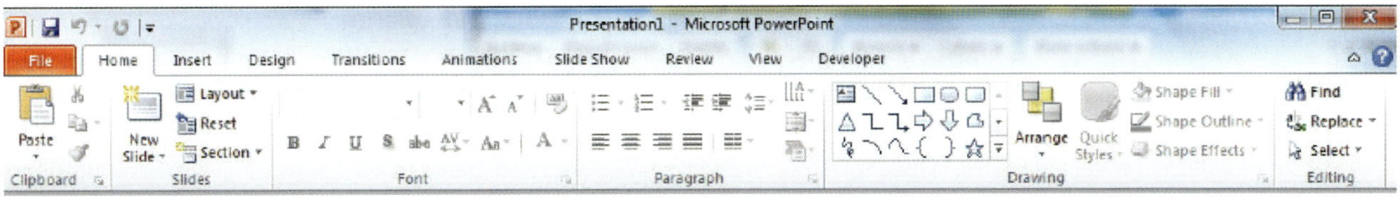

FIGURE 16.10

Use the *Insert* tab to insert items such as tables, shapes, charts, and headers/ footers into your document. See Figure 16.11.

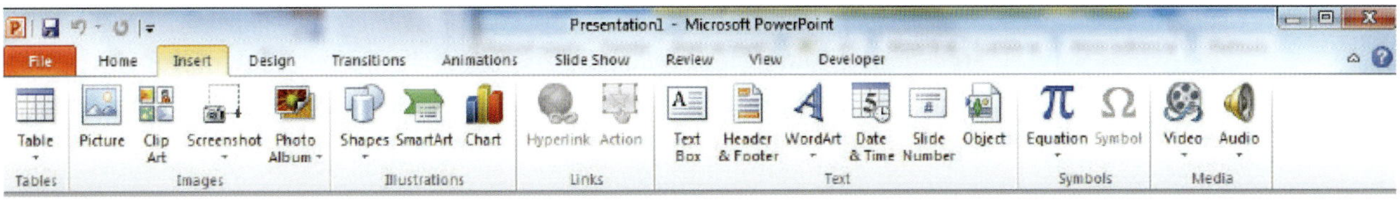

FIGURE 16.11

Customize the background of your presentation from the *Design* tab. You can also change the theme design and colors, and modify the page setup of your presentation. See Figure 16.12.

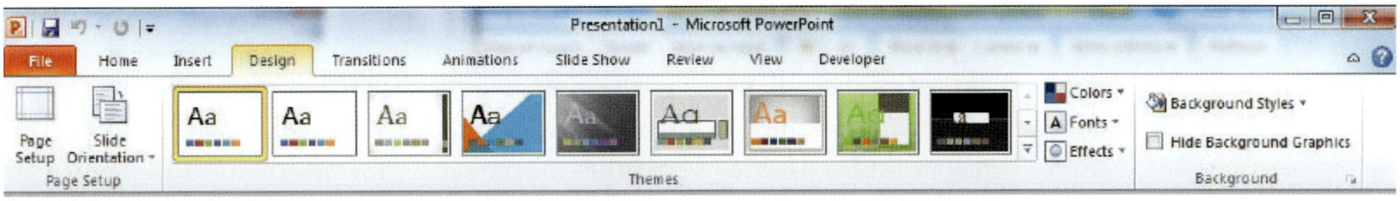

FIGURE 16.12

The *Transitions* tab allows you to control what happens on the screen when a presenter moves to the next slide. For example, you can use a slow fade, a spiral effect, or a wipe from top to bottom. Sounds played during the presentation and settings to advance from slide to slide are also set here. See Figure 16.13.

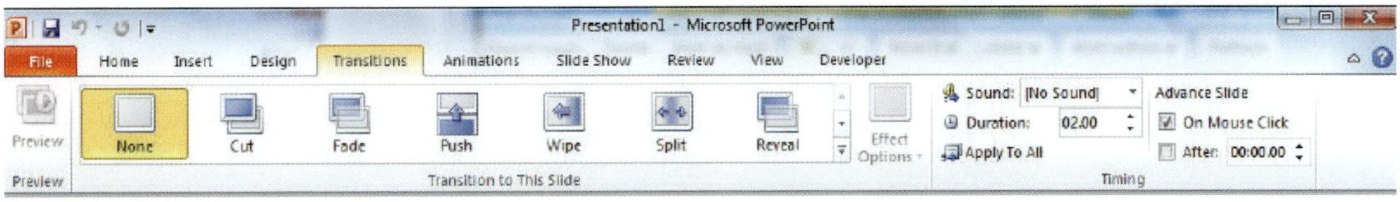

FIGURE 16.13

Use the *Animations* tab to create movement on the screen when the slide is displayed. You can apply, change, or remove animations to objects on this tab. See Figure 16.14.

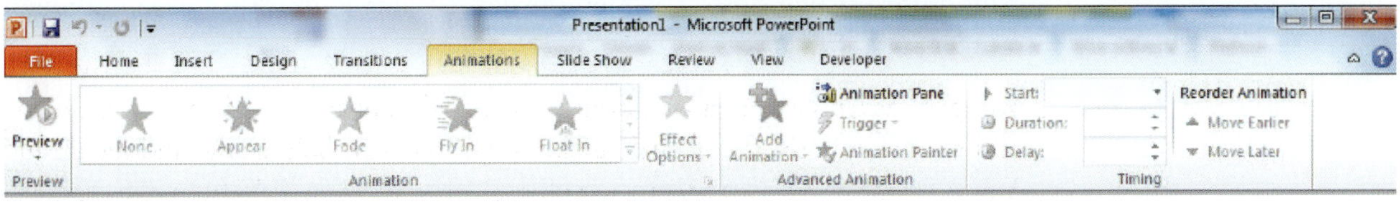

FIGURE 16.14

To control the presentation of your slide show, use the *Slide Show* tab. From here, you can set up a repeating slide show and hide slides for a given presentation. See Figure 16.15.

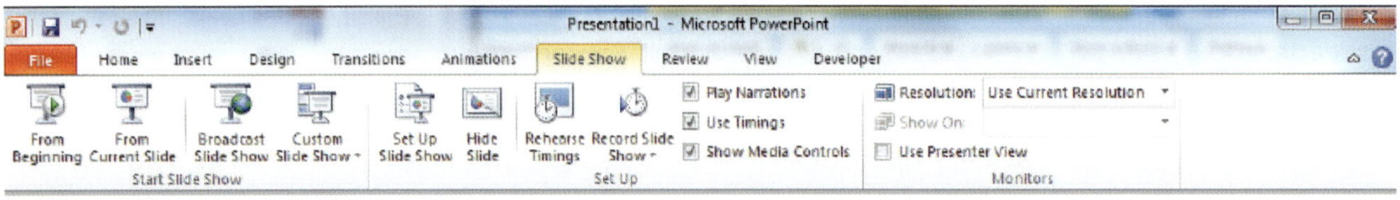

FIGURE 16.15

The *Review* tab includes commands to check the accuracy of your presentation, such as a spelling and grammar check and the Compare feature that lets you compare one presentation to another, marking any changes. See Figure 16.16.

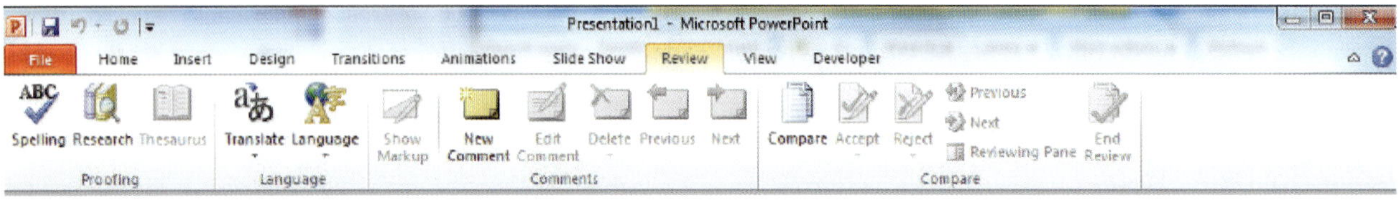

FIGURE 16.16

Make global changes to the appearance of your presentation using the Slide Master in the *View* tab. Zoom in and out, display rulers, display gridlines, and show drawing guidelines on the screen for precise measurements. See Figure 16.17.

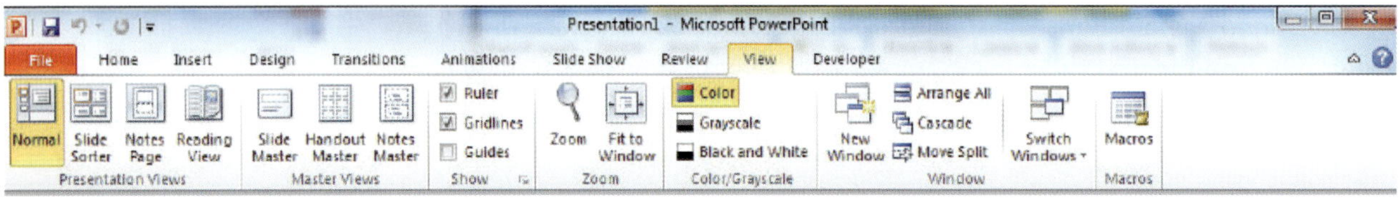

FIGURE 16.17

As with most other applications, scroll bars on the right side of the screen allow you to move up or down in the window.

Views in PowerPoint

When you open PowerPoint, the presentation displays in Normal view. Normal view is the typical working view of a presentation. A pane on the left of the window includes a *Slides* tab and an *Outline* tab. The *Slides* tab displays thumbnails of the existing slides. Click on the desired slide to quickly navigate through a presentation.

When you click on a slide, it displays in the larger Slide Pane to the right. This is where you create or edit each slide. The *Outline* tab displays only the text of the presentation arranged in an outline layout, and is useful when you want to focus on writing and editing text content. See Figure 16.18.

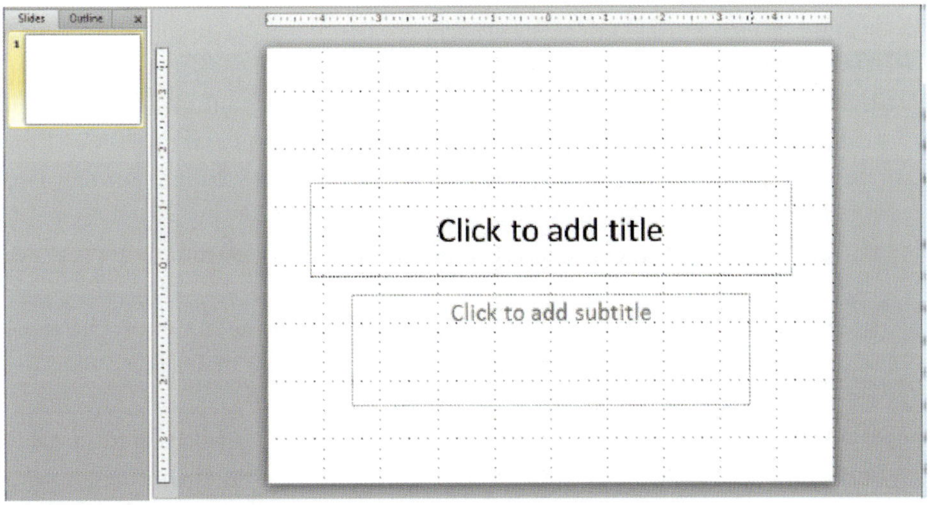

FIGURE 16.18

Use the Slide Pane to enter and edit text, graphics, and other objects in your presentation. Notice it includes areas outlined with dotted lines, which are called **placeholders.** Placeholders are areas set aside to make it easy to enter text or insert objects, such as charts, tables, or clip art graphics. The two placeholders on the default title slide created with a new blank presentation are labeled **Click to add title** and **Click to add subtitle.** As you will see shortly, you will do exactly that to add content to this slide.

In addition to the *Slides* tab, *Outline* tab, and Slide Pane, Normal view includes a Notes Pane below the Slide Pane. You can type notes for yourself for prompts or a script when you present the slide show. You can also type notes to print for your audience's reference. Initially, the Notes Pane is very shallow (see Figure 16.19). To make it larger, position your pointer over the top of the Notes Pane, so that your pointer changes to a two-headed arrow shape. Hold down the mouse button and drag up to allow more space for notes.

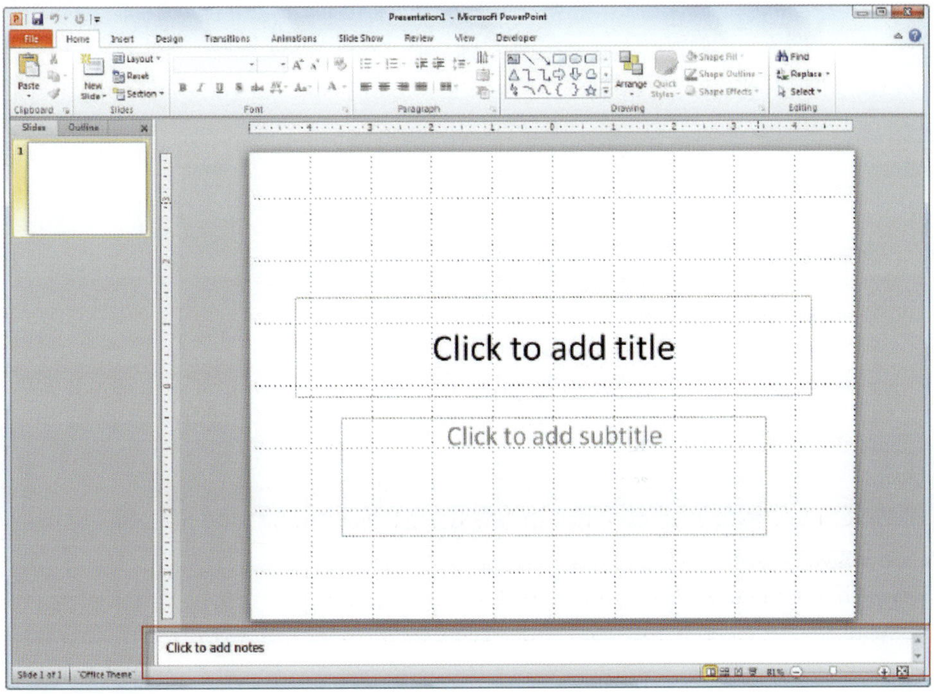

FIGURE 16.19

Status Bar Options

The left side of the status bar in PowerPoint tells you the slide number of the selected slide along with the total number of slides in the presentation and the name of the currently applied document theme. On the right of the status bar are buttons used to switch between the following views:

- *Normal view*—The default edit view for working with slide content. See Figure 16.20A.
- *Slide Sorter view*—A view that allows you access to all slides on the same screen. In Slide Sorter view, you can drag slides to change their order, copy, and delete slides. See Figure 16.20B.
- *Reading view*—A presentation view that lets you run the presentation as a slide show on a PC, rather than on a projector in front of an audience. It includes navigation arrow keys on the status bar to navigate through the slide presentation. This view makes it easy to switch back to Normal or Slide Sorter view for editing. See Figure 16.20C.
- *Slide Show view*—This view runs the slide presentation as a slide show, using your full screen and advancing as you click the mouse, press the **Page Down** or **Enter** key, or click a remote controller. Press the **Esc** key to return to Normal view. See Figure 16.20D.

These views, along with others that allow more specific control of the slide show and set global choices for formatting, are also available from the *View* tab. The status bar also includes a zoom slider at the bottom right for you to zoom in or out on slide content, making it larger or smaller by moving the slider bar.

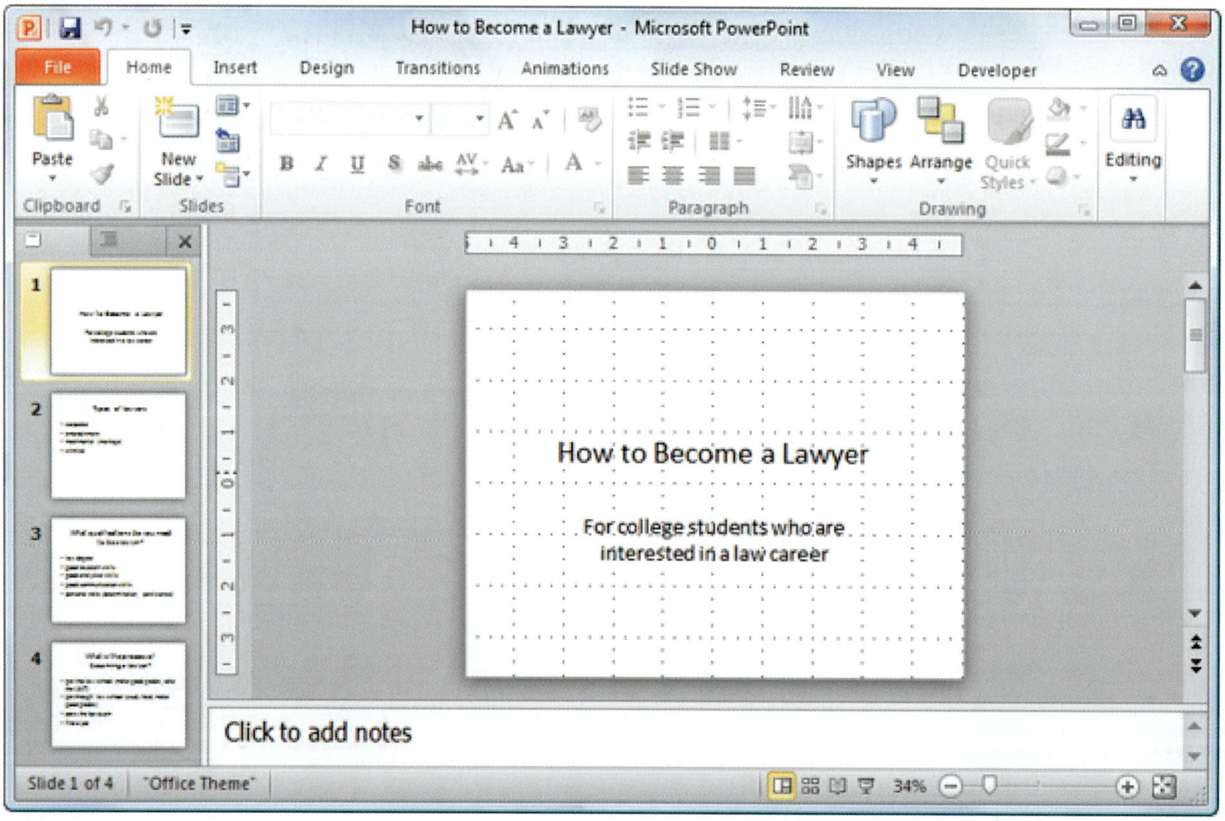

FIGURE 16.20A

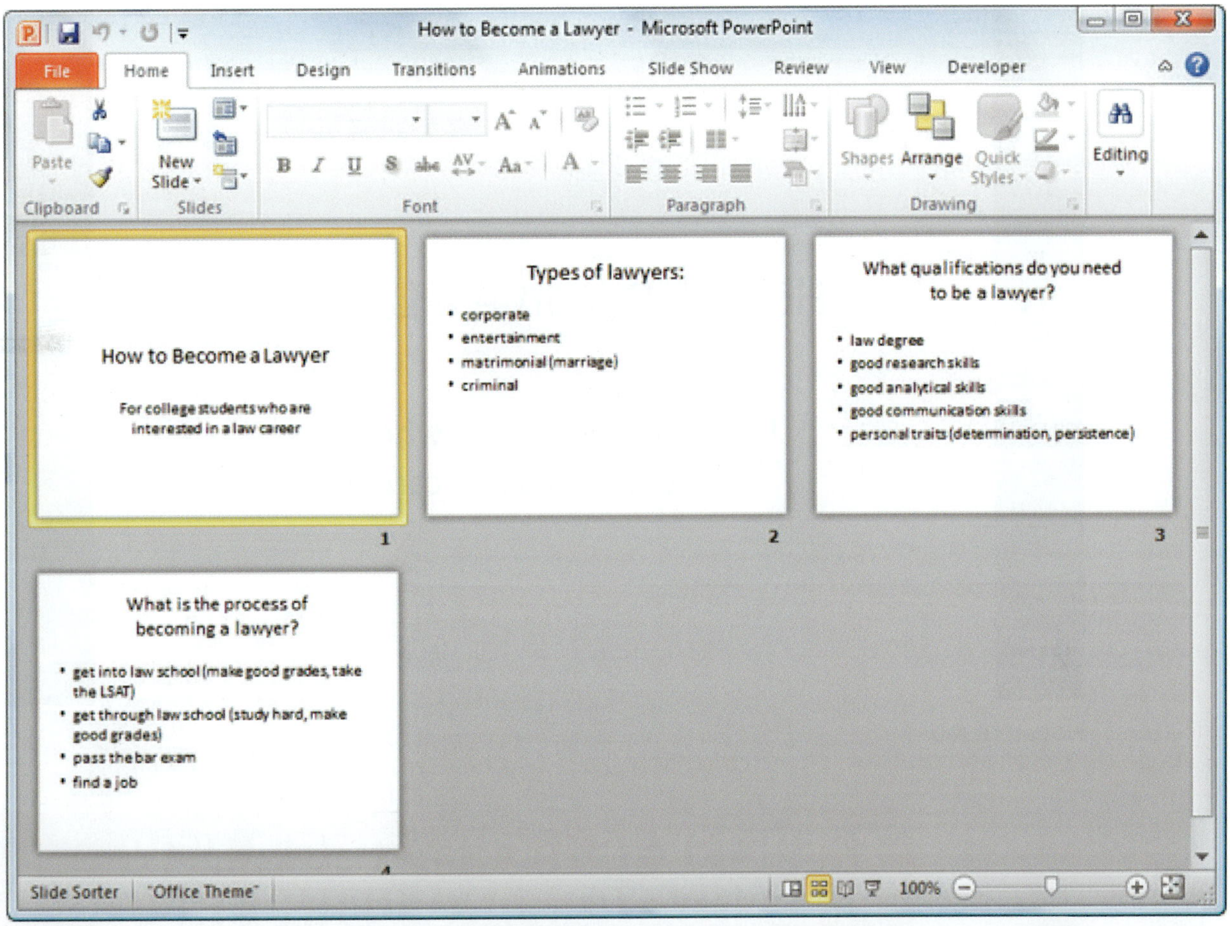

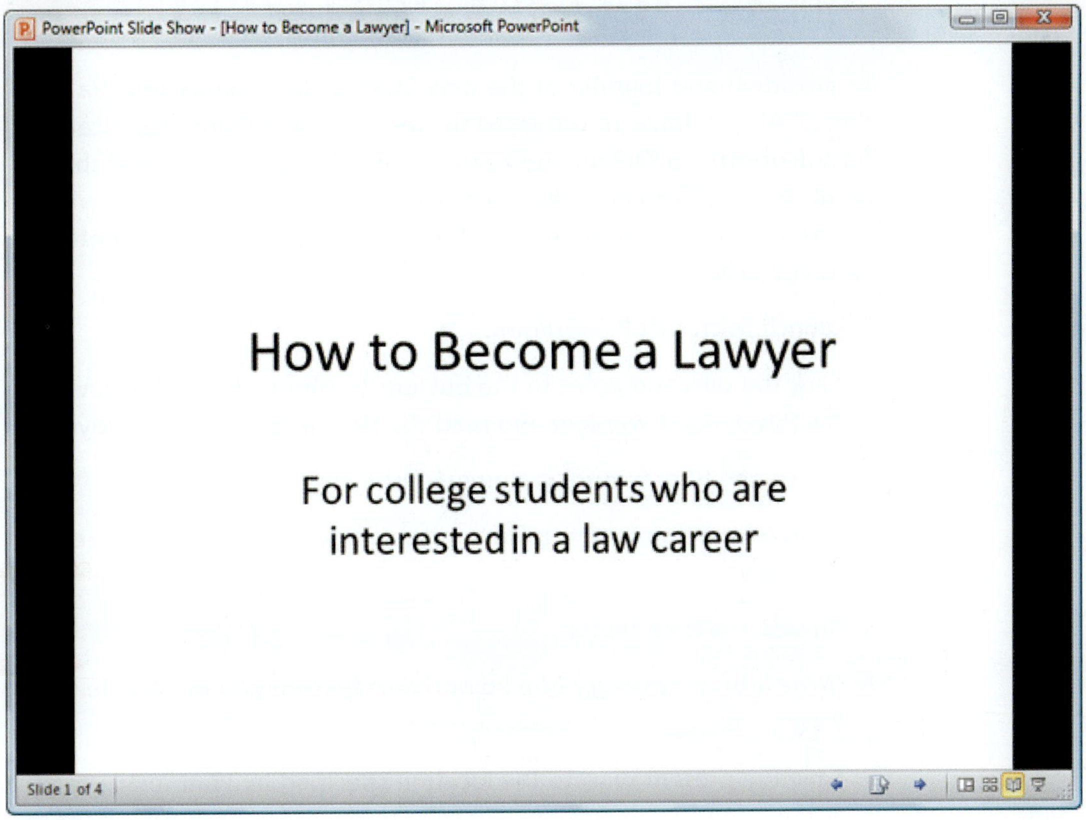

FIGURE 16.20C

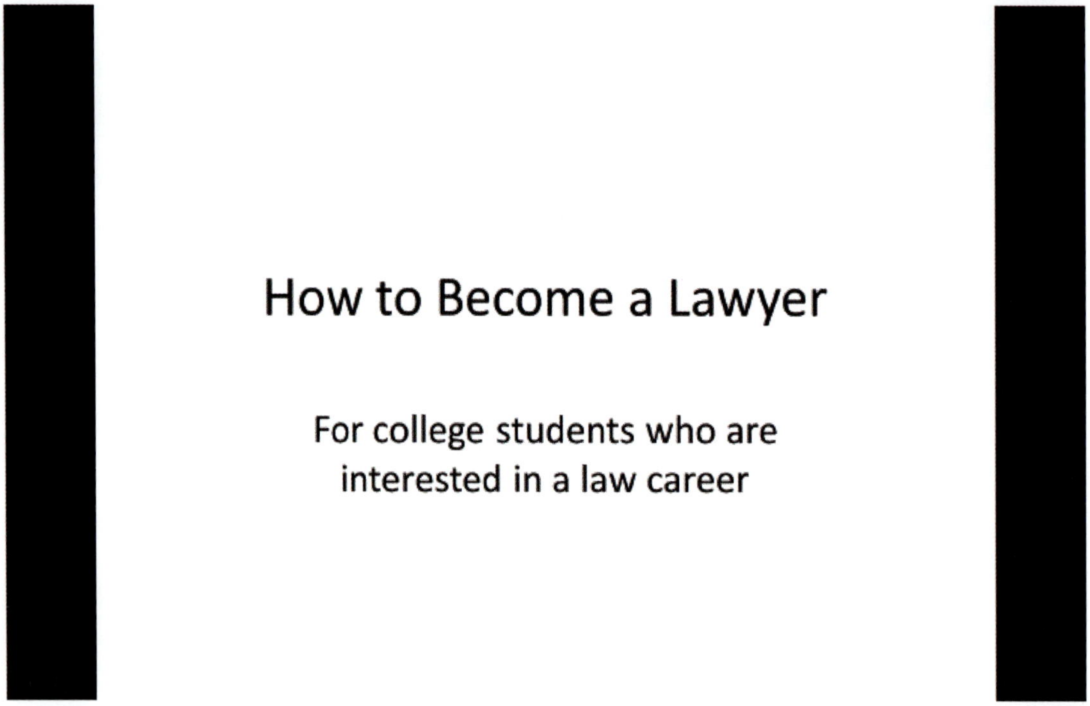

FIGURE 16.20D

EXERCISE 16.1: CREATING A NEW PRESENTATION AND USING THE HELP FEATURE IN POWERPOINT

As president and founder of the new Student Technology Association (STA), you have volunteered to create a PowerPoint presentation for the upcoming Technology Fair at your college. Not only will this promote the STA to potential members, it will also provide you with a chance to experiment with PowerPoint and improve your presentation software skills.

1. Launch Microsoft PowerPoint.
2. Click the tabs and point to the buttons (without clicking) to review the PowerPoint window and read the Help information displayed.
3. Access the Help feature in PowerPoint.
4. Search for help on how to save, close, and open files if you need a review.
5. Browse the Help feature.
6. Write a brief summary of a PowerPoint feature you want to learn how to use.
7. Save the presentation to the location specified by your instructor. Name it "STA Presentation." Close it or leave it open for the next exercise.

Entering Text in PowerPoint

When you create a new default presentation in PowerPoint, the Title Slide layout is the first thing you see on the screen. As you add more slides to the presentation, you can choose from eight additional slide layouts that define the general structure of the slide by the placeholders they include and their placement on a slide. For example, there are placeholders to add bulleted text, tables, graphics, or movies to a slide, accessed by a click of your mouse. Most slides also contain a title slide placeholder at the top of the slide.

To enter text on a slide, click inside of the placeholder and type your desired text. For example, imagine that small business owner Lee Schuster needs to prepare a presentation for the new staging component of his interior design business. After creating a new presentation, Lee clicks on the **Click to add title** placeholder. The placeholder changes to contain a blinking insertion point to show Lee that he can enter text. Selection handles also appear around the placeholder object. Lee types "Home Staging Presentation" and notices that the text is centered automatically within the placeholder and the slide. He clicks the **Click to add subtitle** placeholder and types the name of his company, "Interior Furnishings, Inc." See Figure 16.21.

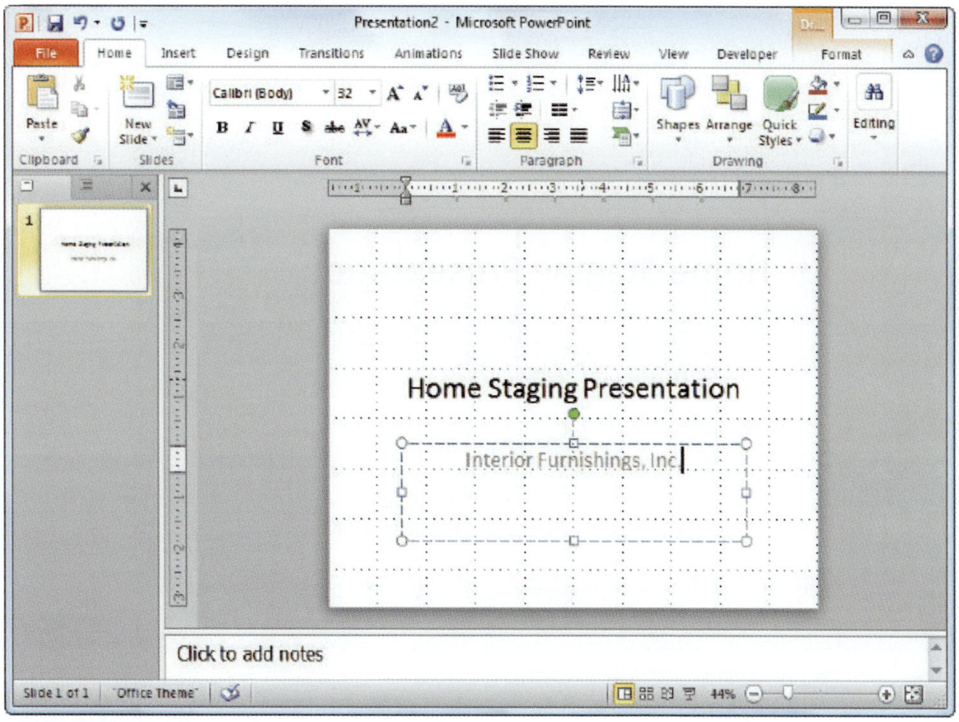

FIGURE 16.21

Selecting in PowerPoint

You select text and objects on a PowerPoint slide for the same reason you select them in other applications—to mark them as the relevant content for the action or command you choose next, such as deletion, copy and paste, or reformat.

Hold the mouse button down and drag over the text to select it. You can also click to place the insertion point at the beginning of the text to select, then hold down the **Shift** key and click at the end of the text to select. Many of the shortcuts you learned using Microsoft Word® work in PowerPoint too, such as double-clicking on a word to select it and triple-clicking a paragraph to select the paragraph.

Click an object on a PowerPoint slide to select it. When you click a placeholder object, a dashed borderline and small selection handles appear around the object. To select multiple objects (i.e., text boxes, graphics) on a slide, hold down the **Shift** key as you click on each object in turn.

PowerPoint also allows you to select objects using the Selection and Visibility task pane from the Ribbon, which is helpful when you have many objects on a slide, possibly overlapping. The Selection and Visibility task pane is also available in Microsoft Excel 2010©.

To select objects using the Ribbon:

1. Click the *Home* tab.
2. In the *Editing* group, click **Select.**
3. Click **Selection Pane.** See Figure 16.22.
4. From the Selection and Visibility task pane, click the item or items you want to select.

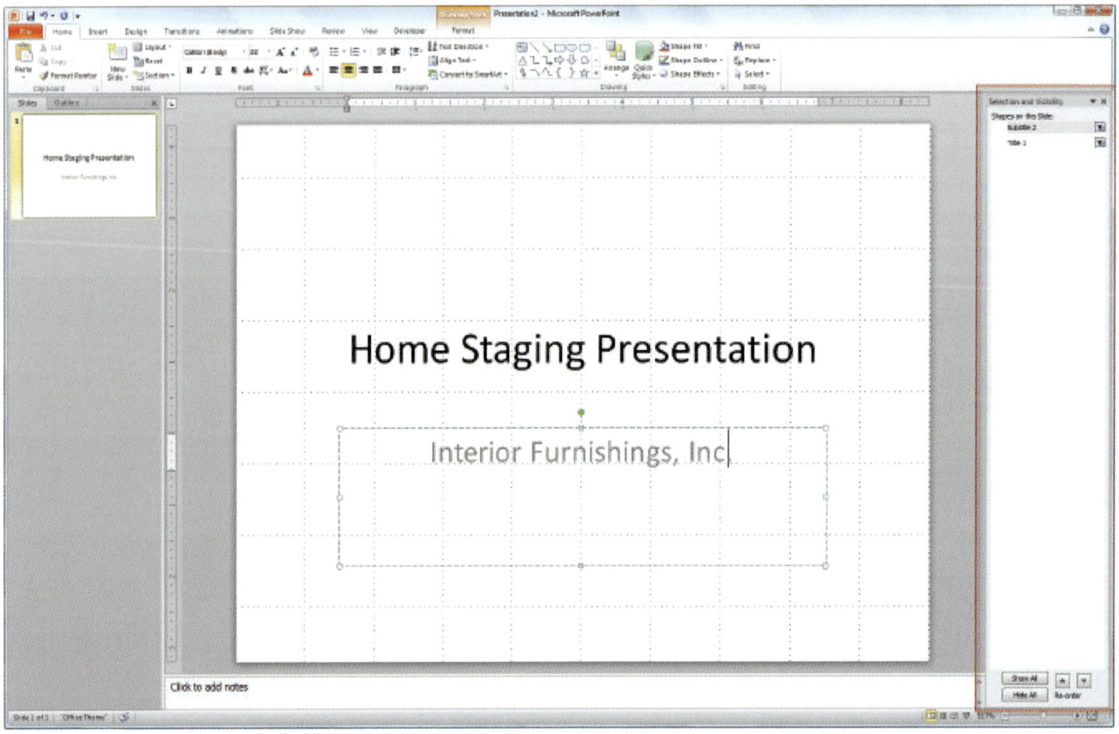

FIGURE 16.22

Editing Text in PowerPoint

Editing text in PowerPoint is similar to editing in Microsoft Word. For instance, to insert a word into an existing sentence, click to place the insertion point where the word should appear. To delete letters or numbers one at a time on a slide, click to place the insertion point at the beginning of the text to delete and press the **Delete** key, or click to place the insertion point at the end of the text to delete and press the **Backspace** key. Pressing **Delete** or **Backspace** with text selected will delete all the selected text. Typing with text selected will replace the selected text with any text you type.

The procedure for moving or copying text within a presentation is also consistent with the procedure in Word. To cut or copy and paste text:

1. Select the text.
2. Click the *Home* tab.
3. In the *Clipboard* group, click **Copy** to copy the text, or click **Cut** to remove the text, and place it on the internal clipboard for the next step. (Or use the keyboard shortcuts **Ctrl+C** to copy and **Ctrl+X** to cut.)
4. Click to place the insertion point where the copied or cut text should appear, and then in the *Clipboard* group, click **Paste.**

Global Find and Replace

You can also edit text in PowerPoint by automatically replacing it with other text. This can be done one word at a time or throughout the entire presentation, globally. For example, imagine that legal assistant Marisa Abrogar has completed her 25-slide presentation, "How to Become a Lawyer"—and then she decides that she would rather use the word "attorney" instead of "lawyer." Marisa can use the global Find and Replace function in PowerPoint to make all of the substitutions at once, instead of searching each slide of the presentation for the word "lawyer."

To find each occurrence of a word or phrase and replace it with another:

1. Click the *Home* tab.
2. In the *Editing* group, click **Replace** (see Figure 16.23).
3. In the Find what box, type the text that you want to search for and replace.
4. In the Replace with box, type the replacement text.
5. Click **Find Next,** and then one of the following:

- Click **Replace** to replace the highlighted text and find the next time it occurs in the document.
- Click **Replace All** to replace all instances of the text in your document.
- Click **Find Next** to skip this instance of the text and proceed to the next time it appears in the document.

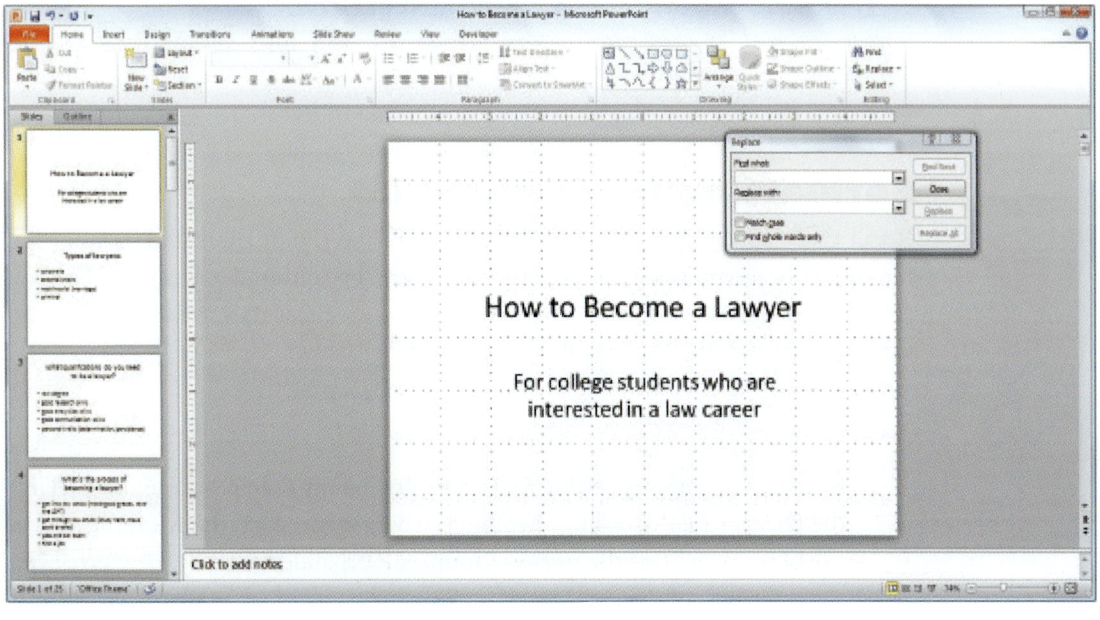

FIGURE 16.23

EXERCISE 16.2: ENTERING TEXT ON A SLIDE

The dean of students asks you to speak at the upcoming Technology Fair about the variety of technology resources available to students on campus. Your goal is to create a lively, interesting slide show to accompany your 20-minute lecture. It will also post to the campus website, so accuracy and a professional appearance are very important.

1. **On paper, outline the points you will cover in your presentation. Consider topics such as the campus computer lab(s), WiFi locations on campus, the college's elearning portal, student discounts on hardware and software, and so on. Collaborate with your classmates and consult with your instructors as needed.**
2. **Divide your outline into the content for your presentation's slides. Draft an introductory slide to follow the title slide and a summary slide to end the presentation. You need approximately 10 slides for the 20-minute lecture.**
3. **Think of an engaging title for your presentation, one that explains its purpose in an intriguing way.**
4. **Open the STA Presentation.pptx file you created in the last exercise, if necessary.**
5. **Enter your title in the title placeholder and enter your name in the subtitle placeholder.**
6. **Save the changes to your presentation.**
7. **Close it, or leave it open for the next exercise.**

Formatting in PowerPoint

Recall that you can use document themes in a PowerPoint presentation, and that the theme imposes consistent colors, fonts, sizes, background art, and so on. You can choose a document theme when you create a new presentation, or apply it to an existing presentation. The default theme is Office Theme.

To change the document theme:

1. Click the *Design* tab.
2. In the *Themes* group, point to various document theme buttons to preview the changes that choosing them will make. If you click the **More** button in the bottom right of the *Themes* group, the expanded Gallery view gives you more themes to preview. See Figure 16.24.
3. Click the theme you like best and apply it to all the slides of your presentation. Next, set it as the default for new slides you add.

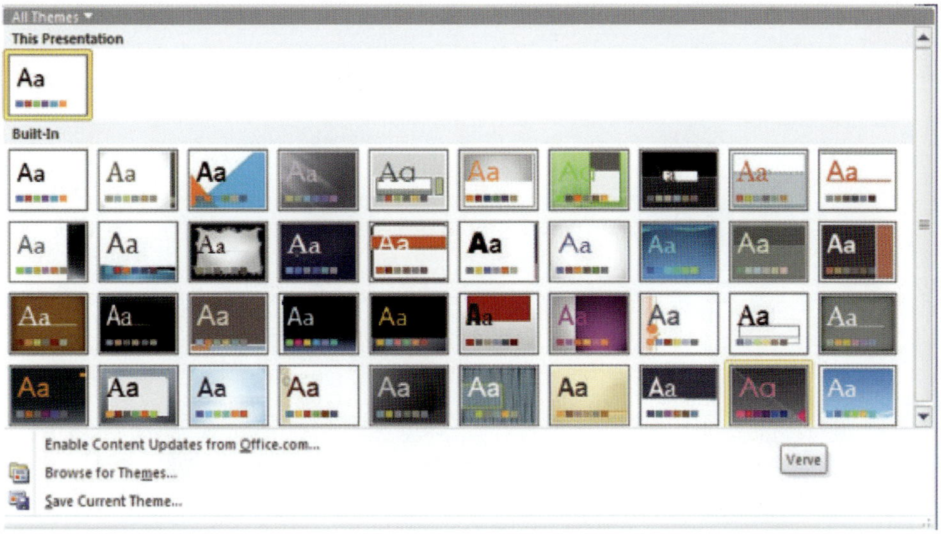

FIGURE 16.24

For example, interior designer Lee Schuster wants to make his "Home Staging Presentation" more visually appealing. He expands the Themes gallery of the *Design* tab, and after previewing several options, selects the Aspect theme. See Figure 16.25.

FIGURE 16.25

Here are some examples of Marisa's "How to Become a Lawyer" title slide with various themes applied. Notice that the text does not change; instead, only the arrangement of the placeholder text, the fonts and font formatting, and the colors used are changed. See Figures 16.26A–C.

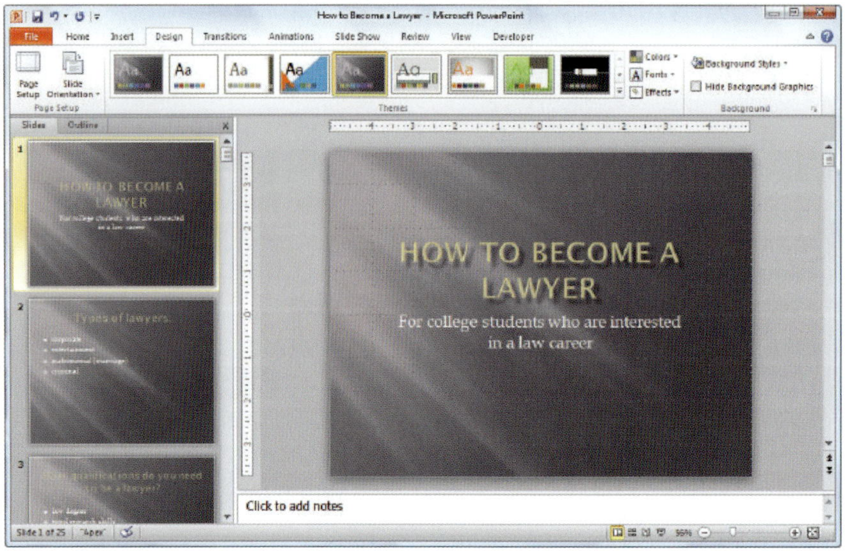

FIGURE 16.26A

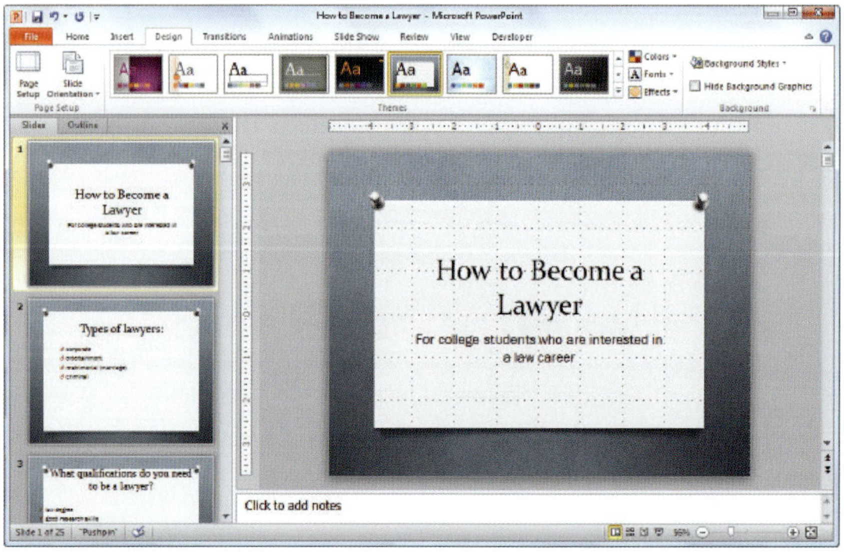

FIGURE 16.26B

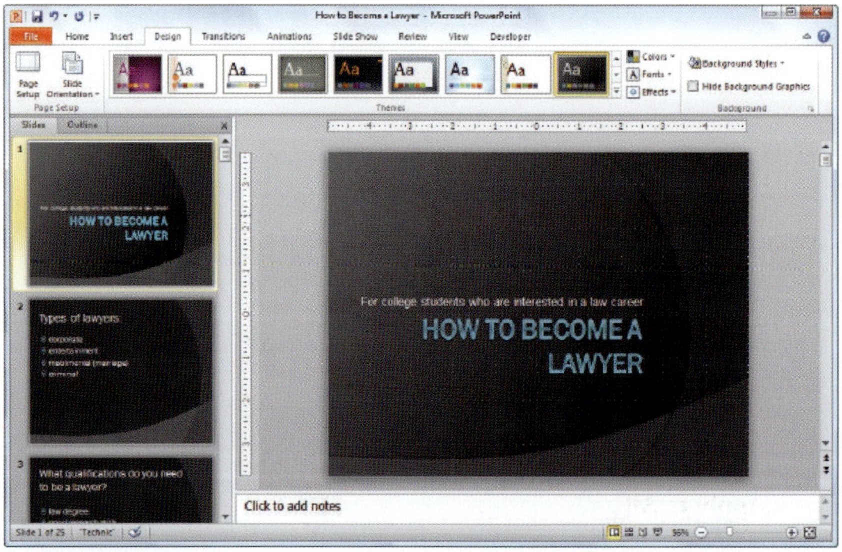

FIGURE 16.26C

Marisa and Lee can reformat slides based on their own preferences, of course. If Lee wants to experiment to draw more attention to his company name, he can select Interior Furnishings, Inc. and click the **Increase Font Size** button from the *Font* group on the *Home* tab a few times to see if he likes it larger. If he decides that he does not, he can click the **Decrease Font Size** button, or he can click the **Bold** button with the company name selected to see if he prefers to put emphasis on the words.

To change the appearance of existing characters:

1. Select the text you want to change.
2. Click the *Home* tab.
3. In the *Font* group, click the button for the desired effect.

Remember that the small arrow in the bottom right of the *Font* group is a dialog box launcher. Click it for more character formatting choices.

Paragraph Formatting

Paragraph formatting in PowerPoint includes commands to change the line spacing, indentation, text direction, and alignment.

To change the appearance of existing paragraphs:

1. Select one or more paragraphs you want to change.
2. Click the *Home* tab.
3. In the *Paragraph* group (see Figure 16.27), click the button(s) for the desired effect(s).

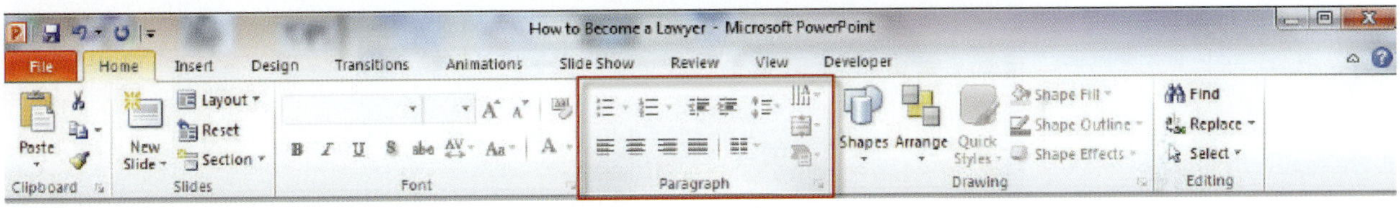

FIGURE 16.27

Background Formatting

You can reformat many elements of the slide's appearance, including the slide background. You can use backgrounds made of solid color, textured patterns, and pictures. See Figures 16.28A (solid color) and 16.28B (pattern fill) to see slide backgrounds for the slide presentation on home staging. Changing background styles affects all slides in a presentation.

To modify background styles:

1. Click the *Design* tab.
2. In the *Background* group, click the *Background Styles* drop-down arrow.
3. Choose from the available preset background styles. Notice the color and pattern choices are limited to those that combine well with the theme already chosen for the presentation.
4. For more options, click the *Format Background* from the drop-down list. The *Fill* tab on the left lets you choose a solid or gradient (shaded) fill, or a picture or texture to use as a fill.
5. Click **Apply to All.**

The button choice makes it clear that changes made to the background are applied to all the slides in a presentation, but what about other formatting changes,

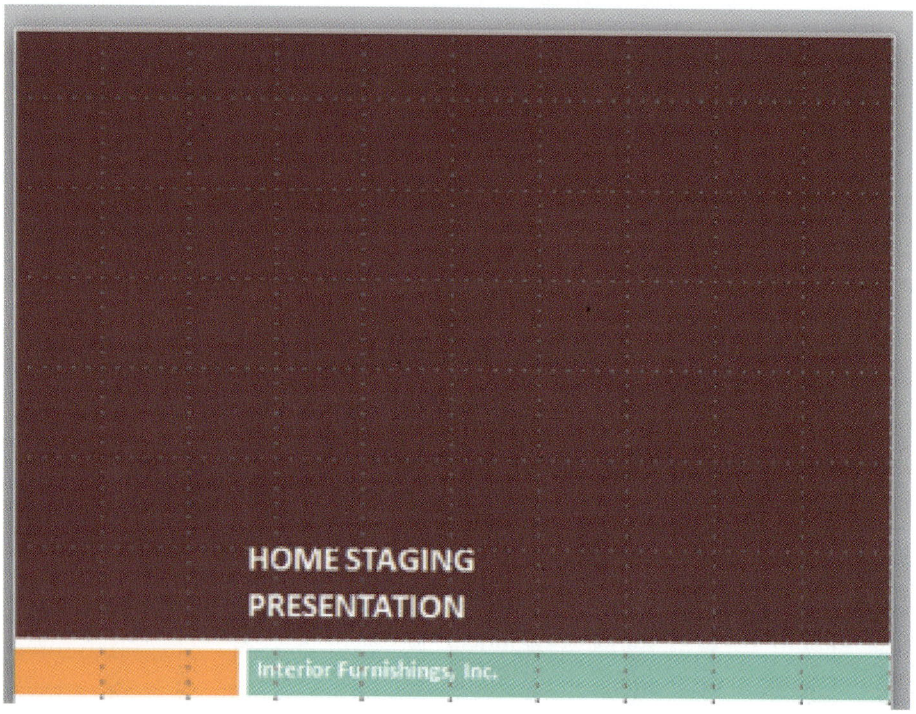

FIGURE 16.28A

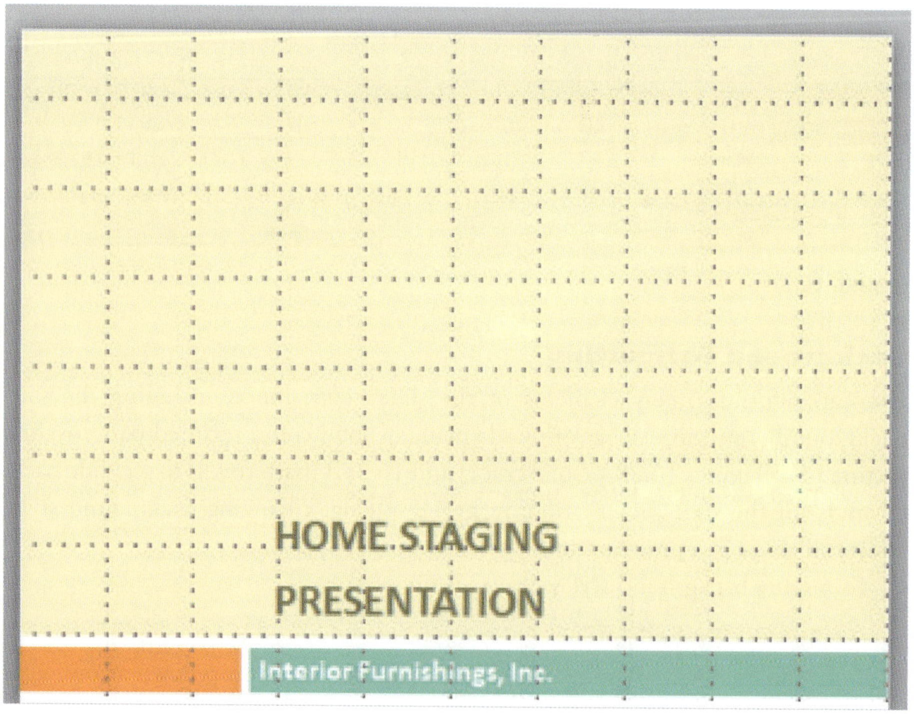

FIGURE 16.28B

such as making all the title placeholders on all slides of a presentation italic, or increasing the line spacing of bulleted lists on each slide? You might assume that you must make these changes on each and every slide. However, you can make the changes on a "behind-the-scenes" slide called the Slide Master and ensure changes will be made globally throughout the presentation and help keep the look of your slides consistent.

To use the Slide Master:

1. Click the *View* tab.
2. In the *Master Views* group, click **Slide Master.**
3. The Slide Master thumbnail appears, along with thumbnails of individual masters for various slide layouts. The *Slide Master* tab also displays (see Figure 16.29).
4. To make global changes, click the top thumbnail and make necessary font, color, and layout changes in the master slide to the right, using the options on the *Slide Master* tab.
5. When you finish, click **Close Master View** in the *Close* group.

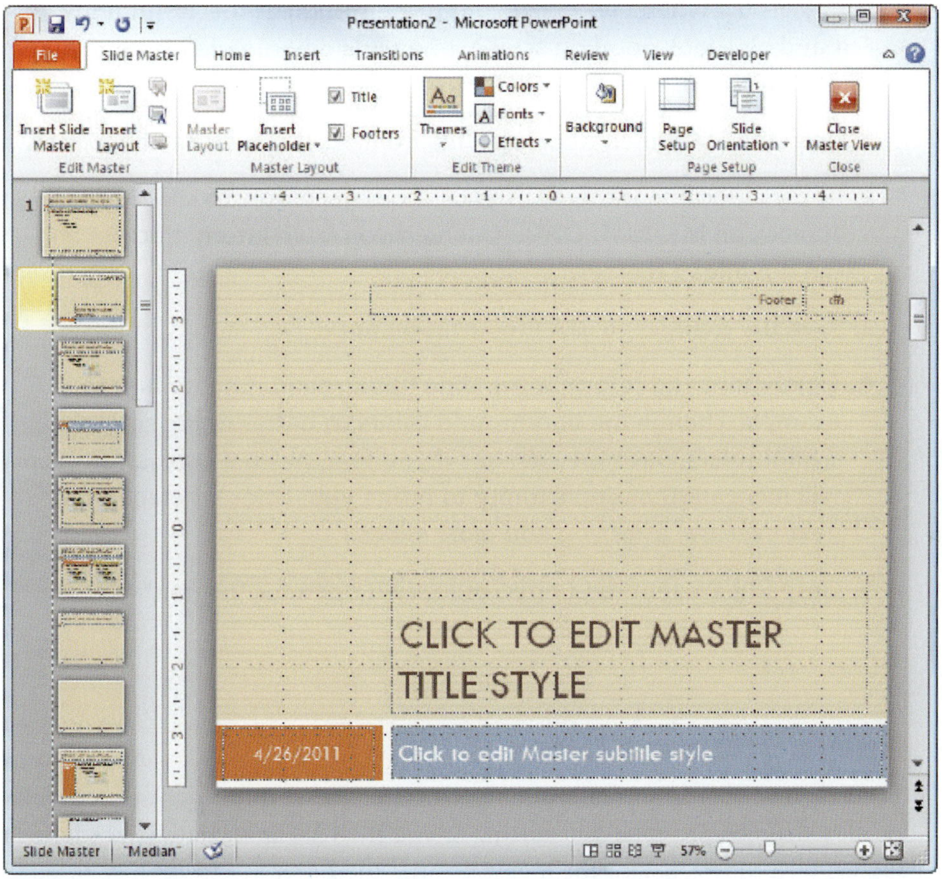

FIGURE 16.29

If you have already made some formatting changes by hand on individual slides of your presentation, changes made in the Slide Master do not override your previous choices.

Using action buttons within a presentation makes navigation easy as you can click a button directly on the slide to move within a presentation. To insert action buttons using the Slide Master:

1. Click the *View* tab.
2. In the *Master Views* group, click **Slide Master.**
3. The Slide Master thumbnail appears, along with thumbnails of individual masters for various slide layouts.
4. On the *Slide Show* tab, select **Action Buttons.**

5. Choose the navigation you want to apply to your presentation: *Home, Back* or *Previous Slide*, and so on.
6. Save your presentation.

EXERCISE 16.3: FORMATTING A PRESENTATION

You are ready to select an eye-catching combination of fonts, colors, and placeholder arrangements for your presentation. These must be highly visible when you make your presentation at the Technology Fair and also look good on screen when it is downloaded from the campus website.

1. **Open the STA Presentation.pptx file from the last exercise, if necessary.**
2. **Apply a document theme of your choice. Feel free to click More Themes on Microsoft Office Online if you have Internet access and can download themes.**
3. **Save the changes to STA Presentation.pptx.**
4. **Experiment and reformat the slide background if necessary; for example, change the background colors to better represent your school colors. Save the changes if you feel they are successful. (You will have another opportunity to refine your color scheme in the next exercise, after you add more slides.)**
5. **Close STA Presentation.pptx, or leave it open for the next exercise.**

Adding New Slides

As noted, new blank presentations typically begin with a title slide. You add slides for the remaining presentation content. As you show the presentation, a new slide displays each time you click the mouse or press the **Enter** key to advance through the slide show.

Changing the Slide Layout

When you add a slide to a presentation, you choose from one of nine built-in slide layouts. The slide layout you choose depends on the intended purpose of the slide. See Figure 16.30.

To insert a slide:

1. In Normal view, click the thumbnail of the slide preceding the slide you will insert.
2. Click the *Home* tab.
3. In the *Slides* group, click the drop-down arrow in the bottom half of the **New Slide** button.
4. Click a slide layout (see Figure 16.31).

SLIDE LAYOUT	PURPOSE
Title Slide	Contains a title and subtitle placeholder, used to begin a presentation
Title and Content	Contains a title placeholder and a content placeholder, used to enter bulleted text or to insert a table, chart, or picture
Section Header	Used as an optional divider slide to begin a new section of the presentation
Two Content	Similar to Title and Content, but with two content or bulleted text areas
Comparison	Similar to Two Content, but with extra text placeholders for explanatory text describing the differences between the content
Title Only	Contains a title placeholder; the rest of the slide used to draw graphics or paste content
Blank	Adds a completely blank slide to draw graphics, paste content, or create your own custom slide layout
Content with Caption	Similar to Comparison, but with only one title placeholder, content area, and text placeholder for explanatory text
Picture with Caption	Similar to Content with Caption but specifically for picture content

FIGURE 16.30 **Slide Layouts and Their Purpose**

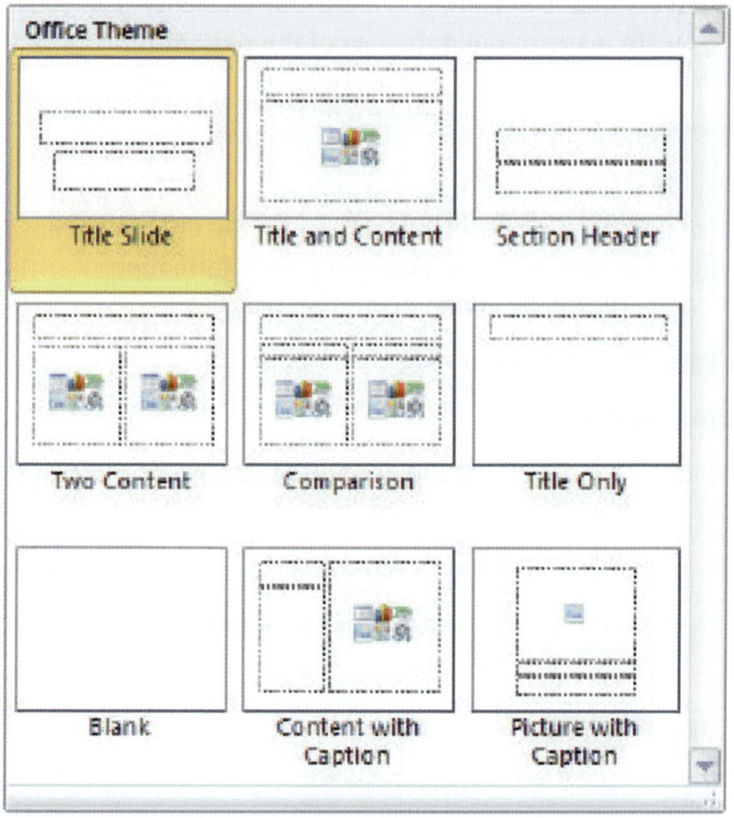

FIGURE 16.31

You can change a slide's layout at any time. For example, if Lee Schuster adds a Blank slide as the second slide of his presentation and later realizes that a Title and Content slide is more helpful for adding bulleted text, he can change the Blank slide to a Title and Content layout. If he adds a slide and then changes his mind, he can always delete it.

To change a slide layout:

1. In Normal view, click the thumbnail of the slide you want to change.
2. Click the *Home* tab.
3. In the *Slides* group, click the drop-down arrow next to the **Layout** button.
4. Click a slide layout.

To delete a slide:

1. In Normal view, click the thumbnail of the slide you want to delete.
2. Press the **Delete** key on the keyboard.

The Title and Content slide layout is the most commonly used layout; a title followed by bulleted text is a popular arrangement for on-screen information. Its content placeholder includes a bullet followed by the instruction **Click to add text.** After you click and type the first line of the slide, press the **Enter** key to create a new line with a bullet. If you prefer, you can click the *Outline* tab in the pane to the left, and type the content there.

EXERCISE 16.4: ADDING SLIDES

Now that you have a theme in place and a draft of the content of your presentation, you are ready to build the rest of the presentation by adding slides with bulleted text.

1. **Open your STA Presentation.pptx file from the last exercise, if necessary.**
2. **Add slides for the text content of your presentation. Choose from the slide layouts as needed to best present your information. (Slides with graphics will be added in another exercise.)**
3. **Type your bulleted text on each slide.**
4. **Save the presentation.**
5. **Experiment with new document themes and reformatting. Note the effect on each slide of the presentation.**
6. **Save the changes if you feel they are successful.**
7. **Close STA Presentation.pptx, or leave it open for the next exercise.**

Graphics in PowerPoint

"A picture is worth a thousand words." That is even true when creating PowerPoint slides. Combining images and text on a slide makes for a much more interesting presentation for your audience.

Images

You have learned that you can use content placeholders to add bulleted text to a slide. You can also use content placeholders to add images. Just click their icons in the center of the placeholder. Click the icon with the green arrow to add a SmartArt diagram. Click the icon with a landscape to insert a picture from a file, or click the icon with small images to insert a clip art image. See Figure 16.32.

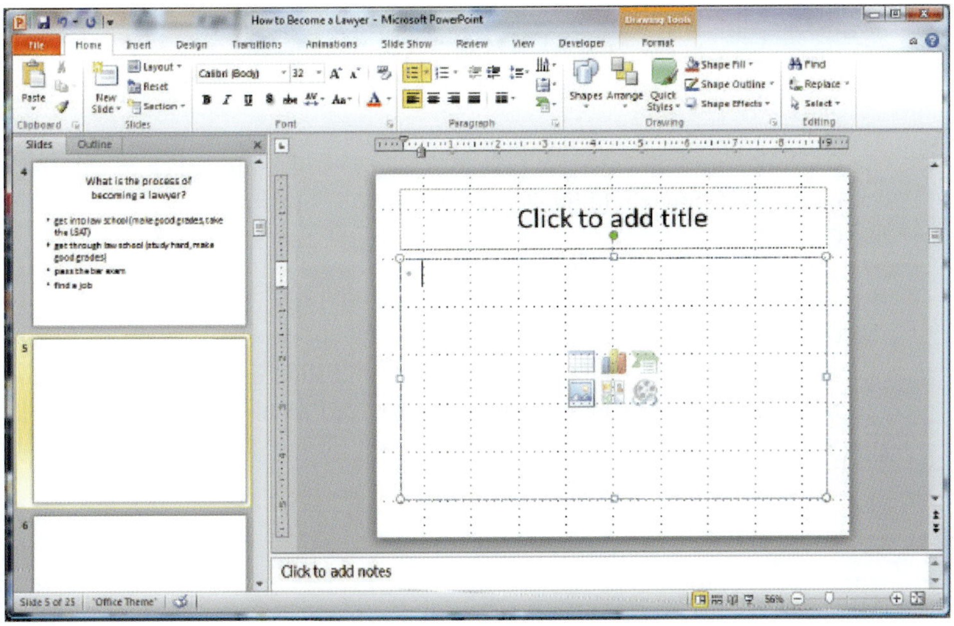

FIGURE 16.32

Click the **Clip Art** icon, for example, to open a task pane on the right where you can type in a keyword for the type of image you want and search for it from clip art images saved on your computer or found on the Internet. See Figure 16.33.

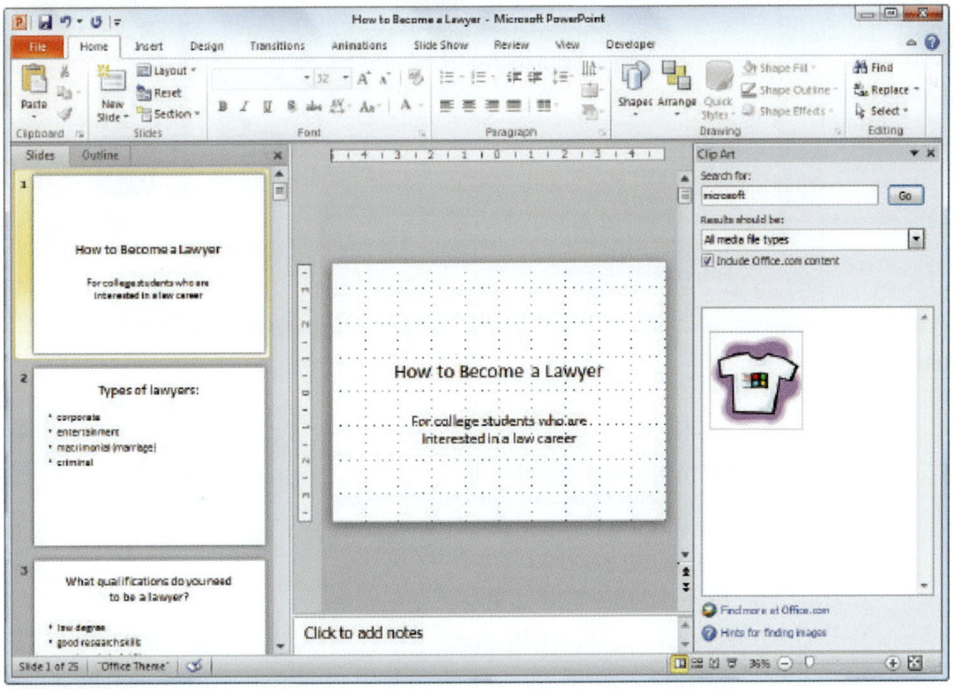

FIGURE 16.33

To insert images using a placeholder:

1. Add a slide with a content area layout, such as the Title and Content or Two Content layout.
2. Click the **Clip Art** icon in the center of the content area.

3. In the Clip Art task pane, type a keyword or phrase that describes the image that you are looking for.
4. Click the drop-down arrow next to *Search in* to specify the source of the images.
5. Click the drop-down arrow next to *Results should be,* and click to check the media types you would like to use.
6. Click **Go.**
7. Click a clip art image to insert it.

You are not limited to adding images based solely on the arrangement of content areas on the slide layout. The content of the second slide in Marisa's presentation could be laid out with images rather than text, and would look something like Figure 16.34.

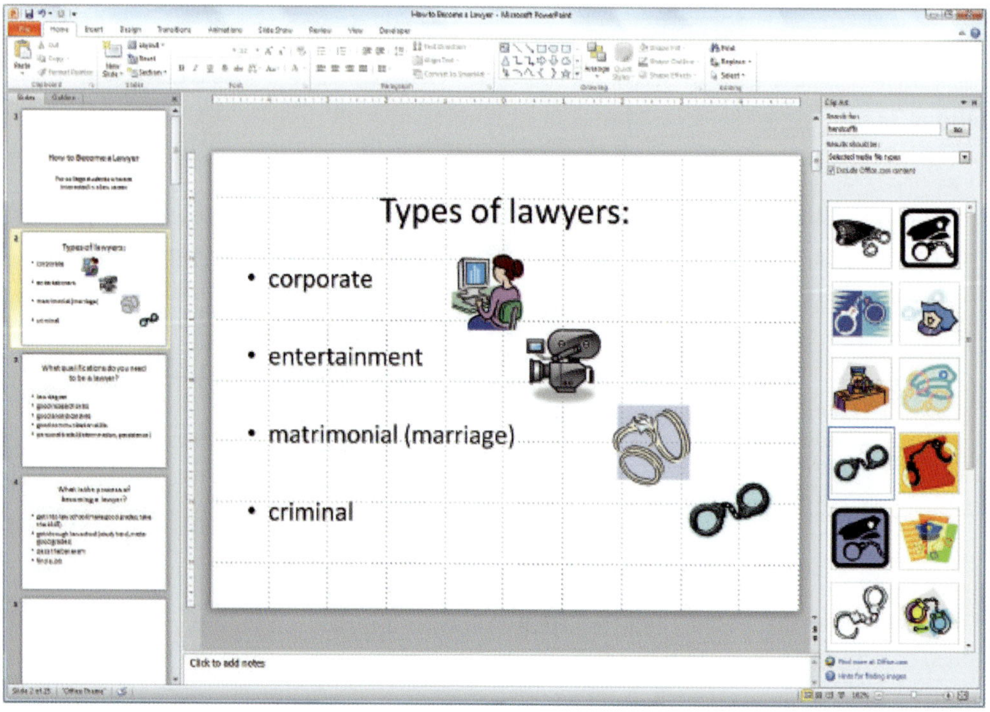

FIGURE 16.34

To insert images without a placeholder:

1. Add a slide without a content area layout, such as a Title Only or Blank Slide layout.
2. Click the *Insert* tab.
3. In the Images group, click **Clip Art.**
4. In the Clip Art task pane, type a keyword or phrase that describes the image that you are looking for.
5. Click the drop-down arrow next to *Search in* to specify the source of the images.
6. Click the drop-down arrow next to *Results should be,* and click to check the media types you would like to use.
7. Click **Go.**
8. Click a clip art image to insert it.

After you add the image, you will most likely need to resize and position it on the slide.

- To resize an image, click to select it and then position the pointer over one of the small selection handles that appear. Your pointer will take the shape of a two-headed arrow. Hold down the mouse button and drag to resize the image. Dragging a selection handle on the corner of the image will resize it while keeping the proportions intact.
- To move an image, place your pointer directly on top of the image, so that it takes the shape of a four-headed arrow. Hold down the mouse button and drag to move it to a new location on the slide. See Figure 16.35.

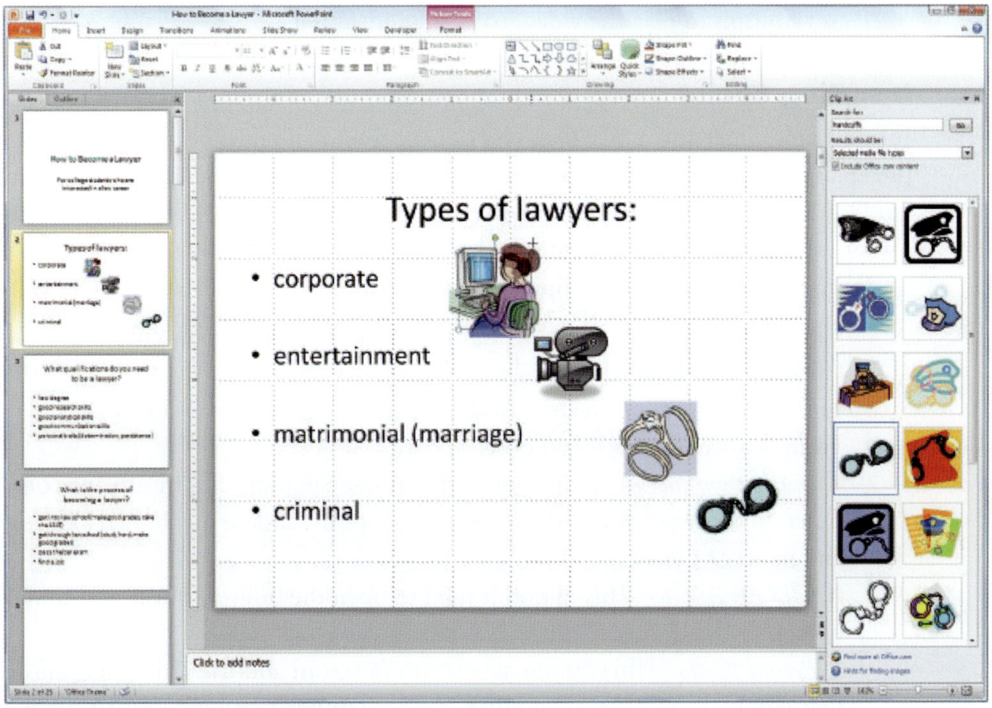

FIGURE 16.35

Inserting Movie Clips and Sound

Use movies and sound files in slide presentations to give them life and make them exciting to view.

Inserting Movie Clips

Movie clips (video files) consist of a few seconds to several minutes of video. Supported video file formats include Adobe Flash Media (with the extension .swf), Windows Media file (.asf), Windows Video file (.avi), Movie file (.mpg or .mpeg), and Windows Media Video file (.wmv). Videos in the .mp4, .mov, and .qt formats are compatible if the Apple QuickTime player is installed.

Click the **Insert Media Clip** icon in the center of a content area to insert a movie clip into your presentation, or follow the steps below.

To insert a movie clip into a slide presentation (see Figure 16.36):

1. Click on the slide where you want to insert the video.
2. Click the *Insert* tab.

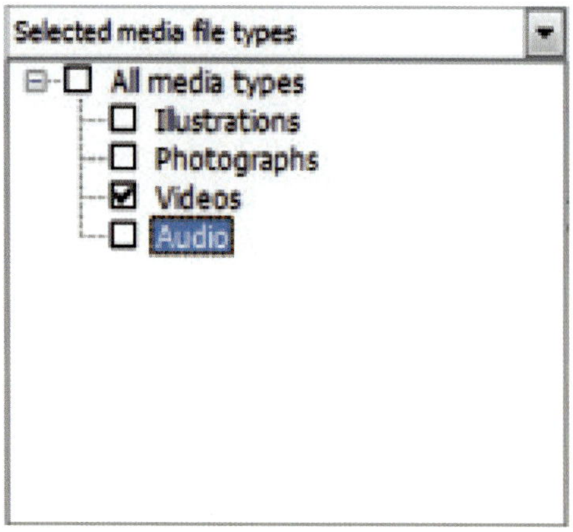

FIGURE 16.36

3. In the *Media* group, click **Video** to reveal a drop-down list. From the drop-down list, choose:
   - *Video from file*—use this option to pick a movie file from your computer.
   - *Video from website*—choose this option to link to an uploaded movie on a video sharing website such as YouTube.
   - *Clip Art Video*—this option allows you to choose a video file from the PowerPoint built-in library displayed in the task pane on the right side of the document window. In the task pane, you can search for a sample video by keyword, choose the type of video, and search the Office.com website for more samples.

A video inserted on a slide has controls displayed beneath it. Use the controls to play the video, pause it, and stop it.

Inserting Sound

In addition to inserting movie files, you can use sound and music clips in your slide presentations. Compatible formats for sound and music files include AIFF Audio (.aiff), AU Audio (.au), MIDI (.mid or .midi), MP3 Audio (.mp3), Windows Audio (.wav), and Windows Media Audio (.wma).

To insert sound and music clips into a presentation:

1. Click the slide where you want to insert the sound and music clip.
2. Click the *Insert* tab.
3. In the *Media* group, click the **Audio** button to reveal a drop-down list.
4. From the drop-down list, choose:
   - *Audio from file*—Use this option to choose an audio file from your computer. In the Insert Audio dialog box that appears, choose the desired location and name of the file.
   - *Clip Art Audio*—This option is used to open the built-in music and sound library.
   - *Record Audio*—This option allows you to record and use sound and music that you record on your computer. Your computer must have a microphone to create the file. In the Record Audio dialog box that appears, click on the red button (RECORD) to record the sound. Once the recorder is on, speak or play music into your computer's built-in or plug-in microphone. While recording, you will see a "total sound length" message. When you are finished recording, click on the blue square button to stop recording.

PowerPoint inserts an icon on the slide for the sound. Click the icon to display controls for audio settings.

Inserting Pictures

You can insert pictures from files on your computer with the *Insert* tab on the Ribbon or click the **Insert Picture from File** icon in the center of a content area.

To insert a picture into a slide presentation:

1. Click the slide where the picture will appear.
2. Click the *Insert* tab and the **Picture** button. Or, click the **Insert Picture from File** icon in the center of a content area.
3. In the Insert Picture dialog box, navigate to the folder location of the image you want to use.
4. Click on the desired picture and then click **Insert.**

FAQ: COPYRIGHTED IMAGES

A copyright is a legal right given to an author to share and make copies of created work. Copyrights are provided for books, writings, images, movies, fine art, and any created work. When you work with images in PowerPoint, it is important to note whether that image has a copyright that protects it from unauthorized use, or if the image is *public domain* and available for free use.

If an image is copyrighted, you must obtain permission from the creator of the image or pay a fee (sometimes called a license) to copy and use the image in your PowerPoint presentation. There are many places to find copyright-free images and images in the public domain. In fact, the U.S. government manages one of the most comprehensive websites of this material.

If you have a budget to pay for copyrighted images, you could use one of many stock image companies. Most of these companies require a per image fee to be paid for a one-time use of the image. These companies will also allow you to pay a set fee to download multiple copyrighted images when needed. Veer, Corbis Images, and Getty Images are a few of the many stock photo companies that offer copyrighted images for a fee.

Correcting Images: Brightness and Contrast

In general, you will resize and move pictures following the procedures described above for images. You can adjust their brightness and contrast with the *Picture Tools* tab.

To adjust picture images:

1. Click on the picture to select it. A *Format Picture Tools* tab appears (see Figure 16.37).
2. In the *Adjust* group, click **Corrections.**
3. Point to the various images to preview the corrections available and then click on the picture that shows the desired levels of sharpness, brightness, and contrast for the image on your slide.

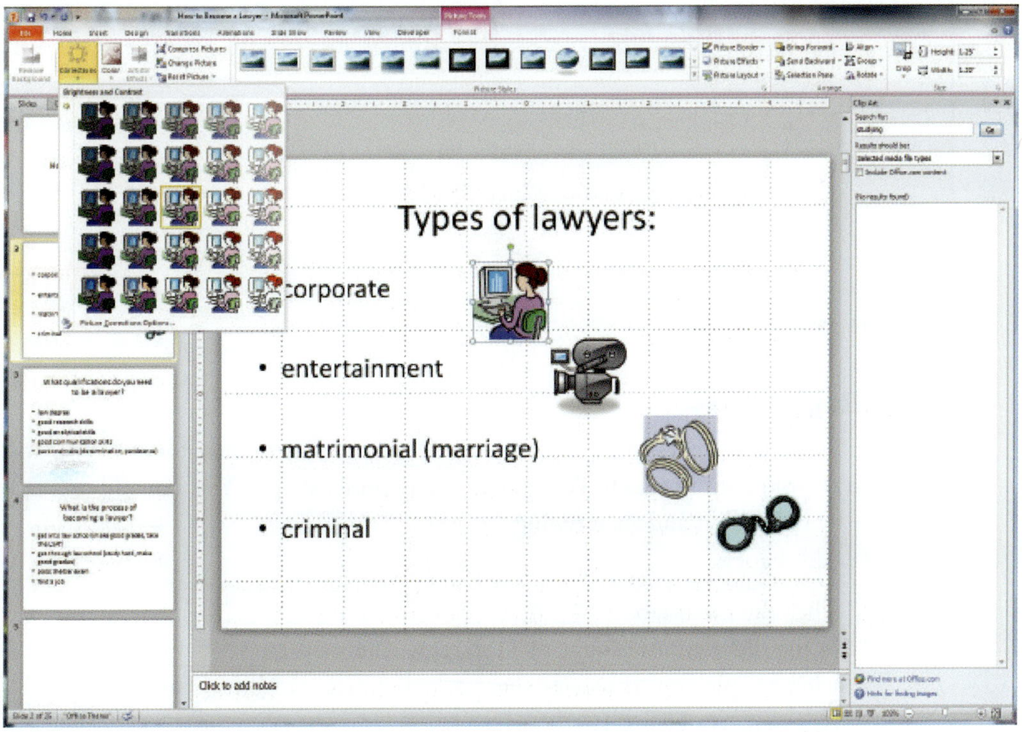

FIGURE 16.37

Compressing Images

When using image files such as color photos, it is very important to reduce or compress the file size of the images. A typical PowerPoint presentation could include images from backgrounds, icons, bullets, clip art, and photos. In addition to these images, the slide presentation would contain text of different sizes and many colors. Add sounds, transition effects, and slide animations to the above list and the file size of the presentation increases considerably. Large PowerPoint presentations with huge file sizes can run extremely slowly. Slow presentations are not ideal as they can be boring to audience members.

To compress embedded media files (see Figure 16.38):

1. Click the *File* tab.
2. Click **Info.**
3. Click **Compress Media** on the right.
4. Click the level of quality you wish to preserve for the presentation from the options **Presentation Quality, Internet Quality,** and **Low Quality.**
5. A dialog box will display to show you the progress of the compression. Click **Close** when it is complete.

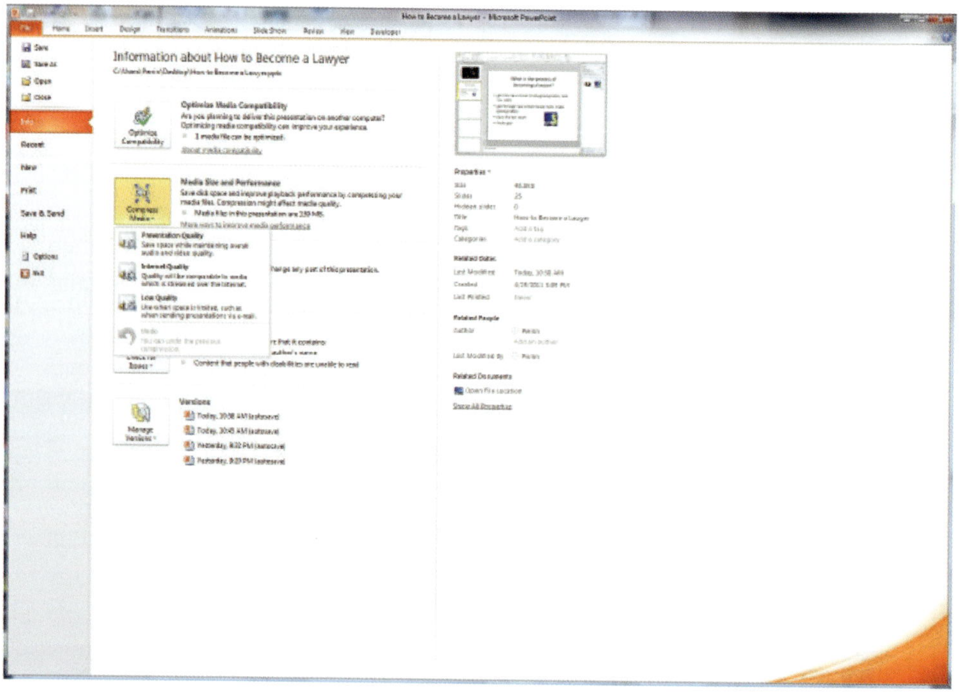

FIGURE 16.38

Adding Shapes

Sometimes the images provided by clip art or pictures do not meet your needs. You can draw your own images in PowerPoint using preset shapes. You can add text to a shape by selecting it and then typing.

To add shapes:

1. Click the *Insert* tab.
2. In the Illustrations group, click **Shapes.**
3. Click to "pick up" the shape that you want to draw. Your pointer appears as a plus sign. See Figure 16.39.
4. Click on the slide, hold down the mouse button, and then drag to draw the shape.

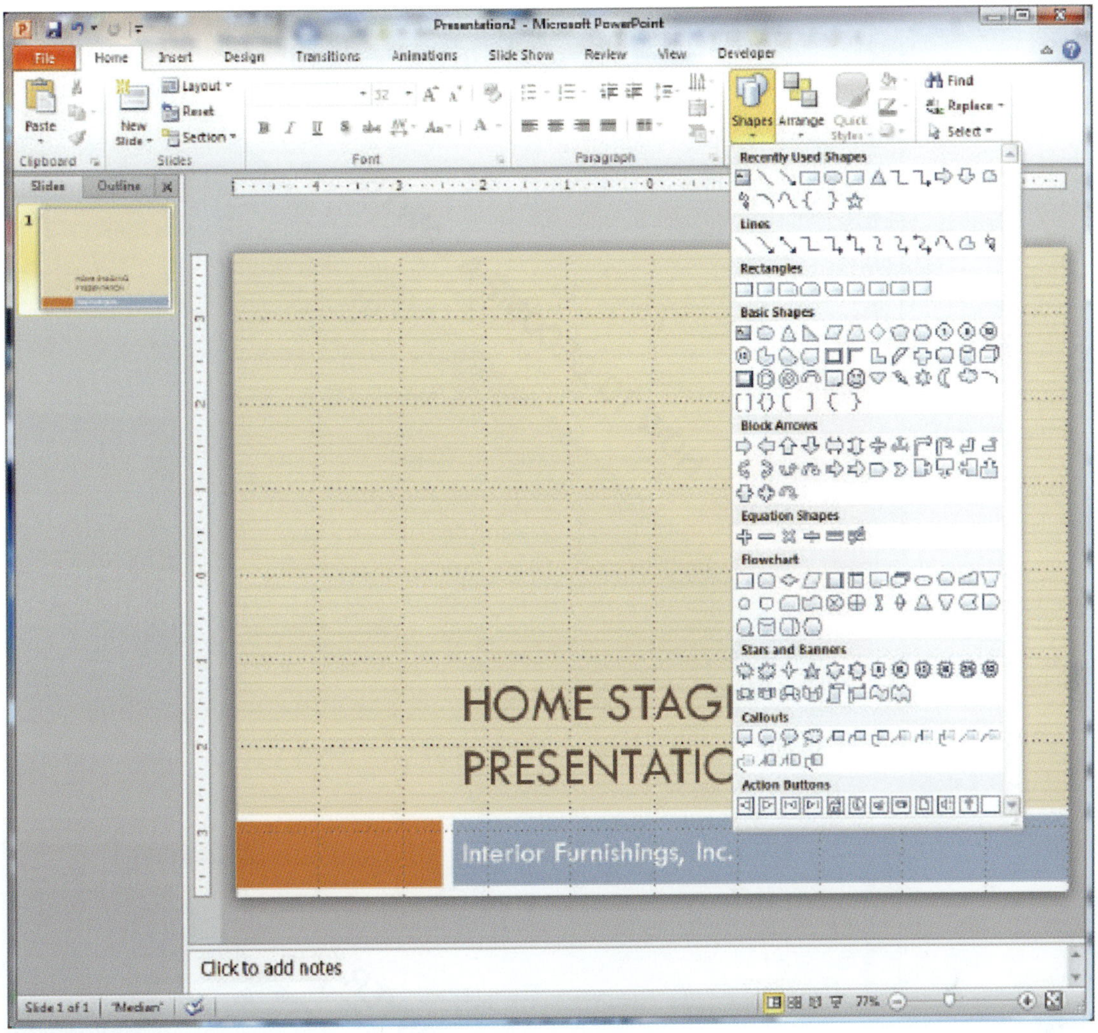

FIGURE 16.39

If you hold down the **Shift** key while you drag to draw a shape, you can constrain the dimensions of the shape. For example, holding the **Shift** key while dragging a circle creates a perfectly round circle; holding it while dragging a line draws a straight line; and holding it while dragging a rectangle draws a perfect square.

Adding Borders

Borders are a good way to make sure objects stand out within a slide. Marisa created the two slides shown in Figures 16.40A and 16.40B for her "How to Become a Lawyer" presentation. She added a border to the subtitle placeholder in Figure 16.40B. Which do you think calls more attention to the subtitle?

To add borders around an object:

1. Click the object to select it.
2. Click the *Home* tab.
3. In the *Drawing* group, click **Shape Outline.**
4. Click the weight drop-down to choose a border thickness.
5. Click the color box to choose a color for the border.

PowerPoint has a variety of preset Quick Styles for images that combine borders, colors, and special effects.

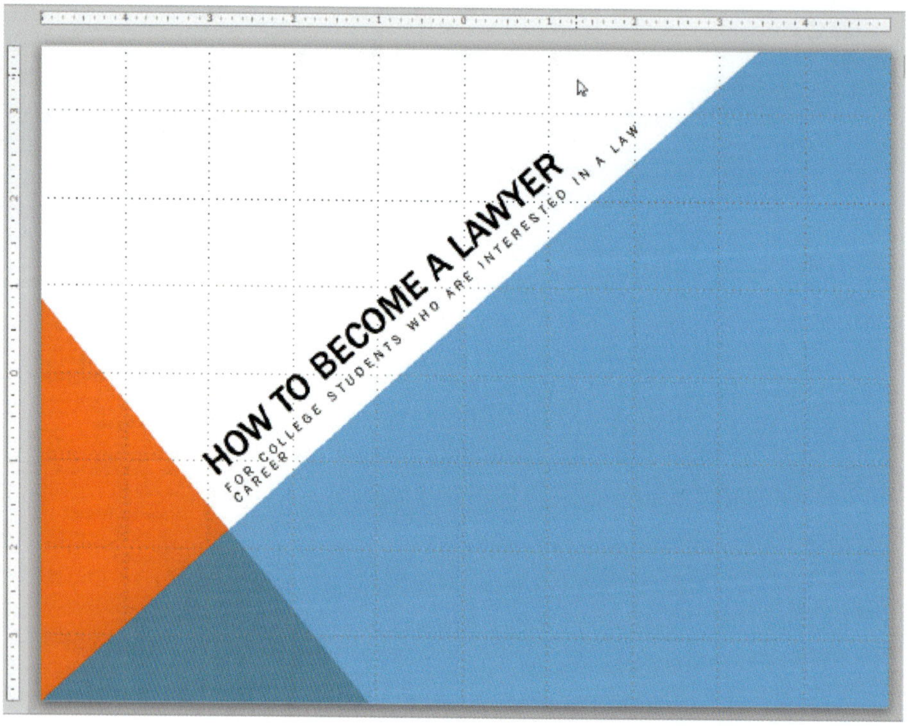

FIGURE 16.40A

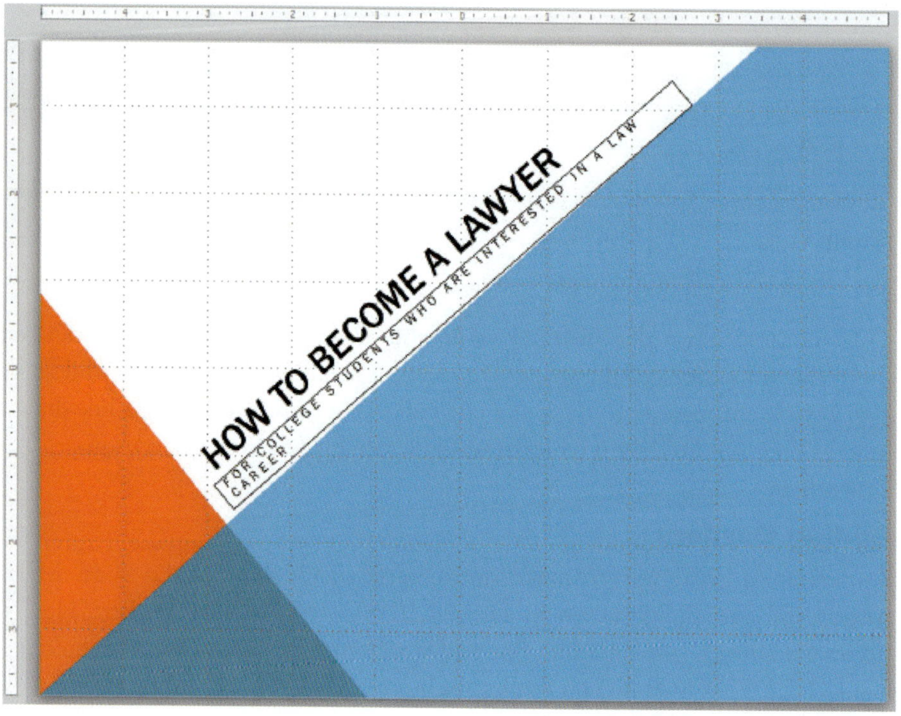

FIGURE 16.40B

To apply a preset Quick Style image:

1. Click an object to select it.
2. Click the *Home* tab.
3. In the Drawing category, click the **Quick Styles** button to show the available border styles.
4. Click a style to apply it to your object.

EXERCISE 16.5: ADDING GRAPHICS

One of your goals with this presentation is to improve your PowerPoint skills, so you decide to experiment with images added to slides.

1. **Open the STA Presentation.pptx file from the last exercise, if necessary.**
2. **Add at least two slides that include images—clip art, pictures, SmartArt diagrams, or shapes—that help communicate the information in your presentation.**
3. **Add relevant images to at least two of your bulleted list slides.**
4. **Save the presentation.**
5. **Close STA Presentation.pptx, or leave it open for the next exercise.**

Using the Notes Pane

Notes included in PowerPoint presentations provide your audience with additional information such as references or footnotes that cannot fit onto the slide itself. Or, use them to write a script for the presenter to refer to during the presentation. The presenter may print a hard copy of the notes for distribution or reference.

To add notes to a slide:

1. Display the slide in Normal view or in the Notes Pages view from the *View* tab.
2. Click in the Notes pane at the bottom of the screen and type the notes for that slide.

Working with Slides

Slide Sorter View shows thumbnails of the slides in your presentation and provides a very convenient way to add, delete, and rearrange them. Click the **Slide Sorter View** button on the bottom right side of the status bar or on the *View* tab to change to this view.

To rearrange slides in Slide Sorter View:

1. Switch to Slide Sorter View.
2. Point to the slide you want to move and hold down the mouse button. Drag the slide to a new location.
3. You will notice a vertical line appears as you drag. When it is positioned appropriately, release the mouse button to drop the slide in that location.

As with the other Microsoft Office applications, it is a good idea to right-click on an element to modify in PowerPoint. The right-click displays a context menu of commands that it makes sense to choose from, depending on what you clicked. For example, you can right-click a slide in Slide Sorter View and choose **Delete Slide** to remove it. Or right-click and choose **Hide Slide** to leave it in the presentation, but skip it when running the slide show.

To add new or duplicate slides in Slide Sorter View:

1. Switch to Slide Sorter View.
2. Right-click on the slide and choose **New Slide.** A blank slide with the same slide layout is added after the slide you right-clicked.
3. You can also right-click on the slide and choose **Duplicate Slide.** Now a copy of the slide is added after the selected slide.

In Normal view, right-clicking on slides in the slide list pane on the left of the screen provides a similar set of commands.

A slide number in PowerPoint is similar to a page number, often appearing in the footer area at the bottom right of the slide. Slide numbers are useful for presentations because they make it easier for audience members to refer to slides when asking questions to the presenter.

To insert a slide number on a slide (see Figure 16.41):

1. Click the *Insert* tab.
2. In the *Text* group, click **Slide Number.**
3. In the Header and Footer dialog box that appears, click the *Slide* tab.
4. Check *Slide Number* to insert the slide number to the bottom right.
5. Slide numbers are usually not displayed on the title slide. Check *Don't show on title slide* to leave the number off.
6. Click **Apply to All,** or **Apply** if you want to display the number on the selected slide only.

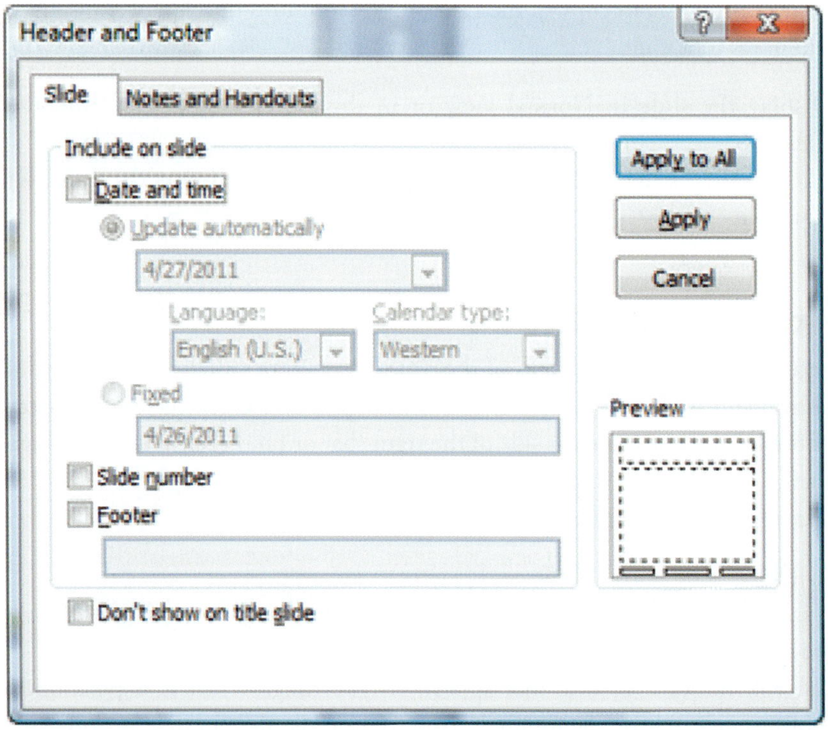

FIGURE 16.41

Adding Transitions

Once you finish your slides, you can add transitions between them that instruct PowerPoint how to display each slide when you run the slide show. Transitions are small animations that deliver each slide in a unique and interesting way. It is recommended that you keep transitions consistent within a presentation, changing them only to call attention to an important slide.

Some available transitions in PowerPoint are shown in Figure 16.42.

Cut	After the current slide displays, the next slide comes in quickly.
Fade	After the current slide displays, it fades out and the next slide comes in.
Wipe	After the current slide displays, it leaves the screen as the next slide comes in.

FIGURE 16.42

To add a transition between two or more slides:

1. Select the slide or slides to which you want to add transition effects.
2. Click the *Transitions* tab.
3. Click the **More** button in the bottom right of the *Transition to this Slide* group to display the full gallery of options.
4. Point to a slide transition to preview its effect, then click the one you would like to apply.

Several options for slide transitions are available from the *Timing* group.

To apply timing options:

1. Select the slide or slides to which you want to control timing.
2. Click on the *Transitions* tab.
3. In the *Timing* group, click the sound drop-down to add sound effects to slide transitions. Click the duration arrows to set the duration of the slide transition in seconds.

Viewing a Slide Show

Before delivering your presentation, run it as a slide show to evaluate its appearance and practice speaking with it. To run a slide show, click the Slide Show view on the status bar, or click the **Slide Show** button on the *View* tab. For more control, click the *Slide Show* tab and choose a button from the *Start Slide Show* group. To stop a slide show and return to Normal view, press the **Esc** key on the keyboard.

You have several options to advance the slide show manually as it runs.

- *Option #1.* Use the arrow keys (or the **Enter** and **Backspace** keys, or **Page Up** and **Page Down**) on your computer keyboard to advance the slides in the presentation. This approach is suitable if you give your presentation from a lectern or smart podium (laptop connected podium) in front of an audience. If you choose to walk around during the presentation, you will have to come back to the podium each time you advance the presentation.
- *Option #2.* Use the connected mouse to advance the slides in the presentation. This approach is similar to the first option because you have to be near the computer during the presentation.
- *Option #3.* Use a wireless mouse to advance the slides in the presentation. This option provides you with more flexibility while presenting the slide show because you can be a certain distance away from the computer. The limitation is that there cannot be any obstructions between the mouse and computer.

You may choose to run the presentation automatically with the PowerPoint software itself. To do this, you must set up the presentation as a show that will run using settings that you apply.

To set up an automatic slide show:

1. Click the *Slide Show* tab.
2. In the *Set Up* group, click **Set Up Slide Show.**
3. In the Set Up Show dialog box, check the appropriate boxes to apply your desired settings for the show. For instance, under Show type:
   - For a normal speaker at a podium with an audience, choose **Presented by a speaker (full screen).**
   - For a presentation to be viewed on a PC, choose **Browsed by an individual (window).**
   - For a presentation at an exhibit or convention, choose **Browsed at a kiosk (full screen).**
   - Under Show options:
     - Check **Loop continuously until 'Esc'** to play the presentation repeatedly until the **Esc** key is pressed.
   - Under Show slides:
     - Click **All** to play the entire presentation.
     - Click **From slide # to slide #** to play a portion of the presentation.
   - Under Advance slides:
     - Click **Manually** to advance manually with the keyboard or mouse.
     - Click **Using timings, if present** to advance slides after preset times.

EXERCISE 16.6: RUNNING THE SLIDE SHOW

You are ready for the speaking engagement but want to add slide transitions and preview your slide show to see what improvements you can make.

1. **Open the STA Presentation.pptx file from the last exercise, if necessary.**
2. **Add slide transitions to all slides.**
3. **Run the slide show and make any necessary improvements.**
4. **Run the slide show for a classmate and incorporate his or her suggestions as you see fit.**
5. **Save the presentation.**
6. **Your instructor may ask you to present your slide show in class.**
7. **Close STA Presentation.pptx.**

Printing a Presentation

You can print PowerPoint presentations as handouts and distribute them for an audience to follow along with the presenter, or print the slides themselves on one page each for reference or distribution. These printouts are sometimes called *decks.* You may also want to print the notes of your final PowerPoint presentation as a script for the speaker to follow.

To print the slides of a presentation:

1. Click the *File* tab.
2. Click **Print.**
3. Under Print Range, click **All** to print all of your slides. Or, to print only the slide that is displayed, click **Print Current Slide.** Or, to print specific slides, click **Custom Range,** and then enter the numbers of individual slides or a range of slides.
4. Under Other Settings, click **Color** and click the option that you want.
5. Click **Print.**

To print Notes:

1. Click the *File* tab.
2. Click **Print.**
3. Under Settings, click the arrow next to **Full Page Slides,** then click **Notes Pages.**
4. Click **Print.**

Handouts

Creating handouts with readable slides and a notes section for your audience is important when your goal is to provide appealing materials for your presentation. Audience members will appreciate handouts that do not contain too many pages and at the same time, contain pages with readable text. For instance, if your slides have charts and graphics on them, choose a print layout that involves fewer pages, such as a two per page, three per page, or four per page layout.

To print handouts (see Figure 16.43A and 16.43B):

1. Click the *File* tab.
2. Click **Print.**
3. Click the *Full Page Slides* drop-down list.
4. Under Handouts, click the number of slides to print per page, and whether they should appear in order vertically or horizontally.
5. Click **Print.**

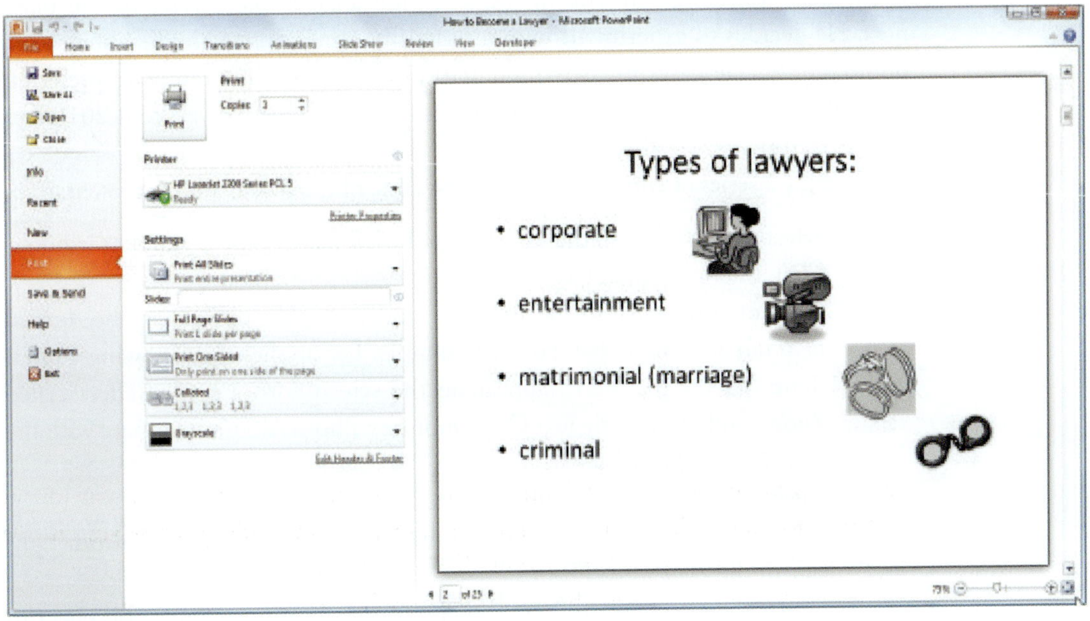

FIGURE 16.43A

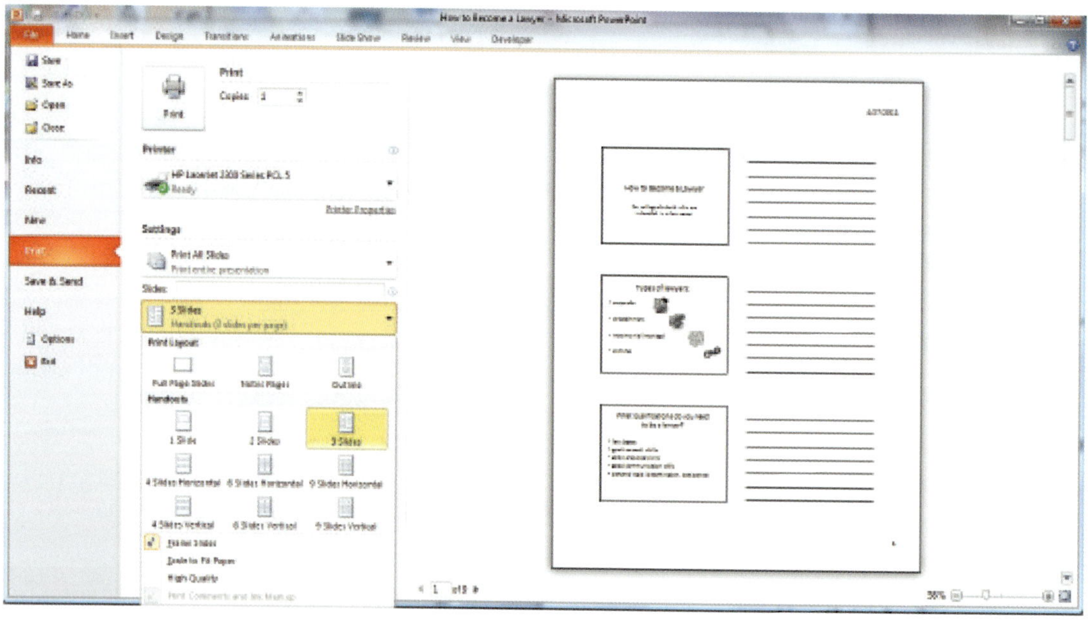

FIGURE 16.43B

ADVANCED TOPICS IN POWERPOINT

Custom Animations

Custom animations in PowerPoint add excitement and movement to objects on individual slides in a presentation. Use the Animation Pane to add animations to selected elements on a slide. You can create animations that affect how objects in a slide will:

- Appear on the screen (entrance)
- Disappear from the screen (exit)
- Move across the screen (motion paths)
- Behave while on the screen (effects)

For example, imagine that Lee Schuster needs to compile an album of his most successful designs to run in the reception area of his interior design business. He decides to experiment with a series of animations to the first slide for a photo album. He bases his new presentation on the six-slide template presentation called "Contemporary Photo Album" that comes with PowerPoint 2010 (see Figure 16.44).

To apply a series of animations to the first slide of the photo album presentation:

1. Select the first slide in the slide list on the left pane of the document window.
2. Click the *Animations* tab.
3. Click on any object in the slide and notice that the options in the *Animations* tab are now active. For this example, Lee applies the following animations: Set the picture to appear on the screen with a special effect called Zoom, and set the title text Contemporary Photo Album to appear with the special effect Float In.
4. Click the picture on the slide to select it.
5. In the *Animation* group, click the small down arrow on the bottom right side of the *Animation* group.
6. Under the Entrance options, click the **Zoom** button to apply this effect to the picture. A small number 1 appears to the left of the picture.

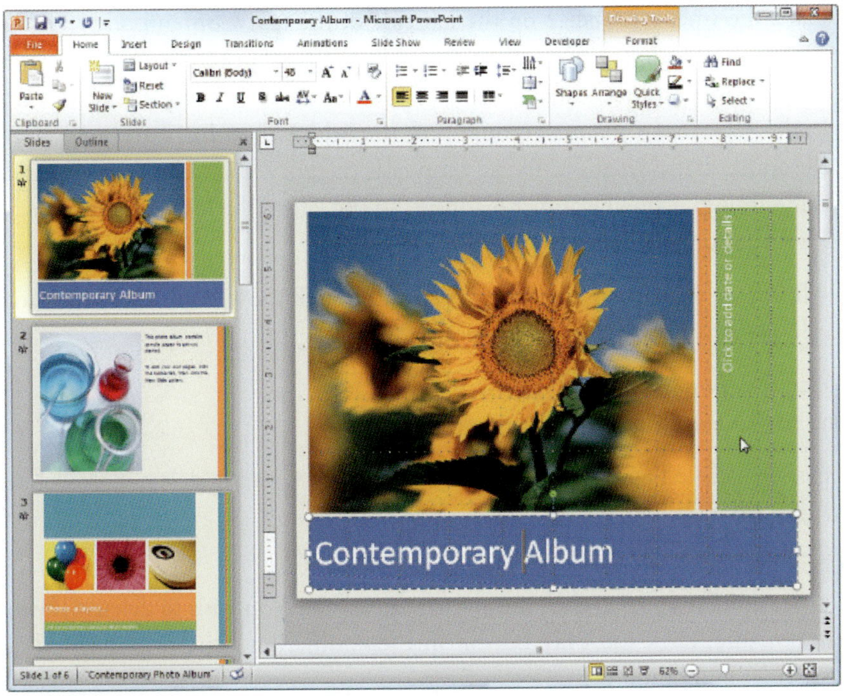

FIGURE 16.44

7. Select the text Contemporary Photo Album at the bottom of the slide.
8. Under the *Animation* group, click the small down arrow on the bottom right side of the *Animation* group.
9. Under the Entrance options, click the **Float In** button to apply this effect to the text. A small number 2 appears to the left of the picture. See Figure 16.45. Next, Lee also wants to add an underlining animation effect to the text Contemporary Photo Album so that after the text floats into the slide, it appears underlined for emphasis.

FIGURE 16.45

10. Click the small number 2 on the left side of the text Contemporary Photo Album. The animation number and object appear in the Animation Pane with a border around them.
11. In the *Advanced Animation* group, click the **Add Animation** button to select the additional animation. In the Emphasis category, click **Underline** to add underlining. A small number 3 appears to the left of the text Contemporary Photo Album on the slide.

Lee will not see the animations until he runs the slide show or previews the animations. To preview the series of animations:

1. Click the *Animations* tab.
2. In the *Preview* group, click **Preview.**

If Lee is not satisfied with the custom animation effect, he can delete it. To delete an animation from a slide:

1. Click the slide containing the animations.
2. In the Animation Pane, click the animation number you wish to delete. (If you are not sure, click the **Play** button in the Animation Pane to preview that particular animation.)
3. With the animation selected in the Animation Pane, click the down arrow to the right of the selected animation. From the drop-down list, click *Remove.*

Copying, Importing, and Exporting Slides

Copy and Import a Slide

When you create a slide presentation, you can insert an existing slide into a new slide presentation instead of creating a slide from scratch.

To import a slide from another PowerPoint presentation:

1. Click on the slide before the place where you want the new slide to appear.
2. Click the *Home* tab.
3. In the *Slides* group, click **New Slide.**
4. Click **Reuse Slides.** The Reuse Slides task pane opens on the right side of the window. See Figure 16.46.
5. Click the **Browse** button at the top of the Reuse Slides pane and choose **Browse File.** The Browse dialog box opens.
6. Navigate to the presentation with the slide(s) you want to reuse.
7. Click **Open.** All of the slides in the imported presentation display in the Reuse Slides task pane.
8. Click the slide(s) that you wish to import into the existing slide presentation. The selected slide(s) from the Reuse Slides pane now appears after the slide you selected in your presentation.

Export a Slide

PowerPoint also allows you to save slides in different formats for use in other types of software programs. For instance, you can save one or more PowerPoint slides from a presentation in Windows Media Video format; graphics formats such as GIF, JPEG, PNG, TFF; or a PDF format.

To save a slide or entire slide presentation into a different format:

1. Click the slide you want to export.
2. Click the *File* tab.

FIGURE 16.46

3. Click **Save As.**
4. In the Save As dialog box, click the drop-down arrow next to *Save as Type* and choose the desired file format from the drop-down list.
5. Type a file name in the File name field.
6. Click **Save.**
7. In the dialog box that appears, click the buttons for **Every Slide** (if you want the entire presentation) or **Current Slide Only** (if you want only one slide). If you choose Every Slide, PowerPoint creates a new folder and adds all the picture files to the folder. If you choose Current Slide Only, PowerPoint saves the picture in the chosen format.

Comment Feature

In PowerPoint, you can insert comments on slides in a presentation. Comments assist with editing. Insert them to provide additional information or alert a colleague of a slide from a shared presentation to be edited. Comments appear like footnotes at the bottom of the page when printed. Inserted comments appear on the slide labeled with your user name and initials followed by the comment number, and the date you inserted the comment. See Figure 16.47.

To insert a comment onto a slide of a presentation:

1. Click the *Review* tab.
2. In the *Comments* group, click **New Comment.**
3. In the small textbox that appears, type in the text for the comment.
4. When finished typing the comment, click anywhere on the slide to exit the comment box.

To edit an existing comment:

1. Click the comment you wish to edit.
2. Click the *Review* tab.
3. In the *Comments* group, click **Edit Comment.** Or, double-click on the comment number.

FIGURE 16.47

To delete a comment:

1. Click the comment you wish to delete.
2. Click the *Review* tab.
3. In the *Comments* group, click **Edit Comment** or double-click on the comment number and press the **Delete** key on the keyboard.

INTEGRATION: SENDING HANDOUTS TO WORD

One advantage to using the Microsoft Office suite is the smooth integration of the output from one application into another. For example, PowerPoint has the ability to convert your slide presentation to a handout in Microsoft Word. From Word, you can save it as a Word document, edit and format it using Word features, and then print it or e-mail it to your audience. The PowerPoint slides appear in the Word document as large thumbnails displayed alone on a page or next to blank lines for your audience members to use for notes pages. You choose how many slides will appear on a handout page: one, two, or three for each. To convert a PowerPoint presentation to a Word handout:

1. Click the *File* tab.
2. Select **Save & Send.**
3. Click **Create Handouts.**
4. In the pane on the right, click **Create Handouts.**
5. In the Send to Microsoft Word dialog box, choose a layout option: **Notes next to slides; Blank lines next to slides; Notes below slides; Blank lines below slides;** or click **Outline only** to send the text of your presentation to Word.
6. Click **OK.**

FAST TRACK PRACTICE: CREATING A SALES PRESENTATION

Mark Sonnerheim is a medical equipment salesman for MedStatic Equipment, Inc. and needs to create an effective sales presentation to present his latest sales numbers and information to his superiors at the company's corporate headquarters. The presentation must contain the following information and data arranged in an interesting, manageable format for the audience of senior-level executives.

Slide 1: Title

- Mark Sonnerheim
- MedStatic Equipment, Inc.
- Medical equipment sales report
- Year to date 2011

Slides 2, 3, 4: Medical Equipment Suppliers

- Supplier names
- Supplier location (city and state)
- Supplier equipment
- Number of units supplied to MedStatic

Slide 5: Sales from Medical Equipment

Year	Sales (in millions)
2010	5.4
2009	5.6
2008	4.2
2007	4.1
2006	4.0

Slide 6: Recommendations for Next Year to Save Money

- Increase size of territories for each sales force
- Require sales force to check in with main offices more frequently to receive assignments
- Add teleconferencing to avoid sales force coming into main office

Slide 7: Closing

- "Thank you" to the audience
- Mark Sonnerheim's contact information
- E-mail: mark.sonnerheim@MedStatic.com

Include the following features in the final sales presentation:

- Appropriate backgrounds, graphics, and bulleted text
- Animations within slides
- Slide transitions
- Headers and footers on each slide

Also, final slides should be:

- Visually appealing
- Professional
- Consistent in the use of fonts, headings, layout, and graphics such as bullets

SUMMARY

Organizations use presentation software to visually communicate business ideas to colleagues, employees, customers, and potential clients. Originally created to run on large mainframe computers, presentation software gained more popularity and use throughout the 1990s as the use of personal computers and digital projectors increased. Like most software booms, there were early forerunners of presentation software, but Microsoft's PowerPoint software quickly became the most popular presentation graphics software on the market.

PowerPoint is a graphics presentation software application that is widely used by many types of businesses and in many industries. Business professionals create attractive and engaging business presentations that include text of all sizes, shapes, colors, and effects. Presentations can also include graphics to engage an audience while imparting valuable information in an easy to understand visual manner. The graphics may be clip art images, pictures, diagrams, charts, tables, and drawn shapes.

PowerPoint slide shows are often enhanced with special effects known as transitions as, within a presentation, one slide replaces the next. Custom animations, as well as sound effects, music, and embedded videos, are added to grab an audience's attention.

Although PowerPoint presentations may contain lots of bells and whistles, it is wise for PowerPoint users to plan and create presentations carefully. Effective presentations are succinct, to the point, and targeted to a specific audience and delivery method. In a professional setting, presentations should use appropriate, relevant graphics and slide transitions. An additional feature of PowerPoint is the ability to print presentations as handouts for audience members. Printouts can include handouts with sections for audience members to annotate.

Mastering PowerPoint is a useful skill in any career you pursue. Basic PowerPoint skills include the ability to enter, edit, and format text on slides using document themes, adding appropriate graphics and special effects, and printing presentations in various formats. More advanced skills include adding custom animations, reusing slides, and adding comments for editing.

CHAPTER 17

Modes of Delivery

KEY CONCEPTS

1. Public speaking is often required at work or other events. See page 214.

2. The four modes of delivering a speech are extemporaneous, manuscript, impromptu, and memorized. See page 215.

3. Speakers should rehearse all four modes of delivery. See page 215.

4. When delivering a speech, nonverbal communication is as important as content and verbal communication. See page 219.

Like death and taxes, public speaking is inevitable," Aaliyah's public speaking instructor said with a laugh as he assigned the class's first speech. This sentiment did not calm Aaliyah's nerves—to say the least. Of course, she knew that she would need to speak in front of an audience for her college courses and at her job.

In fact, Aaliyah's boss had her give an impromptu speech at the last department meeting. Just thinking of the experience made her cringe. She had stumbled over every word and ended up playing with the bracelet on her wrist in an attempt to calm herself down. She could easily think of what she wanted to say—but figuring out *how* to say it and how to prepare for the situation was a different story. For her next public speaking experience, Aaliyah wants to be prepared and take plenty of time to practice.

MODES OF DELIVERY

Aaliyah is wise to think carefully about what she will say and how she will deliver her speech. The four methods or manners in which a person gives a speech are called the **modes of delivery**:

- Extemporaneous
- Manuscript
- Impromptu
- Memorized

Effective speakers are aware of these modes and prepare for each situation.

There are many misconceptions about how to prepare for a speech. Some people advocate not practicing a speech, because they believe you will become bored with it when it comes time to get in front of your audience. Others advise packing your speech with more information than you can use in the time allotted so you will not run out of things to say.

People who are very knowledgeable about their presentation topics might think, "I know my topic, so I don't need to prepare a formal presentation. I'll do better if I just wing it." On the other hand, some people become excessively tied to their written speeches and decide to simply read them because they are afraid that they may forget the information otherwise. In reality, it is best to practice each of the four modes as much as possible. The type of speech chosen should be appropriate for the content and the time allotted for delivering the speech.

Above all, the best advice is, "Practice makes perfect." The more you rehearse your speech, the more comfortable you will become with it. The more comfortable you are with the content, the more comfortable you will be with the delivery. As you rehearse, you will probably think of new ideas to insert or new ways to present the information. Sometimes these last-minute ideas will be the ones that truly win over an audience.

The audience typically is **empathetic**, meaning they want to be kind and considerate toward the speaker. They are gathered because the speaker has useful information to share that may help them in some way, such as by increasing their knowledge or helping them do their jobs better. The audience is not expecting a flawless speech in perfect Standard English, but they do want to see a fellow human being doing the best he or she can to share information. The audience members know how frightening or uncomfortable it can be to speak in front of a group of people, so the audience usually has empathy for the speaker.

Finally, keep in mind that the anxiety you feel is actually good! Have you ever hosted a dinner party and become stressed about preparing the menu and cleaning your house? You know that the planning and the stress are part of the process, and usually they are well worth the effort. The reward comes when you and your guests enjoy a memorable evening together. Likewise, it is rewarding when you present information to your appreciative audience. Learning to harness the anxiety you feel about public speaking and do your best to prepare can empower and energize you to do well.

Extemporaneous

The majority of speeches fall into the **extemporaneous** category. In these speeches, the content is offered in a way that makes the speaker seem relaxed and comfortable, and makes the speech almost conversational. The speaker focuses on the main message and supporting points rather than delivering a word-by-word recitation of a prepared statement.

Rehearsing

The quality of the presentation you will give is directly related to rehearsing your speech. A speaker should not just wing it or decide that their conversational skills and knowledge are so great that they can forego rehearsal. To best prepare for an extemporaneous speech, you should first create an outline of the main talking points. You may want to write down these points in the form of notes that you can refer to during the presentation.

Practice delivering the content out loud to get a feel for whether it meets the needs of the audience and if the organization flows logically. Often extemporaneous speeches offer opportunities for audiences to ask questions, so prepare for this by thinking about questions your audience may have and how you will respond.

Presenting

Now that you have rehearsed the content of your speech, take time to practice the techniques that will help you deliver the speech. How you will enter the room and command the audience's attention? How will you remain relaxed and comfortable? If there will be a podium, will you stand behind it or in front of it? Or, will you walk among the audience members?

Keep your words simple; use everyday speech rather than trying to impress your audience with big words. No matter how large the audience, practice your presentation as if you are having an informal conversation with a small group of associates. Make use of body language that comes naturally to you; a speech is typically not the place for exaggerated gestures and expressions. Consider rehearsing these skills in front of a practice audience or even a mirror.

Manuscript

The **manuscript** method is not as common and is reserved for formal situations when accuracy of information is imperative. For example, many fields hold professional conferences where members deliver speeches on topics of interest using the manuscript mode.

Frequently, the manuscript of the speech is considered for publication in a journal where complete accuracy is expected. Often, a consideration for presentations delivered using the manuscript method is whether the speech will become part of some sort of permanent record. In the case of famous speeches, such as Martin Luther King, Jr.'s "I Have a Dream" speech, you can likely find published copies.

If the situation calls for a manuscript delivery, the speech should be written with the same seriousness as an academic or professional paper, including conducting the same level of research and revision. Then, the speech should be adjusted slightly for oral delivery.

You may want to rehearse and include some effective speaker's notes to guide you as you give the speech (for example, indicating when you will pause for effect). When you rehearse, be sure that the speech is written so that you can read it with the least amount of distraction to your audience (consider, for example, printing the speech in large font). The audience should not notice you turning the pages or flipping through your notes. Make frequent eye contact and interact with the audience as you share the information formally.

Impromptu

Impromptu speeches take place when someone is suddenly called upon to speak about a certain topic. Imagine that you are in a history class and the professor turns to you and says: "Take us quickly through three important factors that led us into the war in Iraq." The response you give is an impromptu speech. In a professional context, your boss might ask you to stand up at a meeting and provide a brief overview of events that occurred the previous day.

It can be nerve-wracking to be called on to speak at a moment's notice, but you should remember that this is simply the way everyday conversation works. When you are with friends, at school, or at work, you converse with others continually without preparation. Therefore, stay composed the moment you are called upon to speak. You can often stall for a moment by expressing your appreciation for the chance to speak. While you are thanking your supervisor or professor for the opportunity to express your point of view, use that brief moment to gather your thoughts.

Most impromptu situations require a very concise reply, so focus on the main point ("Three important factors that caused us to get into a war in Iraq are…") and its main supporting points ("…one, the belief that there were weapons of mass destruction hidden there; two, the growing concern over terrorist activities originating from Iraq; and three, the protection of valuable oil reserves"). Concentrating on the thesis and two or three key points will help you stay focused. Once finished, you can again thank the person who invited you to speak as a way to bring the impromptu response to a close.

Memorized

For a **memorized speech**, the speaker memorizes the presentation word-for-word and delivers it to an audience without the use of an outline or notes. As with manuscript delivery, the memorized speech requires a speaker to write and rehearse a presentation until it is committed to memory. Once the speech is memorized, it should flow naturally from the speaker. It may be helpful to record yourself giving the speech and then listen to the recording repeatedly until you have committed the words to memory. Consider practicing with a partner who can prompt you when you get stuck.

DID YOU KNOW?

Most celebrities and politicians do not memorize their speeches. Some rely on teleprompters or wear an earpiece through which they are prompted about what to say. Many people who are constantly in the public eye are used to giving speeches, though they often do not prepare them entirely on their own. A speechwriter usually conducts the research and then provides the speaker with the main talking points and the facts to back them up. After that, it is up to the speaker to deliver the information.

Speakers also have a few tricks that anyone can use. For example, they may insert greetings, some background information, or pauses to give themselves a few moments to gather their thoughts. They will often jot down a few ideas, and bring their own personality into the delivery.

VOICE

As a speaker, you must carefully consider *how* you use your voice. Practice is the best way to work on vocal techniques for using the sound of speech effectively. One effective way is to record yourself on a webcam and play back the recording in order to experience your voice first hand.

Volume

Obviously, **volume**, the loudness with which you project your voice, should be carefully considered and practiced. You want all the audience members to be able to hear you without straining, no matter where they are sitting in the room, but of course, you also do not want them to feel like they are being shouted at.

If you can, rehearse in the room where the presentation will be given so that you will have a good idea of how loudly you need to speak so that everyone in the room can easily hear you. Practice projecting the sound of your voice and maintaining its strength for an amount of time equal to the length of the presentation. It can also be helpful to practice with a few people who can provide feedback on how well they can hear you.

Pitch

As a speaker, practice varying the **pitch** of your voice, that is, how deep or high you speak. For example, draw your audience's attention to the seriousness of a point by speaking in a deeper voice, or use a higher pitch to add some humor to another point.

Note that pitch is a part of intonation—the way speakers vary the overall sound of their voices to project the emotion behind what they are expressing. For example, when speakers ask questions, they will raise the pitch of their voices at the end, just as you do when you ask a question in normal conversation. Overall, you should focus on a natural level of deepness and speak at a level that will be easily heard and understood.

Rate

The **rate** or speed with which a speech is delivered should be carefully monitored. Most people speak more rapidly when they are nervous, but a presentation is not a race; it is a conversation with the audience. Take your time and maintain that conversational atmosphere.

Keep in mind that the best speed for delivering a speech often feels abnormally slow or awkward; practicing with a few people can help you determine which speed is best for audience comprehension. You can also vary the speed to achieve a purpose and to help maintain the audience's interest. For instance, if a concept is difficult for the audience to understand, slow your rate of speaking to give the audience time to absorb each idea. On the other hand, you may want to speed up your speaking if the speech seems to be dragging or you notice the audience losing interest. However, using a normal rate of speaking is best for most of the presentation.

Pauses

Sometimes what a speaker does not say carries as much weight as what the speaker articulates. You may have heard the term "pregnant pause," which refers to when a speaker stops speaking briefly to allow the listener time to absorb what was just said and to think about the possible meanings and ramifications. When a speaker pauses, this allows the audience individually and collectively to join in the speaker's thought process. Listeners may think about what the speaker will say next, and the pause gives the audience time to reflect on and to better comprehend and assimilate the content of the speech.

The pause is also a great time to insert appropriate humor or to take a quick look around the room to make sure that everyone is engaged in the speech. A glance with a pause makes the audience wonder what the speaker will do next. The audience may assume that whatever that next thing is will include them, and as a result they might respond by making eye contact, smiling, or signaling to the speaker in some other way that they are paying attention.

Vocal Variety

Vocal variety refers to a number of vocal qualities including volume, pitch, tone, rate, and pauses. Make use of these voice characteristics and techniques to add variety to your speaking voice. Avoid speaking in a monotone, which is difficult for the audience to listen to and may convey to the audience that you are bored.

Vocal techniques should be used with a specific purpose in mind and in a way that seems natural. Study some of the speeches easily available online, or listen to professional speakers such as television broadcasters. How does each speaker maintain a professional voice while inserting variety to maintain the listeners' interest? Can you identify and imitate their techniques?

Articulation

One final consideration for using your voice during a speech is the **articulation** of the words. Articulation refers to the pitch, nasal quality, and breathing patterns in your voice. Be sure to use the standard pronunciation of words and avoid mumbling; practice the complete and proper sounds of words by taking advantage of online articulation practice activities.

NONVERBAL COMMUNICATION

As you plan and practice your speech, consider the various forms of **nonverbal communication**. Often people limit their consideration of nonverbal communication to just body language and gestures, but your appearance is an important aspect of nonverbal communication as well. Your audience will respond to the impression you make with your appearance.

Dress and groom yourself appropriately for the context of the presentation. A presenter with messy hair, wearing a T-shirt and jeans with sandals, will probably not command the attention of a meeting room full of potential business clients who are wearing suits. Although your classmates may be more accepting of the T-shirt and sandals for a classroom presentation, dressing in business casual style will enhance everyone's impression of you and your message.

For some speaking occasions, you might adjust your appearance in unexpected ways. If you are presenting on the life of the famous poet Emily Dickinson, for example, you might dress in attire from the time period. Whatever choice you make, however, your appearance should enhance—not distract from—your presentation.

Another important part of nonverbal communication is body language. Use body language appropriately and in ways that you would in normal conversation. Face the audience and make frequent eye contact with those in the room to let them know you are connecting with them. However, be aware that some cultures do not feel comfortable with direct eye contact, so use your discretion when deciding how much eye contact to use.

A smile on your face can help the audience feel more comfortable with you. It can also enhance their experience of a presentation and the sense of community that you generate as a speaker. Incorporate more serious facial expressions to emphasize important points to the audience. Do not be afraid to be yourself or to show your personality; use the gestures and facial expressions that come most naturally to you. Audiences will see through a gesture or expression that contradicts your true feelings, so be genuine.

Another nonverbal communication skill that can be very effective is moving around the room to hold the audience's attention. Consider walking around among your listeners if this is appropriate for the context and the audience. Also, you might involve the audience in the presentation. For example, invite someone to stand up and role-play with you for a few minutes, or ask a couple of people to assist with a manipulative used to illustrate a key point. There may also be cultural differences to consider (in terms of personal space, for example), so be aware of the cultural make-up and values of your audience.

Consider how you can use nonverbal communication to repeat or emphasize a key point. For example, if you are presenting a list of the key benefits a potential client would derive from buying your company's product and you have the benefits listed on a white board, you can quietly walk over to the white board and tap each reason after you explain it. Following that up with eye contact and a knowing smile will emphasize to your audience that they should pay special attention to the point you are making. Likewise, if you invite an audience member to role-play with you, you could alter your body language to better exemplify the character or role you are playing.

Finally, do not be a distraction in your own presentation. You may be nervous, but avoid jingling your keys, playing with your jewelry or hair, chewing gum, or using any body language or movements that do not fit the presentation. Be careful that your body language does not unintentionally express something contrary to what you intend. For example, an audience may think you are bored with your presentation if they notice that you are slouching.

It may be helpful to record yourself rehearsing your presentation to see where your nonverbal communication techniques are strong and where they could be improved. Overall, nonverbal communication should be carefully practiced, and speakers should maintain a businesslike demeanor throughout their presentations.

SUMMARY

- Speakers can be better prepared by understanding which mode of delivery they will use for a speech.
- The four modes of delivery are extemporaneous, manuscript, impromptu, and memorized.
- It is important to practice the use of your voice, including volume, pitch, rate, pauses, vocal variety, and articulation.
- The delivery of a speech, its content, and nonverbal communication are three factors to consider when preparing for a speech.
- Consideration should be given to cultural norms and variations when preparing for a speech.
- Nonverbal communication reinforces the message of a speech and includes general appearance and mode of dress, facial expression, and body movement.

CHAPTER

18

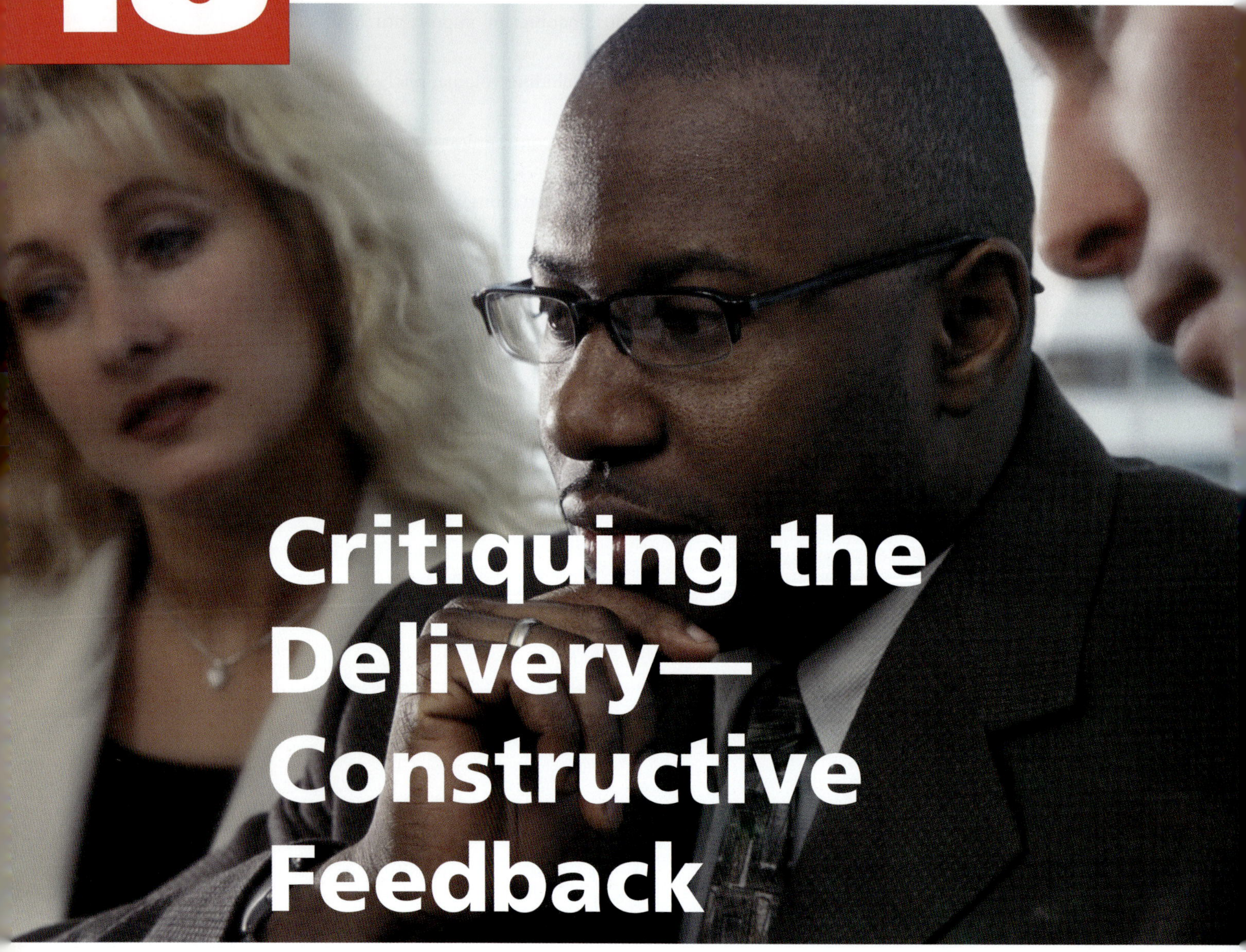

Critiquing the Delivery—Constructive Feedback

Janet, a manager in the human resources department of a toy manufacturer, is training a new employee, Shirin. After Shirin has spent a few weeks getting to know the company and its policies, Janet asks Shirin to give a presentation to employees about health benefits.

During Shirin's presentation, one of the audience members rests her head in her hands, and few of the other audience members make eye contact with Shirin. After the speech, no one asks questions, and everyone seems quite eager to leave the room.

After the speech, Janet tells Shirin that she is disappointed in how the presentation went. Janet says that the audience appeared bored. She also lists a number of criticisms of Shirin's speech—she spoke too softly and too quickly, she failed to make adequate eye contact with her listeners, and she seemed unprepared for the presentation. Janet's advice may help Shirin improve presentations in the future, but you may be surprised to learn that Janet's responses are actually examples of ineffective feedback.

KEY CONCEPTS

1. Learn when it is appropriate to critique. See page 224.
2. Know how to ask for permission to critique. See page 227.
3. Be aware of appropriate and inappropriate forms of feedback. See page 227.
4. Learn the differences between general and specific feedback. See page 228.
5. Give credit for strong points, but offer constructive feedback for weak points. See page 228.
6. Learn how to highlight areas for improvement. See page 229.

CRITIQUING THE DELIVERY: CONSTRUCTIVE FEEDBACK

Constructive feedback is a critical part of evaluating and improving communication. Any occasion for communication, no matter how formal or informal, can benefit from reflection and evaluation, but learning how to become an effective communicator—and how you can help others do so—takes time.

Certain strategies can ensure that you provide others with meaningful, positive feedback and avoid giving harmful, negative feedback. It is your responsibility to learn and practice these strategies, and you will also need to adjust these strategies for specific situations. If you are providing feedback for a friend or someone you know really well, your feedback might take a different tone than if you are providing feedback to someone you do not know personally.

CONSIDERATIONS OF CRITIQUE

It is often acceptable to provide a critique of a speaker—and it is often unacceptable. Students in a public speaking class should be aware that the instructor and their fellow students are going to evaluate them. First-year teachers are often evaluated on their presentation techniques in the classroom. Many business presentations are critiqued by upper management.

As an audience member, however, you should only offer feedback on the quality of the presenter's public speaking if you know for sure that it is welcome. Never volunteer a critique unless the speaker has specifically requested an evaluation. Engaging with the speaker's content—for example, asking questions of clarification—are appropriate ways of communicating with a speaker, but evaluating the speaker's delivery and organization is only appropriate when the speaker invites comments.

If you *are* asked to provide an evaluation of a speaker's performance and organization, you must first:

- Take the time to provide a fair critique that is purposeful and deliberate. If someone has asked you to evaluate a speech or performance, he or she is expecting you be honest and tactful.
- Learn how to be a more effective active listener.
- Learn what it takes to be an excellent evaluator.

All people respond to criticism differently, so the relationship you have with a speaker will affect whether he or she will ask you to provide feedback—and it will also affect how you provide it. There are few occasions, for example, when it would be acceptable to ask a boss or instructor if you may critique him or her. As these people are your supervisors, you should not volunteer such input on your own.

However, it may be appropriate to provide an evaluation of those close to you because you have formed a more personal relationship with them. A friend, for instance, may ask you to evaluate her presentation for a class because she trusts your judgment and is comfortable knowing that you are invested in the success of her speech. Successful, effective listeners know when it is appropriate to offer feedback.

Examine the set of sample evaluation forms in the box on this page for some effective ways to critique a presentation by a peer.

PEER EVALUATION FORM

Topic: Pit bulls

Speaker: ?

Evaluator: Steve

Scale: 5 Excellent 4 Good 3 Average 2 Fair 1 Poor

INTRODUCTION

__5__ Gained the audience's attention.

__5__ Established credibility.

__5__ Explained how the topic was relevant to the audience.

__5__ Previewed main points.

BODY OF THE SPEECH

__5__ Stated three to five main points.

__5__ Used effective transitions.

__5__ Cited an appropriate number of credible sources.

__5__ Maintained the audience's attention.

CONCLUSION

__5__ Provided summary of main points.

__5__ Activated audience response.

DELIVERY

__5__ Used correct volume, rate, tone, enunciation, pronunciation, and pauses.

In this section, the evaluator must highlight what the speaker did especially well and highlight areas for improvement. The evaluator will give constructive suggestions for improvement.

The speaker did a good job of organizing and delivering her speech

—Steve

(*continued on next page*)

PEER EVALUATION FORM

Topic: Pit bulls

Speaker: Matilda

Evaluator: Lonnie

Scale: 5 Excellent 4 Good 3 Average 2 Fair 1 Poor

INTRODUCTION

__4__ Gained audience's attention.

__3__ Established credibility.

__3__ Explained how the topic was relevant to the audience.

__3__ Previewed main points.

BODY OF THE SPEECH

__5__ Stated three to five main points.

__4__ Used effective transitions.

__1__ Cited an appropriate number of credible sources.

__5__ Maintained the audience's attention.

CONCLUSION

__1__ Provided summary of main points.

__4__ Activated audience response.

DELIVERY

__4__ Used correct volume, rate, tone, enunciation, pronunciation, and pauses.

In this section, the evaluator must highlight what the speaker did especially well and highlight areas for improvement. The evaluator will give constructive suggestions for improvement.

Matilda used statistics in her attention-getter to grab the audience's attention—which she did, for the most part. Her delivery through most of the speech was great. She spoke loud enough, her rate of speech was appropriate, and she worked hard on pronunciation and enunciation. Matilda's three main points were especially well developed, balanced, and organized.

However, it was difficult to hear Matilda during the introduction. She only cited one source, and this affected her credibility. Matilda needed to emphasize the transitions between all of the main points. She did not provide a clear summary during the conclusion.

Overall, Matilda did a fine job on her speech. She seemed nervous at times, and this can be remedied by practicing more. Matilda also needs to speak up through the entire speech. I recommend that she practice in front of others so she can modify her volume. It is easy to forget the summary, and practice will help her remember to include a strong summary.

—Lonnie

Checklist of Peer Evaluation Model

As you can see from the evaluation forms in the box, two students provided very different evaluations of Matilda's performance. Steve, the first evaluator, did not take the time to learn the speaker's name, and his remarks were informal and general. The evaluator assigned perfect scores in all categories, even though the second evaluator, Lonnie, identified specific weaknesses in Matilda's presentation. Steve's overall feedback is insufficient, and his comments do not provide any useful information that Matilda can use to improve her next speech. The evaluation process benefitted neither the speaker nor the evaluator.

On the other hand, Lonnie actively listened and assigned distinct scores for each category. Lonnie's summary evaluation began with what Matilda did well, explaining why he had given her high scores in certain areas. Next, he discussed what Matilda needed to improve. Lonnie provided an equal amount of positive feedback and negative feedback. Often, the most valuable part of an evaluation for the speaker is the suggestions for improvement.

In order to provide adequate feedback, an evaluator must be honest with a speaker, but honesty should always be delivered with tact. When giving an evaluation, issue the speaker fair scores and always take the time to describe both the positive and the negative qualities of the speech. While it is not always necessary to do so, it is often helpful to begin with the positive qualities of a speech. If you do, presenters are naturally more receptive to your constructive criticism and feedback, and you establish trust. They are aware that you listened closely to the speech and that you know that speakers' time, effort, and thought was invested in the presentation. Always try to help the speaker by providing suggestions for improvement. See Figure 17.1.

Appropriate

- Be truthful but tactful.
- Offer a fair assessment—if you are asked to provide a grade, be honest.
- Begin with the speaker's strengths.
- End with the speaker's weaknesses.
- Always offer suggestions for improvement.
- Ask permission to critique in appropriate situations.
- Never provide a critique unless it is asked of you.

Inappropriate

- Make rude or blunt statements.
- Offer an unwarranted exceptional assessment (providing all perfect grades to be nice).
- Focus on the strengths and ignore the weaknesses.
- Overemphasize the weaknesses and neglect to discuss the strengths.
- Neglect to include suggestions for improvement.
- Critique all of the speakers you hear, regardless of the situation.

FIGURE 17.1 Appropriate and Inappropriate Feedback

SPECIFIC VERSUS GENERAL FEEDBACK

Specific feedback addresses particular positive and negative qualities of a speaker's presentation. A speaker might excel, for example, at preparing effective visual aids for a speech, but his ability to execute an effective presentation by using these aids might need improvement. He may not maintain eye contact, may speak too fast, or may be difficult to hear at times. **General feedback** provides information about the overall quality of the speech. For example, general feedback could focus on how effectively the speaker conveyed his main message.

As a rule, specific feedback is more helpful to a speaker than general feedback. Comments that are specific and refer to details of a speaker's presentation provide concrete steps to take in order to improve. General feedback may be useful, but it does not provide focused takeaways the speaker can use to develop skills and remedy weaknesses. Someone who hears "You spoke too quickly when discussing your conclusions" knows exactly what she needs to work on for her next speech. Someone who hears "Your speech was great, but it could have been better" does not have a clear plan of action.

STRONG POINTS

In order to develop a tone that is constructive and positive, always begin your evaluation with the speaker's strengths or strong points. When evaluators first discuss negative qualities of a presentation, a speaker may be less willing to accept criticism as a means to improve.

Every speaker has strengths, and the evaluator must actively listen in order to identify speaker strengths. Some speakers excel at certain areas of delivery, while other speakers are great at creating and organizing speeches. You can practice evaluating speeches (and improve your own public speaking skills at the same time) by watching speakers on television or on the Internet. Think about what makes their speeches effective or ineffective. The more familiar you are with the qualities of successful speeches, the better you will be able to critique and present speeches yourself.

You must always balance the speaker's strengths and weaknesses. If you list three particular strengths, list three weaknesses or areas of the speech that need improvement. Speakers enjoy hearing what they do well, and they are more likely to use your constructive criticism. Listing strengths first is a great way to ease into discussing the weak points.

WEAK POINTS

Hearing about imperfections can be difficult, and some people may respond defensively to criticism. Evaluators must carefully word criticism in a way that is constructive. This does not mean that your critique cannot be honest—even if it means discussing failures—but it should never be unnecessarily harsh. Evaluators must be honest, but tactful. Always exercise empathy when issuing feedback. If you struggle with the same weakness, for example, the speaker may feel more at ease knowing that you understand what he or she is going through.

Any criticism that touches on the ineffective qualities of a speech should be grounded in specific details. Speaking generally about a presentation in a negative tone can be hurtful. Specific examples that support a point, however, will help the speaker understand that the criticism may be justified. If you comment on a speaker's delivery, for example, you must explain what specific details need improvement. Did the speaker maintain eye contact? Was the volume and tone appropriate for the topic and audience? Did the speaker use pauses effectively?

AREAS FOR IMPROVEMENT

After discussing the speaker's strengths and weaknesses, effective evaluators cast weaknesses as areas for improvement. Once you describe a weakness to a speaker, you should follow up with brainstorming methods to overcome that specific weakness. After all, the rationale behind evaluating a speech is to help the speaker present a more effective speech the next time.

After reviewing an evaluation, speakers should have clearly defined steps that they can take to plan and give a better speech. Your evaluation should always list a variety of tactics that the speaker can use to hone his or her craft. If the speaker's nervousness is affecting his or her delivery, for example, suggest some strategies that may help overcome nervousness, such as practicing or visualization techniques.

Many rush through the evaluation process because they find it tedious, but peer evaluation is vital to a speaker's improvement. It is difficult for a speaker to be self-reflective while attending to all of the details of giving a speech. Until a peer points out what worked well and what did not, speakers often do not have a strong sense of what they can do to make their presentations more effective.

Evaluation should not rest solely on an instructor's shoulders, because public speaking involves an audience. Learning how to properly diagnose areas for improvement for your fellow students takes effort, but it is an indispensible part of the process. You will appreciate the input of your fellow students as you work to become a confident and successful public speaker.

SUMMARY

- Be mindful of the considerations involved with critiquing another person.
- It is important to ask the speaker if you can critique them tactfully.
- It is more helpful to provide specific feedback in most situations.
- Discuss the speaker's strong points but provide constructive feedback for remedying his or her weak points.
- Always discuss how the speaker can improve.

APPENDIX A

APA STYLE

APA style is a set of rules and guidelines for manuscript preparation based on the psychology literature that was developed by the American Psychological Association (APA). APA style is a standard format for academic research writing and is used extensively in the social sciences. The *Publication Manual of the American Psychological Association* (2010) is the style's official guide. The information in this chapter comes from the sixth edition of the *Publication Manual* and its affiliated website.

The *Publication Manual* provides guidelines for formatting a research paper and referencing sources. It provides specific information about organizing the content of the research paper; using effective writing style and avoiding bias in language; employing Standard English grammar and punctuation; and using tables, figures, and graphs to illustrate a research paper. The *Publication Manual* also guides authors through the process of submitting papers for publication. The purpose of this appendix is to focus on the guidelines the *Publication Manual* sets forth for most undergraduate papers.

The *Publication Manual* also includes detailed information about documenting sources—giving credit to the sources that were used to prepare a manuscript. Following these guidelines can help a writer avoid plagiarism. Every type of source used in a research paper must be cited, from journals and books to music and videos. The APA's website (http://apastyle.org) and its accompanying blog (http://blog.apastyle.org) are among the best resources for the most up-to-date information on citing electronic sources.

FORMATTING A PAPER

Each research paper should have four core components:

- Title page
  - Includes the title of the work, running head, and byline
  - May also include school and instructor information
- Abstract
  - Provides a short summary of research and findings
- Body text
  - Includes an introduction with a background of literature consulted, method of research, results, and a discussion of the results
- References
  - Includes all sources referenced in the paper

The following basic guidelines should be used when formatting a paper:

- Use 8½ × 11 in. (22 × 28 cm) paper (standard)
- Use double spacing between lines
- Use a 12-point serif font, such as Times New Roman
- Number each page on the right-hand side at the top of the page
- Use 1-inch margins on each side
- Indent the first line of each paragraph to ½ in. (1.3 cm)
- Align the text to the left, leaving the right margin ragged and unjustified
- Present a title page, abstract, body text, and references, in that order

Some papers may feature other collateral items, such as appendices, author notes, footnotes, tables, figure captions, and figures. They should be placed in this sequence after the references.

Organization is important to help the reader follow the flow of ideas from existing research to original findings. The APA has established common formatting styles to create uniformity in published material that is recognizable to a broad readership. Perhaps most important is that writers remember to not worry about perfectly formatting the paper in APA style until the revision stage. Becoming preoccupied with formatting early on will slow writing progress.

Title Page

The title page includes the title of the paper centered in the upper third of the page. This is followed by a byline, which includes the author's name. In the upper-left corner of the title page, the running head (see the next section for more information) should be identified. Also include a page header that includes the running head to the left and the page number in the upper-right corner.

Running Head

The research paper's title page should include a page header, called a running head, that will appear on each page of the document. Usually a shortened version of the paper's title (two to three words, no more than 50 characters) is used as the running head. For example, if the title of the document is "Everything You Need to Know about APA Citations," an appropriate running header might be "APA CITATIONS." The running head should be flush left in all caps. In the top-left corner of the title page, type "APA CITATIONS" flush left and the page number flush right.

Abstract

An abstract is a summary of the research paper and its findings. It is an extremely important paragraph that allows readers to immediately determine if they are interested in reading the paper. This section begins on page 2 with the header "Abstract" centered on the page with an initial capital A followed by lowercase letters. Abstracts should be brief and usually range between 150 and 250 words. The text should be flush left (without an indention) beneath the title and Arabic numerals should be used for any numbers.

Headings

Using levels of headings provides a hierarchy for the sections in a paper; in effect, they provide the reader with an outline of the paper. Avoid use of only one subsection heading or one subsection within a section. The same level of heading should be given to all topics of equal importance (e.g., Method, Results). At least two subsection headings should be used within a section; otherwise, none should be used. A heading structure for all sections should use the same top-to-bottom progression, regardless of the number of levels of subheading. APA style uses five possible levels of headings, which follow each other sequentially. Thus, if only one level is used, use Level 1; if two are used, use Levels 1 and 2 (the most common combination in most research papers), in that order; if three are used, use Levels 1, 2, and 3, in that order, and so on.

Level 1: Centered, boldface, initial capital letters on important words; on the line above the paragraph

Example:

BASIC FINDINGS

Level 2: Flush left, boldface, initial capital letters on important words; on the line above the paragraph

Example:

Demographic Analysis

Level 3: Indented, boldface, sentence-case heading followed by a period, on the same line of copy as the beginning of the paragraph that follows.

Demographic analysis. The demographic analysis shows that among participating physicians...

Level 4: Indented, boldface, italicized, sentence-case heading followed by a period, on the same line of copy as the beginning of the paragraph that follows.

Demographic analysis. The demographic analysis shows that among participating physicians...

Level 5: Indented, italicized, sentence-case heading followed by a period, on the same line of copy as the beginning of the paragraph that follows.

Demographic analysis. The demographic analysis shows that among participating physicians...

Punctuation and Spacing

Punctuation provides the pace for a sentence and tells the reader where to pause (commas, colons, or semicolons), stop (periods, question marks, or exclamation points), or deviate (parentheses, dashes, or brackets). The different kinds of punctuation in a sentence usually designate different kinds and lengths of pauses. Modern word-processing programs provide the appropriate space for each character, so hit the spacebar only once after commas, colons, and semicolons. Do not add extra spaces around dashes, parentheses, or brackets.

APA style suggests—but does not require—two spaces after punctuation marks at the end of a sentence in draft manuscripts. Because requirements vary across publications, when submitting a manuscript for publication, consult the publication's style guidelines regarding spacing after end punctuation.

Following is a quick guide to some punctuation rules required in APA style.

Period

Periods are used in reference lists after the author's name, the year, the title of a book or article, and the close of the reference; an exception to this close-reference rule is references that end in a website address (electronic references), which do not end with a period.

When in-text citations are used at the end of a sentence, the period should follow the citation. When in-text citations appear at the end of a long, indented quote, periods should not follow the in-text citations. In that case, the period appears at the end of the quote but before the in-text citation. See "Quotations of 40 Words or More," which appears later in this section, for an example.

Colon

Colons appear between the publication location and the publisher listed in individual references. In text, a colon should not be used after an introductory clause that is not a complete sentence. If two independent clauses are separated by a colon, capitalize the word that begins the second clause.

Semicolon

Although semicolons are usually used to separate two independent clauses (complete sentences), a semicolon should also be used to set off items in a series when one or more of these items already includes commas, regardless of whether the items are complete sentences—for example, "The sisters were challenged to ride a bike for two hours; juggle a ball, a book, and a toy car for 10 minutes; and walk on a treadmill for 30 minutes."

Comma

In in-text citations, a comma should be used to set off the year of publication within parentheses. In text, use a comma between all elements in a series of three or more items, including before *and* and *or*.

Quotation Marks

Double quotation marks should be used in the following situations:

- To introduce a word or phrase that is used as slang, a coined expression, or an example of irony
- To identify an article or chapter title in a periodical or book when the title is mentioned in text
- To reproduce or cite material from a published source (only up to 40 words)

Double quotation marks should not enclose quotations of 40 words or more.

Quotations of 40 Words or More

Quotations of 40 words or more should be in a paragraph by themselves, should be indented five spaces without the customary first-line indent, and should not include quotation marks. These block quotations should also be followed by a citation that includes a page number. The citation is presented after the closing punctuation of the block quotation. If the quoted text contains quotation marks, double quotation marks should be used. Note the following example:

> Candy manufactured at the offshore facility was tainted, but testing of product made domestically revealed that it was safe. Representatives from the manufacturer claimed that the company was unaware of any problems with ingredients or machinery at the offshore plant prior to the discovery of the poisoned product. (Bradenforth, 2007, p. 238)

Italics

Use italics for introduction of a new, technical, or key term (but only on first use of the word; do not italicize the word again if it is used in subsequent sentences). Also use italics in the following instances:

- Letters used as statistical symbols
- Periodical volume numbers in the reference list
- Anchors on a scale (e.g., a survey asks respondents to rate customer service on a scale of *1* to *5*).

Parentheses

Parentheses are used in the following circumstance:

- To set off reference citations in text
- To separate letters that identify terms in a series within a sentence or paragraph
- To enclose the citation or page number of a direct quote
- To introduce an abbreviation
- To enclose numbers that represent formulas, equations, statistical values, or degrees of freedom

Avoid use of back-to-back parenthetical text.

Hyphens

A hyphen should not be used on common fractions used as nouns (e.g., Two thirds of the students missed class); however, a hyphen should be used when the fraction is used as a descriptor (e.g., The student council requires a two-thirds majority to pass a new rule). Hyphens should also be avoided in compounds in which the first word is an adverb (e.g., The nearly vetoed legislation has finally passed) and in situations where there is no possible way a compound term could be misread without it (e.g., The health care industry lobbied Congress for this law). Do not use a space before or after a hyphen.

Dashes

APA distinguishes em dashes (two hyphens placed side by side with no space in between: —) from en dashes (which are slightly longer than a hyphen: –). Note that some word-processing programs include em dash and en dash symbols, often a combination of keystrokes or accessible from the symbols menu. As shown in the examples in the paragraphs that follow, do not add spaces before or after em dashes and en dashes.

An em dash should be used to either highlight a clause or to indicate a diversion from the sentence's primary clause (e.g., The test subjects—who were unaware of the change—disliked the nature of the treatment).

An en dash is used between words of equal weight in a compound adjective (e.g., "medication–nutrient interaction") and between page ranges (e.g., 112–114).

Using Numbers in a Document

Generally, APA style uses numerals to express numbers 10 and larger and words for numbers one through nine. One primary exception to this rule is when a number greater than 10 begins a sentence. In this case, the word should be spelled out (e.g., Forty-eight men were surveyed).

There are several exceptions in which numbers less than 10 are listed in numeric form, generally related to presenting a specific quantity measurement, such as in the following instances:

- When the numbers precede a unit of measurement or a percentage symbol
- When the numbers are used for a mathematical or statistical function
- When used to represent time, dates, ages, scores, or points on a scale
- When placed in a numbered series, parts of book chapters or tables, or in a numbered list of four or more
- When included in a research paper's abstract

If the number of days, months, or years are an approximation, write out the numbers (e.g., The ships takes approximately eight days to reach Portugal). A zero should be written before decimals and numbers that are less than one, except in decimal fractions where the number cannot be greater than one. Plurals of numbers should be written by adding *-s* or *-es*, without an apostrophe.

Abbreviations

APA style recommends minimal use of abbreviations, as they can often cause more confusion than clarification and can hinder reader comprehension. Generally, an abbreviation should be used only if (a) it is well known and a reader would be familiar with it, or (b) it saves considerable space and prevents repetition.

A writer must decide whether to spell out an expression or group name every time or spell it out initially and abbreviate it thereafter. If abbreviating, the term must be written out completely the first time, followed by its abbreviation in parentheses. Afterward, the abbreviation can be used without any further explanation.

Do not write out standard abbreviations for units of measurement on first use, but do not use the abbreviation if a specific measurement is not given (e.g., It was 3 cm in length; It was measured in centimeters).

A sentence can begin with an abbreviation or acronym that appears in all capital letters but not if it is all lowercase letters. Some abbreviations are accepted as words in APA style and do not require explanation, including the following well-known terms: IQ, REM, ESP, AIDS, and HIV.

Periods are used with abbreviations for initials of names (e.g., William S. Sanderson), to abbreviate the United States when used as an adjective (e.g., U.S. Navy), in identity-concealing labels for study participants (e.g., participants S. P. and J. M.), and with Latin and reference abbreviations (e.g., i.e., etc.).

Periods should not be used with abbreviations of state names, capital letter acronyms, or metric and nonmetric measurements; one exception is the abbreviation for inch (in.), which includes a period because of the likelihood of its confusion with the word "in."

In general, use Latin abbreviations only in parenthetical material and use the English translations of Latin abbreviations in running text (e.g., use "e.g." in parentheses and use "for example" in text). However, "et al." (and others) and "v." (for versus) should be used for citations, both parenthetical and in text (APA, 2010, pp. 106–111).

Percent and Percentages

The symbol for percent (%) should be used only when it is preceded by a numeral (e.g., 5%). The word "percent" should not be spelled out after a numeral. When a number is not given, the word "percentage" should be used (e.g., a significant percentage of women in the group preferred the reformulated product). In table headings or legends, use a percent symbol in lieu of the word "percentage" to conserve space.

Lists

Elements or ideas in a series can be enumerated to clarify their relationship. This is particularly important when a sequence is lengthy or difficult to understand. Three different forms are possible: a within-sentence list, a numbered list, or a bulleted list.

Example of a within-sentence list:

The student's three choices were (a) living in the dorm with a roommate, (b) living alone in the dorm, or (c) living at home.

Listing within a Sentence with Internal Commas

When listing items within a paragraph or sentence with items that include commas, use lowercase letters in parentheses and semicolons, as shown in the following example:

The respondents were broken into three groups: (a) high communication apprehension, scoring more than 35; (b) moderate communication apprehension, scoring between 18 and 35; and (c) low communication apprehension, scoring below 18.

Numbered Lists

To list paragraphs in a numbered sequence, such as itemized conclusions or successive steps in a procedure, number each paragraph or sentence with an Arabic numeral followed by a period, as shown in the following example:

1. We divided the study sample into three groups based on income.
2. We further subdivided these three groups into subgroups based on race/ethnicity.
3. We calculated the average monthly income for each of these subgroups.

Bulleted Lists

Numbered lists may imply an unintended and unwanted hierarchy such as chronology or importance. In such cases, a bulleted list, as shown in the following example, is an option:

The physicians were asked questions about the following factors:

- How long they have been in practice
- How many patients they see per week on average
- How many of those patients have private insurance

Each item in the bulleted list should be indented. Items in a bulleted list may be complete sentences or parts of a longer sentence introduced with a colon, but all items in the list should be parallel (e.g., they should all start with the same part of speech or same conjugation, form, or tense of a verb).

REFERENCES AND INTERNAL CITATION STYLE

Proper documentation of sources includes two important steps: creating a reference list and using internal citations. APA guidelines require a structured reference list and parenthetical in-text citations of each source listed in the references. It is critical to carefully follow APA guidelines for placement and style of citations and references. Footnotes and endnotes are occasionally used, but they are secondary to parenthetical citations. Content footnotes are used to clarify or expand on information in the text, and copyright permission footnotes are used to identify the source of quotations. Neither type should be used in place of parenthetical citations in an APA-style research paper.

Citation Style

For parenthetical citations, include author name(s) and year of the publication. If using a direct quotation or paraphrasing a particular passage, the page number must also be included. APA style offers a variety of acceptable citation formats. Example 1 illustrates an effective way to mention the authors in the text of the sentence; it is particularly useful if the writer wishes to describe the cited author in some way. The style of Example 2 results in a complete statement without using the cited author's name in the sentence. Example 3 shows a direct quote from the reference material coupled with mention of the author's name in the sentence. Example 4 combines a direct quote and a complete statement that does not mention the author's name in the sentence.

Example 1:
According to Booth, Colomb, and Williams (2003), you should avoid plagiarism.

Example 2:
You should avoid plagiarism (Booth, Colomb, & Williams, 2003).

Example 3:
According to Booth, Colomb, and Williams (2003), "In all fields, you plagiarize when you use a source's words or ideas without citing that source" (p. 202).

Example 4:
Many authorities have commented on the topic, but this is one of the most effective descriptions: "In all fields, you plagiarize when you use a source's words or ideas without citing that source" (Booth, Colomb, & Williams, 2003, p. 202).

If a source has two to five authors, use all the names of the authors in the first citation, but in later citations, refer to secondary authors with the abbreviation "et al." If a source has six or more authors, in all citations—including the first—list only the first author followed by "et al." and the date (e.g., Smith et al., 2007). Note that if citing the same source more than once in the same paragraph, it is not necessary to include the year in the succeeding citations. See Example 5 for an illustration.

Example 5:
Plagiarism can harm your career (Booth et al., 2003). Several prominent historians have lost credibility because they had plagiarized from the works of others (Weaver et al., 2009). It is best to create your own original content and exercise caution when quoting and summarizing the content of others (Booth et al.).

Some citation styles do not meet the criteria listed previously, including the following:

- Personal communications
- Anonymous works
- Works without publication dates
- Classical works

See Figure A.1 for examples of these unusual styles.

Reference Style

The APA reference style is preferred for many reasons, but primary among them is that APA style is perhaps the most common form of organizing, citing, structuring, and verifying information in universities today. APA reference style provides all the basic building blocks that make it easier to learn other styles, such as MLA, Turabian, and Chicago style, and underscores the importance of professionalism and rigor in writing. All references should be listed in alphabetical order by the first author's last name or, if no author is listed, by the title of the source.

Assembling a Reference List

An APA reference list is more than just a simple listing of works cited. Each type of reference—a journal article, a book, a website, or a newspaper article, for example—has its own unique style. The idea behind the reference list is to give readers as much information as possible to seek out the references and gain a deeper understanding of the logic expressed in the paper by reading them. The following are general guidelines for an APA reference list:

- Sources should be arranged alphabetically by the author's last name. If there is no identified author, alphabetize the reference listing by the first main word of the title, excluding "A," "An," or "The."
- Double space or leave one blank line between each line of type in a reference list.
- The first line of a reference is set flush left, but any subsequent lines in the same reference are indented one-half inch (known as the hanging indent).

REFERENCE TYPE	IN-TEXT CITATION STYLE	REFERENCE STYLE	EXPLANATION
Personal communications that include letters, memos, e-mail, nonarchived discussion groups, personal interviews, and telephone conversations	S. H. Hanson (personal communication, January 1, 2007), or (S. H. Hanson, personal communication, January 1, 2007)	Not included in reference list	Cite personal communication in the text only
No publication date given	(Hamilton, n.d.)	Hamilton, G. (n.d.). *Hope is the verb.* Boston, MA: Cambridge Press.	When no date is given, write n.d. in parentheses for in-text and reference list mentions
A work with no identified author, not designated as anonymous	("College Bound," 2007)	College bound. (2007). *Journal of Teacher Education, 45*(3) 26–31.	In the reference list, alphabetize by title
Works with group authors	(American Psychological Association, 1994)	American Psychological Association. (1994). *The APA manual of style.* Washington, DC: Author.	Alphabetize group authors, such as associations and universities, by the first significant word of the name
A work's author is designated "anonymous"	(Anonymous, 2007)	Anonymous. (2007). *Let's build bridges.* New York, NY: Prentice Hall.	In the reference list, only a work that is explicitly identified as written by "Anonymous" includes the word, which is alphabetized as such.
Classical works	(Plato, trans. 1938), or (Freud, 1931/1997)	Not required	Reference entries are not required for major classical works. That includes ancient Greek and Roman works and the Bible. In cases of the Bible, identify which version was used in the first in-text citation—for example," (1 Cor. 13:1) [King James Version]."

FIGURE A.1 **APA Citation Style for Unusual References**

- Periods separate most parts of a reference, including (a) after the author name(s), (b) after the date, (c) after the closing parenthesis for the date of publication, and (d) at the end of the reference (except for an electronic reference, which requires no period). Periods should also be used after the first and middle initials of each author.
- Commas are used between the author's last name(s) and initials; to separate authors; between the book or periodical title and the volume number; after an issue number and before a page number; and between a volume number and page number. A colon is used to separate the city of publication and the publisher's name.
- The author's names in a reference should be listed as last name first, followed by a comma, and then the first and middle initials, and finished with a period. When there are eight or more authors, list only the first six and abbreviate the remaining authors using ellipsis points ("…"), followed by the final author. If a group or entity is the author, spell out its full name as the author. If a second author of a book or magazine is listed with the word "with," he or she should be listed in the reference in parentheses—for example, "Porter, J. (with Rutter, K. L.)." To reference an edited book, list the editor's name in the author position and follow it with the abbreviation "Ed." or "Eds." in parentheses. If there is no author, the title of the work should be moved to the beginning of the reference.
- The year the work of a reference was copyrighted should follow the authors' names (or title, if there are no authors), appear in parentheses, and have a period at the end outside of the parentheses. For magazines, newspapers, or newsletters, the year, followed by the exact date (month and date) of the publication should be listed in parentheses. If no date is available, "n.d." should be written in parentheses and should be followed by a period.

- The title of an article or chapter comes after the date, followed by the title of the work, periodical, or book. Only the first word of the title and subtitle (if there is one) should be capitalized. The title should not be italicized or have quotation marks around it. All nonweb references should end with a period. Web-based references should include as much of the previously listed information as possible and the digital object identifier (DOI) if available or the web address of the source. If the last item in the reference is a DOI or a website address, it should not end with a period.
- The city of publication follows the title of any book or brochure. Regardless of how well-known a city is, write a comma and the appropriate two-letter abbreviation for the state or territory that is used by the U.S. Postal Service. Spell out country names. A colon should follow the city, state, or country of publication. If the publisher is a university that has the same name as the state or province (e.g., Ohio State), do not repeat the state or province in the publisher location.
- The publisher's name follows the city of publication. The name of the publisher should be as brief as possible, eliminating terms such as "Inc.," or "Co.," but the words "Books" and "Press" should be kept in the reference. If two or more publisher locations are given, give the first listed or the publisher's corporate office, if specified. A period should follow all listings.
- "Page" and "pages" should be cited as "p." and "pp." in instances where book chapters are listed. Periodical page numbers go at the end of the reference, following the title of the journal, and "p." or "pp." is not used. Book page numbers go between the title and the city of publication. All page numbers should include the entire article or chapter, and the beginning and end numbers should be separated by an en dash. Page numbers for entire books are not listed.
- Appropriate abbreviations for use in reference section and in-text citations include the following:
  - chap. = chapter
  - ed. = edition
  - Rev. ed. = revised edition
  - 2nd ed. = second edition
  - Ed. (Eds.) = editor (editors)
  - Trans. = translator(s)
  - n.d. = no date
  - p. (pp.) = page (pages)
  - Vol. = volume (as in Vol. 4)
  - Vols. = volumes (as in four volumes)
  - No. = number
  - Pt. = part
  - Suppl. = supplement
  - Tech. Rep. = technical report
- U.S. states and territories should be indicated with the appropriate two-letter abbreviation used by the U.S. Postal Service. City names and country names should not be abbreviated (APA, 2010, p. 187).

Examples of References

Refer to the *Publication Manual* or its companion website (http://apastyle.org) if citing a resource that is not included among the examples that follow. Different sources have different requirements and rules. Books, journal articles, magazine articles, websites, and other sources each have particular requirements that give proper credit and help readers locate the reference material. If any part of the reference is not included, this amounts to failure to properly credit a source. The following 13 examples illustrate some of the more common reference styles.

Example 1: A book with a single author.

Klein, N. (2000). *No logo*. New York, NY: Picador.

Book author: The author's last name is listed first, followed by the author's first and middle initials (if applicable). The period that follows the initial is also the period that follows the first element (author's name) of the References citation.

Date of publication: The year the book was published is included in parentheses, followed by a period.

Book title: The title is italicized with all words except the first in lowercase. If there is a colon in the title, the first word following the colon is also capitalized. If the book has several editions, the edition of the text goes in parentheses following the title. This element is followed by a period.

Publication information: For all cities, include the state (e.g., Newbury Park, CA), even if the city is well known. A colon is placed after the state and followed by the name of the publisher. Omit superfluous terms such as "Publishers," "Co.," or "Inc.," but keep the words "Books" or "Press."

Example 2: A book with two to seven authors.

Rubin, R. B., Rubin, A. M., & Piele, L. J. (2000). *Communication research: Strategies and sources* (5th ed.). Belmont, CA: Wadsworth.

Book author: The author's last name is listed first, followed by the author's first and middle initials (if applicable). A comma follows the name of the first author, even when there are only two authors to list. Type "&" before the last author is listed. Authors are listed in the order they are listed on the book cover.

Date of publication, book title, and publication information: Follow the format applied in Example 1.

Example 3: A book with eight or more authors.

Brown, L. V., Ecks, T. Z., Walters, F. A., Zim, A., Ricks, J., Bynum, C. T., ... Olsen, L. (2007). *Research methods for undergraduate students.* New York, NY: Text Press.

Book author: The author's last name is listed first, followed by the author's first and middle initials (if applicable). With more than seven authors, list only the first six authors and abbreviate the remaining authors using ellipsis points ("..."), followed by the final author. Do not type "&" before the final author.

Date of publication, book title, and publication information: Follow the format applied in Example 1.

Example 4: An article with only one author in a scholarly journal.

Kramer, M. W. (2005). Communication in community theatre groups. *Journal of Applied Communication Research, 33,* 159–182.

Article author: The author's last name is listed first, followed by the author's first and middle initials (if applicable).

Date of publication: The year the article was written is included in parentheses, followed by a period.

Article title: The article title is not italicized nor enclosed in quotation marks, and only the first word of the title and the subtitle should be capitalized. The title is followed by a period.

Journal title: The journal title is italicized and all words in the title are capitalized except articles and prepositions ("a," "the," "and," "an," "of").

Publication information: Provide the volume number (in italics) and the page numbers (not italicized) of the article. If the periodical uses successive pagination in its volumes, it is not necessary to include the issue number. If the pagination is not successive, the issue number should be included in parentheses and not italicized—for example, *Consulting Psychology Journal: Practice and Research*, *45*(2), 10–36.

Example 5: An article with multiple authors in a scholarly journal.

Rosenfeld, L. B., Richman, J. M., Bowen, G. L., & Wynns, S. L. (2006). In the face of a dangerous community: The effects of social support and neighborhood danger on high school students' school outcomes. *Southern Communication Journal, 71*, 273–289.

Article author: The author's last name is listed first, followed by the author's first and middle initials (if applicable). Type "&" before the last author is listed. Authors are listed in the order they appear on the article. With more than seven authors, list only the first six authors and abbreviate the remaining authors using ellipsis points ("..."), followed by the final author. Do not type "&" before the final author.

Date of publication, article title, journal title, and publication information: Follow the format applied in Example 4.

Example 6: A magazine article.

Marano, H. E. (2004, August). Rock around the doc. *Psychology Today, 9,* 47–52.

Article author: The author's last name is listed first, followed by the author's first and middle initials (if applicable).

Date of publication: The year and month the article was written is included in parentheses as "(year, month)."

Article title: The article title is not italicized, and only the first word of the title and subtitle should be capitalized.

Periodical title: The periodical title is italicized, and all words in the title are capitalized except articles and prepositions ("a," "the," "and," "an," "of").

Publication information: Provide the volume number (italics) and the page numbers of the article (not italicized). If the periodical uses successive pagination in its volumes, do not add the issue number. If the pagination is not successive, the issue number should be included in parentheses and not italicized—for example, *Communication Connection*, *2*(2), 3–7.

Example 7: An online magazine or news article.

Marano, H. E., & Schwartz, B. G. (2004, August). Rock around the doc. *Psychology Today, 9,* 47–52. Retrieved from http://www.psychologytoday.com

Article author, date of publication, article title, periodical title, and publication information: Follow the format applied in Example 6.

Retrieval information: The rule for electronic resources is to list the information that will help readers find the resource. Do not include the date the document was retrieved unless there is an expectation that the material cited will change over time. Some documents include a digital object identifier (DOI), which is a number that provides a consistent means to find an online document. If the cited publication has a DOI, it is usually prominently displayed at the top of the online document. If the research document includes a DOI, include it at the end of the reference, after the page numbers. For example, Marano, H. E., & Schwartz, B. G. (2004, August). Rock around the doc. *Psychology Today, 9,* 47–50. doi:10.1187/0142-9052.78.1.298. If no DOI is available, give the home web page for the periodical, not the specific link to the article. Web pages often disappear or change, and this avoids citing expired web addresses.

Example 8: An article from a newspaper database.

Russell, P. R. (2007, May 11). Saving energy is a hot topic: Energy to develop ways to conserve. *New Orleans Times-Picayune,* p. Money 1. Retrieved from www.timespicayune.com

Article author: Follow the format applied in Example 7.

Date of publication: The year, month, and day the article was written are included in parentheses (year, month, day).

Article title, periodical title: Follow the format applied in Example 6.

Publication information: Follow the format applied in Example 7.

Retrieval information: The rule for electronic resources is to list the information that will help the reader find the resource. Do not include the name of the database where the article was found; instead list the newspaper's home web page address. Do not close the web page address with a period.

Example 9: An article from a newspaper with one author and nonconsecutive page numbers.

McBride, J. (2007, May 30). Pantex crew returns today: Guards union ratifies 5-year pact. *Amarillo Globe-News,* pp. A1, A6.

Article author: Follow the format applied in Example 7.

Date of publication: Follow the format applied in Example 8.

Article title, periodical title: Follow the format applied in Example 6.

Publication information: For newspapers, include the section and page number. Unlike journal citations, newspaper references do require a "p." or "pp." before the section and page number(s). If the pages are not continuous, list the page on which the article begins, insert a comma and a space, and then list the page where the article continues (e.g., pp. A1, A6).

Example 10: An article with no author, from a newspaper.

Asarco gets approval to auction land in Salt Lake City. (2007, May 30). *Amarillo Globe-News,* p. D6.

Article author: If an article has no author, do not write "Anonymous." The article title is placed first. It is not italicized, and only the first word of the title and subtitle should be capitalized.

Date of publication: Follow the format applied in Example 8.

Article title, periodical title: Follow the format applied in Example 6.

Publication information: Follow the format applied in Example 7.

Example 11: An Internet source.

How to publish with APA. (n.d.). Retrieved from American Psychological Association website: http://www.apastyle.org

Heading title: Websites and web pages often do not have identified author(s). In such a case, the website section heading is used at the beginning of the reference. It is not italicized, and only the first word of the title and subtitle should be capitalized.

Date of publication: A date is also not often available, so it is acceptable to reference that there is no date identified by typing (n.d.) after the heading title.

Internet site title: Identify the publisher of the resource as part of the retrieval information.

Retrieval information: The rule for electronic resources is to list the information that will help readers find the resource. Only include the complete web page address if the home page of the organization housing the document does not have a search function or if the website is large and hard to navigate, making it unlikely that the reader will be able to find the document from the home address. Do not close the web page address with a period.

Example 12: A picture from a website.

Pollock, J. (1953). *Greyed rainbow* [Painting]. Retrieved from http://www.artic.edu/aic/collections/artwork/83642?search_id=1

Artist or photographer: Follow the format applied to authors in Example 6.

Title: The title of the picture is italicized and only the first word of the title should be capitalized. The title is followed by the medium (e.g., painting, photograph, etc.) in brackets.

Retrieval information: Follow the format applied in Example 8.

Example 13: A picture from a book.

Pollock, J. (1953). *Greyed rainbow* [Painting]. In E. G. Landau, *Jackson Pollock* (p. 230). New York, NY: Abradale Press.

Artist or photographer: Follow the format applied to authors in Example 6.

Title: Follow the format applied in Example 12.

Book author and title: The word "In" is followed by the author's name. First and middle initials (if applicable) precede the author's last name, which is followed by a comma. The title of the book is italicized and only the first word and any proper nouns are capitalized. The page number(s) or plate number for the artwork is set in parentheses and is not italicized.

Publication information: Follow the format applied in Example 1.

APPENDIX B

MLA FORMATTING

Another format used as the standard for research writing at colleges and universities is MLA style, a set of rules and guidelines for manuscript preparation developed by the Modern Language Association of America (MLA). MLA style is a standard of writing used extensively in the humanities. The *MLA Handbook for Writers of Research Papers* and the *MLA Style Manual and Guide to Scholarly Publishing* are the style's official guides. The information in this section comes from the seventh edition of the *MLA Handbook* (2009) and the third edition of the *MLA Style Manual* (2008).

Both books provide guidelines for formatting a research paper and referencing sources. The *MLA Handbook* is geared toward high school and undergraduate students and provides step-by-step advice on all aspects of writing and presenting papers, from choosing a topic and conducting research to devising a thesis statement and creating an outline. The *MLA Style Manual* is tailored to graduate students, scholars, and professional writers. The *Manual* guides authors through the process of writing and submitting papers for publication and explains the peer-review process in detail. The two guides provide specific information about organizing the content of the research paper; using effective writing style and avoiding bias in language; employing standard English grammar and punctuation; and using tables, figures, and graphs to illustrate a research paper. This section will focus on the guidelines the *MLA Handbook* (2009) sets forth for most undergraduate papers.

The *MLA Handbook* and *MLA Style Manual* also include detailed information about documenting sources—giving credit to the sources used to prepare a manuscript. Following these guidelines can help with avoiding plagiarism. Every type of source used in a research paper must be cited, from journals and books to music and videos. Note that this book uses MLA style in its reference lists.

FORMATTING A PAPER USING MLA

Each research paper using MLA style should have three core components:

- A heading and title
- Body text
- A list of works cited

The first page of the research paper begins with the title of the work, the author's name, and the date. The body text is the heart of the paper and should include an introduction and a conclusion. Finally, a works cited section includes all sources in the paper.

The following basic guidelines should be used when formatting a paper:

- Use 8½ × 11 in. (22 × 28 cm) paper (standard)
- Use double spacing between lines
- Use a 12-point serif font, such as Times New Roman
- Number each page on the right-hand side, one-half inch from the top of the page, flush with the right margin
- Use 1-inch margins on each side
- Indent the first line of each paragraph ½ in. (1.3 cm)
- Align the text to the left, leaving the right margin ragged and unjustified
- Include a works cited page

Some papers may feature other collateral items, such as appendixes, author notes, and footnotes. Tables, illustrations, and figures should be placed as close as possible to the related text in the body of the paper.

Organization is important to help the reader follow the flow of ideas from existing research to original findings. The MLA has established common formatting styles to create uniformity in published material that is recognizable to a broad readership. Perhaps most important for writers to remember is that perfecting the paper's MLA formatting is not necessary until the revision stage. If a writer becomes preoccupied with formatting early on, it will slow the writing process. There will be ample time during the revision stage to ensure that the formatting is accurate.

Heading and Title

In MLA style, no separate title page is needed. Instead, at the top of the first page, the writer should type his or her name, the instructor's name, the number of the course, and the date—each on a separate line, double spaced. Next, type the title of the paper on the next line, centered, with headline style capitalization (capitalizing the first letter of main words). Do not italicize, boldface, or underline the title. Double space and begin typing the body of the paper, indenting the first paragraph one-half inch. Spacing after paragraphs should be set to zero.

Header and Page Numbers

Every page of the research paper should have a header that includes the writer's last name and a consecutive page number. The page number should be one-half inch from the top of the page in the upper right-hand corner, flush with the right margin. In the header, type the last name followed by a space before the page number.

Headings

Research papers and scholarly articles in the humanities often do not have formal headings. If a break is needed between ideas, some authors insert an extra blank line between paragraphs. If this method is used, be sure that the extra line does not appear at the bottom or top of a page, where it may be overlooked by the reader. If this occurs, add three asterisks, centered, on the blank line, and use this method consistently throughout the paper, regardless of where in the text the other blank lines appear.

Using levels of heading, however, can provide a transition between unified sections of thought and aid in the flow of a paper. If using headings, do not also use blank lines to signal a break between paragraphs. In MLA style, it is acceptable to use headings labeled with numbers, words, or both. When numbering headings, use consecutive Arabic numerals. If using only numbers, center them on the page. If using only words or a number and words, the heading should be flush left. Do not add extra blank lines above or below a heading.

Punctuation and Spacing

Punctuation provides the pace for a sentence and tells the reader where to pause (commas, colons, or semicolons), stop (periods, question marks, or exclamation points), or deviate (parentheses, dashes, or brackets). The different kinds of punctuation in a sentence usually designate different kinds and lengths of pauses. Modern word-processing programs provide the appropriate space for each character, so type the spacebar only once after commas, colons, and semicolons. Do not include extra spaces around dashes, parentheses, or brackets. Put only one space between sentences. Following is a quick guide to punctuation rules required by MLA format.

Period

Periods are used in reference lists after the author's name, the title of a book or article, the year, the type of medium, and the close of the reference. When in-text citations are used at the end of a sentence, the period should follow the citation. When in-text citations occur at the end of a long, indented quote, periods should not follow the in-text citations. In that case, the period occurs at the end of the quote but before the in-text citation. See "Quotations of More Than Four Lines," which appears later in this section, for an example.

Colon

Colons are used in references between the publication location and the publisher. In the works cited list, use a colon between the title and subtitle of a book or article.

In text, a colon should not be used after an introductory clause that is not a complete sentence. Use a colon to introduce a quotation only if the introductory clause is a complete sentence.

Semicolon

Although semicolons are usually used to separate two independent clauses (complete sentences), a semicolon should also be used to set off items in a series when one or more of these items already includes commas, regardless of whether the items are complete sentences—for example, "The sisters were challenged to ride a bike for two hours; juggle a ball, a book, and a toy car for 10 minutes; and walk on a treadmill for 30 minutes."

Comma

A comma should be used in the works cited list between the publisher and the year. Do not use a comma to set off the page numbers of in-text reference citations. If the title of a work is required in the parenthetical citation, put a comma between the author name and the work title.

In text, use a comma between elements in a series of three or more items, including before *and* and *or*.

Quotation Marks

In addition to use in expressing direct quotations, double quotation marks should be used in the following situations:

- To introduce a word or phrase that is used as slang, a coined expression, or an example of irony
- To identify an article or chapter title in a periodical or book when the title is mentioned in text
- To reproduce or cite material from a published source
- To introduce a translation of a foreign word or phrase

Double quotation marks should not enclose quotations of more than four lines.

Quotations of More Than Four Lines

Quotations that take up more than four lines of text should be in a paragraph by themselves, presented as a block quotation, indented one inch from the left margin without the customary first-line indent. They should be double-spaced and should not include quotation marks. They should also be followed by a citation that includes a page number. The citation is presented after the closing punctuation of the block quotation. If the quoted text contains quotation marks, double quotation marks should be used.

Block quotations are generally introduced by a colon, though some situations may require no punctuation or a different punctuation mark. If the quotation includes more than one paragraph, indent the first line of each paragraph one-half inch.

Example:

> Candy manufactured at the offshore facility was tainted, but testing of product made domestically revealed that it was safe. Representatives from the manufacturer claimed that the company was unaware of any problems with ingredients or machinery at the offshore plant prior to the discovery of the poisoned product. (Bradenforth 238)

Italics

Use italics for introduction of a new, technical, or key term (but only on first use of the word; do not italicize the word if again it is used in subsequent sentences). It is acceptable to use italics for emphasis, but do so sparingly, as this can quickly become distracting and ineffective.

Italics are also necessary in the following contexts:

- Letters or words that are referred to as letters or words (e.g., "Some street signs leave off the *e* in *Clairemont.*")
- Foreign words in an English text not typically found in an American dictionary
- The names of books, plays, poems published as books, pamphlets, periodicals, websites, films, TV and radio broadcasts, CDs, dance performances, paintings, ships, aircraft, and spacecraft discussed in the body of the paper

Parentheses

Parentheses are used in the following ways:

- To set off reference citations in text
- To enclose the citation or page number of a direct quote
- To introduce an abbreviation
- To enclose the year of a periodical entry in a works cited list

Hyphens

A hyphen should not be used on common fractions used as nouns (e.g., "Two thirds of the students missed class"); however, a hyphen should be used when the fraction is used as a descriptor (e.g., "The student council requires a two-thirds majority to pass a new rule"). Hyphens should also be avoided in compounds in which the first word is an adverb (e.g., "The nearly vetoed legislation has finally passed") and in situations where there is no possible way a compound term could be misread without it (e.g., "The health care industry lobbied Congress for this law"). Do not use a space before or after a hyphen.

Dashes

In MLA style, type two hyphens to make a dash or use the dash symbol available in most word processing programs' symbol menus. Do not add space before or after the dash. A dash should be used to either highlight a clause or to indicate a diversion from the sentence's primary clause (e.g., "The test subjects—who were unaware of the change—disliked the nature of the treatment").

Using Numbers in a Document

MLA style differentiates between papers that frequently use numbers and ones that seldom use them. Most papers in the humanities, such as those focused on literature, history, or philosophy, use numbers infrequently. For such papers, spell out numbers that are expressed in one or two words; otherwise, use numerals (e.g., two, forty-seven, three hundred, fifty thousand, but $4\frac{3}{4}$; 405; 2,425; 55,000).

For papers that frequently include numbers, such as a technical scientific study that discusses many measurements or one that uses statistical data, use numerals before units of measure (e.g., 4 centimeters, 47 kilowatts) and when numbers are introduced together to refer to related things (e.g., "The membership of the city council rose from 7 to 15 over the last ten years." Notice in this example that "ten" is spelled out because it is not presented with related figures.). In other instances, spell out numbers that are expressed in one or two words.

One primary exception to these rules is when a number expressed in more than two words begins a sentence. In such a case, the words should be spelled out (e.g., "Two hundred and three men were surveyed").

There are several exceptions in which numbers of one or two words would be listed in numeric form, generally related to specific quantity measurements, such as the following:

- To express decimal fractions
- With abbreviations or symbols
- To represent dates, scores, or points on a scale
- With most times of the day, except when time is expressed in quarter-hours or half-hours or in hours followed by "o'clock" (e.g., 4:50, 10:05, half past three, a quarter to nine, two o'clock)
- To show divisions (e.g., page 9; year 4 of the project)

When expressing large numbers, combine words and numerals (e.g., 5.7 billion). In a range of large numbers, give only the last two digits of the second number unless the first digit of the second number is not the same as the first digit of the first number (e.g., 245-57, 1567-91, 295-314, 1989-2004). Write out the century using lowercase letters (e.g., twenty-first century). Plurals of numbers should be written by adding *-s* or *-es*, without an apostrophe (MLA 2008, 81–85).

Abbreviations

MLA style recommends minimal use of abbreviations in the body of a paper, as they can often cause more confusion than clarification and can hinder reader comprehension. Generally, an abbreviation should be used only if (a) it is well known and a reader would be familiar with it, or (b) it saves considerable space and prevents repetition.

The writer must decide whether to spell out an expression or group name every time or spell it out initially and abbreviate it thereafter. A term must be written out completely on first use, followed by its abbreviation in parentheses. Afterward, the abbreviation can be used without any further explanation. Generally, MLA requires that abbreviations do not use periods after letters or spaces between letters (e.g., UK, US, CIA, CD, BA, URL). Exceptions to this guideline include the following:

- Use a period and a space after initials used in a person's name (e.g., J. D. Salinger)
- Use a period after most abbreviations that end in lowercase letters (e.g., Czech Rep., dept., govt., misc.)
- Use a period but no space between letters in most abbreviations in which lowercase letters each represent a word (e.g., p.m., i.e., n.p.)

Other guidelines for in-text abbreviations in MLA style include the following:

- Spell out the names of months, but abbreviate them in the works cited list, except May, June, and July
- Most words expressing units of time are spelled out (e.g., second, minute, month, year) with a few exceptions (e.g., a.m., AD, BC)
- Spell out the names of US states and countries, with a few exceptions (e.g., USSR, US, UK)
- Use Latin abbreviations only in parenthetical material. In running text, use the English translations of Latin abbreviations (e.g., use "e.g." in parenthetical text but use "for example" in the text)

Percent, Percentages, and Monetary Figures

Expressing percentages and amounts of money follow a similar format to that of numbers in MLA style. For a paper that uses numbers infrequently, spell out percentages and amounts of money that can be written in three words or fewer (e.g., thirty-four percent, two hundred Euros, four thousand dollars, forty-eight cents).

In papers that frequently use numbers, use numerals with the appropriate symbols (e.g., 28%, 60%, $2.75, ¥5,000, $0.94). The symbols for percent and for various currencies should be used only in combination with a numeral (e.g., "5%, €205"). The word "percent" should not be spelled out after a numeral.

When a number is not given, the word "percentage" should be used (e.g., a significant percentage of women preferred the reformulated product). In table column or row headings or legends, however, use a percent symbol instead of the word "percentage" to conserve space.

REFERENCES AND INTERNAL CITATION STYLE

Proper documentation of sources includes two important steps: creating a works cited list and using internal citations. MLA guidelines require a structured works cited list and parenthetical in-text citations of each source listed in the works cited list. It is critical to carefully follow MLA guidelines for placement and style of citations and references. Footnotes and endnotes are occasionally used, but they are secondary to parenthetical citations. Content footnotes are used to clarify or expand on information in the text, and bibliographic notes are sometimes used to add evaluative comments about sources. Neither type should be used in place of parenthetical citations in an MLA-style research paper.

Citation Style

Parenthetical citations include the author name(s) and usually the page number for the information referenced. When using a direct quotation or paraphrasing a particular passage in a work, include the page number where it appeared in the source document. Do not include a page number when citing an entire work rather than referencing a particular portion of it.

Citations can be formatted in a variety of ways. Example 1 illustrates an effective way to mention the authors in the text of the sentence; it is particularly useful when the aim is to describe the author in some way. The style of

Example 2 results in a complete statement without using the author's name. Example 3 shows a direct quote from the reference material coupled with mention of the author's name in the sentence. Example 4 combines a direct quote and a complete statement that does not mention the author's name.

- *Example 1:* According to Colomb, Booth, and Williams, you should avoid plagiarism.
- *Example 2:* You should avoid plagiarism (Colomb, Booth, and Williams).
- *Example 3:* According to Colomb, Booth, and Williams, "In all fields, you plagiarize when you use a source's words or ideas without citing that source" (202).
- *Example 4:* Many authorities have commented on the topic, but this is one of the most effective descriptions. "In all fields, you plagiarize when you use a source's words or ideas without citing that source" (Colomb, Booth, and Williams 202).

If a source has more than three authors, list all the names of the authors in the citations or list only the name of the first author followed by "et al." However, whichever style is used must also be applied to the citation in the works cited list. See Example 5 for an illustration of these citation options.

- *Example 5:* Plagiarism can harm your career (Colomb, Booth, and Williams). It is best to create your own original content and exercise caution when quoting and summarizing the content of others (Sampson et al. 77).

If the works cited list includes more than one work by the same author, add the title of the work—shortened or in full—with a comma after the author name(s) to clarify which of the author's works the citation is referencing.

- *Example 6:* Many authorities have commented on the topic, but this is one of the most effective descriptions: "In all fields, you plagiarize when you use a source's words or ideas without citing that source" (Colomb, Booth, and Williams, *Plagiarism* 202).

Some works have no listed author. In those cases, use an abbreviated version of the article title in the citation.

- *Example 7:* In 2005, Philadelphia City Schools suspended 215 children because of incidents of plagiarism ("Cheating on the Rise").

Reference Style

The MLA reference style is more accommodating than other styles, including APA, Turabian, and Chicago style. Typically, references are listed in alphabetical order, usually by the authors' last names; if no author is listed, entries are alphabetized by the title of the source. However, MLA offers some flexibility in preparing the list of works cited. If the paper is a historical piece in which the chronology of the sources is important, the writer may decide to arrange the reference list chronologically. Similarly, if, for example, the paper compares various forms of ancient mythology, the writer may choose to group entries by subject matter (e.g., Greek Mythology, Roman Mythology, Norse Mythology).

Entries within the works cited list have similar flexibility. For example, if the paper focuses on a particular music producer, it is acceptable to list associated albums not by artist name, as would be the norm, but by producer name (followed by "prod."). Similarly, if the paper is about a children's book illustrator, the writer can list the associated books' references with the illustrator's name (followed by "illus.") rather than the authors' names.

When creating a list of works cited, think carefully about why the particular sources were chosen and document them in a way that is appropriate for the subject and for the readers' needs.

Assembling a List of Works Cited

An MLA reference list, as the name implies, is a listing of works cited in the text. Each type of reference—a journal article, a book, a website, or a newspaper article, for example—has its own unique style. The idea behind the list of works cited is to give the reader as much information as possible to seek out the references used and gain a deeper understanding of the writer's logic by reading them. Following are general guidelines to the elements included in an MLA works cited list. Note, however, that items included in the citation are ordered and punctuated differently, depending on the type of source:

- On a new page at the end of the paper, title the references section "Works Cited," centered, an inch from the top of the page.
- Double-space the entire works cited list, both between and within individual references.

- The first line of a reference is set flush left, but any subsequent lines in the same reference are indented one-half inch.
- Entries in the works cited list are usually alphabetized by author's last name (or by article title if no author is given). If the list includes more than one work by the same author, alphabetize these entries by article title. In the first entry, include the author's first name, last name, and middle initial (if applicable). For subsequent entries by the same author, it is acceptable to substitute the author's name with three hyphens followed by a period. Only do so if the author's name is *exactly* the same in each entry. If there are different co-authors, do not abbreviate the entry.
- Periods separate most parts of a reference. They should be present after the author name(s), after article titles, after publication date, after type of medium, after page numbers of book chapters, and at the end of the reference. Periods should also be used after the middle initials of each author. Commas are used between the author's last and first name(s), to separate authors, and between the book publisher and date. A colon is used to separate the city of publication and the publisher's name.
- The first author's name in a reference should be listed last name first, followed by the first name and middle initials, and finished with a period. All subsequent author names should appear in typical order (first name, middle initial, last name). When there are more than three authors, list all authors in the order they appear in the original publication or list the name of the first author only followed by "et al." To reference an edited book, insert the editor's name in the author position and follow it with the abbreviation "ed." If there is no author, the title of the work should be listed first.
- The title of an article or chapter comes after the author name, followed by the title of the work, periodical, or book. Put the article title in double quotation marks, and capitalize all important words in the title and subtitle (if there is one). The title should not be italicized.
- The city of publication follows the title of any book. The state, province, or country after the name of a city is not required. A colon is placed after the city name.
- The publisher's name follows the city of publication. Make the publisher's name as short as possible while still ensuring that the reader can identify the publisher. Omit articles (a, an, the) and descriptive words (e.g., "books, publishers, press"). Abbreviate whenever possible (e.g., "Univ., Assn., Acad."). Place a comma after the publisher's name.
- The year a book was copyrighted should follow the publisher of the book. Place a period after the date. For journals, the date goes inside parentheses after the volume and issue number, followed by a colon. For newspapers, magazines, and online sources, the date goes after the source name (newspaper, magazine, or website name). In these cases, the day, month, and year are included, in that order, if applicable, with no added punctuation. Months—except May, June, and July—are abbreviated. If no date is available, insert "n.d." (for "no date").
- Include page numbers for periodical articles, book chapters, and online sources, if applicable. Do not use "p." or "pp." before the page numbers and provide only the last two digits of the second number unless the first and last numbers within the range do not start with the same digit (e.g., 197-99 but 197-204). Page numbers for entire books are not listed. If paragraphs are numbered (for example, in an Internet article), use of "par." or "pars." is acceptable.
- The type of medium is always included in an MLA reference. This indicates the type of source consulted (e.g., Print, CD, Web, LP, Television, Film). The type of medium is always capitalized and is always followed by a period.
- For Internet sources, always include the retrieval date. List the day, month (abbreviated unless May, June, or July), and year—in that order, without added punctuation (e.g., 5 Feb. 2010)—that the source was last accessed.
- Appropriate abbreviations for use in the reference section and in-text citations include the following:
  - cond. = conductor
  - conf. = conference
  - illus. = illustrator
  - introd. = introduction
  - narr. = narrator

- trans. = translator(s)
- n.d. = no date
- n.p. = no place of publication, no publisher
- n. pag. = no pagination
- vol. = volume
- ed. = editor
- par. = paragraph
- pref. = preface
- prod. = producer
- qtd. = quoted
- supp. = supplement
- U = University
- UP = University Press
- writ = written by

Examples of References

If a source does not match any of the examples provided in this section, refer to the *MLA Handbook* (2009) or the *MLA Style Manual* (2008). Both publications offer similar instructions for citing and referencing sources; however, the *MLA Style Manual* provides more detail about types of sources most likely to be used by professors and graduate students.

MLA style imposes different requirements and rules on different types of sources. Books, journal articles, magazine articles, websites, and other sources each have particular requirements that give proper credit and help readers locate the reference material. The following 15 examples illustrate the format for referencing some of the more common types of sources.

Example 1: A book with a single author.

Klein, Nathan. *No Logo*. New York: Picador, 2000. Print.

Book author: The author's last name is listed first, followed by the author's first name and middle initials (if applicable).

Book title: The title is italicized with all important words capitalized. If there is a colon in the title, the first word following the colon is always capitalized.

Publication information: It is not necessary to include a state, province, or country after the name of a city. A colon is inserted after the city and followed by the name of the publisher. Make the publisher's name as short as possible while still ensuring that the reader can identify the publisher. Omit articles (e.g., a, an, the) and descriptive words (e.g., books, publishers, press). Abbreviate whenever possible (e.g., Univ., Assn., Acad.).

Date of publication: The year the book was published follows the publisher's name.

Type of medium: Include, with initial caps, the type of medium of the publication consulted (e.g., Print, Web, CD, Audio Cassette, Microfilm, Performance, Laser Disc).

Example 2: A book with two or three authors.

Rubin, Rhonda B., Alfred K. Rubin, and Lynnette J. Piele. *Communication Research: A Study in Strategies and Sources.* 5th ed. Belmont: Wadsworth, 2000. Print.

Book author: The first author's last name is listed first, followed by the author's first name and middle initials (if applicable). A comma follows the name of the first author, even when there are only two authors to list. All subsequent author names are presented in usual order (first name, middle initial [if applicable], last name). Type "and" before the last author is listed. Authors are listed in the order they appear on the book.

Book title, publication information, date of publication, type of medium: Follow the format applied in Example 1. (Note that edition numbers follow book titles.)

Example 3: A book with more than three authors.

Brown, Lester V. et al. *Research Methods for Undergraduate Students.* New York: Columbia UP, 2007. Print.

Brown, Lester V., Thomas Z. Ecks, Fatima Walters, Adian R. Zim, Akiko Yashimoto, and Jason P. Bynum. *Research Methods for Undergraduate Students.* New York: Columbia UP, 2007. Print.

Book author: The author's last name is listed first, followed by the author's first name and middle initials (if applicable). With more than three authors, it is acceptable to write out the names of all the authors or to list only the first author followed by the abbreviation "et al." Whichever approach is used, the same style must be applied to the in-text parenthetical citations.

Book title, publication information, date of publication, type of medium: Follow the format applied in Example 1.

Example 4: A translated chapter in a multi-author book.

Tocada, Rieko. "Pottery of the Meiji Era." Trans. Ginger Farriday. *The Arts in Japan, 1868–1912.* Ed. Samuel Jensen. London: Wadsworth, 2006. 247-91. Print.

Article author: The author's last name is listed first, followed by the first name and middle initials (if applicable). If applicable, the name of the translator follows the author name.

Article title: The article title is in double quotation marks and is not italicized. Capitalize all important words. If there is a colon in the title, the first word following the colon is always capitalized. A period follows the title, inside the quotation marks.

Book title: Follow the format applied in Example 1.

Book editor: The editor's name is not inverted. If there is more than one editor, use the abbreviation "Eds." (MLA 2009, 157).

Publication information, date of publication: Follow the format applied in Example 1.

Page numbers: After the date, list the page numbers of the chapter. Do not use "p." or "pp." before the page numbers and provide only the last two digits of the second number unless the first digit of both numbers in the range is not the same.

Type of medium: Follow the format applied in Example 1.

Example 5: An article with only one author in a scholarly journal.

Kramer, Micah W. "Communication in Community Theatre Groups." *Journal of Applied Communication Research* 33.2 (2005): 159-82. Print.

Article author: The author's last name is listed first, followed by the author's first name and middle initials (if applicable). For articles with multiple authors, follow the format applied in Examples 2 and 3.

Article title: The article title is in double quotation marks and is not italicized. Capitalize all important words. If there is a colon in the title, the first word following the colon is always capitalized. A period inside the quotation marks follows the title.

Journal title: The journal title is italicized, and all important words in the title are capitalized. If the journal title starts with an article (the, a, an), unless it is a foreign title (e.g., *La Familia*), omit it. No punctuation follows the journal title.

Publication information: Provide the volume number and the issue number (if any) separated by a period, with no intervening spaces. The year the article was written is included in parentheses after the volume and issue number. After the closing parenthesis, add a colon and a space; then include the page numbers of the article. Do not use "p." or "pp." before the page numbers and provide only the last two digits of the second number unless the first digit of both numbers in the range is not the same.

Example 6: A magazine article.

Marin, Helena E. "Proust's Reflective Imagery." *Literary World* 15 June 2004: 47-52. Print.

Article author: The author's last name is listed first, followed by the author's first name and middle initials (if applicable).

Article title: Follow the format applied in Example 5.

Periodical title: The periodical title is italicized, and all important words in the title are capitalized. If the periodical title starts with an article (the, a, an), unless it is a foreign title (e.g., *La Familia*), omit it. No punctuation follows the periodical title.

Date of publication: If applicable, the day, month, and year that the article was published, in that order, follow the periodical title. Put a colon after the year.

Publication information: Do not provide a volume or issue number, even if they are listed. Provide page numbers for the article. If the pagination is not successive, give the first page number and a plus sign.

Example 7: An article from a newspaper.

McBride, Jenna. "Tornado Rips through City Hall Complex." *Globe News* [Topeka] 30 May 2007: A1+. Print.

Article author, article title: Follow the format applied in Example 6.

Periodical title: The newspaper title is italicized, and all important words in the title are capitalized. If the newspaper title starts with an article (the, a, an), unless it is a foreign title (e.g., *Le Monde*), omit it. If the newspaper name does not include the city of publication (e.g., *Globe News* rather than *Chicago Tribune*), add it in brackets after the name, in roman (not italic). If the newspaper is published nationally (e.g., *USA Today*), no city is needed. Do not include a state name unless it is part of the newspaper's title. No punctuation follows the newspaper title.

Date of publication: Follow the format applied in Example 6.

Publication information: For newspapers, include the section and page number. Do not write "p." or "pp." before the section name (if applicable) and the starting page number. If the article continues past the first page, add a plus sign.

Type of medium: Include the type of medium of the publication consulted (e.g., Print).

Example 8: An article with no listed author, from a newspaper.

"Asarco Gets Approval to Auction Land in Salt Lake City." *Amarillo Globe-News* 30 May 2007: D6. Print.

Article author: If an article has no listed author, do not insert "Anonymous." The article title is placed first. The article title is in double quotation marks and is not italicized. Capitalize all important words. If there is a colon in the title, the first word following the colon is always capitalized. A period inside the quotation marks follows the title. If the title begins with an article (a, an, the), alphabetize the entry according to the first letter of the first important word.

Article title, date of publication: Follow the format applied in Example 6.

Periodical title, publication information, type of medium: Follow the format applied in Example 7.

Example 9: An online magazine or news article.

Marano, Hyram E., and Beatrice G. Schwartz. "Proust's Reflective Imagery." *Literary World.com.* U. of Texas, June 2004. Web. 24 Feb. 2008.

Article author: Follow the format applied in Example 6.

Article title: Use double quotation marks around the title if it is part of a larger work. If the article is independent, italicize the title and do not use quotation marks.

Publication information: List the title of the overall website in italics, if it is distinct from the article title. Next include the publisher or sponsor of the website; if none is available, insert "n.p."

Date of publication: If applicable, the day, month, and year that the article was published, in that order, follow the publisher. If no date is available, insert "n.d."

Retrieval information: Insert "Web" as the type of medium. List the day, month, and year of retrieval, in that order.

Example 10: An article from a periodical database.

Russell, Pierre R. "Saving Energy Is a Hot Topic: Energy to Develop Ways to Conserve." *New Orleans Times-Picayune* 11 May 2007: Money 1. *LexisNexis.* Web. 5 Jan. 2009.

Article author, article title, periodical title, date of publication: Follow the format applied in Example 6.

Publication information: Follow the format applied in Example 7.

Retrieval information: Include in italics the name of the database where the article was found, followed by a period. Next, insert "Web" as the type of medium. List the day, month, and year of retrieval, in that order.

Example 11: An Internet source.

"Oklahoma Housing Trends, June–Dec. 2009." Chart. *Baystreet Realty.com.* America First Home Loans 2009. Web. 18 Feb. 2010.

Heading title: Websites or web pages often do not have identified author(s). In such a case, the website section heading is listed at the beginning of the reference. The heading is in double quotation marks and is not italicized. Capitalize all important words. If there is a colon in the title, the first word following the colon is always capitalized. A period inside the quotation marks follows the title. If the title begins with an article (a, an, the), alphabetize it by the first letter of the first important word used. If applicable, include a word to describe the type of document (e.g., chart, map, editorial, home page).

Publication information, retrieval information, date of publication: Follow the format applied in Example 9.

Example 12: A film or video recording.

Summer Morning. Dir. Cesar Patino. Perf. John Frisko, Lynn Bosworth, and Tina Dunmore. RKO, 1938. Film.

Film title: Usually the title of the film is listed first in italics. However, if the paper focuses on a particular aspect of the film—such as the prop design, the movie studio, or an actor or director—it is acceptable to insert this information at the beginning of the citation. Think carefully about why the sources were selected and write the entry appropriately for the subject. Include any information that is relevant to the paper.

Director name: Use the abbreviation "Dir." before the director's name. Do not list the last name first.

Performer names: It is acceptable to include the names of the key actors in a film or video recording.

Distributor name: Include the name of the distributor, followed by a comma. Make the distributor's name as short as possible while still ensuring that the reader can identify it.

Year of release: The year the film was released follows the distributor's name.

Type of medium: Include the type of medium (e.g., Film, Video recording, DVD, Laser disc).

Example 13: A personal interview.

Tomlin, Simon. Skype interview. 19 Feb. 2010.

Name of interviewee: In the author position, place the name of the person interviewed, last name followed by a comma then the first name, followed by a period.

Type of interview: Indicate how the interview was conducted (e.g., Telephone interview, Personal interview).

Date of interview: List the day, month, and year of the interview, in that order.

Example 14: A picture from a website.

Pollock, Jackson. *Greyed Rainbow.* 1953. Art Institute of Chicago. *The Art Institute of Chicago*. Web. 6 June 2011.

Artist or photographer: Follow the format applied to authors in Example 1.

Title: Follow the format applied in Example 1.

Date: List the year of completion or n.d. if no date is known.

Collection: List the name of the institution or collection that owns the picture.

Retrieval information: Follow the format applied in Example 9.

Example 15: A picture from a book.

Pollock, Jackson. *Greyed Rainbow.* 1953. Art Institute of Chicago. *Jackson Pollock*. By Ellen G. Landau. New York: Abradale Press, 2010. 230. Print.

Artist or photographer and title: Follow the format applied to authors in Example 14.

Book title: Follow the format applied in Example 1.

Book author: The author of the book appears in standard format of first name followed by last name. The first name is spelled out and middle initials included (if applicable).

Publication information: Follow the format applied in Example 1.

Page or plate number: Following the publication information, list the page or image/plate number for the picture.

APPENDIX

C

PowerPoint Essentials: PowerPoint Shortcuts

CREATING A NEW PRESENTATION

There are two ways to create a new presentation with Microsoft PowerPoint 2010® presentation software. You can base your presentation on a template or base your presentation on a theme.

To create a presentation based on a template, use the following steps:

1. Click the *File* tab on the Ribbon.

2. Click *New*.

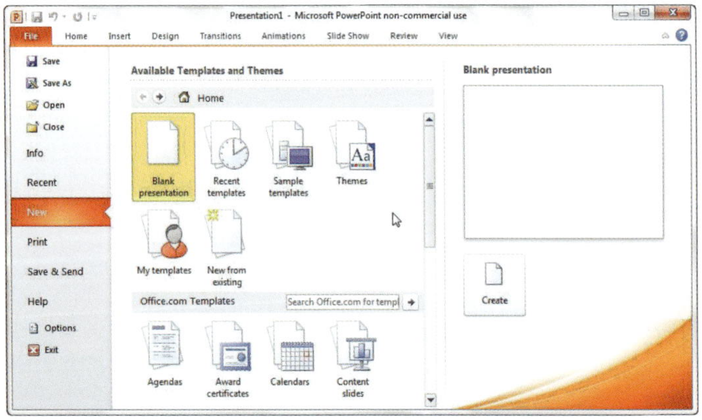

3. Select an available template under Available Templates and Themes.

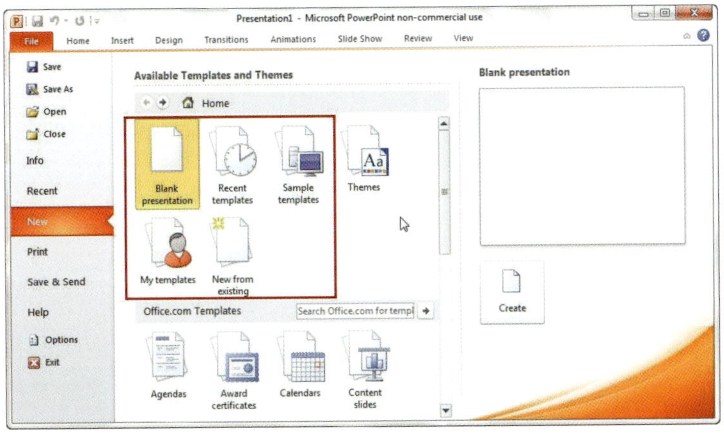

4. Click **Create.**

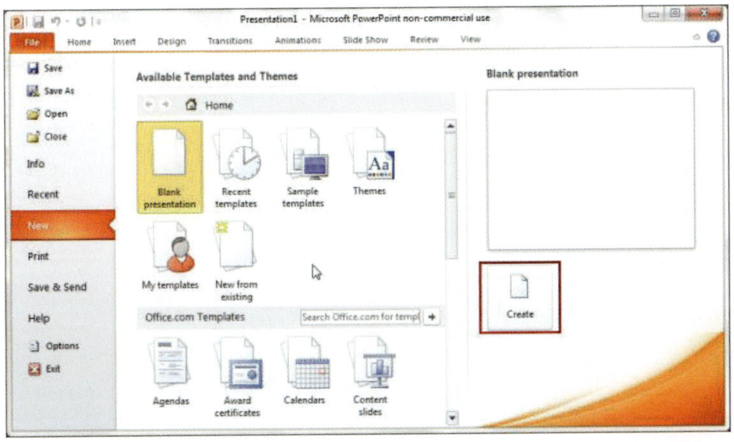

To create a presentation based on a theme, use the following steps:

1. Click the *File* tab on the Ribbon.

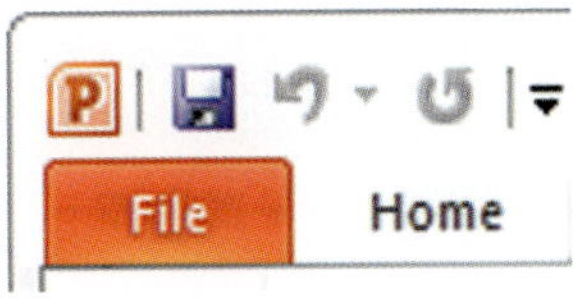

2. Click *New*.

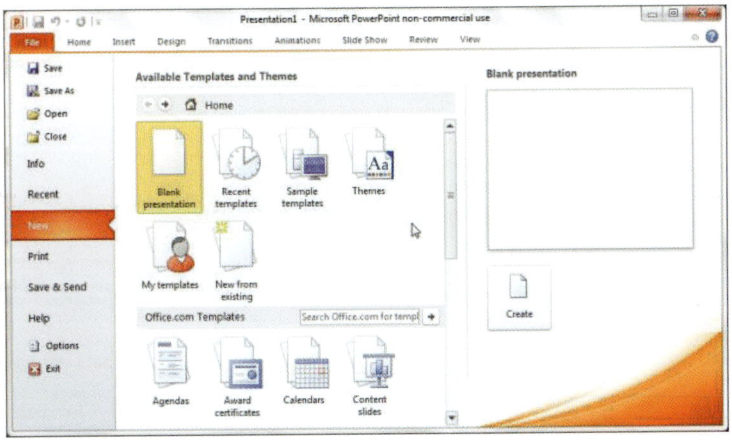

KEY CONCEPTS

1. Creating a New Presentation
2. Entering, Selecting, and Editing Text
3. Formatting Slides
4. Adding and Deleting Slides
5. Viewing a Slide Show
6. Printing a Presentation

3. Select **Themes** under Available Templates and Themes.

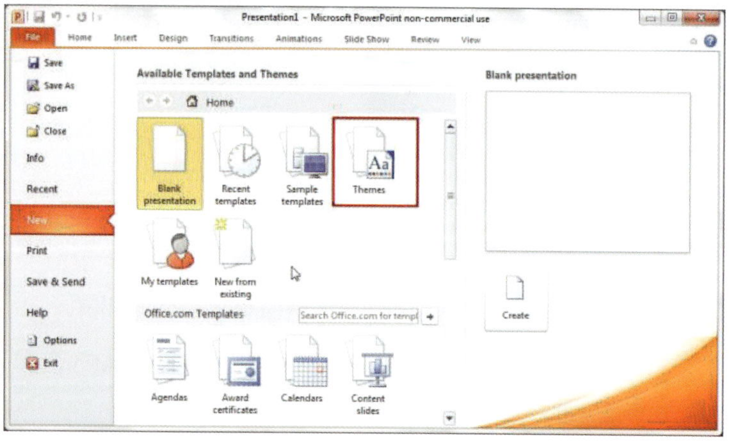

4. Click **Create.**

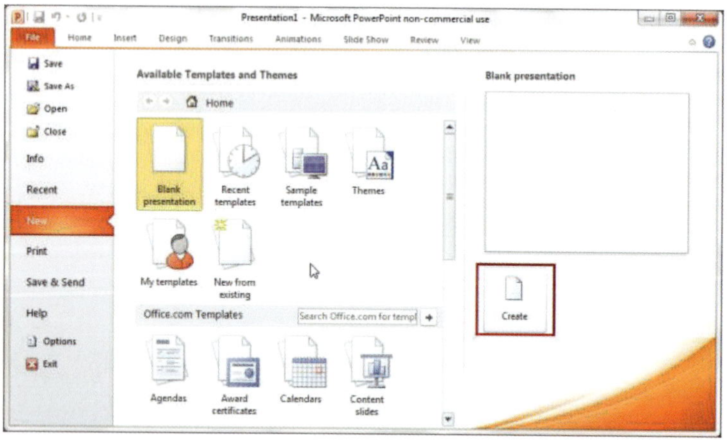

ENTERING, SELECTING, AND EDITING TEXT

Entering Text

To enter text into a PowerPoint slide, click inside the text placeholder box and begin typing.

Selecting Text and Objects

Hold down the left mouse button and drag over the text or double-click on a word to select text in PowerPoint. Triple-click inside a paragraph to select the entire paragraph.

To select an object in PowerPoint, click on the object. To select multiple objects, press the **Shift** key as you click on each object.

Editing Text

Editing text in the PowerPoint application is similar to editing text in the Microsoft Word 2010® word processing software application. To insert a word into an existing sentence, click to place the insertion point of the new word and type the new word. To delete individual characters, click the insertion point at the right of the letter and press the **Backspace** key. To delete a word, select the entire word and then press **Delete** or **Backspace.** To replace text, select the text and type over it.

FORMATTING SLIDES

You can format slides in PowerPoint a number of ways.

To change the theme of a presentation, use the following steps:

1. Click the *Design* tab.

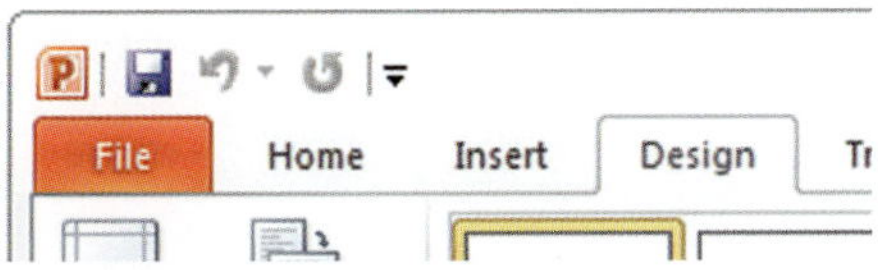

2. In the Themes section, select a desired slide design. Click the down arrow to the right of the theme selections to view more slide choices.

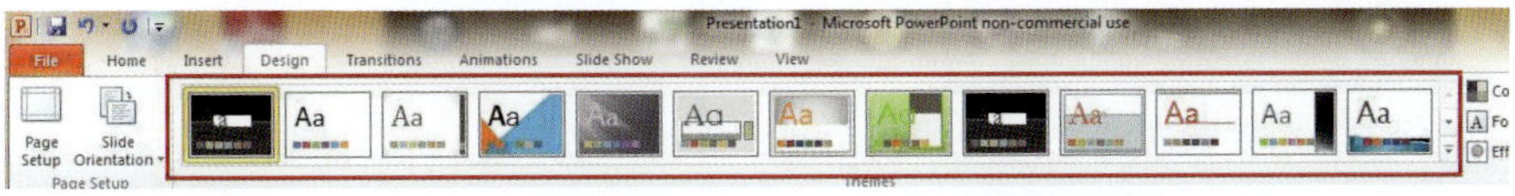

3. Click a slide design to apply the theme to the entire presentation.

To change the appearance of existing characters, use the following steps:

1. Select the text you want to format.
2. Click the *Home* tab.

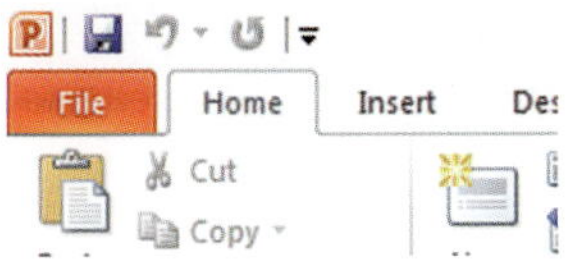

3. Under the Font section, use the appropriate menu options to format the selected text.

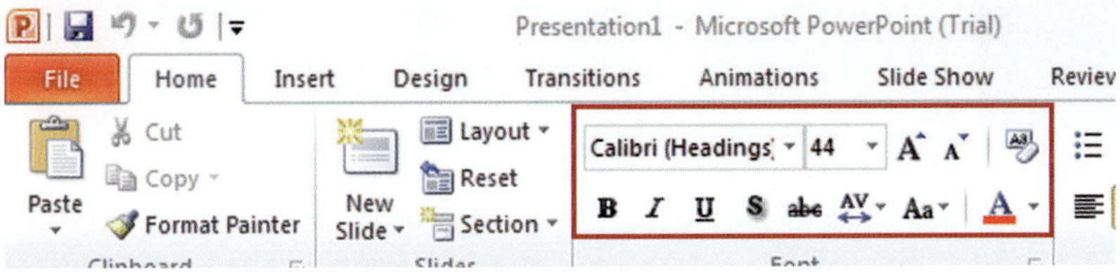

To change the appearance of existing paragraphs, use the following steps:

1. Select the paragraphs you want to format.
2. Click the *Home* tab.

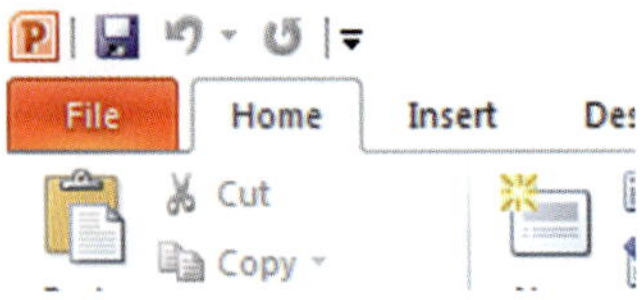

3. Under the Paragraph section, use the appropriate menu options to format the paragraphs.

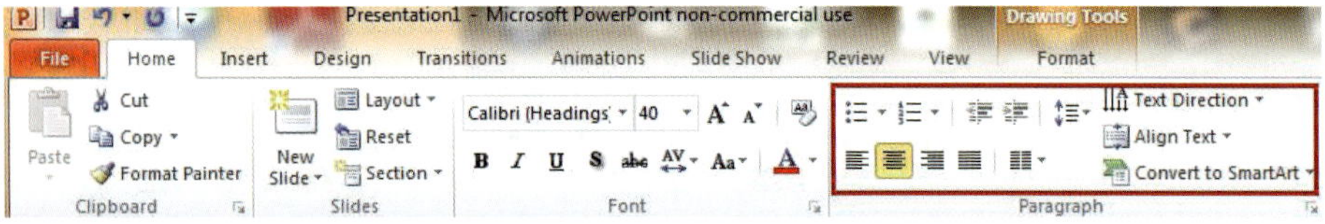

To change the background style of a presentation, use the following steps:

1. Click the *Design* tab.

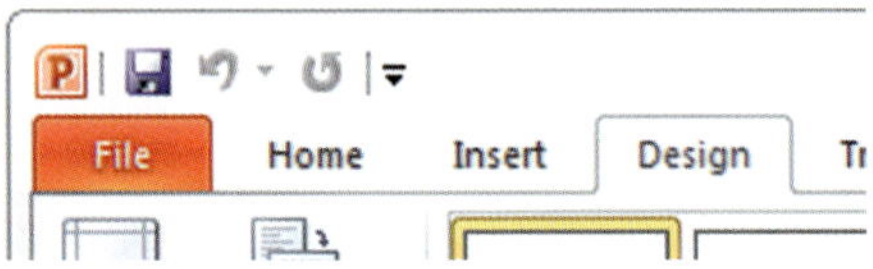

2. Click the **Background Styles** button on the right side of the Ribbon.

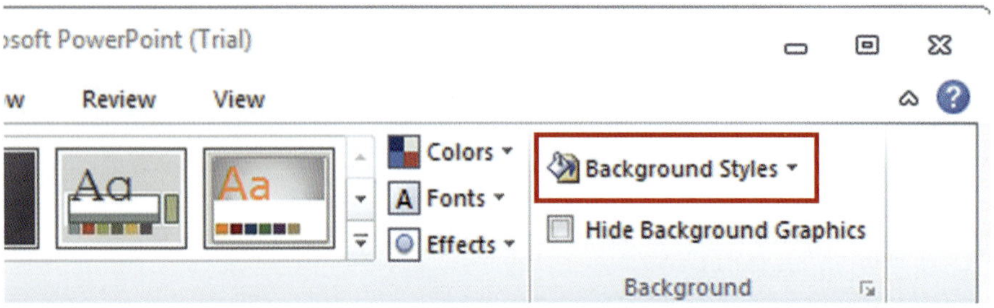

3. Click on a desired background style from the gallery.
4. For more background options, click the **Format Background** button.

5. Modify the fill settings to achieve the desired effect. Then, click **Apply to All.**

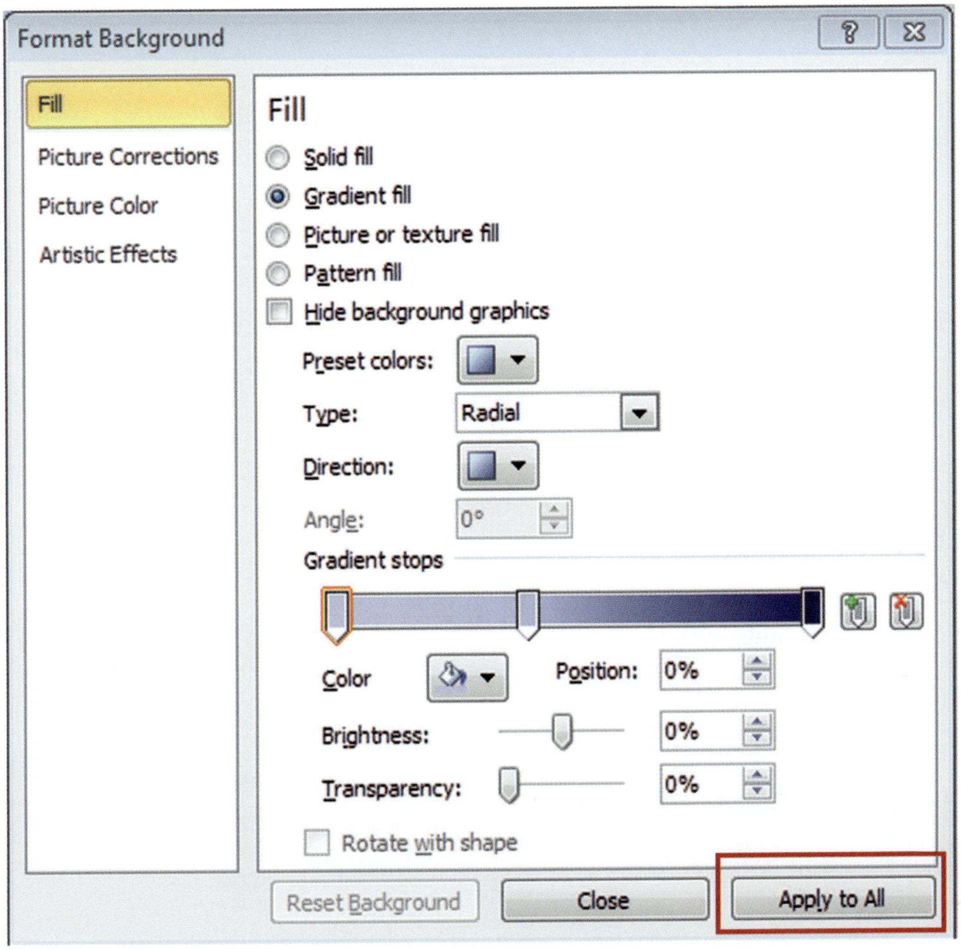

ADDING AND DELETING SLIDES

To add a new slide to a presentation, use the following steps:

1. Click the *View* tab. Then, click **Normal.**

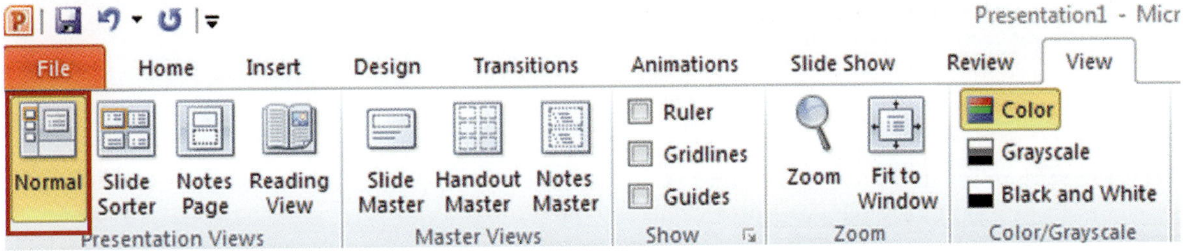

2. Click the *Home* tab.

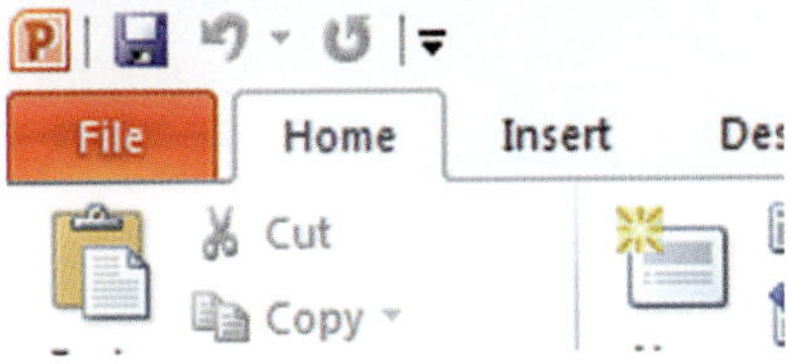

3. In the Slides pane on the left side of the window, click the slide thumbnail of the slide preceding the slide you will insert.

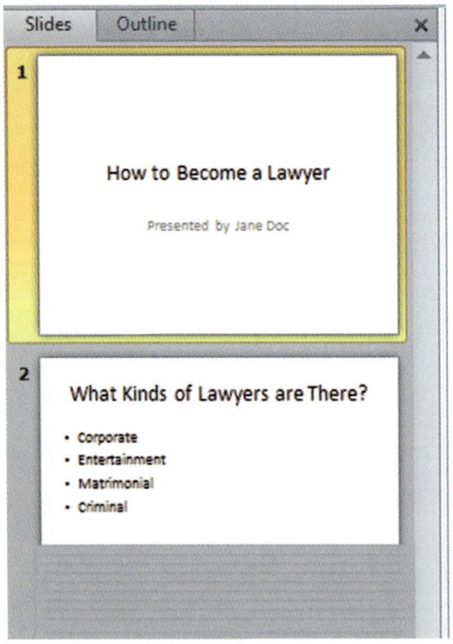

4. Click the down arrow inside the **New Slide** button.

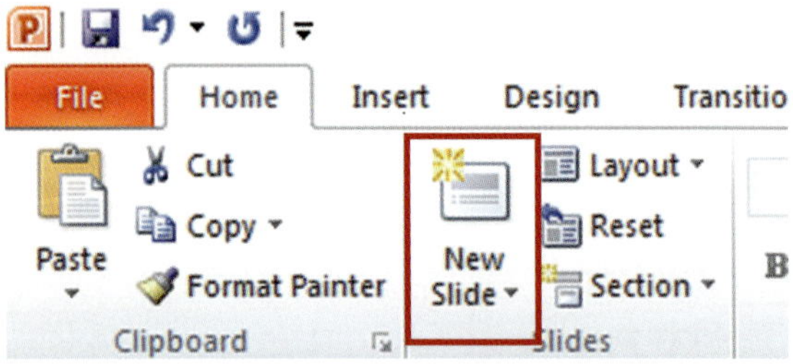

5. Select and click a desired slide layout from the list of slides.

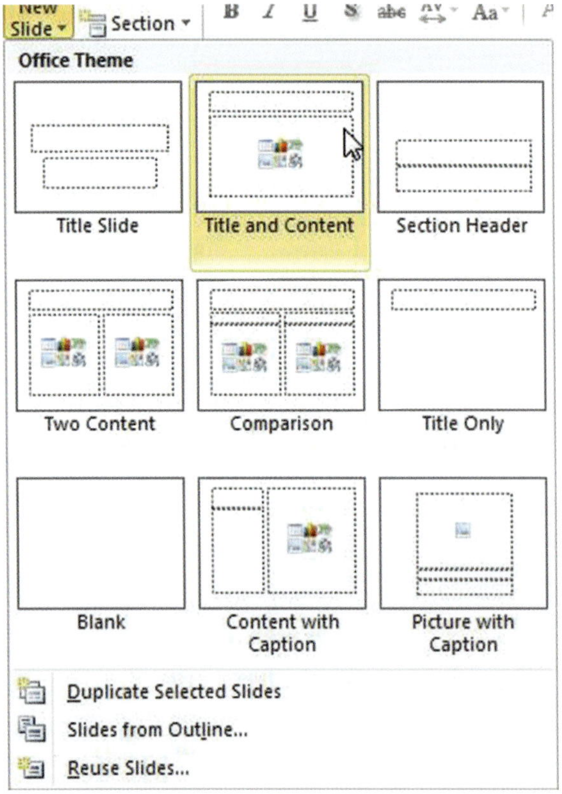

To delete a slide from a presentation, use the following steps:

1. Click the *View* tab. Then, click **Normal.**

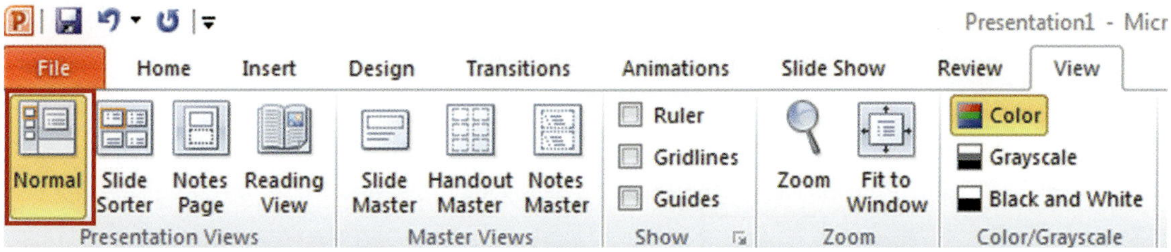

2. In the Slides pane on the left side of the window, click the slide thumbnail you want to delete.

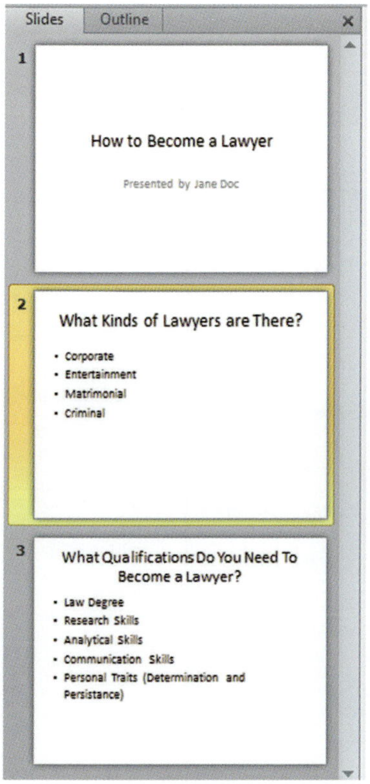

3. Press the **Delete** key.

VIEWING A SLIDE SHOW

PowerPoint allows the user to advance slides either manually or automatically when presenting a slide show.

To advance slides manually, use the following steps:

1. Click the *Slide Show* tab and then click **From Beginning.**

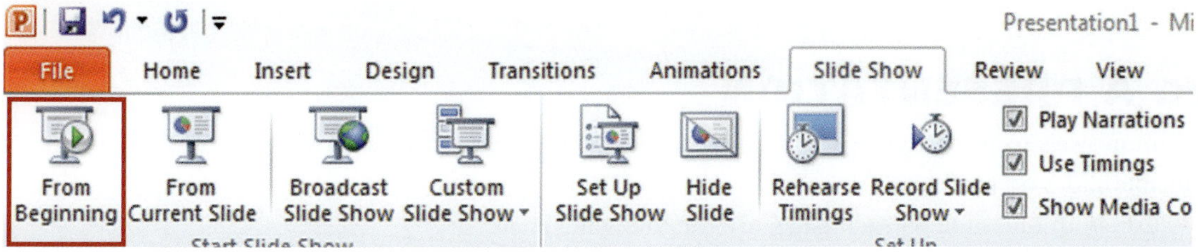

2. To advance the slides, press the left and right arrow keys or **Enter** (page up) and **Backspace** (page down) keys.
3. To terminate the slide show at any time, press **Esc.**

To advance slides automatically, use the following steps:

1. Click the *Slide Show* tab and then click the **Set Up Slide Show** button.

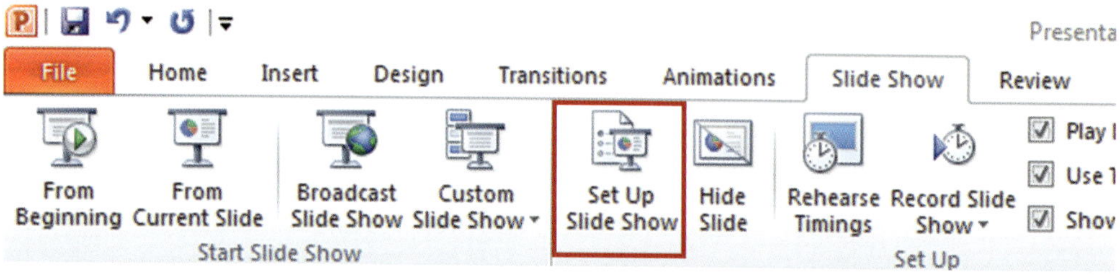

2. Select the appropriate slide show settings in the dialog box and click **OK.**

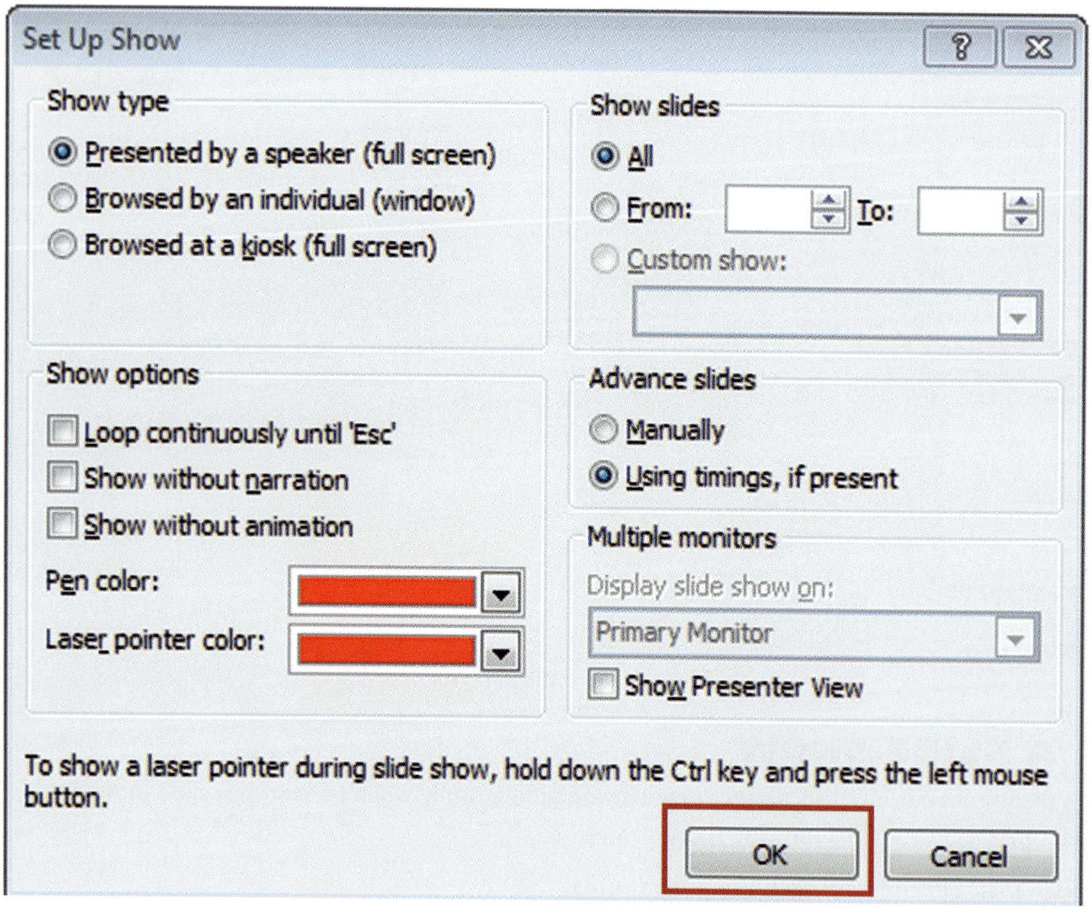

PRINTING A PRESENTATION

The two most common ways to print a presentation in PowerPoint are to print out each slide on a full page or as a handout with multiple slides on one page.

To print a presentation with one slide on each page, use the following steps:

1. Click the *File* tab.

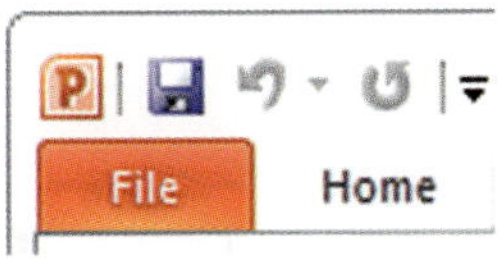

2. Click *Print*.

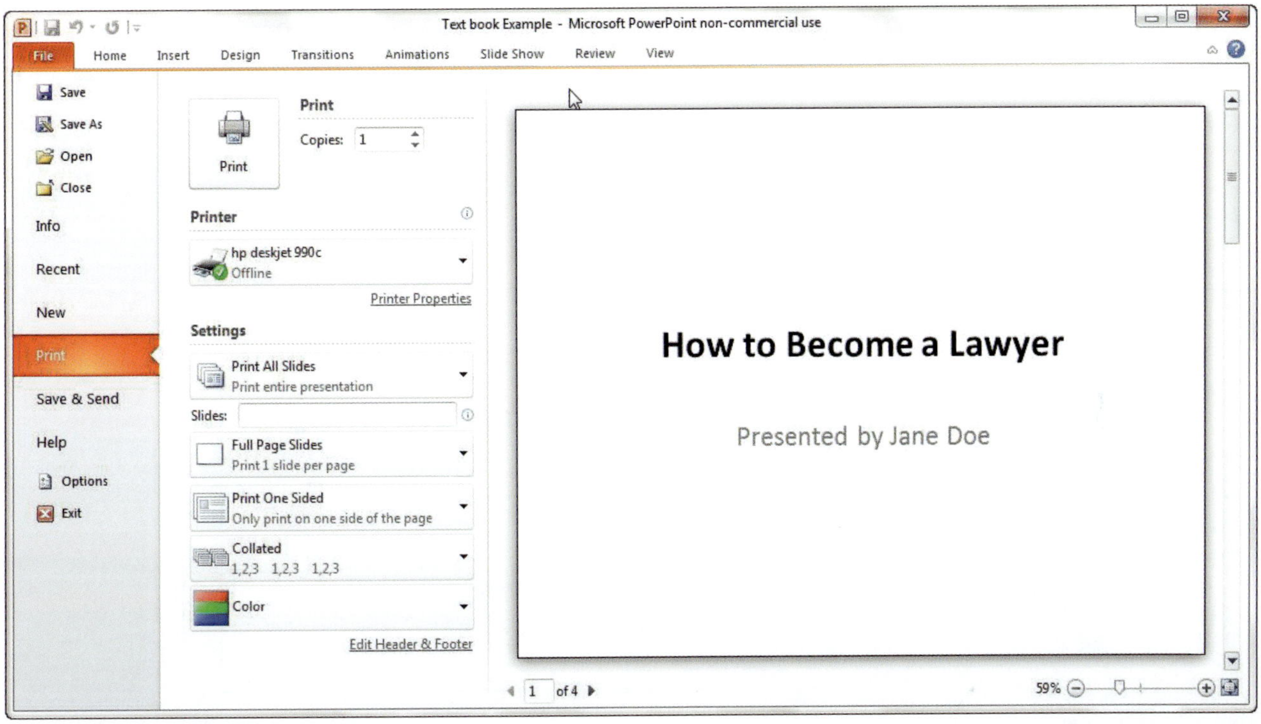

3. Select **Print All Slides** and then click **Print.**

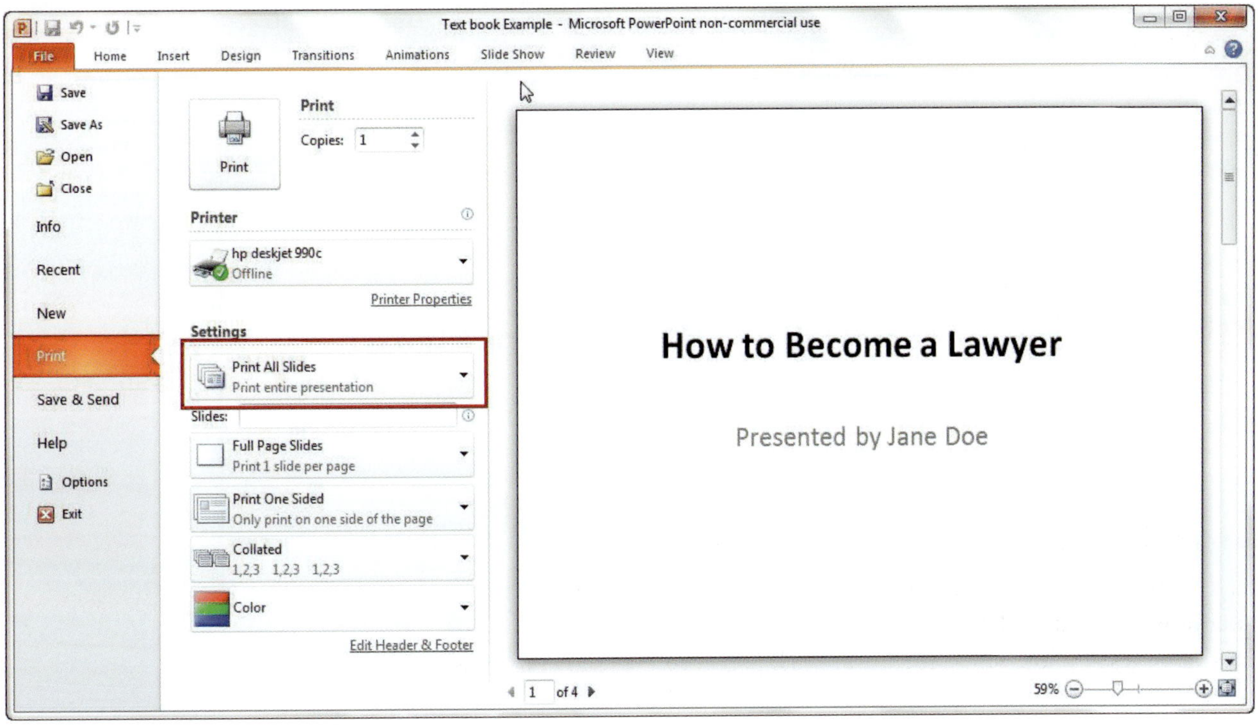

To print a presentation as a handout, use the following steps:

1. Click the *File* tab.

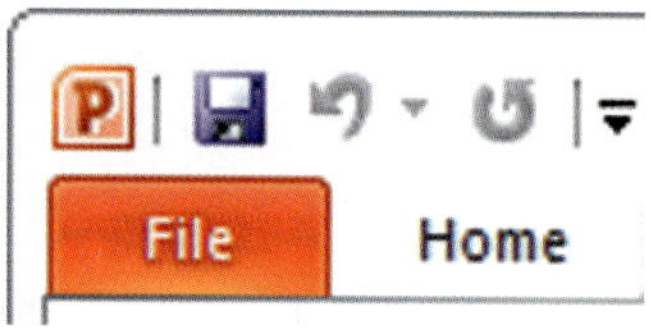

2. Click *Print*.

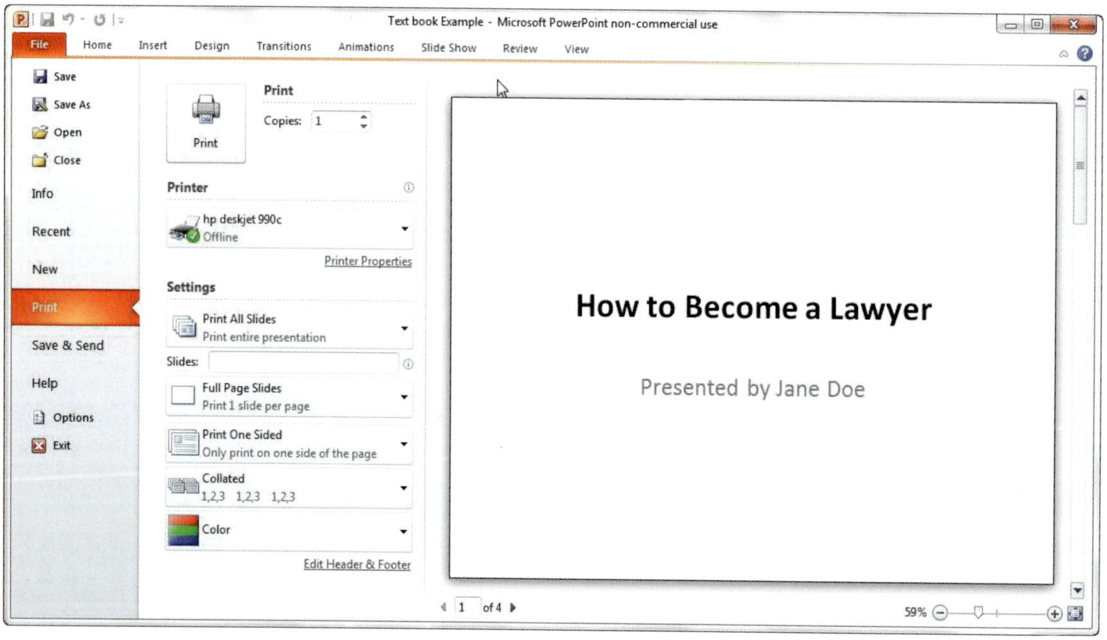

3. Click **Full Page Slides.**

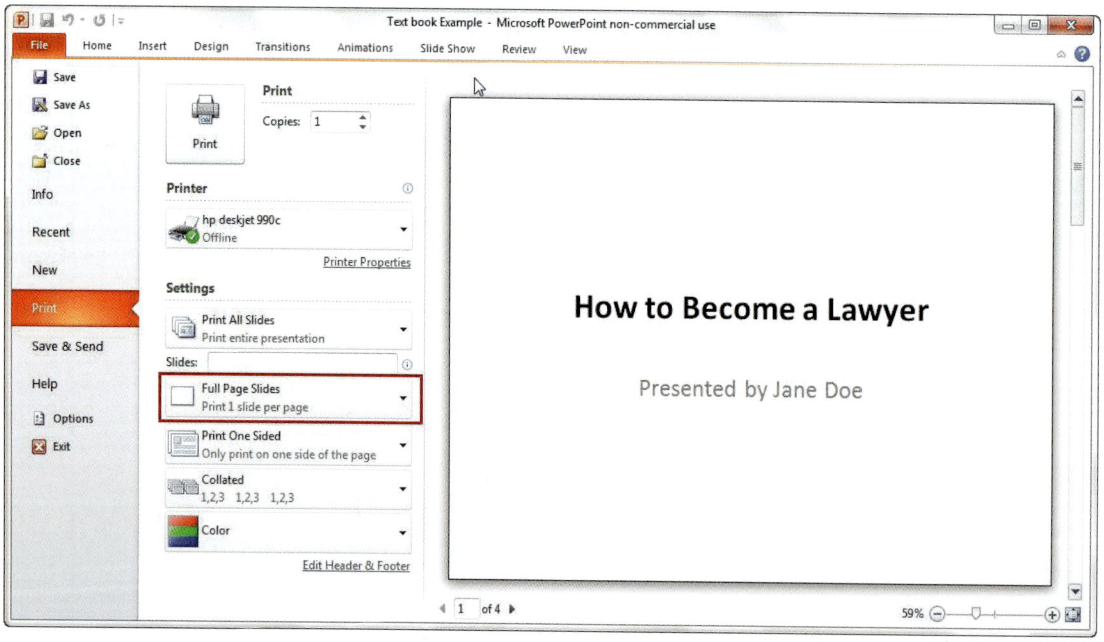

4. Select the appropriate slide layout configuration under Handouts.

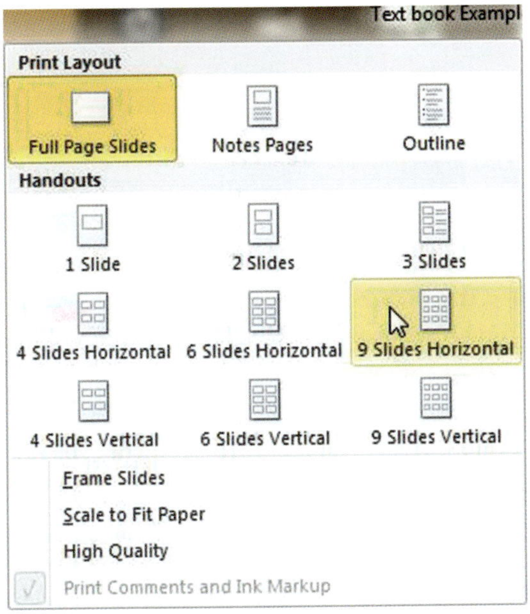

For information on adding notes to a presentation, see Using the Notes Pane in the chapter, "Productivity Software: Presentations."

APPENDIX D

COMMUNICATION ANXIETY

OVERVIEW

It is an unfortunate reality—many people suffer from a debilitating phobia that impairs their ability to speak comfortably in front of others. If you happen to be comfortable talking to groups, this may seem like an irrational fear, but is a very real problem for countless people. In truth, everyone experiences some level of anxiety when faced with speaking in public, but most people can learn to deal with communication anxiety or apprehension.

Communication apprehension is a fear or nervousness associated with communicating with one other person or a group of people. Researchers Scott Myers and Carolyn Anderson found that people have high, moderate, or low communication apprehension levels. Their research indicated that those who are high in communication apprehension feel intimidated in almost every speaking situation (even in front of intimate groups of two or three people), and those who are low in communication apprehension rarely experience it. Those who have moderate levels of communication apprehension are occasionally intimidated but tend to be rather flexible in their approach to speaking opportunities. Most researchers will agree that there are many different types of communication anxiety. However, this appendix will focus on the most common issues such as situational and trait communication anxiety.

Situational Anxiety

People with situational anxiety experience communication apprehension during certain situations and not others. Their fear of communicating is very real, but this fear becomes much more intense in particular situations. This situational type of communication apprehension is quite normal, as everyone is anxious about communicating in certain situations (most notably, in situations in which they are unsure of their subject material or on occasions when they must deliver bad news). Even veteran speakers get nervous, but their knowledge and experience helps them deal with this anxiety. It is always best to admit to yourself that the anxiety exists in order to cope with it.

Imagine that you are a very confident speaker because you have been involved in public speaking situations since high school, when you served as student body president. Today, you frequently give presentations to potential customers as part of your job. Because of your extensive experience, you are generally comfortable speaking to large groups of people, even groups of strangers.

Now you have been invited to present a toast at your cousin's wedding, and you are very nervous about this speaking situation—mostly because you do not know the bride's family well and you want to make sure you do the right thing for your cousin and family. This is a classic example of situational anxiety—despite the fact that you are generally comfortable speaking to groups, the fact that this occasion is of particular importance to you and your family has led to some apprehension on your part about the speech.

Trait Anxiety

Some people are inherently afraid of speaking in any speaking situation. Those who do not have much experience speaking in public lack the knowledge and training to overcome their fears. Communication apprehension only becomes stronger if a person avoids speaking in front of groups. The longer an anxiety-provoking situation is avoided, the more nervous the person will become. Eventually, it can become an enduring part of one's personality—a phenomenon known as trait apprehension.

Consider the following example: Meredith has never given a speech in any class or at any event. She has always managed to avoid speaking in public. Her fear of public speaking has become trait-based due to her lack of experience. Meredith's fear has become a phobia, and she admits that speaking in public is one of her greatest fears. Her advisor has insisted that she take a communication class in which she would have to give a presentation, and she is terrified. Meredith has tried everything to get out of the class, but Public Speaking 101 is a requirement for her major.

Overcoming Communication Anxiety

In order to overcome the fear of speaking in public, first realize that communication apprehension is quite normal. Then, consider the following approaches to tackling the anxiety.

Emotional Reframing

It is possible to transform your fear into excitement. Excitement helps people focus on the task ahead. Athletes, for example, are very aware of the positive effects of the adrenaline that come along with nervous excitement. Think of your anxiety as excitement, and use it to your advantage to help you perform better under pressure.

Self-Monitoring

You have learned how to critique yourself in communicative situations, and now you can use this to your advantage. However, doing so can become debilitating if you are too hard on yourself—most people think that they perform worse than they actually do.

Acknowledge that you have specific strengths and weaknesses. Telling yourself that you are horrible at public speaking while you are in the middle of a presentation is detrimental to your self-esteem, not to mention your speech. You are engaged in "self-talk" throughout your presentation, constantly giving yourself internal messages while you speak. Pay attention to whether these are positive or negative, and replace the negative thoughts with positive ones.

Consider this example: Mark has enrolled in a public speaking class. He has given speeches in the past, but nonetheless he is quite nervous about speaking in public. Mark was very quick to tell his instructor that he is horrible at public speaking, thus focusing on his negative qualities rather than using his strengths to boost his self-confidence.

Halfway through his first speech, Mark realizes that he is sending himself negative messages. He is extremely critical of himself: He realizes that he is rushing through the speech, including missing some key points. He completely misses the fact that his delivery has great volume and tone. The content of his speech is terrific, but he is quick to overlook this strength. He also avoids eye contact with his audience and shakes his head a number of times, disappointed that he is making mistakes. Mark must learn to manage his negative self-monitoring.

Controlling Physical Responses

Everyone reacts to stress in different ways. Some people perspire, shake, fidget, blush, and avoid eye contact—and public speaking opportunities are hardly exempt from these symptoms of stress. It is difficult to address these responses unless you are aware of them.

When rehearsing a speech, ask a friend to point out your physical responses to stress since you are unlikely to notice them yourself. People have a natural "fight or flight" response to certain stimuli: When you encounter something you fear, you tend to either stand your ground or run. Unfortunately, you cannot run away from your obligation as a speaker. Learn that you have this instinct to fight or run, but reprogram yourself to think

DID YOU KNOW?

Techniques to Help You Cope

Many students are terrified of speaking in public; as a result, they often postpone taking required public speaking courses until the very end of their college experience. However, a public speaking class definitely can help students in their other courses and experiences.

It is very normal to experience communication apprehension, but some people actually need therapy to help them overcome severe cases of communication anxiety. Biofeedback is one tool that is used to help people with this phobia. Visualization techniques and breathing exercises are also used to help overcome communication anxiety. The fear of speaking in public can be also be helped by extensive practice speaking in front of groups.

of the stimuli (these natural stress responses) as nonthreatening. Consider these other tips to help you maintain your poise:

- Project confidence through your posture.
- Approach the front of the room with certainty rather than uncertainty. Quiet self-assurance occurs when you use your body to convey confidence.
- If you are seated during the presentation, be sure that you sit up straight.
- Use natural gestures. It is not uncommon to use unnatural gestures when you are nervous, but become aware of any distracting gestures you use and try to eliminate them from your speaking style.
- Try stretching before the speaking event to help your muscles relax and focus your concentration.
- Incorporate breathing activities to prevent hyperventilating. Hyperventilation can occur when you speak for long periods of time while breathing abnormally. Remember to pause and take deep breaths before you speak.

PROFESSIONALISM

Gestures and eye contact are critical components of effective public speaking. A lack of eye contact with your audience during the presentation may communicate nervousness or lack of interest to them. Maintaining eye contact with your audience forms an intimate bond between speaker and listener.

Do not focus on a familiar face or a specific area in the room. Maintain eye contact with your entire audience. Public speaking is a reciprocal activity that requires participation from both the speaker and the listener, and eye contact is the link.

The most important thing to remember about gestures is to keep them simple and natural. Do not incorporate gestures that might seem inauthentic. Watch effective speakers to learn how they use gestures effectively. Strive to incorporate appropriate gestures, but do not stray from your speaking style.

Positive Thinking and Visualization

View speaking in public as a positive, rather than a negative, opportunity. Most people do not think of public speaking as a hobby—in fact, most consider public speaking to be one of their least favorite activities. But think of the benefits of delivering an excellent speech: more success at work or school, better social standing, or financial benefits. There are numerous rewards to improving your public speaking skills, so focus on the positive and work to overcome the challenges.

Before a speech, visualize yourself doing a good job. Convincing yourself that you will succeed may be all you need to guarantee success. Telling yourself that you will give a good presentation can be an extremely powerful form of conditioning. You just might find that you will perform the way you have told yourself you will.

Public speakers and athletes both use visualization techniques to help them do well. Before you go to sleep the night before the presentation, visualize yourself speaking confidently. Repeat the process immediately after waking the next morning, and repeat it again twice more before you begin the presentation. During each of these visualization exercises, review in your mind all of the stages of presenting your speech, from the beginning to the end.

Preparation

One of the best ways to improve your public speaking skills is to prepare yourself before the event. Some people need more rehearsal than others, but you can never be too prepared. Use whatever strategies work best for you. Some people practice in front of a mirror to help them with their gestures and facial expressions. Other people rehearse before friends and families. The more you practice, the more confident you will become. If you are using presentational aids, make sure that you rehearse with them as well.

Consider this example: Sandra is preparing her first speech for her public speaking class. She has carefully prepared an outline with great detail because she wants to do a good job. She has put together a number of visual aids for the presentation and feels that she is ready to begin practicing.

Her next goal is to make sure she will be able to complete her presentation in the allotted time. Sandra has learned from experience that she has trouble staying within time limits. Her preparation involves practicing until she consistently completes the presentation within the appropriate time limit.

Sandra's friends take turns timing her throughout the week. After three complete practice runs, Sandra believes she is fully prepared to deliver the speech.

REFERENCES

Grice, G. L., & Skinner, J. F. (2009). *Mastering public speaking* (7th ed.). Boston, MA: Allyn and Bacon.

Hybels, S., & Weaver, R. L. (2011). *Communicating effectively* (10th ed.). Boston, MA: McGraw-Hill.

Myers, S. A., & Anderson, C. M. (2008). *The fundamentals of small group communication.* Thousand Oaks, CA: Sage.

Wood, J. T. (2010). *Communication mosaics: An introduction to the field of communication* (6th ed.). Belmont, CA: Thomson Wadsworth.

GLOSSARY

A

abstract generalities: Words and examples that cannot be readily understood by using the physical senses.

acquaintance: Type of relationship that occurs when two people like one another; usually based on a commonality between the two people such as how close they live or work to one another; communication is at a less intimate level than deeper friendships or relationships.

active listening: Focusing on what the other person is saying and demonstrating an understanding of the content of the message and the feelings underlying the message.

adjourning: Situation in which groups gradually disband and go their separate ways.

apathetic: Uncaring.

articulation: The pitch, nasal quality, and breathing patterns in your voice.

artifacts: Tangible items such as jewelry, pictures, or other items that communicate something about a person.

assumption: An idea or opinion that someone adopts that is not based on a complete understanding of the facts in a given situation.

asynchronous course: A course allowing students to enter the class whenever it is convenient for them to complete a task rather than at an appointed time.

attachment style: How a person responds to communication experiences based on how he or she was raised in childhood; four types are secure, fearful or unlovable, rejecting or dismissive, and anxious.

attending: Devoting concentration to a given speaker or another verbal or visual resource.

audience: The spectators, listeners, or viewers of the presentation.

audience analysis: Taking a close look at who you will be speaking to and evaluating the audience's attitudes, opinions, needs, and wants.

authority: The power to influence thought or behavior.

autonomy: The state of controlling yourself; independence; in relationships, dependency is the opposite of autonomy.

B

bar graph: A visual graph figure used to compare amounts and quantities; the direct comparison of values is the principal purpose for bar graphs.

bias: Preferential treatment of one group over another.

blog: Derived from the words *web* and *log;* an Internet site where hosts post information and updates related to a particular theme.

build-up: A stage in relationships when people begin to know more about each other and develop a trust and confidence in one another.

C

case studies: More formal studies involving in-depth interviews, polls, surveys, questionnaires, focus groups, observations, and the collection of additional relevant data.

charts: Graphics that visually convey information to an audience.

chronemics: Perception of time, which includes promptness and willingness to wait.

citation: A location where a source may be found.

clincher: A statement at the end of a presentation, often factual, that definitively closes the topic.

co-culture: Reflects the reality that people can be part of more than one culture; in communication, also denotes a subculture within a larger group.

code: Types of nonstandard language such as slang or jargon that are letters or words with arbitrary meanings arranged by the rules of syntax and used to communicate.

codependent: Term used to describe a relationship in which one person depends on the other to control or make decisions for him or her.

cognitive dissonance: An attitudinal obstacle to effective listening; a discrepancy between what a person believes, knows, and values, and persuasive information that calls those beliefs into question.

collective system of meaning: Considering your own culture's values, expectations, perceptions, communication styles, and history.

colloquialisms: Informal phrases often used in ordinary conversation.

common formulas: Patterns to organize your speech effectively.

common ground: A speaker's attempt to identify ways in which he or she is like the audience.

communication channels: The means, methods, vehicles, modes, and techniques used to send messages.

concrete details: Words and expressions that describe something that can be perceived by one of the five senses.

conscience: A sense of one's own moral duty and an awareness of one's conduct in relation to it.

constructed messages: Highly thoughtful, carefully formulated messages.

constructive feedback: A critical part of evaluating and improving communication.

constructivism: The practice of organizing perceptions based on past experiences; a process by which people naturally attempt to understand the world around them.

contexts: Also referred to as settings; environments where communication takes place.

continuation: Situation in which two people realize that they want to stay in the relationship and it continues to grow.

credibility: The ability of the speaker to elicit the audience's belief in the speaker's words and actions.

cultural norms: Certain belief systems, practices, and teachings that become an agreed-upon method of operation.

cultural relativism: The belief that people think, feel, and act based on their cultural upbringing.

cultural universals: Situation in which norms become the standard for most cultures.

culture: Group or community with which a person shares common experiences that shape the way he or she understands the world; includes gender, race, or national origin, and groups a person joins or becomes a part of.

D

decode: Making sense of the message by using one's knowledge of language from personal experience.

definition: An organizational pattern for a speech that is a brief statement of what something is.

demographics: The statistical data about a particular population's makeup.

demonstration speech: Speech involving an active showing of its subject.

deterioration: Situation in which a relationship begins to come unraveled.

diagram: A specific type of graphic that shows how the parts of a whole fit together.

dialectical tension: A conflict that arises from two ideas or forces that conflict with one another.

dialogue: Conversation.

diction: Choice and use of words and phrases.

doublespeak: Language that deliberately distorts or manipulates the meaning of the words.

E

eloquence: The ability to express yourself in a persuasive and powerful way.

emoticons: Representations of facial expressions or shapes created via characters or abbreviations frequently used in text messaging.

empathetic: Feeling kind and considerate.

encode: A sender putting the message into his or her own words or meaning.

ethics: The moral principles that guide a person's conduct.

ethnicity: A social group that shares a common national or cultural tradition.

ethos: The distinguishing beliefs or character of the speaker.

etiquette: The ground rules of polite, civil communication.

euphemism: The substitution of an unpleasant or disagreeable phrase or word with an inoffensive one; a type of doublespeak.

expertise: Skill or knowledge in a particular area.

extemporaneous: Speeches in which the content is offered in a way that makes the speaker seem relaxed and comfortable and makes the speech almost conversational.

external noise: Sometimes called "physical noise"; includes environmental factors such as sounds and visual stimuli that distract from the intended message.

F

facial affect: An observable expression of emotion on your face.

facial expression: A physical gesture of nonverbal communication.

fair use: A concept relating to copyright and the ownership of intellectual property.

feedback loop: The space in which the sender adjusts the message based on responses from the receiver.

flip chart: A visual aid that is useful for showing a series of pictures, words, or diagrams that need to be shown in order, one visual at a time.

forming: The first step of putting together a group presentation.

G

general feedback: Information about the overall quality of the speech.

geographically dispersed team (GDT): A team of individuals who work from various geographical locations.

H

haptics: The study of touch.

human perception: Gathering external information using the five senses (smell, touch, taste, sound, and sight), and using that information to make conclusions about your surroundings.

I

identity script: Something you tell yourself that then becomes part of your identity.

impromptu: Speeches that take place when someone is suddenly called on to speak about a certain topic without preparation.

inflection: Quality of one's voice that moves up and down the scale naturally.

informative speeches: Typically divided into four types: speeches about objects, events, processes, or concepts.

initiator: The sender who begins the communication process.

internal noise: Includes psychological distractions such as thoughts, feelings, or reactions that interfere with the communication process.

interpersonal communication: Communication between or among two or more people; the prefix *inter-* means *between*.

intimate distance: A closeness usually reserved for communicating with family members or romantic partners; typically defined as one-and-a-half feet or less.

intranet: A computer network accessible only to a defined group of people such as a corporation or a university.

intrapersonal communication: A dialogue within yourself; the prefix *intra-* means *within*.

J

jargon: Words that are specific to a type of work or profession.

L

least to most important: One of the ways to organize information for a speech where the least important information is conveyed first, and the speech ends with the most important point or information.

line graphs: A visual figure that effectively displays developments, trends, or variances over time.

logos: Evidence that is presented by a speaker and how that evidence is shared.

M

manipulatives: Props that the audience can perceive with their senses.

manuscript: A written document; formal speeches are often delivered from manuscript so quotes, figures, and statistics are as accurate as possible.

maps: Ideal visual aids when the occasion for them arises.

mass communication: Any message destined for many receivers that must travel through some means other than directly from the sender to the receivers, and receivers may not be able to provide feedback.

media richness theory: Theory categorizing communication channels that ranks them according to their "richness," with face-to-face conversation being the most rich and channels such as brochures, web pages, or letters and e-mail messages being the least rich.

mediated communication: A communication that is facilitated by someone or something in the middle of and in addition to the communicators.

memorized speech: Speech in which the speaker memorizes the presentation word-for-word and delivers it to an audience without the use of an outline or notes.

message: Any piece of information passed along from a sender to a receiver; the sender's goal is to convey this piece of information to the receiver.

mindful listening: Being aware in the present moment, attentive, nonjudgmental, and involved in the acts of receiving and responding.

mnemonics: A strategy to improve memory that uses rhymes, memory aids, and other devices to help remember important information.

moderate: In a webinar, the ability of the meeting host to view a participant's post before it is published to the group and decide whether to accept or reject it.

modes of delivery: The four methods or manners in which a person gives a speech: extemporaneous, manuscript, impromptu, and memorized.

monotone: Quality of a person's voice in which the voice stays at the same pitch without varying.

most to least important: A viable organizational pattern starting with the most important information and ending with the least important information.

mourning: The process of remembering and expressing grief about someone or something lost.

N

neutral: Having no preference one way or another about a topic.

noise: The distractions and unwanted background input, interference, or any other barriers that may cause complications or distort a message for both sender and receiver.

nonverbal communication: Body language, facial expression, gestures, and behavior that transmit meaning.

nonverbal cues: Information communicated through body language and other unspoken hints.

norming: Situation in which each member of a group embraces a clear role and function for the benefit of the group and the project's success.

O

organizational chart: A chart that shows the structure of a company or organization and reveals the hierarchy of the staff and shows who reports to whom.

outline: A summation of the parts of the speech that focuses on its structure rather than writing out word-for-word what the presenter intends to say.

P

paralanguage: *How* something is said, not *what* is said.

paralinguistics: The various qualities of speech that involve your voice: how loudly you speak and whether you take long pauses.

paraphrasing: Most common form of feedback; a method of active listening that summarizes or serves as an interpretation of a message.

passive listening: A form of attending to what someone is saying without registering every word.

pathos: The act of engaging the audience in the presentation.

patterns of organization: Four basic approaches to organizing material for a speech: definition, process, most to least important and least to most important, and general to specific and specific to general.

pauses: Moments of silence between thoughts or main points; an important part of paralanguage.

perception: Becoming aware of something through the senses.

performing: During this stage, the group usually first practices and then delivers the presentation.

personal space: The space that you consider yours; the distance between people when they are communicating with one another.

photograph: An excellent visual aid to command audience attention and show exactly what a speaker is verbally discussing.

pie or circle graph: A visual figure that helps to show the relative proportions of parts of a whole.

pitch: A characteristic of sound that fluctuates with the changes of vibration in a human's vocal chords.

plagiarism: Taking credit for someone else's work or stealing someone's intellectual property.

poker face: An expression that shows no indication of what the person is thinking or feeling.

primary sources: Original documents that were created by the person or people you are researching.

principle of coordination: Principle that states each main point is equal to the others in significance, breadth, and depth.

principle of subordination: Principle that demonstrate visually a subordinate or lesser position in the content.

proxemics: The study of personal space, the use of which is instrumental to the act of listening.

pseudolistening: Attitudinal obstacle that can prevent effective listening.

public communication: Typically applies to groups of 20 or more people; the most formal environment for communication.

public space: More formal setting in which there is a sense of detachment or separation between the speaker and the audience; generally considered between 12 and 25 feet.

public speaking: Any speaking engagement before an audience of 20 or more listeners.

purpose: The reason for sharing or communicating.

R

rate: Speed with which a speech is delivered.

receiver: The interpreter of the message.

reflected appraisal: How a person sees him- or herself reflected through other people's eyes.

regionalism: A characteristic quality that is specific to a certain area; in speech, verbal accents can indicate where someone grew up.

relationship: How two or more people are connected.

resistant: Not wanting to hear about the topic or even from someone representing it.

rhetorical modes: Three methods of communication: self-introduction, informative speech, and persuasive speech.

rhetorical sensitivity: How you choose language and present ideas to appeal to your audience.

rhetorical triangle: The interdependence of the speaker, the situation, and the audience.

S

schema: Someone's prior knowledge and experience that affects how he or she responds to situations and communicated messages.

scripted messages: Messages used over and over again without putting much thought into them.

secondary sources: Commentary or evaluation of material from a primary source, including encyclopedias, biographies, or magazine articles.

select stimuli: One of the three main stages in the process of human perception where sensory details influence perception.

self-awareness: A level of knowledge and understanding about one's own biases, prejudices, motives, intentions, triggers, perceptions, and cultural filters.

self-concept: How a person thinks about him- or herself.

self-esteem: How a person feels about him- or herself.

self-image: Who you are and how you define who you are using your unique set of experiences.

sender: An initiator; the person who encodes or puts the message into words.

setting analysis: Consideration of both the abstract situation and the physical conditions of the speech.

settings: Environments where communication takes place.

situation: Also called the context of the speech; where and why the speaker and audience have come together.

slang: Nonstandard words.

small-group communication: Formal or informal communication that usually involves a group of at least 3 and no more than 20 people.

social exchange theory: A concept based on economics, psychology, and sociology that suggests all relationships are based on a cost-benefit analysis that each one of us has for ourselves.

social interaction: The way groups or cultures interact or influence one another.

social penetration theory: A concept that says as people get to know one another in intimate personal relationships, they learn more and more about each other's personal and private lives.

social space: The amount of personal space reserved for impersonal business or casual social interactions.

spatial organization: How the speaker moves through a description section by section according to space.

speaker: The person who delivers a speech.

speaker's outline: An expansion of the brief outline designed to help the speaker remember some of the key aspects not only of the content but also of the delivery.

specific feedback: Responses that address particular positive and negative qualities of a speaker's presentation.

spontaneous messages: Messages blurted out without thinking.

standard English: English that uses correct spelling, punctuation, and grammar.

standard vocabulary: Words that are universally understood and that most people know and accept.

status quo: The state of how conditions are at the present; also a speech that suggests that making a change or taking a certain action may be detrimental.

stereotyping: Making assumptions about people or groups of people based on preconceived ideas about a particular characteristic such as race or religion.

storming: A time of transition for a team in which members disagree and then reach consensus.

subpoints: Points in an outline that are clearly indicated by labels and indentation.

supporting details: The facts, statistics, and other pieces of evidence mostly from outside sources.

supporting sentences: Statements that help provide proof or further explanation.

T

tables: Columns of figures arranged in an order that helps the audience pick out specific information.

termination: A stage of a relationship when a relationship ends.

texting: A type of virtual communication conducted by using the keypad of a cell phone to send written messages.

theme: The message the speaker wishes to convey; explains what the audience needs to know most about a topic.

thesis statement: A directly stated topic, typically containing a preview of the main points.

tone of voice: An indication of the communicator's mood and attitude about the receiver of the message and the topic.

topic: The broad subject area of information that a speech addresses that is different from the speech's theme or purpose.

topic sentence: Sentence that summarizes and previews the main point of the section of an outline.

transactional: Used to describe a communication process that is completely integrated, simultaneous, and interrelated.

U

understanding: Decoding a message to determine its meaning.

URL: Uniform resource locator.

V

virtual team: A group of coworkers who are not located in the same office building.

vocalized pauses: The fillers used in everyday speech to keep the conversation going externally while a person tries to process the next idea to express in the conversation.

vocal variety: Vocal qualities including volume, pitch, tone, rate, and pauses.

volume: The loudness with which a speaker projects his or her voice.

W

webinar: Another type of virtual communication that combines the voice capabilities of a telephone conference with a shared view of a computer screen and an instant-message written "chat" feature.

white space: The area on a page or image that does not contain graphics, images, or writing.

PHOTO CREDITS

Chapter 1 Opener, p. 2: © Gino Santa Maria (Fotolia); p. 4: © auremar (Fotolia); p. 7: © tlorna (Fotolia); p. 8: © Nikolai Sorokin (Fotolia); p. 11: © pressmaster (Fotolia); p. 12: © barneyboogles (Fotolia); p. 14: © memo (Fotolia); p. 15: © diego cervo (Fotolia); p. 16: © Lisa F. Young (Fotolia); p. 18: © Pavel Losevsky (Fotolia).

Chapter 2 Opener, p. 22: © Thomas Perkins (Fotolia); p. 24: © imabase (Fotolia); p. 25: © Nikolai Sorokin (Fotolia); p. 26: © Andrew Kazmierski (Fotolia); p. 28: © WavebreakMediaMicro (Fotolia); p. 29: © hfng (Fotolia); p. 30: © Iriana Shiyan (Fotolia).

Chapter 3 Opener, p. 32: © claudiaveja (Fotolia); p. 34: © CandyBoxPhoto (Fotolia); p. 37: © Frank Jr (Fotolia); p. 38: © air (Fotolia); p. 39: © Rudolf Kotulán (Fotolia); p. 41: © Leah-Anne Thompson (Fotolia); p. 45: © Monkey Business (Fotolia).

Chapter 4 Opener, p. 48: © diego cervo (Fotolia); p. 50: © vgstudio (Fotolia); p. 51: © Kablonk Micro (Fotolia); p. 52: © WavebreakMediaMicro (Fotolia); p. 53: © Jason Stitt (Fotolia); p. 54: © Bryan Creely (Fotolia); p. 55: © vgstudio (Fotolia); p. 57: © Edyta Pawlowska (Fotolia); p. 58: © Vladimir Mucibabic (Fotolia); p. 59: © roza (Fotolia).

Chapter 5 Opener, p. 62: © AVAVA (Fotolia); p. 64: © Mariusz Prusaczyk (Fotolia); p. 65: © imabase (Fotolia); p. 66: © WavebreakMediaMicro (Fotolia); p. 67: © Peter Galbraith (Fotolia); p. 68: © Anyka (Fotolia); p. 71: © heliac (Fotolia); p. 72: © Darrin Henry (Fotolia).

Chapter 6 Opener, p. 74: © Aramanda (Fotolia); p. 76: © Jason Stitt (Fotolia); p. 77: © Yuri Arcurs (Fotolia); p. 78: © Junial Enterprises (Fotolia); p. 80: © goodluz (Fotolia); p. 82: © Yuri Arcurs (Fotolia); p. 83: © fred goldstein (Fotolia); p. 84: © iofoto (Fotolia); p. 86: © godfer (Fotolia); p. 88: © Eduard Titov (Fotolia); p. 90, top: © nyul (Fotolia); p. 90, bottom: © Rido (Fotolia).

Chapter 7 Opener, p. 94: © Rob (Fotolia); p. 96: © Fedels (Fotolia); p. 98: © microimages (Fotolia); p. 99, top: © nyul (Fotolia); p. 99, bottom: © Monkey Business (Fotolia); p. 100: © Stefano Neri (Fotolia); p. 101: © Lev Dolgatsjov (Fotolia); p. 102: © iQoncept (Fotolia); p. 103: © AVAVA (Fotolia); p. 105, top: © Junial Enterprises (Fotolia); p. 105, bottom: © drx (Fotolia); p. 107: © cyrano (Fotolia); p. 108: © Paylessimages (Fotolia).

Chapter 8 Opener, p. 112: © Andres Rodriguez (Fotolia); p. 114, top: © Couperfield (Fotolia); p. 114, bottom: © Kablonk Micro (Fotolia); p. 115: © treenabeena (Fotolia); p. 116: © N-Media-Images (Fotolia); p. 118, top: © vlorzor (Fotolia); p. 118, bottom: © AVAVA (Fotolia); p. 119: © treenabeena (Fotolia); p. 120: © JJAVA (Fotolia); p. 121: © AVAVA (Fotolia).

Chapter 9 Opener, p. 126: © Vadim Ponomarenko (Fotolia); p. 129: © Yuri Arcurs (Fotolia); p. 133: © jack ruston (Fotolia).

Chapter 10 Opener, p. 136: © Helder Almeida (Fotolia); p. 139: © iofoto (Fotolia): p. 140: © Kurhan (Fotolia); p. 141: © Lom (Fotolia); p. 142: © iofoto (Fotolia).

Chapter 11 Opener, p. 146: © max blain (Fotolia); p. 149, top: © Monkey Business (Fotolia); p. 149, bottom: © Yuri Arcurs (Fotolia); p. 150: © Pavel Losevsky (Fotolia); p. 152: © Kablonk Micro (Fotolia).

Chapter 12 Opener, p. 154: © FotolEdhar (Fotolia); p. 156: © alexsalo images (Fotolia); p. 157: © iofoto (Fotolia); p. 159: © Fotograv A. Gravante (Fotolia); p. 160: © Rod Ferris (Fotolia); p. 162: © Stephen Coburn (Fotolia); p. 163: © James Steidl (Fotolia); p. 167: © Kelly Young (Fotolia).

Chapter 13 Opener, p. 170: © Helder Almeida (Fotolia); p. 172: © Dmitry Vereshchagin (Fotolia); p. 173, top: © Yuri Arcurs (Fotolia); p. 173, bottom: © Kablonk Micro (Fotolia); p. 175: © David Gilder (Fotolia); p. 176: © Bronwyn Photo (Fotolia); p. 180: © Elenathewise (Fotolia).

Chapter 14 Opener, p. 184: © Philip Date (Fotolia); p. 186: © Rob (Fotolia); p. 187: © Emin Ozkan (Fotolia); p. 188: © Monkey Business (Fotolia); p. 191: © enens (Fotolia); p. 193: © Vibe Images (Fotolia).

Chapter 15 Opener, p. 198: © alexsalo images (Fotolia); p. 200: © ALEKSANDER CLAPINSKI (Fotolia); p. 203, top: © edbockstoc (Fotolia); p. 203, bottom: © Monkey Business (Fotolia); p. 205, top: © Michael Ransburg (Fotolia); p. 205, bottom: © Alex Kalmbach (Fotolia); p. 210: © xalex (Fotolia).

Chapter 16 Opener, p. 212: © surpasspro (Fotolia); p. 213: © nyul (Fotolia); p. 214, top: © C© Tomas Skopal (Fotolia); p. 214, bottom: © chungking (Fotolia).

Chapter 17 Opener, p. 260: © picsfive (Fotolia); p. 262: © FOTOCROMO (Fotolia); p. 264: © Lucy Clark (Fotolia); p. 265: © pressmaster (Fotolia); p. 267: © Anton Gvozdikov (Fotolia).

Chapter 18 Opener, p. 270: © Vibe Images (Fotolia); p. 272: © Kablonk Micro (Fotolia); p. 275: © microimages (Fotolia); p. 276: © Blair Bunting (Fotolia); p. 277: © Dmitry Vereshchagin (Fotolia).

Appendix C Opener, p. C-2: © Yuricami (Fotolia).

REFERENCES

Chapter 1

Beebe, S., Beebe, S., & Ivy, D. K. (2009). *Communication: Principles for a lifetime*: Vol. 4. *Presentational speaking* (portable ed.). Needham Heights, MA: Allyn & Bacon/ Pearson Education.

Brenner, D. M. (2007). *Move the world: Persuade your audience, change minds, and achieve goals*. New York, NY: John Wiley & Sons.

Brignall, M. (2007). Describing the transactional communications model. Retrieved from http://www.wisc-online.com/objects/ViewObject.aspx?ID=oic100

Capp, G., Capp, C., & Capp, G. R. (1990). *Basic oral communication* (5th ed.). Englewood Cliffs, NJ: Prentice-Hall.

Cherney, L. R. (2005). Communication. In G. Albecht (Ed.), *Encyclopedia of disability* (Vol. 1, pp. 279–282). Thousand Oaks, CA: Sage.

Christians, C. G. (2007). Communication ethics. In *Encyclopedia of science, technology and ethics*. Farmington Hills, MI: Gale Cengage (Macmillan Reference).

Communication; Nonverbal communication. (2008). In *International encyclopedia of the social sciences* (2nd ed.). Farmington Hills, MI: Gale Cengage (Macmillan Reference).

Communication channels; Speaking skills in business. (2007). In *Encyclopedia of business and finance* (2nd ed.). Farmington Hills, MI: Gale Cengage (Macmillan Reference).

Dellinger, S., & Deane, B. (1980). *Communicating effectively: A complete guide to better managing*. Radnor, PA: Chilton Book Company.

Duckworth, C., & Frost, R. (2008). Noise pollution. In *Gale encyclopedia of science* (Vol. 4). Farmington Hills, MI: Gale Cengage (Macmillan Reference).

Hargrave, J. (2007). Listening skills in business. In *Encyclopedia of business and finance* (2nd ed.). Farmington Hills, MI: Gale Cengage (Macmillan Reference).

Harris, T., & Sherblom, J. (2011). *Small group and team communication* (5th ed.). Needham Heights, MA: Allyn & Bacon/Pearson Education.

Headrick, D. (2005). Communication overview. In *Berkshire encyclopedia of world history*. Retrieved from http://www.scribd.com/doc/36159228/Ency-of-World-Hist

Hu, Y., & Sundar, S. (2007). Computer-mediated communication (CMC). In J. J. Arnett (Ed.), *Encyclopedia of children, adolescents, and the media* (pp. 200–202). Thousand Oaks, CA: Sage.

King, L., & Gilbert, B. (1994). *How to talk to anyone, anytime, anywhere: The secrets of good communication*. New York, NY: Crown/Three Rivers Press/Random House.

Liepmann, L. (1984). *Winning connections: A program for on-target business communication*. Indianapolis, IN: Bobbs-Merrill Press.

LoCicero, J. (2007). *Business communication*. Cincinnati, OH: Adams Media (F+W).

Lucas, S. E. (1998). *The art of public speaking*. New York, NY: McGraw-Hill.

Merrier, P. (2006). *Business communication*. Cincinnati, OH: Thomson South-Western College Publishing.

O'Neil, S., Evans, J., & Bigley, H. (2007). Communications in business. In *Encyclopedia of business and finance* (2nd ed.). Farmington Hills, MI: Gale Cengage (Macmillan Reference).

Oberg, B. C. (2003). *Interpersonal communication: An introduction to human interaction*. Colorado Springs, CO: Meriwether.

Reardon, K., & Christopher, N. (2010). *Comebacks at work*. New York, NY: HarperBusiness.

Ross, R. (1983). *Speech communication: Fundamentals and practice*. Englewood Cliffs, NJ: Prentice-Hall.

Rothwell, J. D. (2009). *In mixed company: Communicating in small groups and teams* (7th ed.). Farmington Hills, MI: Gale Cengage (Thomson Wadsworth).

Simmons, A. (2007). *Whoever tells the best story wins*. New York, NY: Amacom Press.

Verderber, R. F., Verderber, K. S., & Sellnow, D. (2009). *Communicate!* (13th ed.). Retrieved from http://www.cengagebrain.com/shop/content/verderber36403_1439036403_01.01_toc.pdf

Windley, C., & Skinner, M. (2007). Selecting a topic. University of Idaho. Retrieved from http://www.class.uidaho.edu/comm101/chapters/selecting_topic/selecting_topic_printable.htm

Chapter 3

Hornby, L., & Le, Y. (2009, December 22). China to require Internet domain name registration. Retrieved from http://www.reuters.com/article/2009/12/22/us-china-internet-idUSTRE5BL19620091222

Chapter 4

Center for Media Literacy. (2002–2011). Military doublespeak: How jargon turns gore into glory. Retrieved from http://www.medialit.org/reading-room/military-doublespeak-how-jargon-turns-gore-glory

National Institute on Deafness and Other Communication Disorders. (2011, July 5). Retrieved from http://www.nidcd.nih.gov/health/hearing/asl.html

Sussman, L. (n.d.). Effective communication. Retrieved from http://cobweb2.louisville.edu/faculty/regbruce/bruce//mgmtwebs/commun_f98/chronemics.htm

Chapter 5

Demographics of the United States. Retrieved from https://www.cia.gov/library/publications/the-world-factbook/geos/us.html

DuPraw, M. E., & Axner, M. (2003–2007). Working on common cross-cultural communication challenges. Retrieved from http://www.pbs.org/ampu/crosscult.html

Willcoxson, L., & Millett, B. (2000). The management of organisational culture. *Australian Journal of Management and Organisational Behaviour, 3*(2), 91–99.

Chapter 6

Lewicki, R. J., & Tomlinson, E. C. (2003, December). Trust and trust building. Retrieved from http://www.beyondintractability.org/essay/trust_building/

University of Texas at Dallas Counseling Center. (2011, January 19). Self-help: Coping with a breakup. Retrieved from http://www.utdallas.edu/counseling/breakup/

Chapter 7

Adler, R. B., & Proctor, R. F. (2007). *Looking out, looking in* (12th ed.). Belmont, CA: Thomson Wadsworth.

Canary, D. J., Cody, M. J., & Manusov, V. L. (2008). *Interpersonal communication: A goals-based approach* (4th ed.). Boston, MA: Bedford/St. Martin's Press.

Hybels, S., & Weaver, R. L. (2009). *Communicating effectively* (9th ed.). New York, NY: McGraw-Hill.

McCornack, S. (2007). *Reflect and relate: An introduction to interpersonal communication.* Boston, MA: Bedford/St. Martin's Press.

Wolff, F. I., & Marsnik, N. C. (1993). *Perceptive listening* (2nd ed.). Fort Worth, TX: Harcourt Brace.

Wood, J. T. (2010). *Communication mosaics: An introduction to the field of communication* (6th ed.). Belmont, CA: Thomson Wadsworth.

Chapter 8

Allen, E., & Seaman, J. (2010, November). *Class differences: Online education in the United States, 2010.* Retrieved from http://sloanconsortium.org/sites/default/files/class_differences.pdf

Boyd, D. M., & Ellison, N. B. (2007). Social network sites: Definition, history, and scholarship. *Journal of Computer-Mediated Communication, 13*(1), article 11. Retrieved from http://jcmc.indiana.edu/vol13/issue1/boyd.ellison.html

Brown, J. E. (2010). An empirical look at the relationship between personality type and the challenges of telecommuting (Doctoral dissertation). Retrieved from Proquest. (Publication No. 3415608)

Chapter 9

Beebe, S., Beebe, S., & Ivy, D. K. (2009). *Communication: Principles for a lifetime: Vol. 4. Presentational speaking* (portable ed.). Needham Heights, MA: Allyn & Bacon/Pearson Education.

Brenner, D. M. (2007). *Move the world: Persuade your audience, change minds, and achieve goals.* New York, NY: John Wiley & Sons.

Brignall, M. (2007). Describing the transactional communications model. Retrieved from http://www.wisc-online.com/objects/ViewObject.aspx?ID=oic100

Capp, G., Capp, C., & Capp, G. R. (1990). *Basic oral communication* (5th ed.). Englewood Cliffs, NJ: Prentice-Hall.

Cherney, L. R. (2005). Communication. In G. Albecht (Ed.), *Encyclopedia of disability* (Vol. 1, pp. 279–282). Thousand Oaks, CA: Sage.

Christians, C. G. (2007). Communication ethics. In *Encyclopedia of science, technology and ethics.* Farmington Hills, MI: Gale Cengage (Macmillan Reference).

Communication; Nonverbal communication. (2008). In *International encyclopedia of the social sciences* (2nd ed.). Farmington Hills, MI: Gale Cengage (Macmillan Reference).

Communication channels; Speaking skills in business. (2007). In *Encyclopedia of business and finance* (2nd ed.). Farmington Hills, MI: Gale Cengage (Macmillan Reference).

Dellinger, S., & Deane, B. (1980). *Communicating effectively: A complete guide to better managing.* Radnor, PA: Chilton Book Company.

Duckworth, C., & Frost, R. (2008). Noise pollution. In *Gale encyclopedia of science* (Vol. 4). Farmington Hills, MI: Gale Cengage (Macmillan Reference).

Hargrave J. (2007). Listening skills in business. *Encyclopedia of Business and Finance* (2nd ed.). Farmington Hills, MI: Gale Cengage (Macmillan Reference).

Harris, T., & Sherblom, J. (2011). *Small group and team communication* (5th ed.). Needham Heights, MA: Allyn & Bacon/Pearson Education.

Headrick, D. (2005). Communication overview. In *Berkshire encyclopedia of world history.* Retrieved from http://www.scribd.com/doc/36159228/Ency-of-World-Hist

Hu, Y., & Sundar, S. (2007). Computer-mediated communication (CMC). In J. J. Arnett (Ed.), *Encyclopedia of children, adolescents, and the media* (pp. 200–202). Thousand Oaks, CA: Sage.

King, L., & Gilbert, B. (1994). *How to talk to anyone, anytime, anywhere: The secrets of good communication.* New York, NY: Crown/Three Rivers Press/Random House.

Liepmann, L. (1984). *Winning connections: A program for on-target business communication.* Indianapolis, IN: Bobbs-Merrill Press.

LoCicero, J. (2007). *Business communication.* Cincinnati, OH: Adams Media (F+W).

Lucas, S. E. (1998). *The art of public speaking.* New York, NY: McGraw-Hill.

Merrier, P. (2006). *Business communication.* Cincinnati, OH: Thomson South-Western College Publishing.

O'Neil, S., Evans, J., & Bigley, H. (2007). Communications in business. In *Encyclopedia of business and finance* (2nd ed.). Farmington Hills, MI: Gale Cengage (Macmillan Reference).

Oberg, B. C. (2003). *Interpersonal communication: An introduction to human interaction.* Colorado Springs, CO: Meriwether.

Reardon, K., & Christopher, N. (2010). *Comebacks at work.* New York, NY: HarperBusiness.

Ross, R. (1983). *Speech communication: Fundamentals and practice.* Englewood Cliffs, NJ: Prentice-Hall.

Rothwell, J. D. (2009). *In mixed company: Communicating in small groups and teams* (7th ed.). Farmington Hills, MI: Gale Cengage (Thomson Wadsworth).

Simmons, A. (2007). *Whoever tells the best story wins.* New York, NY: Amacom Press.

Verderber, R. F., Verderber, K. S., & Sellnow, D. (2009). *Communicate!* (13th ed.). Retrieved from http://www.cengagebrain.com/shop/content/verderber36403_1439036403_01.01_toc.pdf.

Windley, C., & Skinner, M. (2007). Selecting a topic. University of Idaho. Retrieved from http://www.class.uidaho.edu/comm101/chapters/selecting_topic/selecting_topic_printable.htm

Chapter 10

American Communication Association. (2011). *The ACA open knowledge guide to public speaking.* Retrieved from http://www.textcommons.org/node/2

Chapter 11

Fear of public speaking statistics. (2011, February 13). Retrieved from http://www.speech-topics-help.com/fear-of-public-speaking-statistics.html

Nielsen Company. (2011). *Nielsen: A world of insights. Retrieved from http://www.nielsen.com*

Chapter 12

Beebe, S., Beebe, S., & Ivy, D. K. (2009). *Communication: Principles for a lifetime: Vol. 4. Presentational speaking* (portable ed.). Needham Heights, MA: Allyn & Bacon/Pearson Education.

Brenner, D. M. (2007). *Move the world: Persuade your audience, change minds and achieve goals.* New York, NY: John Wiley & Sons.

Brignall, M. (2007). Describing the transactional communications model. Retrieved from http://www.wisc-online.com/objects/ViewObject.aspx?ID=oic100

Capp, G., Capp, C., & Capp, G. R. (1990). *Basic oral communication* (5th ed.). Englewood Cliffs, NJ: Prentice-Hall.

Cherney, L. R. (2005). Communication. In G. Albecht (Ed.), *Encyclopedia of disability* (Vol. 1, pp. 279–282). Thousand Oaks, CA: Sage.

Christians, C. G. (2007). Communication ethics. In *Encyclopedia of science, technology and ethics.* Farmington Hills, MI: Gale Cengage (Macmillan Reference).

Communication; Nonverbal communication. (2008). In *International encyclopedia of the social sciences* (2nd ed.). Farmington Hills, MI: Gale Cengage (Macmillan Reference).

Communication channels; Speaking skills in business. (2007). In *Encyclopedia of business and finance* (2nd ed.). Farmington Hills, MI: Gale Cengage (Macmillan Reference).

Dellinger, S., & Deane, B. (1980). *Communicating effectively: A complete guide to better managing.* Radnor, PA: Chilton Book Company.

Duckworth, C., & Frost, R. (2008). Noise pollution. In *Gale encyclopedia of science* (Vol. 4). Farmington Hills, MI: Gale Cengage (Macmillan Reference).

Hargrave, J. (2007). Listening skills in business. *Encyclopedia of business and finance* (2nd ed.). Farmington Hills, MI: Gale Cengage (Macmillan Reference).

Harris, T., & Sherblom, J. (2011). *Small group and team communication* (5th ed.). Needham Heights, MA: Allyn & Bacon/Pearson Education.

Headrick, D. (2005). Communication overview. In *Berkshire encyclopedia of world history.* Retrieved from http://www.scribd.com/doc/36159228/Ency-of-World-Hist

Hu Y., & Sundar, S. (2007). Computer-mediated communication (CMC). In J. J. Arnett (Ed.), *Encyclopedia of children, adolescents, and the media* (pp. 200–202). Thousand Oaks, CA: Sage.

King, L., & Gilbert, B. (1994). *How to talk to anyone, anytime, anywhere: The secrets of good communication.* New York, NY: Crown/Three Rivers Press/Random House.

Liepmann, L. (1984). *Winning connections: A program for on-target business communication.* Indianapolis, IN: Bobbs-Merrill Press.

LoCicero, J. (2007). *Business communication.* Cincinnati, OH: Adams Media (F+W).

Lucas, S. E. (1998). *The art of public speaking.* New York, NY: McGraw-Hill.

Merrier, P. (2006). *Business communication.* Cincinnati, OH: Thomson South-Western College Publishing.

O'Neil, S., Evans, J., & Bigley, H. (2007). Communications in business. In *Encyclopedia of business and finance* (2nd ed.). Farmington Hills, MI: Gale Cengage (Macmillan Reference).

Oberg, B.C. (2003). *Interpersonal communication: An introduction to human interaction.* Colorado Springs, CO: Meriwether.

Reardon, K., & Christopher, N. (2010). *Comebacks at work*. New York, NY: HarperBusiness.

Ross, R. (1983). *Speech communication: Fundamentals and practice*. Englewood Cliffs, NJ: Prentice-Hall.

Rothwell, J. D. (2009). *In mixed company: Communicating in small groups and teams* (7th ed.). Farmington Hills, MI: Gale Cengage (Thomson Wadsworth).

Simmons, A. (2007). *Whoever tells the best story wins*. New York, NY: Amacom Press.

Verderber, R., F., Verderber, K. S., & Sellnow, D. (2009). *Communicate!* (13th ed.). Retrieved from http://www.cengagebrain.com/shop/content/verderber36403_1439036403_01.01_toc.pdf

Windley, C., & Skinner, M. (2007). Selecting a topic. University of Idaho. Retrieved from http://www.class.uidaho.edu/comm101/chapters/selecting_topic/selecting_topic_printable.htm

Chapter 14

Janszen, E. (2007, July 7). Ten surprising facts about the homeless in the U.S. Retrieved from http://www.itulip.com/forums/showthread.php/1672-Ten-Surprising-Facts-about-the-Homeless-in-the-US

Chapter 15

Adobe Systems Incorporated. (2011). Adobe Captivate 5.5. Retrieved from http://www.adobe.com/products/captivate/

GoogleDocs. (n.d.). Retrieved from https://docs.google.com/

Grice, G. L., & Skinner, J. F. (2009). *Mastering public speaking* (7th ed.). Boston, MA: Allyn and Bacon.

Hybels, S., & Weaver, R. (2011). *Communicating effectively* (10th ed.). Boston, MA: McGraw-Hill.

Prezi. Retrieved from http://prezi.com/

SlideRocket. Retrieved from http://www.sliderocket.com/

Appendix D

Grice, G. L., & Skinner, J. F. (2009). *Mastering public speaking* (7th ed.). Boston, MA: Allyn and Bacon.

Hybels, S., & Weaver, R. L. (2011). *Communicating effectively* (10th ed.). Boston, MA: McGraw-Hill.

Myers, S. A., & Anderson, C. M. (2008). *The fundamentals of small group communication.* Thousand Oaks, CA: Sage.

Wood, J. T. (2010). *Communication mosaics: An introduction to the field of communication* (6th ed.). Belmont, CA: Thomson Wadsworth.

INDEX

D

E

F

G

H

I

J

K

L

M

N

O

P

R

S

T

U

V

W

Y

Notes

Notes

Notes

Notes

Notes

Notes

Notes

Notes

Notes

Notes

Notes

Notes